A LATIN AMERICAN COMMON MARKET?

A LATIN AMERICAN COMMON MARKET?

SIDNEY DELL

Issued under the auspices of the
Royal Institute of International Affairs
OXFORD UNIVERSITY PRESS
LONDON   NEW YORK   TORONTO
1966

Oxford University Press, Ely House, London W.1

GLASGOW NEW YORK TORONTO MELBOURNE WELLINGTON
CAPE TOWN SALISBURY IBADAN NAIROBI LUSAKA ADDIS ABABA
BOMBAY CALCUTTA MADRAS KARACHI LAHORE DACCA
KUALA LUMPUR HONG KONG

*Printed in Great Britain
by The Broadwater Press Ltd, Welwyn Garden City, Hertfordshire*

PREFACE

The Latin American quest for economic integration is of much more than local importance: its lessons are of deep significance for the political economy of the underdeveloped world as a whole. There are more than one hundred underdeveloped countries throughout the world, and over ninety of them have populations of under 15 million, while more than sixty have less than 5 million. The rate at which these countries are able to move towards tolerable living standards may depend to a great extent on their ability to form larger and more viable economic units. The present study has been written with these broader implications in the background.

The author's first and most important debt is to the rich literature provided by the Secretariat of the Economic Commission for Latin America, headed for many years by Dr Raúl Prebisch, and more recently by Dr José Antonio Mayobre. ECLA has pioneered many germinal ideas in the study of the growth process in underdeveloped countries, but none of greater potential than the idea of economic integration as a dynamic stimulus to the advance of these countries.

The author also gratefully acknowledges valuable comments by Andrew Shonfield, who originally suggested the study, and by Benjamin Hopenhayn; and the meticulous editing of Katharine Duff.

The views expressed in this volume are those of the author alone, and do not necessarily represent the views of the United Nations Secretariat, to which he belongs.

S. D.

New York
April 1965

CONTENTS

TABLES

APPENDICES

ABBREVIATIONS

AID	Agency for International Development (USA).
ALALC	Asociación Latinoamericana de Libre Comercio (LAFTA).
BNCE	Banco Nacional de Comercio Exterior (Mexico).
CEMLA	Centro de Estudios Monetarios Latinoamericanos.
ECLA	United Nations, Economic Commission for Latin America.
EEC	European Economic Community (Common Market).
EFTA	European Free Trade Association.
EPU	European Payments Union.
IBRD	International Bank for Reconstruction and Development.
ICA	International Co-operation Administration (USA).
IMF	International Monetary Fund.
LAFTA	Latin American Free-Trade Association.
OAS	Organization of American States.
PAU	Pan American Union.
UNCTAD	United Nations Conference on Trade and Development.

NOTE ON REFERENCES

Many of the basic documents on Latin American integration, including the various treaties, and reports of new developments, are to be found in the following publications, referred to subsequently by the abbreviations indicated:

Title	Abbreviation
1. ECLA, *Multilateral Economic Co-operation in Latin America*, 1962.	*Multilateral Co-operation*
2.(a) ALALC, *Tratado de Montevideo, Resoluciones de la Conferencia.* Montevideo, 1963.	*Resoluciones*[1]
(b) Banco de México, *Resoluciones adoptadas por la Conferencia de las Partes Contratantes del Tratado de Montevideo en los años de 1961, 1962, y 1963.* Mexico City, 1964.	*Resoluciones*[1]
(c) Banco Nacional de Comercio Exterior, *Resoluciones del cuarto período ordinario y del segundo extraordinario de sesiones de la Conferencia de las Partes Contratantes de la ALALC. Suplemento de Comercio Exterior.* Mexico City, December 1964.	*Resoluciones*[1]
3. ALALC, *Resoluciones del Comité Provisional de Montevideo, Resoluciones del Comité Ejecutivo Permanente.* Montevideo, 1963.	*Resoluciones* (Comité)
4.(a) Banco Nacional de Comercio Exterior, *Comercio Exterior*, Mexico City, monthly.	*Comercio Exterior*
(b) — *Tres años en el camino de la integración, Suplemento de Comercio Exterior,* June 1964.	*Tres años*
5. CEMLA, *Boletín Quincenal.* Mexico City, fortnightly.	*Boletín Quincenal*

[1] Publications 2(a) and 2(b) are alternative sources for resolutions of the Contracting Parties to the Treaty of Montevideo adopted in 1961 and 1962. 2(b) also includes resolutions adopted in 1963. 2(c) contains resolutions adopted in 1964. The relevant session is indicated in all cases by the roman numeral in brackets that follows the resolution number.

CHAPTER I

THE BACKGROUND

Social Variety and Inequality

Is integration possible or even desirable in Latin America? In a world of super-powers, it has become fashionable to regard the merging of small countries as an end in itself, and nationalism as a luxury fit to be enjoyed only by those able to measure their military strength in nuclear megatons. Perhaps the broad sweep of history will indeed bring about the progressive homogenization of men and nations, and perhaps we are witnessing the early stages of this process. But whether this is so or not, the reality of today is diversity, not homogeneity, and no political, economic, or sociological analysis can afford to overlook this simple fact.

Latin America is a cross-section of virtually every stage of human history. Every phase of civilization is encompassed—aboriginal tribes, societies living under conditions similar to those that must have prevailed before the Spanish Conquest, the feudal populations on the great landed estates, and finally the urban complexes associated with contemporary industrialization. The most primitive peoples are in the Amazon region, where headhunters and cannibalism are still occasionally to be found. In the mountainous regions of Colombia, Ecuador, Peru, Bolivia, and the north-east of Argentina there are millions of people still living in Inca-type communities, maintaining ancient social traditions and institutions as in the days of the Inca Empire. Next in terms of historical evolution come the great feudal estates or *latifundios*—which had their hey-day during the colonial period and still dominate the agriculture of the region. Finally, there are the modern industrial communities, of which the most remarkable, perhaps, is São Paulo, a city of bustling industry and skyscrapers that is almost more American than anything to be found in the United States itself. A more extraordinary demonstration of the social immobilities characteristic of underdeveloped countries could scarcely be found than the fantastic contrast between the industrial workers of São Paulo and the aborigines of the Amazon basin. It is always important to bear these diversities in mind when thinking of Latin America. When we speak of Latin America we are not referring to a homogeneous entity, but rather to a spectrum of societies ranging from the most primitive to the most advanced.

The remarkable breadth of this spectrum is associated with extreme disparities in levels of living, health, education, and cultural achievement. It has been estimated that 2 per cent of the people of the continent own more than half of its wealth, while a major part of the rest live in conditions of the most dejected poverty.

The extreme inequality of land tenure in Latin America is one of the most basic of the underlying causes of poverty and social tension. It has been estimated that nearly three-quarters of all farms in the region are less than 20 hectares in size, and account for under 4 per cent of the total arable area. At the other extreme, 1·5 per cent of all farms exceed 1,000 hectares in size and account for no less than 65 per cent of the cultivable land area. This is a far greater degree of concentration of ownership than obtains in any other region of the world of comparable size.[1]

The impoverishment of the smallholders is scarcely surprising under these conditions—even if they adopted more modern techniques and had sufficient resources to be able to make use of better seed, fertilizer, and equipment, their farms are usually too small for efficient operation. As matters stand, a miserable subsistence is all that most of these smallholders can expect of life. Even less tolerable, perhaps, are those *latifundios*, or large estates, where opportunities for modern methods of cultivation are rarely exploited, and large areas lie idle because the owners are too wealthy to be bothered, or because the land is held for mainly speculative purposes.

Consider, for example, the situation in Honduras, by no means the poorest country in Latin America. It is estimated that as a partial consequence of the pattern of land tenure, *90 per cent of good flat land in Honduras lies unused*, while the peasantry ekes out an abject existence by cultivating the hillsides. Five out of six of the small Honduran farms do not even have a wooden plough. Of the total of 117,000 farms of less than 25 acres, only 184 have steel ploughs and none have tractors. The general picture is a pathetic one:

---

[1] Thomas F. Carroll, 'The Land Reform Issue in Latin America', in Albert O. Hirschman, ed., *Latin American Issues* (N.Y., 1961), pp. 164–5.

Everywhere one finds scrawny cattle grazing untended plains, while beans and corn are being cultivated on the nearby bare slopes. This does not make sense for the landowner, the small farmer or the economy as a whole, yet it is a common condition not only in Honduras, but throughout Latin America.[2]

It is true that inequality in the distribution of wealth and income has not always been an obstacle to economic advancement. In eighteenth- and ninteenth-century Europe and North America, for example, the distribution of income was exceedingly inequitable, but it was this inequality that made it possible for the rich to hold down the consumption of the poor and devote large resources to investment and expansion. In the typical Latin American economy of today, on the other hand, the rich use their command over resources not to stimulate the growth of the economy but rather to provide themselves with the luxuries that they see around them when they visit New York, Paris, and London. It appears, in fact, that the proportion of national income allocated to luxury consumption may be several times as high in some of the Latin American countries as in the United States or Western Europe.[3]

It is necessary to take these inequalities into account in evaluating the significance of the available information on average Latin American incomes. It is estimated that in 1960 the total output of the Latin American region amounted to some $80 billion, equivalent to about $400 per head.[4] Although this figure of per capita output represents only one-seventh of the comparable average in the United States, or two-fifths of that in Western Europe,[5] it is nevertheless quite high in relation to per capita output in some of the countries of Africa and Asia. This means that Latin America starts off from a potentially more favourable position than do most of the African and Asian countries, because substantial resources are there to be mobilized if the will and energy to do so can be found. Despite this, however, inequalities are such that the depths of poverty to be found in Latin America are probably almost, if not quite, as great

[2] Vincent Checchi and others, *Honduras; a Problem in Economic Development* (N.Y., Twentieth Century Fund, 1959), pp. 52–53.

[3] Nicholas Kaldor, 'Will Under-developed Countries Learn to Tax?', *Foreign Affairs*, Jan. 1963.

[4] ECLA, *Economic Survey of Latin America, 1963* (E/CN.12/696), vol. i, Table 1.

[5] Inter-country comparisons of per capita output are subject to serious conceptual and statistical limitations, especially where there are marked differences in the patterns of output and prices between the areas compared, as in these instances. The comparisons are therefore intended to be indicative rather than precise.

B

as anything to be found anywhere in the world. It is believed that about half of the population of Latin America has an average personal income of only $120 a year.[6]

In 1950, in six countries for which data are available, the percentage of the population living in conventional dwellings ranged from 34 to 68 per cent. In other words, even in the best of the countries for which data are available, over 30 per cent of the population is not living in anything that might be termed a 'conventional dwelling'. At the same time, in five out of seven countries for which data are available, more than 25 per cent of 'conventional dwellings' had densities of three or more persons per room in 1950. Indications are, moreover, that in many countries housing conditions are deteriorating.[7]

A particularly sensitive indicator of living standards is usually the infant mortality rate. According to United Nations estimates, Cuba, Mexico, and Paraguay have an infant mortality rate of about 125 deaths per 1,000 live births; Bolivia, Brazil, Colombia, Dominican Republic, Ecuador, Honduras, Nicaragua, Panama, Peru, and Venezuela have a rate of about 150; and El Salvador and Guatemala have a rate of about 175. The comparable figure in the United States is about 25. For all the Latin American countries listed above, more than one child out of every ten will die before reaching one year of age. These infant mortality rates are closer to those for Asian than for European countries.[8]

The illiteracy rate in Latin America ranges between 14 per cent in Argentina and 89 per cent in Haiti. Twelve countries out of twenty have illiteracy rates above 40 per cent.[9] The average time spent in schools by Latin American children is 2·2 years—one of the lowest figures in the world. Seventy-five per cent of Latin American children do not complete an elementary education.[10]

The scale of effort required to overcome these deficiencies is all the greater in view of the very rapid rate of growth of population. The population of Latin America is now rising at an annual rate of

[6] Raúl Prebisch, *Towards a Dynamic Development Policy for Latin America* (UN Sales No. 64.II.G.4), p. 3.
[7] ECLA, *Provisional Report of the Latin American Seminar on Housing Statistics and Programmes* (E/CN.12/647, Feb. 1963), p. 27.
[8] US, 86th Congress, 2nd sess., *United States-Latin American Relations*; a Study Prepared at the request of the Sub-Committee on American Republics Affairs of the Committee on Foreign Relations, Feb. 1960, pp. 43–44.
[9] ECLA, *Latin American Seminar on Housing*, p. 27.
[10] Data from UNESCO, as reported in *Boletín Quincenal*, 25 Apr. 1963, p. 132.

2·9 per cent, and the rate is expected to go over the 3 per cent mark before the end of the present decade. Some of the Central American and Caribbean countries already have population growth rates around 3·5 per cent per annum, and only two countries—Argentina and Uruguay—have rates below 2 per cent. From a total of about 230 million at the present time, the population of Latin America may reach 300 million before 1975 and 600 million by the year 2000.[11]

Economic Growth and Political Instability

Between 1945 and 1955 considerable economic gains were made in Latin America, and real per capita income rose at an annual rate of 2·7 per cent per annum. Important industrial complexes were created in several parts of the region, continuing the advances that had begun during the 1930s. But the benefits of development have not been widely diffused. The majority of the population have gained little or nothing from the economic development of recent decades[12] and are watching with growing impatience the self-contained prosperity of the social groups that have seized the spoils. At the same time, the position and privilege of the landed aristocracy are being challenged by the new urban classes, in a manner reminiscent of the developed countries in the past.

The relatively rapid rates of growth of the early postwar years— partly the result of favourable prices for Latin American exports, notably of coffee—have not been maintained more recently. From 1955 to 1960 declines in Latin American export prices were accompanied by a marked slowing down in the growth rate of national product to 1·7 per cent per capita, and from 1960 to 1963 the growth rate averaged only 0·7 per cent.[13] Meanwhile food production has not been keeping pace with the population increase.

Although foreign trade difficulties have seriously complicated the development problem of Latin America, the domestic obstacles are even greater. If the domestic forces of development had been

---

[11] ECLA, *Social Trends and Programmes in Latin America* (E/CN.12/645, Feb. 1963), p. 4.
[12] According to Furtado, the rapid economic growth of Brazil has thus far brought no benefit whatever to three-quarters of the population of the country. The gains have been highly concentrated, both socially and geographically (see Celso Furtado, 'Reflexiones sobre la prerevolución brasileña', *El Trimestre Económico* (Mexico City), July–Sept. 1962, p. 373).
[13] ECLA, *Survey, 1963*, vol. i, Table 1.

properly mobilized, much better use could have been made of both internal and external resources.

The fact that purposeful action has been lacking reflects a variety of factors—economic, social, political, and even military. While the struggle for a really radical improvement in living standards in Latin America would seem to call for the utmost unity of purpose and action between the various social groups, the peoples are divided against themselves, unable thus far to achieve such unity. This is mainly the result of the intense economic and social inequality that prevails, and of the determination of the rich to ensure that what they have they shall hold. Under these conditions, the great mass of the population cannot be expected to identify itself wholeheartedly with national objectives. The energies of the people, instead of being directed towards development goals, are engaged in conflict with the overlords, or frustrated in submission to a life of hopeless squalor.

Reference has already been made to the inequalities in land tenure that lie at the root of agricultural stagnation in Latin America. It is idle to talk about regional integration or any other aspect of the external problems of the Latin American countries so long as the forms of land tenure remain as obviously incompatible with economic and social progress as they are today. There are many questions of economic development that remain obscure but the role of land reform is undeniable. In almost all the industrially developed countries of today, land reform, accompanied by the breaking of the political control of the landed aristocracy, was an indispensable prerequisite for industrial growth.

Tax reform is almost equally important. The need for such reform arises not merely because of requirements for adequate financial resources for economic development but 'in order to bring about the degree of social cohesion and co-operation that is essential for the successful functioning of a democratic system'.[14] Governments in any event need large and growing resources in order to provide the infrastructure for development—health, education, communications, utilities, and so forth. Where, in addition, the wealthy are not themselves forward-looking, and prefer a life of indolence to a life of enterprise, governments have no alternative, irrespective of ideological views, to levying resources for capital investment in agriculture and industry.

[14] Nicholas Kaldor, *Essays on Economic Policy* (London, 1964), i. 216.

At the same time tax reform is essential as a means of reducing inequalities in income and wealth. It would be impossible to obtain the co-operation of the people in programmes for economic development, and in the sacrifices that such programmes may involve, in the absence of a fair sharing of burdens, and a sense that such burdens were being graduated according to the capacity to bear them.

The removal of social inequality is also vital. The barriers to social mobility that result from class distinction and racial discrimination seriously impede the operation of purely economic incentives, and are an additional factor preventing unity and cohesion in the pursuit of national objectives. Much greater opportunities for education are a necessary though not a sufficient condition for breaking down these barriers.

Finally, a rapid surmounting of domestic obstacles to development would necessitate the mobilization of all social groups and economic resources in a consistent national programme to this end. Planning involves much more than the drawing up of blueprints for development. Indeed, the drawing up of such blueprints is by far the easier part of the process. Much more difficult is the translation of plans into effective action and the involvement of all people and groups in common effort. Planning in the sense of mobilizing the diverse activities of all members of the community in the direction of generally accepted economic and social targets scarcely exists in Latin America today: and that means that progress is a matter of uncertainty, subject to fits and starts, and a variety of chance factors. Sustained development on the basis of national choice and concerted effort has yet to be attained.

Social conflict and insecurity have been aggravated by repeated intervention by the armed forces in political life. There has been created in each country a concentration of armed power which is much more likely to be involved in domestic politics than in defence against external attack. Postwar experience has been a tedious procession of revolutions and counter-revolutions: from 1948 to 1964 illegal means were used to change governments in no less than seventeen of the Latin American countries, and some countries went through this experience several times over. While in a few instances army control permitted the minimum of reform in the interests of greater stability, in most cases military intervention was frankly designed to crush or forestall such reform. The military expenditure of the Latin American countries is far in excess of their needs or resources, even allowing for the aid received from abroad. During his presidential campaign of 1960, President Kennedy called for an end to the wasteful arms race which, as he pointed out, now absorbs 60 per cent of the budgets of some Latin American nations, dissipates resources which might be used for economic development, and increases tension throughout the hemisphere.[15]

The domestic obstacles to social reform in Latin American countries resulting from the military power continually poised for action in defence of entrenched interests are frequently compounded by the schizophrenic attitude of the international community. On the one hand there is widespread recognition of the need for social reform and there have been efforts to make the granting of aid conditional on such reform. But in the last resort the fear that disturbance to the existing social fabric might open the way to the forces of the Left is apt to gain the upper hand. As Professor Charles E. Lindblom, of Yale, has pointed out:

. . . we confuse Latin American interests with the interests of Latin American ruling minorities. We have also so far failed to reconcile the demands made on American policy by American firms in Latin America with a variety of other American interests in that area, and here the prerequisite adjustment must presumably be on terms less favorable to the American companies than now exist.[16]

With governments continually at the mercy of military power, it is, perhaps, not surprising that the public service in Latin American cuontries is weak, incompetent, and time-serving. The Mexican writer Mariano Azuela, in his novel *The Flies*, has given us a brilliant characterization of the sort of human material that goes into public service in Latin America:

With a feeling that he was dictating his will, Señor Ríos answered: 'Donaciano Ríos, 40 years old; married; two children; government clerk since I cut my eye teeth. Record? Spotless from the moment I began as a junior clerk in a justice's office until I took my present job as Prosecuting Attorney. Work? Like a typewriter. With a little cleaning and overhaul-

---

[15] *The Speeches of Senator John F. Kennedy, Presidential Campaign of 1960* (Washington, D.C., USGPO), p. 1166.
[16] 'A New Look in Latin America', *Atlantic Monthly*, Oct. 1962, as reproduced in *Congressional Record*, 21 Jan. 1963, p. 611.

ing and a bit of oil now and then it will run forever and give satisfaction. Outstanding qualities? Utter abdication of will, unlimited moral flexibility, complete lack of individuality. In short, an ideal public servant.[17]

It is important, in the subsequent discussion, to keep firmly in mind the mounting social tensions in Latin America, and the hostility of prevailing political, military, and administrative forces to the kinds of changes that are indispensable if genuine progress is to be made. Armchair economists addicted to prescribing European or North American remedies for Latin American ills are apt to forget that conclusions or policies that may be valid in a politically stable and economically advanced region may be quite beside the point in the vastly different setting of a continent seeking to reconcile economic development with political reaction and social decay.

External Obstacles to Growth

While the slowing down in Latin America's economic growth in recent years has been largely due to the inability to overcome domestic obstacles, severe problems have also arisen in foreign trade. In particular, Latin American countries, in common with other underdeveloped countries, have encountered increasing difficulties in obtaining the export earnings required to finance the imports they need for development.

This problem of the 'trade gap' of underdeveloped countries has commanded increasing public attention in recent years.[18] Part of the difficulty lies in the fact that world demand for primary commodities, accounting for 90 per cent of the exports of underdeveloped countries, tends to grow very slowly—much more slowly than the demand of the latter countries for the finished manufactures that form the major part of their imports.

The sluggishness of demand for primary products affects both foodstuffs and raw materials. Consumption of foodstuffs in any case rises much more slowly than income in the developed countries, and the domestic farm support programmes adopted by these countries have depressed import needs still further. At the same time the volume of raw materials required to produce a given quantity of manufactures is constantly falling. This is largely the result of technical progress, expressed in the more efficient use and

[17] *Two Novels of Mexico* (Univ. of California Press, 1956), p. 22.
[18] It was, for example, the fundamental issue before the United Nations Conference on Trade and Development at Geneva in 1964.

reduced wastage of raw materials, the discovery of synthetic substitutes with new and desirable properties, and the greater and greater elaboration of the final products of manufacturing industry.

From 1950 to 1962, while the volume of exports of developed countries more than doubled, those of underdeveloped countries advanced only 57 per cent—and of Latin America alone only 53 per cent. In addition, however, the terms of trade deteriorated sharply: for underdeveloped countries as a whole the decline from 1950 to 1962 was 12 per cent, but for Latin America the drop amounted to 21 per cent, reflecting the particularly adverse movements in coffee prices. ECLA has estimated that the loss of income to Latin America in 1955–60 through the decline in prices from the period 1950–4 amounted to $7·3 billion. During the same period, 1955–60, the net inflow of foreign capital amounted to $7·7 billion; and while the loss on terms of trade was, of course, an outright loss, most of the capital inflow consisted of loans requiring repayment.[19]

The combined result of the slow growth in the volume of exports and of the deterioration in terms of trade was that the purchasing power of Latin American exports in terms of goods imported rose by only 23 per cent from 1950 to 1962, or by well under 2 per cent per annum. This rate of growth of external purchasing power was not nearly sufficient to finance the expanding volume of imports needed to sustain the domestic growth rate of over 4 per cent. If anything, the imports of underdeveloped countries tend to rise *more* rapidly than national product rather than less, because the acceleration of development calls for a stepping up in imports of machinery and equipment not available from domestic production.

Moreover, if the Latin American rate of growth were to be increased to the target rate of 5 per cent per annum set by the United Nations General Assembly—not a particularly ambitious target in view of rates of population increase averaging nearly 3 per cent—the demand for imports is not likely to grow at a rate much less than 5 per cent either. Thus even if the terms of trade were stabilized, Latin America, in common with other underdeveloped regions, is faced with a growing excess of import demands over export earnings—a growing 'trade gap'.

While the purchasing power of Latin American exports increased only 23 per cent from 1950 to 1962, the actual volume of imports

[19] R. Prebisch, 'For a Regional Market in Latin America', *Review of the River Plate*, 30 Nov. 1962, p. 330.

advanced by 42 per cent. The additional imports were financed to a considerable extent through the running down of foreign exchange reserves and the accumulation of heavy external debt. This accumulation of debt is of mounting concern in Latin America, especially since the debt has been rising much faster than the capacity to service it.

The total amount of external public debt outstanding in Latin America as a whole doubled from 1950 to 1955, and more than doubled again from 1955 to 1962. At the end of 1962, the amount of such debts outstanding was estimated in the region of $9 billion, or $11·5 billion including commercial arrears, obligations to the International Monetary Fund, and other similar liabilities.[20]

Inflows of capital on this scale, or even on a greater scale, would be all to the good if the ability of Latin American countries to make payments of interest and principal were increasing correspondingly. The result of the very slow expansion of Latin American exports, however, has been that service payments on public external debts have been increasing rapidly as a proportion of exports. In Argentina, Brazil, and Chile, the ratio of service payments on the external public debt to exports exceeded 20 per cent at the end of 1962, and was at a level comparable with that reached in 1931, when exports had already fallen sharply as a result of the great depression.[21]

At the same time a very large proportion of outstanding debt falls due for repayment within the next few years. Of the total indebtedness of Latin American countries on public account outstanding at the end of 1962, including commercial arrears, approximately 65 per cent was due for repayment during the period 1963–7.

The United Nations Secretariat recently estimated the 'trade gap' of underdeveloped countries in 1970 on the assumption that the total output of these countries would increase at an average annual compound rate of 5 per cent during the 1960s as a whole.[22] The projection was based on the relationships between production and trade observed in developed and underdeveloped countries during the 1950s, but it was assumed that there would be no further

---

[20] UNCTAD, *Economic Growth and External Debt—a Statistical Presentation*. Prepared by members of the staff of IBRD (E/CONF.46/40, Mar. 1964), Tables 1 and 6, pp. 5 and 10.

[21] UNCTAD, *Economic Growth and External Debt—an Analytical Framework*. Prepared by members of the staff of IBRD (E/CONF.46/84, Mar. 1964), Table 8, p. 38.

[22] UNCTAD, *Proceedings* (UN Sales No. 64.II.B.16), vi. 91–102.

deterioration in the terms of trade of the latter countries.[23] Within
this framework the total 'gap' for 1970 was estimated at $20 billion
of which the share of Latin America was estimated at $5 billion:
the actual deficit in 1960 was $0·7 billion.

The projected 'gap' for 1970 provides an indication of the order
of magnitude of policy measures required to deal with the mounting
trade problem of underdeveloped countries, on the assumption that
trade with the developed countries maintains something like its
present degree of importance in their economies. Either the 'gap'
will have to be bridged by a suitable expansion of trade and/or aid,
or the underdeveloped countries will have to effect a fundamental
reorientation of their foreign trade pattern and possibly of their
domestic economic policies as well. The only other alternative is a
reduction of overall growth rates by the underdeveloped countries
to the point at which their imports rise no faster than the present
slow rate of expansion of their exports—an alternative that cannot
be considered tolerable.

If prospects for exports of underdeveloped countries to developed
countries do not improve decisively, and if aid cannot be stepped up
very considerably, the only way in which the rate of growth could
be maintained would be through a sharp reduction in the relative
importance of trade with developed countries. At the present time
imports of goods and services by underdeveloped countries from
the rest of the world correspond to about 15 per cent of their gross
domestic product. This ratio would have to fall to about 11 per cent
by 1970 if nothing can be done to bridge the 'gap': and since the
'gap' has been estimated on the basis of unchanged terms of trade,
any further adverse movements in the prices of primary commodities relative to manufactures would necessitate a still greater reduction in the ratio of trade with developed countries.

The difficulty of making a shift of this magnitude by 1970 should
not be underestimated. What it means, in practice, is that in order
to make possible the higher rates of growth (and hence of fixed investment) contemplated, underdeveloped countries would have to
begin producing for themselves much of the heavy engineering products, chemicals, and other goods that they have hitherto counted

---

[23] The further assumptions were made that production in the developed market
economies would increase during the 1960s at the same rate as during the 1950s
(3·7% per annum): and that trade of the centrally planned economies would
rise in accordance with their targets.

on being able to import from the developed countries against exports of primary products. The creation of massive heavy industries in the at present underdeveloped countries must obviously come sooner or later. But whether the necessary enlargement and transformation of industry could be brought about on the scale required by 1970 within the present political, social, and economic framework of the underdeveloped countries seems highly doubtful. Thus far, only the countries of Eastern Europe, China, and the Soviet Union have been able to effect such a build-up of heavy industry within so short a space of time: and it may be doubted whether the underdeveloped countries could bring about the same degree of economic mobilization without undertaking a similar degree of political and social mobilization as well. Thus if the industrially advanced countries remain deaf to the needs of the underdeveloped countries for greater trade and aid, they are thereby sharpening the choice, which the latter countries face in any case, between economic stagnation and revolutionary change.

How far could the 'gap' be bridged by adjustment of aid and trade policies in the developed countries? Aid programmes have been falling into disrepute in several of the developed countries because of impatience with their apparent ineffectiveness, at any rate in their existing form. At the same time, efforts to enlarge market opportunities for the exports of underdeveloped countries encounter the opposition of agricultural and industrial producers in the developed countries. Any major expansion in imports by the developed countries of agricultural commodities competing directly or indirectly with home produce—such as cereals, meat, sugar, and fats and oils —would, it is feared, tend to upset programmes designed to support the prices received by domestic farmers from their marketings. At the same time increases in imports of manufactures from 'low-wage' countries encounter opposition from domestic entrepreneurs and labour unions on the grounds that they may cause 'market disruption' and unemployment.

Faced with difficulties in providing larger access to their own markets, the developed countries have been advising the underdeveloped countries to give greater access to one another, and to form regional groupings to this end. While the formation of such groupings does have much to commend it, as we shall see, it would be idle to suppose that such a policy provides a substitute for improved access to the markets of developed countries. Apart from the

fact that it will take some time to create new channels of trade between countries that have traditionally had much closer links to the
developed countries than to one another, it will be obvious that the
low income levels of the underdeveloped countries prevent them
from providing markets for one another in any way comparable to
those available in the developed countries.

This can be illustrated quite simply by the fact that the total
national expenditure of North America and Western Europe exceeds that of Latin America considerably more than tenfold. An
even greater disparity is evident in the market for manufactures.
The total consumption of manufactures in Latin America amounts
to about 6 per cent of the market for manufactures available in the
developed countries of North America and Western Europe, or
about 4 per cent of the market available in these countries together
with Eastern Europe and the Soviet Union. An increase in manufactured exports from Latin America that would be very large in relation to existing consumption of manufactures in the region itself
would thus be very small as a proportion of the market available in
the industrially developed countries. Hence increased access to the
markets of underdeveloped countries cannot be regarded as a substitute for larger opportunities in the markets of industrial countries.

In short, regional integration is no panacea for Latin America. It
will not diminish the need for political, economic, and social reform,
nor can it bring a beneficial influence to bear without such reform.
Even as regards the problems of external trade its contribution in
the years immediately ahead cannot be more than a limited one and
certainly will not obviate the need for greater access to the markets
of the developed countries. Provided, however, that the energies of
the Latin American peoples are directed towards development
goals more effectively than in the past, the concerting of their efforts
on a region-wide basis could significantly accelerate the attainment of these goals.

CHAPTER II

THE NEED FOR INTEGRATION

Conventional Wisdom on Regional Integration

Until quite recently there was widespread scepticism about the prospects for regional groupings among underdeveloped countries: and it was only as requests for greater access to their own markets began to multiply (and domestic pressures against 'market disruption' were intensified) that the industrial countries began to see merits in such groupings and even indicated a willingness to facilitate the process by relaxing the rather rigorous rules of GATT in this field.

The original pessimism about groupings of underdeveloped countries was based largely on orthodox economic theory, which implied that they would divert much more trade than they would create.

In his well-known study, *The Customs Union Issue*, Professor Jacob Viner held that the primary purpose of a customs union, and its major consequence for good or evil, was to shift sources of supply —and that shift might be either to lower-cost or to higher-cost sources, depending on circumstances.[1] According to this line of reasoning, where two countries both protect a similar range of industries, a customs union between them will tend to concentrate production in the more efficient, lower-cost firms. Where, however, the industries protected in the two countries are essentially dissimilar, the chances are that a customs union will cause each country to shift from low-cost sources of supply in third countries to high-cost sources within the union. In this way Viner arrives at his celebrated conclusion that the balance of advantage and disadvantage in a customs union will depend on how much trade is created and how much diverted.

If we apply this analysis to underdeveloped countries, it looks as though we should have to conclude that these countries should avoid economic unions like the plague: for such unions are almost bound to lead predominantly to shifts from low-cost sources of sup-

[1] (London, 1950), pp. 41–45.

ply for manufactures in the industrial countries of North America and Western Europe to high-cost sources within the underdeveloped countries themselves. This result is all the more certain if, as it appears from most of the plans of this type in existence or under consideration in the underdeveloped countries at the present time, the intention is not to generate undue competition within the union between existing industries; in other words, the intention appears to be maximize trade diversion and minimize trade creation in Viner's terms.

Subsequent refinements of the Viner approach have not yielded conclusions basically different from his in the present context. For example, Professor Lipsey finds

. . . that the sort of countries who ought to form customs unions are those doing a high proportion of their foreign trade with their union partner, and making a high proportion of their total expenditure on domestic trade. Countries which are likely to lose from a customs union, on the other hand, are those countries in which a low proportion of total trade is domestic, especially if the customs union does not include a high proportion of their foreign trade.[2]

Economic unions among underdeveloped countries fall clearly into the latter category, the category showing a balance of losses according to the theory put forward. Apart from the fact that many of them are highly dependent upon foreign trade, the bulk of that trade is carried on with the developed countries rather than with one another. The share of intra-regional trade in the total trade of Latin America is of the order of 10 per cent.

All this unfortunately throws much more light on the state of economic theory than on the problems of underdeveloped countries. One may, incidentally, wonder how adequate the conventional analysis is even for fully developed countries: the economic case for regional integration among such countries depends much more on its dynamic effects on the rate of growth than on its static effects with respect to trade creation and trade diversion.

As regards underdeveloped countries, however, the conventional theory simply misses the basic point. Being designed to explore the problem of optimal allocation of given resources, under given conditions of production, within a competitive framework, it cannot illuminate situations, such as those which arise in underdeveloped

[2] 'The Theory of Customs Unions: a General Survey', *Economic Journal*, Sept. 1960, pp. 508–9.

countries, in which neither resources nor conditions of production can be taken as given, and in which immobility of factors of production obstructs the operation of market forces. For any underdeveloped country contemplating closer economic ties with its neighbours the primary question is not—will this enable us to use our present resources more efficiently? Still less is it a question of whether such associations would lead to a more efficient utilization of world resources as a whole, for underdeveloped countries are surely entitled to look after themselves first and foremost and let the developed countries fend for themselves—as indeed they are very well able to do. The primary question for any potential grouping of underdeveloped countries is whether discriminatory encouragement of trade with one another would tend to accelerate the rate of growth or not.

It is, of course, common ground among economists that protection may be a necessary condition for economic development at the national level.[3] Protection provides a corrective to the operation of market forces where infant industries are to be established, and where the existence of disguised unemployment in agriculture implies a situation in which the real social costs of transferring underemployed labour to industry are much lower than would be indicated by the money costs of the entrepreneurs seeking to employ such labour.

Advantages of Group Protection

The question is therefore not whether protection is an indispensable instrument of policy in underdeveloped countries, but whether group protection offers any advantages over national protection in stimulating the rate of growth. Those who favour regional groupings of underdeveloped countries do so because they see great advantages in securing, for the agricultural and industrial producers of each country, *protected access*[4] *to a region-wide market*, instead of being confined within the limitations of narrow national markets. Such protected access would make it possible (*a*) for countries to use their existing agricultural and industrial capacities more fully in

[3] The form taken by protection may vary. While in some cases, notably the United States, protection traditionally took the form of high tariffs, in other cases the same effect was secured by undervalued exchange rates.
[4] Protected access is secured by the lowering of internal barriers to trade, at the same time as the outer ring of tariff and quota restrictions on imports from the rest of the world is maintained and perhaps even reinforced.

supplying one another's needs; (*b*) for new investment to take place in industries that would not be viable if confined to individual national markets; (*c*) for both old and new industries to reduce costs by benefiting from the economies of scale and specialization: in some cases this might help the industries concerned in the process of becoming fully competitive in world markets, including the markets of developed countries.

Stated in its simplest terms, the case for a common market in Latin America, as in any underdeveloped region, is that future economic growth presupposes a large amount of industrial development and that such development would be facilitated if the barriers to trade within the region could be reduced or eliminated.

While the importance of economies of scale is sometimes exaggerated, it seems clear that the national markets of most of the smaller underdeveloped countries are too restricted to provide an adequate volume of demand for mass-production industries. Productivity in any one country is likely to be lower the greater the number of different industrial products or varieties that it attempts to manufacture and the more its industries are limited to production for the home market alone. Where productivity is low and costs high, the tendency is for industry to seek—and obtain—correspondingly high protection. Yet if each industry in each country is separately entitled to the amount of protection it requires to survive while operating under conditions of low output and high costs, the tendency to regional specialization is necessarily inhibited, and protected inefficiency within small self-contained markets becomes the rule.

Although Latin America is perhaps not as fragmented as Africa, many of the countries in the region are exceedingly small, whether in terms of area, population, or aggregate income. Out of the twenty Latin American republics, only five—Argentina, Brazil, Colombia, Mexico, and Peru—have populations over 10 million. Twelve of them have populations under 5 million. And to these may be added the three Guianas, each with less than 1 million inhabitants, and various islands of the Caribbean, almost all of which likewise have six-figure populations or less.

With their relatively low per capita incomes, the national markets of these countries are exceedingly small, and the purchasing power available after basic needs for food and shelter have been provided is still smaller. Even a country as large as Brazil, with about 80 million people, has a total income of the same order of magnitude as Australia and New Zealand with a combined population of only 14 million.[5]

The markets of most of these countries are much too small to permit the efficient operation of large-scale modern industry at anything like full capacity. That is why, side by side with an overall shortage of industrial capacity in relation to needs, most underdeveloped countries do not fully utilize even such limited capacity as they do have. Vast areas of land remain uncultivated, as already noted, while factories work their machinery at much less than optimum rates.

Thus, for example, only in two of the firms producing trucks in Brazil in 1961 did output exceed 50 per cent of the capacity of one shift, while in the other two firms the rate of utilization was less than 20 per cent of one shift. In cars, jeeps, and utility vehicles, two firms had utilization rates of 70 per cent of one-shift capacity.[6] It has to be borne in mind that two or three-shift operation would be desirable in this particular industry.

Similar situations are to be found in other industries and other countries. In Mexico, for example, it was estimated that in 1962 most industrial establishments were operating at something like 50 per cent of capacity.[7] It is likely that even lower operating ratios are characteristic of the smaller Latin American countries, and that a situation of this sort must be a serious deterrent to investment in new capacity. The discouragement to new investment must be particularly serious in those branches of industry where even a single plant of optimum size would have no prospect of access to a market large enough to ensure economical rates of operation. This is certainly the case for all the many countries and islands in the Western Hemisphere with populations under 5 million.

But, it may be asked, why should it be necessary for Colombia, with a population of 15 million, to join an economic union, when Switzerland, a country with only one-third of Colombia's popula-

[5] As noted earlier, inter-country comparisons of national income are subject to serious limitations, and comparisons of the above type, between developed and underdeveloped countries, may be particularly misleading. In the present context, however, the comparison has a certain validity, being designed to throw light on the total money income available for purchases of industrial products.
[6] ECLA, *Problemas y perspectivas del desarrollo industrial latinoamericano* (E/CN.12/664, Apr. 1963), p. 29.
[7] Estimate by the president of the Confederation of Industrial Associations of Mexico, cited in *Comercio Exterior*, Mar. 1963, pp. 138–40.

C

tion, has been able to achieve a very high per capita income without being a member of an economic union? *A fortiori*, what compelling reasons can there be for countries like Argentina (22 million), Mexico (40 million), and Brazil (80 million) to seek economic integration with their neighbours? The answer is that Switzerland embarked upon its economic development at a time when international trade was still relatively free, and the establishment of new industries could take into account the existence of markets abroad as well as at home. Far different is the present situation confronting the underdeveloped countries. Few of them, in establishing manufacturing industries at the present time, could count on significant export markets. Markets in the industrial countries are closed to them, partly because by now the technological lag is so great that, even though wages in underdeveloped countries are much lower, total costs per unit of output are generally higher because of such factors as low productivity of labour, lack of complementary facilities, or high costs of raw materials, power, or transport: and partly because wherever this is not so, the industrial countries take steps to protect themselves against so-called unfair competition. On the other hand, markets in other underdeveloped countries are also closed to them. Where other underdeveloped countries have competing industries of their own, they have generally protected them in the home market up to the hilt. And where they do not have competing industries of their own, they would rather buy low-cost imports from North America and Western Europe than high-cost imports from their neighbours.

In general, where underdeveloped countries have gained their economic independence, their immediate reaction has often been to associate political nationalism with economic nationalism, and to try and go it alone over the whole range of industry. Moreover, once a broad and comprehensive system of protection has been introduced, the international rule of non-discrimination has prevented any liberalization *vis-à-vis* other underdeveloped countries.

The Industrial Problem of Latin America

During the very first stage of industrial development, this kind of constriction of the channels of trade does not necessarily impede growth to a major extent. Most of the Latin American countries have been able to establish substantial consumer goods industries without looking for markets beyond their own frontiers: and in many of these countries nearly all domestic requirements for manufactured consumer goods are now satisfied from home production.

By the same token, however, these countries have now reached, or are closely approaching, the limit of import saving that is possible in the light industries: and the rate of investment and the growth of income generated in these industries must therefore begin to slow down if it has not already done so. New impetus to industrial investment and expansion, and new opportunities for closing the external gap by import saving will have to come from the development of industries manufacturing intermediate products such as steel and chemicals, as well as durable producer and consumer goods.

There has been a growing consciousness in recent years of the vulnerability of underdeveloped countries that arises from their dependence on the exchange of exported primary commodities for imported manufactures: and this has been accompanied by general acceptance of the need for diversification of production and exports in these countries. What is still not widely understood is that even the industry of these countries is also usually of a semi-colonial or dependent character. For it consists mainly, in most cases, of the elementary processing of crude foodstuffs or raw materials for export to the industrial countries: and of the production of certain relatively simple types of consumer goods, possibly coupled with the final assembly or finishing stages of certain other products, based on imported components. As such, the industry of underdeveloped countries lacks the very simplest and indispensable requirement of independent life—namely the capacity to reproduce itself.

From this standpoint, the industrial development of the at present underdeveloped countries has followed a course somewhat different from that of Western Europe and North America. The Industrial Revolution in Britain meant not only the mechanization of textile production but also the manufacture of the new types of power-generating machinery that were needed in industry and transport. The growth of factory production of consumer goods went hand in hand with the building of mechanical and engineering industries. The same pattern of development was subsequently followed in the United States and on the continent of Europe. Later still in the countries of Eastern Europe, the Soviet Union, and China it was recognized that machine-building industries were the foundation of a self-supporting economy: the emphasis on heavy industry was probably excessive in the early years of development, and too little attention was given to opportunities for specialization and exchange. But the essential approach was based on valid inferences from the past experience of the developed market economies of North America and Western Europe.

It is the lack of machine-building and other intermediate industries that makes the industrial economies of many of the underdeveloped countries so exceptionally vulnerable to the vagaries of the world market for primary commodities. Since machinery and intermediate goods (metal products, chemicals, and other heavy industry products) have largely to be imported, a decline in foreign exchange resources resulting from a downturn in demand for primary commodities reacts immediately on the ability of underdeveloped countries to buy imported materials and equipment.

In the dialogue between the developed and underdeveloped counties, spokesmen for the former are apt to argue that if only the latter would 'put their houses in order', consume less and save more, their problems could be solved. There is no doubt much force in the contention that underdeveloped countries have done far less for themselves than they could have done, and that they may sometimes be tempted to blame others for what are really their own failings. Equally, however, it would be quite false to suppose that attempts to save more in underdeveloped countries would necessarily lead to higher investment and growth. For so long as an expansion of investment presupposes larger imports of machinery from developed countries: and so long as larger imports of machinery depend in turn on a corresponding rise in earnings from exports to (or in financial aid from) the developed countries: and so long, finally, as the latter countries cannot or will not undertake to provide the larger markets or financial aid thus required—so long must any attempts to mobilize additional savings in underdeveloped countries be frustrated by the inability to translate such savings into new productive capacity.

Thus the stagnation of trade between developed and underdeveloped countries has made it essential for the latter countries to stop relying on their traditional pattern of industrial growth, and to seek a more balanced expansion of all the major branches of industry. By this means they may be able to reduce the sensitivity of their economies to outside disturbances while increasing their own

potential for growth. At the same time, however, the very small
national markets of most of these countries make it necessary for
them to seek joint development of those industries in which economies of scale and of regional specialization may be significant. For
however reasonable it may be for small countries to set up industries producing tinned food products, or finished textiles, or foot-
wear, within the limits of their own home markets, they are bound
to be at a serious disadvantage in undertaking the large-scale investments required for many sectors of heavy industry.

As we have seen, light consumer goods industries are already to
be found in all Latin American countries, supplying in many cases
virtually the whole range of domestic requirements in the products
concerned. Capital goods industries, on the other hand, are still in
their infancy, although they have by now attained some significance
in Argentina, Brazil, and Mexico. In the case of Brazil, some two-
thirds of the machinery and equipment used are manufactured in
the country itself: the proportion is somewhat smaller in Argentina,
and much smaller in Mexico.[8] Brazil would, in fact, be much closer
than it is to establishing a capacity for growth independent of outside forces had it not failed thus far to solve the problem of its food
and fuel supplies, which use up much of its available foreign exchange. But apart from Brazil, and to a lesser extent Argentina and
Mexico, Latin America remains a heavily dependent region as far
as the capacity for industrial expansion is concerned.

Some headway has been made in recent years in durable consumer goods industries, which have been growing rapidly in Argentina, Brazil, Chile, Colombia, Mexico, Peru, Uruguay, and Venezuela. In all these cases, however, little or no provision has been
made for regional trade. The situation has become particularly
serious in the automobile industry, which has already developed
rapidly in Argentina, Brazil, and Mexico, while similar development is under way in Chile, Colombia, Peru, and Venezuela.

The sort of problem raised by fragmentation of the Latin American market is strikingly illustrated in this industry: data have already been cited on the low rate of capacity utilization in Brazil.
The total market represented by the above seven countries exceeds
300,000 passenger cars and 250,000 trucks per annum at the present
time. The production of these vehicles is already carried on by about
sixty firms, and new factories or assembly plants are under con-

[8] ECLA, *Problemas y perspectivas del desarrollo industrial*, p. 17.

sideration. Yet the above total market is smaller than that available to such European firms as Fiat (566,000 units per annum), Opel (360,000), Renault (350,000), and Ford of Britain (330,000). As against these latter figures, the largest-scale output for a single firm in Latin America is 20,000 units for trucks and 50,000 for cars.[9]

Available studies of the passenger car industry suggest that cost reductions associated with increasing scale of operations are particularly important up to an annual output of 50,000 units. It will therefore be obvious that most of the Latin American motor vehicle producers are operating on a scale at which unit costs tend to fall rather rapidly as output rises.

It has nevertheless proved extremely difficult to secure any cooperation between countries in the development of this industry. Indeed, some countries, notably Argentina and Brazil, have created a vast amount of unnecessary *internal* duplication of capacity. This has been done by offering such favourable terms and facilities to European and American producers that the latter were able to set up a whole series of local plants almost without regard to the efficiency of operations, with a virtual guarantee that their investment would pay off handsomely.

Another striking example of failure to exploit the economies of scale is to be found in the chemical industry. At the present time Latin America produces about 70 per cent of the chemicals it consumes. An extensive study of the industry by the Secretariat of ECLA has shown that if production were organized on a regional scale, the Latin American countries could bring their prices down below international levels. For example, it is estimated that the chemical industry could bring its prices down to 18 per cent below international prices in Colombia, 14 per cent in Mexico, 10 per cent in Brazil, 9 per cent in Peru, 6 per cent in Argentina, 2 per cent in Chile, and 1 per cent in Venezuela.[10]

The waste, inefficiency, and duplication of the automobile and chemical industries in Latin America are typical of the problems that arise because industries are being built up behind the walls of national protection without regard to the prospects for long-run viability, or the needs and resources of the continent as a whole.

[9] ECLA, *Problemas y perspectivas del desarrollo industrial*, p. 141.
[10] ECLA, *La industria química de Latinoamérica* (UN Sales No. 64.II.G.7), 1963, Table 106.

Proximate Factors in Latin American Integration

The underlying rationale of economic integration in Latin America will now be clear, the main consideration being that access to a region-wide market would make it possible to take advantage of important economies of scale and regional specialization: and this would not merely contribute to more efficient operation of existing industries but would create additional incentives for the establishment of new industries and thus help to speed up the rate of growth.

The widespread understanding that now exists in Latin America of the need for regional economic integration largely reflects the intellectual leadership of the Secretariat of ECLA, headed from 1950 to 1963 by Dr Raúl Prebisch. The task of gaining public and governmental support for such ideas was probably much more difficult than in Europe. Economic considerations alone could scarcely have led to the kind of movement that was needed for the European Economic Community to come into existence in 1957. Much more important was the underlying political momentum: as Professor Hallstein, President of the EEC Commission, has said: 'We are not in business at all: We are in politics.'[11]

While there are certain political overtones in the programme of Latin American integration, it cannot be said that the political pressure for integration is in any way comparable with the corresponding pressures in Europe. As we shall see later, if there are forces tending in the direction of continental solidarity in Latin America, there are equally strong feelings of nationalism. Thus the burden that had to be borne by the intellectual economic arguments was much greater in Latin America than in Europe.

Dr Prebisch and his staff did have one great asset—their intimate contact with the member governments of ECLA. There was hardly a government in Latin America that did not have at least one prominent member, often at Cabinet level, who had served a term on the ECLA staff or in an ECLA training course. Thus the ideas of ECLA were known and understood by government officials who had become acquainted with them as insiders. And ECLA commanded a respect all over Latin America that was quite unrivalled.

It nevertheless seems doubtful whether the influence of ECLA, for all its power and conviction, could alone have been decisive in

[11] Address to the Joint Meeting of Harvard University and Massachusetts Institute of Technology, 22 May 1961.

the absence of certain factors which were simultaneously pushing the Latin American countries in the direction of closer co-operation. The negotiations that led ultimately to the signing of the Treaty of Montevideo, in February 1960, began with quite limited objectives in August 1958 with consultations among experts from four countries only—Argentina, Brazil, Chile, and Uruguay. These countries had for some time previously been trading with one another on a preferential basis, and their mutual trade accounted in fact for the major part of total trade within the Latin American region.

The system of trade between these countries was not based on a preferential system of tariffs, but rather on the employment of exchange and trade controls in a selective manner. For example, Brazil would allocate foreign exchange for imports of fruit from Argentina or Chile and not for corresponding imports from other countries. And Argentina and Chile would reciprocate in their own import policies.

The use of direct controls rather than of tariff preferences for encouraging reciprocal trade in South America partly reflected the fact that tariffs had in many cases ceased to play a significant role in the limitation of imports. In some countries the decline in importance of tariff protection was due to the loss of effectiveness of flat rate duties as a result of rapid inflation. In others it was the rigidity of tariff schedules and the much greater flexibility of quantitative restrictions that induced countries to rely on the latter form of control. The influence of GATT was also important, in two respects. New tariff preferences were contrary to the rules of GATT: and even countries that had not joined GATT found that contractual limitations resulting from agreements with countries outside Latin America prevented them from giving preferential tariff treatment to their neighbours. At the same time, in the course of the early postwar tariff negotiations, certain of the Latin American countries, notably Brazil, were to a considerable extent stripped of their tariff protection, and were thus compelled to resort to all kinds of trade and exchange controls as their balances of payments subsequently came under pressure.

The preferential trading arrangements thus established within the southern group of Latin American countries could therefore be maintained in their existing form only so long as the special trade and payments restrictions on which they depended continued to be employed. From the mid–1950s, however, the countries concerned began, in accordance with policies strongly favoured internationally, to reduce their controls over trade and payments and bring them more closely into line with practices in North America and Western Europe.

Largely as a result of the new policies, trade among the Latin American countries began to decline. Exports of Latin American countries to one another reached their relatively highest point in 1953, when they were equivalent to 12·1 per cent of total exports: by 1961 they had declined to a mere 7·1 per cent of total exports. The highest dollar total of Latin American regional trade was reached in 1955: and from 1955 to 1961, while trade among Latin American countries declined by over 25 per cent, their imports from the rest of the world increased by more than 20 per cent.

It is striking that the entire decline in regional trade was concentrated among the countries that subsequently joined the LAFTA, and particularly among the four southern countries: Argentina, Brazil, Chile, and Uruguay. This may be seen from the following data (in $ millions):

	1955	*1961*	*Decrease*
Exports of all Latin American countries to one another	770	570	200
Exports of LAFTA countries to one another	508	299	209
of which Argentina	190	100	90
Brazil	145	95	50
Uruguay	31	6	25
Chile	58	35	23

It is not surprising, in the light of the above data, that it should have been the four southern countries that took the initiative in drafting a programme of regional co-operation: of the total decline in regional trade amounting to $200 million from 1955 to 1961, the southern four alone accounted for no less than $188 million.

The drastic drop in intra-regional trade at a time when imports from the rest of the world were expanding reflected the progressive abandonment of the instruments whereby Latin American countries had discriminated in favour of one another during the early postwar years. It is also significant that foodstuffs alone accounted for $160 million of the total drop of $200 million in the regional trade of Latin America between 1955 and 1961, while the value of imports of foodstuffs from developed countries, including imports under surplus disposal programmes, was approximately maintained.

The question consequently arose—how could the channels of trade that had been developed under the previous system of discriminatory import and exchange controls be preserved? Thus the practical search for some immediate means of restoring the flow of trade between the four South American countries: Argentina, Brazil, Chile, and Uruguay, coincided with the attempt, on a broader plane and with longer-range objectives, to bring about a greater measure of economic co-operation and even integration within Latin America as a whole. It was, moreover, natural for these two sets of objectives to come together, and for common ground to be sought between them. At a meeting of experts from the four southern countries in April 1959 to consider a draft Agreement, it was pointed out that, apart from the immediate objectives of solving the pressing trade problems that had arisen among the countries of South America, 'the draft Agreement . . . might be the point of departure for discussions at another and more comprehensive instrument in which they considered it highly desirable that all the Latin American countries should take part.' And the experts added that the fact that their four countries had taken the initiative 'would not entitle them to any privilege in relation to countries subsequently joining the system, either through re-negotiation of the Agreement or through accession to the Agreement as it stood.'[12]

At later meetings during 1959, and finally at the meeting at which the Treaty of Montevideo was completed and signed, further steps were taken to broaden the original draft Agreement by including provisions regarding the more permanent objectives of the participating countries. Existing trade among the southern group consisted largely of primary products, while the greatest potential for economic co-operation was likely to lie, as we have seen, in the development of industries on the basis of access to region-wide markets. It was thus necessary to merge the preservation of existing trade with provision for the development of new types of trade, especially in industrial goods.

Participation in the later negotiations was broadened by the joining of Bolivia, Paraguay, and Peru: and the arrival of Mexico during

[12] ECLA, *The Latin American Common Market* (1959), p. 98.

the last stages of negotiation dispelled misgivings that the southern countries might create an exclusive economic group, prejudicial to the interests of Latin America as a whole. The Central American countries stood aside, seeing a need to press forward with their own sub-regional integration plans before they would feel strong enough to face the larger countries of the south within a single grouping. Colombia and Ecuador hesitated, and Venezuela remained aloof partly because of its special position of strength, linked to the export of petroleum, and partly because of the overvaluation of its currency in terms of almost everything other than petroleum.

These various hesitations prevented the countries concerned from participating in the drafting of the Treaty of Montevideo, but they did not rule out ultimate accession to the Treaty. The sense of regional solidarity was sufficiently great for the original signatories to provide, in Article 58, that the Treaty would remain open to accession by the other Latin American states by the simple act of depositing the relevant instrument of accession. In this respect, the Treaty contrasts strikingly with the Treaty of Rome, accession to which involves lengthy and difficult negotiations.

The Scope of Regional Co-operation and the Hemisphere

Why did the Treaty not go further and allow for economic integration on a hemisphere-wide basis? We may pause for a moment on this point before going on to examine the Treaty itself.

No major initiative for economic union with the United States has thus far emerged in Latin America.[13] The idea of such a union has, however, often been suggested in the United States. Indeed, the concept of a Western Hemisphere economic union has probably been gaining ground in the United States in recent years. Such a concept runs directly counter to traditional United States foreign economic policy which has generally sought to gain universal acceptance of the idea of non-discrimination, and the ending of preferential systems such as those of the Commonwealth or the French Community. Throughout the Second World War the United States tried to persuade Britain to do away with Commonwealth prefer-

---

[13] In August 1957, at an economic conference of the OAS in Buenos Aires, Peru proposed the establishment of 'a permanent inter-American commission for the Western Hemisphere common market'. All other Latin American countries, however, favoured exclusively Latin American regional or sub-regional common markets. But see the statement by Dr Prebisch cited at the end of this chapter.

ence, and accepted the preservation of the system after the war only with the greatest reluctance.

The special economic relationships prevailing within the Commonwealth have in fact been very much loosened by postwar developments, and a similar tendency may be observed within the French Community, although there the loosening process has not yet gathered momentum. Indeed, despite the establishment of the European Economic Community and the accession of the former French African colonies to political independence, a considerable—and thus far fairly successful—effort has been made to develop a new form of association between the latter countries and the EEC as a whole.

American interest in a Western Hemisphere economic union may be viewed, in part, as a response to the attempt of the EEC to create the basis for a union between Western Europe and Africa. If the EEC builds Eurafrica, and if Britain seeks a tightening of Commonwealth ties once more, why should not the United States, it may be asked, draw the obvious conclusions regarding its own position in the Western Hemisphere?

In two speeches in June 1960 Governor Nelson A. Rockefeller advanced the idea of a Western Hemisphere Confederation, which would 'make possible a kind of Marshall Plan for Latin America that would work towards long-range industrial development and a Hemisphere Free-trade area, allowing a free flow of men and goods and money from Point Barrow to Tierra del Fuego'.[14]

Although Rockefeller's ideas were not taken up actively by the United States Government at the time, this does not mean that there was no support for them. Professor Hallstein, President of the EEC Commission, following meetings with high level government officials in Washington in May 1961, told the press that there was a tendency in the United States to favour sharing out economic aid according to 'centres of gravity', with each industrialized country paying special, though not exclusive, attention to territories particularly related to it for geographical, historical, cultural, or other reasons. However, the United States would prefer customs preferences to be as small as possible.[15]

---

[14] Governor Nelson A. Rockefeller, *Great Design for Freedom*, an address to the Rotary Club of Binghamton, New York, 21 June 1960. See also his *Western Hemisphere Unity*, an address to the New York Young Republican Club, 12 July 1960.

[15] *Europe* (Luxembourg), 26 May 1961.

A few months later, in September 1961, the Under Secretary of Commerce, Clarence D. Martin, made a public statement in which he expressed the view that the common market arrangements developing throughout the world 'make inevitable a serious consideration of the benefits which could be derived from further economic cooperation within the Western Hemisphere'. And he made it clear that the economic co-operation he had in mind would consist in 'the achievement of a market in which there are no tariffs, quotas, discriminations or other impediments to the movement of goods, services, manpower and invested capital'.[16]

There now began to be signs that there were Latin Americans who might consider some exclusive trading arrangement with the United States in retaliation against the discriminatory features of the association of certain African countries with the EEC. The Secretariat of the ECLA commented significantly that

If it turned out that the EEC system of preferences for African countries must inevitably be renewed, this would be regarded as a precedent that might perhaps enable Latin America to initiate negotiations with the United States for the ultimate establishment of some form of preference in the United States market for certain articles of great actual or potential importance in the balance of payments of Latin American countries.[17]

In October 1963 the Secretariat of the OAS in Washington suggested that while Latin American countries were aware of the shortcomings of regional preferential arrangements, it was likely to take a long time before a more general system of preferences for developing countries could be organized, because of the reluctance of African countries to give up their existing privileged access to the British or EEC market. In these circumstances, the OAS Secretariat proposed that the United States should make unilateral tariff concessions to Latin American countries for products on which the latter were themselves lowering their mutual trade barriers within the framework of their regional groupings[18] (i.e. LAFTA and the Central American common market).

---

[16] US Dept of Commerce, Address by the Honorable Clarence D. Martin, Jr. Under Secretary of Commerce for Transportation, 28 Sept. 1961 (press release).

[17] UN, *Acontecimientos y tendencias recientes en el intercambio de América Latina con la Comunidad Económica Europea*, 22 July 1962, p. 44.

[18] OEA/CIES/369, 19 Oct. 1963 (Spanish text, p. 12).

This was followed by endorsement of the idea of a Western Hemisphere common market by an influential Subcommittee of the United States Congress:

While the concept of a fully developed Western Hemisphere common market seems, at the moment, distant and fenced in by nationalism, it holds a sufficient hope for advancing the economy and industrialization of Latin America and the entire hemisphere to deserve the study of trade experts everywhere.[19]

And the growing independence of Western Europe led Senator Hubert Humphrey to a similar conclusion:

The emergence of a powerful Western Europe—likely to pursue a more independent foreign policy—makes hemisphere co-operation more urgent if the nations of this hemisphere are not only to solve their immediate internal problems but to play a proper role in world affairs in future decades. . . . Trade is essential to the economic prosperity of the hemisphere and we should give careful consideration to the possibility of developing a more cohesive trading area, which would not only bring economic advantages but would also promote the political unity of the hemisphere.[20]

Despite the various indications of growing interest in the possibility of a Western Hemisphere preferential system, it seems unlikely that such a system will ultimately commend itself either to the Latin American countries or to the United States. The Latin American countries could never accept the Rockefeller proposal for 'a free flow of men and goods and money from Point Barrow to Tierra del Fuego' because this would mean complete freedom for United States firms to compete with, and probably overwhelm, the new industries of the region.

The Latin American countries would no doubt be greatly tempted by any United States offer to grant non-reciprocal preferences to imports from Latin America, especially if it became clear that

[19] US Congress, Joint Economic Committee, *Private Investment in Latin America*, a Report of the Subcommittee on Inter-American Economic Relationships (OEA/CIES/369) (1964), p. 25.
[20] Senator Hubert H. Humphrey, 'US Policy in Latin America', *Foreign Affairs*, July 1964. The article was published before Senator Humphrey received the nomination of the Democratic Party for Vice-President of the United States. In his article, Senator Humphrey suggested that the first step in promoting 'a hemispheric trade zone' might be for the United States to lend strong support to the development of LAFTA. Once LAFTA had made significant progress, it would be possible to consider what new trade relationships should be developed between the LAFTA area and the United States and Canada.

African countries were unwilling to agree to the scaling down, progressively, of the preferences they now enjoy in Western Europe. But an arrangement of this sort seems unlikely. For one thing, it is difficult to imagine such an offer being made without any *quid pro quo* of any kind, and the question of the acceptability of such a *quid pro quo* to the Latin American countries would then arise.

On the other hand, the United States, as the leading world power, is likely to ponder carefully the limitations on its influence in Africa, Asia, and indeed, Europe that might follow the introduction of discriminatory ties with Latin America. It would be against the interests of a dominant industrial power to accept any arrangements that would tend to limit its access to any part of the world market: it would thus generally prefer an open system of relatively free trade on a world-wide basis to any restricted system or grouping. Political factors might likewise deter a major world power from granting exclusive privileges to a particular group of countries so long as it wished to retain influence with other groups.[21]

These considerations do not rule out the possibility of some form of special Western Hemisphere programme of economic co-operation: indeed, the Alliance for Progress is just such a programme, providing for the United States to grant financial aid to Latin American countries for the achievement of certain development goals. For the United States to go further and give exclusive privileges to Latin America would imply taking an essentially pessimistic view of the prospects for its future relationships with the Commonwealth and the EEC: and for the Latin American countries to accept such privileges would mean running the risk of creating a dependent relationship, and, if reciprocity were conceded, endangering the prosperity of their newly established industries as well.

A preferential system limited to the Western Hemisphere would also reverse one of the major achievements of the United Nations Conference on Trade and Development of 1964. At that conference it was unanimously agreed that existing preferential arrangements between developed and underdeveloped countries should be abolished *pari passu* with the granting of at least equivalent advantages (in the form of additional aid or market outlets) to the under-

[21] Nevertheless, *Business Week* reported on 23 Jan. 1965 that the State Department was looking 'again' at the question of US trade preferences for Latin America. It was suggested that if the Kennedy round failed to produce significant European concessions to Latin America, US pressure for a US-Latin American preferential system would grow.

developed countries at present participating in such arrangements.[22] There is thus a danger of undoing the progress made at the Geneva Conference in bringing to an end what was essentially a survival of the old colonial systems of economy.

As Dr Raúl Prebisch put the matter in an address to the United Nations Trade and Development Board on 6 April 1965:

One of the main reasons why developing countries have recognized the need to diversify not only the composition but also the destination of their exports is so that they may not have to depend on a single great country or group of countries, but may be able to trade with the entire world. I think that that is of the greatest importance from the political point of view. Unfortunately, there are some symptoms that the spirit of Geneva is not being applied, and that on the contrary there is an aggrava-tion of the tendency towards a system of discriminatory preferences in certain parts of the world. I cannot hide from the Board my great concern at signs in certain Latin American circles, which are manifesting them-selves with increasing force in requests to the United States for a pre-ferential system to be exclusive to Latin American countries. I believe that that is contrary to the spirit of Geneva, and I consider it my duty to call the Board's attention to it. For what Governments do in the near future in this respect may not be of a temporary nature; it will have a tremendous impact on the character and shape of the economic future of the world. Those decisions will mean either the establishment of a new pattern of world integration and world economic unity or the establish-ment of new forms of disintegration of the world by segmentation into zones of influence covering some developed countries and a group of developing countries.[23]

[22] UNCTAD, *Proceedings*, i. 30.   [23] TD/B/9.

U. S. A.

Latin American
Trade Groupings

MEXICO

CUBA
DOMINICAN
REP.
HONDURAS
JAMAICA
GUATEMALA
EL SALVADOR
NICARAGUA
PUERTO
RICO
HAITI

COSTA RICA
PANAMA

TRINIDAD
VENEZUELA
BR.GUIANA
SURINAM
COLOMBIA
FR.GUIANA

ECUADOR

PERU

B R A Z I L

BOLIVIA

PARAGUAY

C H I L E

ARGENTINA
URUGUAY

CMP

Latin American Free
Trade Association

Central American
Integration Programme

0   100
Miles

MAP 1

D

CHAPTER III

THE TREATY OF MONTEVIDEO

General Provisions

The Treaty of Montevideo[1] was signed in February 1960 by Argentina, Brazil, Chile, Mexico, Paraguay, Peru, and Uruguay. The signatory governments deposited their respective instruments of ratification on 2 May 1961, and the Treaty, in accordance with Article 57, entered into force thirty days later. Instruments of accession were subsequently deposited by Colombia on 30 September 1961 and by Ecuador on 3 November 1961. Thus by the end of 1961 the Treaty had entered into force in the whole of the South American continent except Bolivia, Venezuela, and the three Guianas. Of the other Latin American countries, only Mexico has thus far ratified the Treaty (see Map 1).

The Treaty established the Latin American Free Trade Association (LAFTA) with headquarters in Montevideo. The signatory governments expressed their determination 'to establish, gradually and progressively, a Latin American common market', and 'to pool their efforts to achieve the progressive complementarity and integration of their economies on the basis of an effective reciprocity of benefits'.[2]

In pursuit of these goals, the Treaty provides for the establishment of a free-trade area, the members of which undertake to eliminate all tariffs and other restrictions on 'substantially all' of their trade with one another: they do not, however, formally undertake to unify their tariffs against the outside world as the members of a customs union do.

The elimination of internal trade barriers is to be achieved gradually over a period of twelve years—that is, by 1973. To this end, annual negotiations take place so as to bring about reductions in duties by each country on imports from the rest of the group, equivalent each year to not less than 8 per cent of the weighted average duties applicable to third countries: corresponding reductions in

---

[1] The text of the Treaty of Montevideo is contained in *Multilateral Co-operation*, see also below, pp. 228–56.
[2] Treaty of Montevideo, Preamble.

non-tariff import restrictions are also negotiated. These reductions are listed by each country in a National Schedule which must be published by 1 November each year and enter into force from the following 1 January.

Concessions listed in National Schedules may be withdrawn by negotiation among member countries, subject to the provision of adequate compensation: and they may also be set aside under the provisions of various escape clauses, as discussed below. In order to give a greater finality to concessions granted, therefore, the Treaty provides for a Common Schedule. The Common Schedule is to consist of all those products on which LAFTA members agree to eliminate duties, charges, and other restrictions completely *vis-à-vis* one another within the twelve-year period of transition. To this end, provision was made for triennial negotiations to be held among LAFTA members during the third, sixth, ninth, and twelfth years from the effective date of the Montevideo Treaty. The negotiations were to be completed by 30 November of each negotiating year. The items placed on the Common Schedule at the end of the first three-year period were to account for 25 per cent of trade between the participating countries during that period: and this proportion was to rise to 50 per cent at the end of the second three-year period, and 75 per cent at the end of the third three-year period. By the end of the twelve-year period of transition, the Common Schedule of restriction-free items must account for 'substantially all' of the trade between LAFTA members.[3]

The inclusion of products in the Common Schedule is final and the concessions granted in respect thereof are irrevocable, except

[3] This is designed to comply with Art. XXIV para. 8(*b*) of GATT (see below, p. 227). The term 'substantially all' was not defined in the Treaty, and the Contracting Parties of GATT have not agreed upon a definition of the term either. During the consultations that led to the adoption of the Treaty of Montevideo it was assumed by the Latin American representatives that 'substantially all' meant 80%. This was based on a precedent provided by the EEC. At the twelfth session of GATT, the EEC countries maintained that the free-trade area that they had formed with certain African territories would satisfy the provisions of GATT because the system of unrestricted circulation of goods would cover 80% of the trade involved (see ECLA, *The Latin American Common Market*, pp. 96–97). The contention of the EEC countries was neither accepted nor rejected by GATT, although several countries disputed the EEC definition of the term 'substantially all'. Moreover, when the LAFTA countries were subsequently asked by GATT to define this term in the context of the Treaty of Montevideo, they replied that it meant 'between 75 per cent and the whole of the trade' (see *Resoluciones (Comité)*, p. 136, Question 3).

for temporary relief provided under escape clauses. Problems arising in connexion with the establishment of a Common Schedule are
discussed below.

The Montevideo Treaty provides for the immediate application
of unconditional most-favoured-nation treatment to the goods of
each Contracting Party in the territory of the others. In addition, the
products of each LAFTA country are to receive national treatment—
that is, the same treatment as that accorded to domestic products—
in the territories of the other participating countries with respect to
taxes and other internal duties and charges, and are to enjoy freedom
of transit through the territories of the respective member states.

Exceptions to the application of most-favoured-nation treatment
are, however, made for less-developed countries, as indicated below, and with respect to special benefits granted by any Contracting
Party in its border trade whether with LAFTA countries or others.

The Treaty specifies that the negotiation of the National and
Common Schedules shall be 'based on reciprocity of concessions'.[4]
This reciprocity is to be defined in terms of the 'expected growth in
the flow of trade between each Contracting Party and the others as
a whole, in the products included in the liberalization programme
and those which may subsequently be added'.[5]

Provision for cases in which reciprocity is not achieved is made in
the following terms:

> If, as a result of the concessions granted, significant and persistent
> disadvantages are created in respect of trade between one Contracting
> Party and the others as a whole in the products included in the liberalisa-
> tion programme, the Contracting Parties shall, at the request of the Con-
> tracting Party affected, consider steps to remedy these disadvantages
> with a view to the adoption of suitable, nonrestrictive measures designed
> to promote trade at the highest possible levels.[6]

As will be seen subsequently, the interpretation of the principle
of reciprocity raises important problems for the whole programme
of liberalization envisaged under the Treaty of Montevideo.

The Scope of Liberalization

One of the most important issues involved in the interpretation of
the Treaty of Montevideo concerns the extent to which the Treaty
is intended to lead to the freeing not merely of *existing* trade but also

---

[4] Treaty of Montevideo, Art. 10.   [5] Art. 13.   [6] Art. 11.

of trade in all products, whether exchanged among the member countries in the past or not. Article 14 sets forth both objectives: it states that the Contracting Parties shall take steps not only to include in the National Schedules the largest possible number of products in which trade is carried on among the Contracting Parties: but also to add to these Schedules an increasing number of products which are not yet included in reciprocal trade. The significance of this article must, however, be viewed in the light of the rules governing the reduction in duties that has to take place each year following negotiations among the Contracting Parties.

The method whereby the average annual 8 per cent reduction in duties is to be calculated is laid down in Protocol No. 1 to the Treaty. Under this protocol, the products to be taken into account in calculating the annual percentage rate of tariff reduction include those 'originating in the territory of the other Contracting Parties and imported from the Area during the preceding three-year period and further products included in the National Schedule concerned as a result of negotiations'.

In other words, the products to be included in the calculation are those which are already traded among the Latin American countries, together with any others that may be added to the National Schedule as a result of negotiations. Since it is entirely within the discretion of each member country whether or not to include in its National Schedule products which it has not imported from Latin American countries in the past, it appears that the minimum requirements of the Treaty can be satisfied simply by liberalizing existing trade. A country would be under no compulsion to reduce the import duties on particular products whenever such duties were so high (or quantitative restrictions were so stringent) as to exclude all imports from Latin American sources.

If the Treaty were to be interpreted in as restrictive a fashion as this, its significance would be greatly weakened. Indeed, it is rather doubtful whether the arrangement could be regarded as leading to the establishment of a free-trade area in such a case. To illustrate the point, one might envisage a hypothetical case in which, prior to entering a free-trade area, a country imported only one particular product from other members of the area, because of an absolute ban on all other imports. Such a country could fully discharge obligations under the formula described above by simply freeing its imports of that one single product from all tariff and non-tariff restrictions while continuing to prohibit all other imports. Such an interpretation, however, would obviously do serious violence to the whole concept and purpose underlying the Treaty.

Indeed, it is not the trade in traditional primary products that is likely to bring the greatest gains to the Latin American countries from a mutual reduction in trade restrictions. If the Treaty of Montevideo is to make a significant contribution to the economic development of Latin America, it must be by promoting an expansion of trade in semi-finished and finished manufactures, and by creating incentives for the establishment of new industries able to count upon access to the whole of the Latin American market and not simply to the market of a single country. But if this objective is to be achieved, what will count most in the liberalization process are not the products imported from the Area during the preceding three-year period as is provided in Protocol No. 1, but those that have not yet entered significantly into trade within the Area. In fact, the success of the Treaty may be measured by the extent to which it encourages countries to bring new products into the calculation of the annual percentage reductions in mutual tariff barriers.

Agriculture and Industry

Agriculture is subject to quite different treatment from industry under both the Treaty of Rome and the Stockholm Convention (creating the EEC and EFTA respectively) and a similar pattern is followed in the Treaty of Montevideo. In the course of discussions that preceded the adoption of the Montevideo Treaty, it was pointed out that agriculture in Latin America would need to undergo profound changes—involving land reform and the application of modern techniques—before it could be expected to face the pressures of regional competition. It was recognized that market forces could not be expected to operate in a beneficial manner in an environment that was essentially hostile to enterprise, as the subsistence sector of agriculture usually is.

The Treaty of Montevideo therefore provides for special treatment for agriculture. Participating countries are to co-ordinate their agricultural development and agricultural trade policies and will attempt to expand their mutual trade in agricultural products. This is to be done 'without disorganizing the regular productive activities of each Contracting Party'.[7]

[7] Art. 27.

Consequently, participating countries may, during the transition period, limit their imports of agricultural products to the amount required to bridge the gap between domestic production and consumption and may, to this end, take steps to equalize the prices of imported and domestic products. Where countries do have deficits in domestic production, they are required to give priority, 'under normal competitive conditions', to products originating in the territories of the other Contracting Parties, 'due consideration being given to the traditional flows of intra-Area trade'.[8]

During the examination of the Treaty of Montevideo by GATT, LAFTA members were asked whether priority would be given to imports of agricultural products originating in the territories of other LAFTA members even if the prices of supplies from third countries were lower. The reply given was an unconditional 'no'.[9] Thus the granting of priority to imports from other LAFTA suppliers was regarded as dependent on their being able to meet price competition from third countries.

This assurance, though welcome to third countries, appears to go too far. The EEC does not undertake that intra-EEC trade in agricultural products shall be at prices competitive with world market prices—far from it—and it is difficult to see why Latin America should be expected to conform to more rigorous standards than the EEC. Encouragement of intra-regional trade in agricultural products in Latin America could play a vital role in promoting the modernization of the agricultural economy of the region. Since Latin America provides ample scope for all types of land cultivation, whether temperate or tropical, the case for specialization and exchange in agriculture is perhaps even more obvious than the corresponding case in industry. It would be undesirable to place limitations on such specialization because of the competitiveness of supplies from third countries. Achieving competitiveness with supplies from other sources should certainly be a long-range target, but the very attainment of that target depends in part on the creation of region-wide markets for the output of the Latin American countries.

One of the most important provisions of the Treaty of Montevideo is that which authorizes the negotiation of agreements designed to promote industrial development on a co-ordinated region-

[8] Art. 29.   [9] *Resoluciones* (*Comité*), p. 108, Question 190.

wide basis. As we shall see, the overall success of the integration programme may well depend on the effectiveness of joint industrial planning for the Latin American region as a whole.

The preamble to the Treaty of Montevideo states that the participating countries are 'motivated by the desire to pool their efforts to achieve the progressive complementarity and integration of their national economies on the basis of an effective reciprocity of benefits'. For this purpose, the Treaty provides for participating governments to co-ordinate their policies of industrial development and to promote the negotiation of agreements between representatives of particular industrial sectors. The Treaty does not specify the scope or content of such agreements, and there is clearly room for considerable variation in the procedures employed in each case. In some industries the preliminary stages of processing might be carried out in one area and the last stages in another. In others, where two or more countries possess productive facilities in the same industry, regional agreements might take the form of arrangements for inter-country specialization and exchange. Such agreements providing for industrial complementarity on a region-wide basis must take the form of protocols to the Treaty of Montevideo and become effective after the Contracting Parties have determined that they are consistent with the terms of the Treaty.

Less Developed Countries

Of particular interest are the special measures under Chapter VIII of the Montevideo Treaty creating a favoured position for relatively less developed countries within the Free Trade Association. Protocol No. 5 to the Treaty provides for such treatment to be extended to Bolivia (at such time as it may accede to the Treaty) and to Paraguay. Moreover, during its first session in July 1961 the Conference of the Contracting Parties to the Montevideo Treaty approved the extension of special treatment to Ecuador as a less developed country, on joining the Association.

Under the special dispensation of Article 32 of the Treaty, a less developed LAFTA country may receive preferential concessions from other member countries in order to encourage the introduction or expansion of specific productive activities. In other words, a preferential system is created within a preferential system, the less developed countries benefiting from a two-tier preference while the ordinary members receive only the normal reciprocal preferences provided by the Treaty. The less developed countries may also be authorized to reduce their import duties, charges, and other trade restrictions less rapidly than is required of the other parties to the Treaty: and may also take steps to correct an unfavourable balance of payments, subject to fewer limitations and controls than are provided for under the more general escape-clause provision of the Treaty applicable to ordinary members. Permission may further be given to a less developed country to apply appropriate non-discriminatory measures designed to protect the domestic output of products included in the liberalization programme which are of vital importance to its economic development—providing 'that this does not entail a decrease in its customary consumption'. Finally, provision is made in the Treaty for collective arrangements by the LAFTA countries for obtaining financial and technical assistance for the less developed countries, both inside and outside the area, with a view to expanding existing productive activities or encouraging new ones—'particularly those intended for the industrialization of its raw materials'.

Escape Clauses

Any LAFTA country whose production, trade, or balance of payments are adversely affected by concessions granted under the Montevideo Treaty can seek relief under various 'saving clauses' of the Treaty. Mention has already been made of the application of the principle of reciprocity under the Treaty. In accordance with this principle, if a participating country suffers 'significant and persistent disadvantages' because of concessions granted to other LAFTA members, it can request the other Contracting Parties to consider the adoption of suitable non-restrictive measures 'designed to promote trade at the highest possible levels'. Action may similarly be requested if such disadvantages occur for reasons other than the granting of concessions under the Treaty.

In these cases the emphasis is upon 'non-restrictive' measures designed to restore an appropriate balance of advantage among LAFTA members. If, however, such measures prove insufficient to prevent adverse effects upon the production or balance of payments of a member country, the affected party may receive authorization from other members to impose temporary non-discriminatory restrictions on imports of commodities listed in the National Schedules or even in the Common Schedule. These restrictions must not, however, be such as to reduce 'the customary level of consumption' in the importing country.

In cases of emergency, member countries need not wait for specific authorization from the Contracting Parties of LAFTA before introducing the non-discriminatory restrictions required. In such cases, however, information concerning the restrictions applied must immediately be communicated to the Standing Executive Committee, which, 'if it deems necessary, shall convene a special session' of the supreme organ of LAFTA—the Conference of the Contracting Parties. Moreover, if the special restrictions remain in effect for more than one year, the Standing Executive Committee, either on its own motion or at the request of any member, can propose to the Conference 'the immediate initiation of negotiations with a view to eliminating the restrictions adopted'.[10]

Institutions

The Latin American Free Trade Association is a legal entity, with power to contract, acquire, and dispose of property, institute legal proceedings, and hold and transfer funds in any currency.

The supreme organ of LAFTA is the Conference of the Contracting Parties. The Conference is responsible for carrying out the provisions of the Montevideo Treaty, including the holding of periodic negotiations as required by the Treaty, approving the budget of the Standing Executive Committee, adopting its own rules of procedure, and approving those of the Standing Executive Committee.

The Conference is required to hold a regular session once every year, a quorum being two-thirds of the membership. Subject to certain exceptions, the Treaty provided that during the first two years of operations, decisions by the Conference should be adopted by the affirmative votes of at least two-thirds of the Contracting Parties, so long as no negative vote was cast. It was no doubt hoped that it might become possible to dispense with the veto provision over a growing area of decision-making as under the Treaty of Rome. At the end of 1963, however, it was decided to maintain the existing system of voting, including the veto clause: while provision was made for the Contracting Parties to agree on cases in which the veto would no longer be applicable, no time limit for such agreement was laid down and, of course, any decision along these lines would itself be subject to the veto.[11]

[10] Art. 26.   [11] See resolution 68 (III), p. 315 below.

The Standing Executive Committee is the 'permanent organ' of LAFTA, responsible for supervising the implementation of the provisions of the Montevideo Treaty. The Committee has a variety of responsibilities of an executive character, including the convening of the Conference, the preparation of work programmes, budget estimates and studies of various kinds, the presentation of an annual report on its activities and on the results of the implementation of the Treaty for consideration by the Conference, and the submission to the Conference of such recommendations as it deems appropriate for the effective implementation of the Treaty. The Committee also represents LAFTA in dealings with third countries and international organs and entities, as well as in contracts and other instruments of public and private law.

The Standing Executive Committee may request the technical advice and co-operation of individuals and of national and international organizations. In this connexion, a special status is given to the Secretariats of ECLA and of the Inter-American Economic and Social Council of the OAS. Protocol No. 3 to the Treaty provides that representatives of these two Secretariats shall attend the meetings of the Standing Executive Committee when the business to be discussed is, in the Committee's opinion, of a technical nature.

The Standing Executive Committee has a Secretariat headed by an Executive Secretary, who is elected by the Conference for a three-year term with the possibility of re-election. The Executive Secretary attends the plenary meetings of the Committee without the right to vote, and also serves as the General Secretary of the Conference. The Executive Secretary and the Secretariat are international civil servants, forbidden to seek or receive instructions from any government or other national or international entity.

The Treaty of Montevideo remains open to accession by any Latin American state by the simple device of depositing the relevant instrument of accession. For such acceding states, the Treaty enters into force thirty days after the deposit of the instrument of accession, and at the next session of the Conference following the date of deposit, the new member state enters into negotiations so as to comply with the requirements of the Treaty regarding the reduction of trade barriers.

Thus, for example, Colombia, which had ratified the Treaty during the latter part of 1961, conducted negotiations with the seven other member countries during the early months of 1962, leading to the granting of mutual concessions which became effective on 1 April 1962. Ecuador also acceded, and conducted negotiations in the manner required. However, Cuban ratification was rejected in 1962, as indicated below.

Under the Treaty, new members benefit from concessions already in effect as a result of previous negotiations only after they themselves have lowered their own trade barriers by 8 per cent for each year since the Treaty went into force.[12] If, therefore, a new member were to join at a relatively late stage in the twelve-year transition period, it would be faced with the need for a very substantial measure of liberalization: and it might well prove necessary to adopt some means of graduating the reduction in trade barriers so as to avoid undue economic dislocation.[13]

Although the Treaty is of unlimited duration, it provides for a withdrawal procedure, and is therefore in this respect unlike the Treaty of Rome. A country wishing to withdraw informs the other Contracting Parties at a regular annual session of the Conference, and formally submits its instrument of denunciation at the following regular session. The rights and obligations of the denouncing government with respect to reductions in duties, charges, and other restrictions, received or granted under the liberalization programme, remain in force for a period of five years from the date on which the denunciation becomes formally effective, unless the Contracting Parties consent to a shorter period.

The Rejection of Cuba

When Cuba announced its intention, in 1962, of complying with the procedure for accession laid down in Article 58, the LAFTA members met to consider the matter. They decided that although Article 58 provides that any Latin American country, without exception, may join LAFTA by following the procedure laid down, they could not permit accession by any country maintaining an economic régime incompatible with the Treaty of Montevideo. They decided further that there was an 'absolute incompatibility' between the Cuban economic system and the Treaty of Montevideo, and that the accession of Cuba would therefore not be

[12] Art. 59.
[13] When, however, the LAFTA members were asked in GATT whether they thought that a country joining LAFTA after six years would be able to effect a 48 per cent reduction in its tariffs in a single stage, the answer given was 'Obviously yes' (see *Resoluciones (Comité)*, p. 150, Question 142).

accepted so long as it maintained its existing economic régime.[14] No attempt was made to define the precise character of the incompatibility referred to. Ostensibly, it was not of a political nature, since the relevant resolutions refer only to 'technical' and 'economic' compatibility.

It is possible that LAFTA members could have sought to justify Cuba's exclusion on the grounds that Cuba could not literally maintain free trade with other Latin American countries without abandoning its whole system of foreign trade planning and control; and that Cuba would not be in a position to comply with those clauses of the Montevideo Treaty that call for encouragement to private enterprise. That the governments were not, however, prepared to say all this in so many words probably reflected a concern on the part of some of them that findings of this sort might be used in future against countries seeking to extend the scope of state enterprise or control. Had not President Adolfo López Mateos of Mexico himself stated that 'We must conceive of the Latin American economy as a planned economy'.[15]

The Cuban case has therefore left behind it an important area of uncertainty as to the point at which public regulation or control of a country's economy might be held to raise a possible question of incompatibility with the Treaty of Montevideo.

The Hesitation of Venezuela

Bolivia and Venezuela were the only two independent countries of South America that had not joined LAFTA by the end of 1964. The case of Bolivia will be examined in Chapter VII in connexion with the discussion of problems of less developed countries. There remains the case of Venezuela.

Ever since the beginning of the negotiations that ultimately led to the signing of the Treaty of Montevideo, successive governments in Venezuela have been faced with a dilemma. On the one hand, they could see the opportunities for accelerated growth that participation in a scheme of regional integration might offer to their country. On the other hand, they were aware that Venezuela, a country of very high costs, might be placed at a disadvantage compared with other Latin American countries.

The explanation for the high cost structure of the Venezuelan economy is to be found in the fact that the level of industrial wages is

[14] *Resoluciones*, 36 (II) and 37 (II). [15] *Comercio Exterior*, Nov. 1961, p. 649.

determined essentially by the productivity of the petroleum and iron ore sectors. These sectors are so productive as to be able to pay relatively high wages, and this tends to influence the wage levels of other sectors where productivity is much lower. Consequently while wage costs per unit of output may be low in the sectors producing petroleum and iron ore they are very high elsewhere. This means that Venezuela might be in an inferior competitive position in relation to other countries within LAFTA except for petroleum, iron ore, and perhaps a few other products. As the Bank of Venezuela pointed out in September 1960:

> Any common market or free trade area will leave us producing nothing but petroleum and iron ore, and importing everything else. Our textiles cannot compete with Brazilian textiles, our coffee cannot compete with Colombian coffee and our meat cannot compete with Uruguayan meat. For us a free trade area is utopian at the present time.[16]

For these reasons the government of Venezuela took the view that participation in a common market would not be possible without special treatment that would allow for the particular difficulties in which Venezuela found itself.

The problem of Venezuela in this respect differs in degree but not in kind from that of other Latin American countries. It is, indeed, a quite general characteristic of underdeveloped countries that they are competitive on world markets in respect of a few primary commodities produced for export, and uncompetitive in relation to almost everything else, notably industrial goods. It is not only Venezuela but all underdeveloped countries that have generally high costs in industry, necessitating protection in one form or another. Venezuela is therefore not a special case but rather an extreme one within a broad spectrum of countries ranging from those in which the export sector is exceptionally productive to those in which it is not.

For all these countries, the problem is that the particular exchange rate that enables them to sell their primary commodities in world markets is set too high to enable them to export manufactures. And the greater the differential between productivity in primary commodity production and in manufacturing, the more is an exchange rate set in terms of primary commodities apt to be overvalued in terms of locally produced manufactures.

---

[16] Banco de Venezuela, *Boletín de Economía y Finanzas*, Sept. 1960.

It is this latter consideration that accounts for the paradox that Venezuela, one of the richer countries of Latin America and one of the most comfortably placed in terms of import capacity and the balance of payments, should have sought special treatment for itself before joining LAFTA. Because of the exceptional gap in productivity between the petroleum and iron ore sectors and the rest of the economy, Venezuela was maintaining an exchange rate overvalued in terms of almost everything except these two products.

In effect, Venezuela was asking for special favours from LAFTA because of the impact on its economic structure of its riches in petroleum. But the other LAFTA countries could scarcely be expected to see the matter that way. As far as they were concerned, Venezuela would have to choose between an exchange rate policy that had been geared to its traditional lopsided dependence on one or two export commodities, and a policy that would permit participation in a joint programme of industrial development in Latin America.

On the other hand, it was not unnatural for Venezuela to take the view that it could hardly set its exchange rate with reference to the small amount of trade that it was likely to do with other Latin American countries. When, towards the end of 1960, Venezuela undertook a partial devaluation of its currency, this was a response to a weakening in its general trade and payments position rather than an attempt to create the necessary conditions for joining LAFTA. Nevertheless the partial devaluation did help to bridge the gap with LAFTA and the government began to reconsider the possibility of acceding to the Treaty of Montevideo.

It is not quite clear how far President Leoni's announcement in June 1964[17] that Venezuela would join LAFTA within a matter of months reflected a continuing expectation that it should qualify for special treatment. The President expressed the view that no disruption of the Venezuelan economy would occur, because of the flexibility and gradualism characteristic of the Treaty of Montevideo. No doubt it was expected, at the least, that under the 'flexible' arrangements of LAFTA, Venezuela would be eligible for membership of the intermediate group of countries, along with Chile, Colombia, Peru, and Uruguay.[18]

[17] The President's statement followed by only a few days a decision by the Chamber of Industry of Caracas to oppose the entry of Venezuela into LAFTA as being contrary to national economic interests (*Boletín Quincenal*, 25 June 1964, pp. 202–3).

[18] The special position accorded to this group is discussed below in ch. vii.

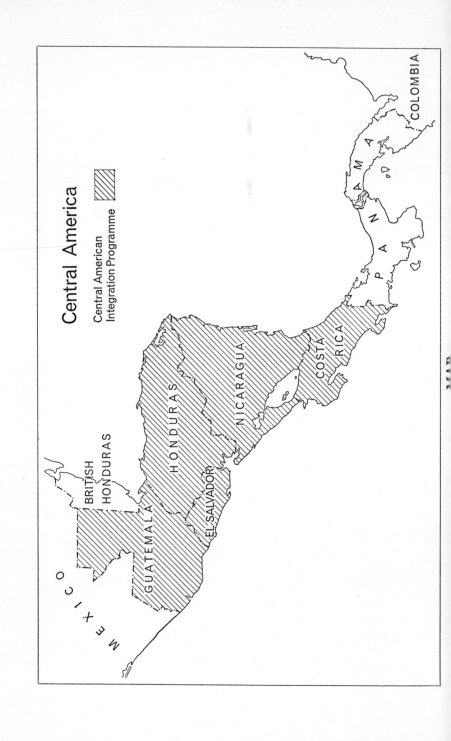

Central America

Central American
Integration Programme

COLOMBIA

PANAMA

COSTA RICA

NICARAGUA

HONDURAS

BRITISH
HONDURAS

EL SALVADOR

GUATEMALA

MEXICO

CHAPTER IV

THE CENTRAL AMERICAN
INTEGRATION PROGRAMME

Steps to Integration

Before going further with our analysis of trends and problems in the LAFTA area, it may be useful to turn aside for a moment to examine the Central American integration programme, which offers a number of interesting points of comparison and contrast.

The five Central American countries—Costa Rica, El Salvador, Guatemala, Honduras, and Nicaragua—have reached a stage of economic co-operation that is in many ways more advanced than that attained by the members of LAFTA. To some extent this reflects the greater sense of regional solidarity prevailing among these countries than in Latin America as a whole. The Central American countries are linked by historical, social, and cultural bonds reaching back to the days before independence was achieved in 1821.

Although the winning of Central American independence was followed by a break-up into separate states, the idea of Central American unity was never lost and there were times when reunification seemed close to realization.[1] During the 1930s and 1940s, however, the unification movement received a setback, and not until 1950 did circumstances again become favourable for a new move towards unity.

In October 1951 the foreign ministers of the five Central American countries met and adopted the Charter of San Salvador establishing an Organization of Central American States (Organización de Estados Centroamericanos, known as ODECA). The first steps towards economic integration were taken in the same year, when ECLA approved the establishment of the Central American Com-

---

[1] In *The Central American Republics* (London, OUP for RIIA, 1964), p. 82, Prof. Franklin D. Parker suggests that the attempts made to foster Central American unity in 1906–7 might have cut fifty years off the unification timetable had it not been for the involvement of the United States in Central American politics.

E

mittee for Economic Co-operation. It was this committee that directed the evolution of the integration programme.

The need for Central America to unite before considering entry, as a single unit, into any broader Latin American association derives essentially from the lower level of development of the countries in the area and their relatively small size compared with some of the LAFTA countries.

Nowhere, perhaps, are the advantages of economic integration so abundantly clear as in Central America.[2] Here is a region of five contiguous countries with a population totalling only 12 million persons, a population growth rate of over 3 per cent per annum, and a per capita income of less than $200. Over half of the region's income is obtained from agriculture; and coffee, bananas, cotton, and cocoa account for 90 per cent of all exports. Inadequate as the industry of the region is, there is a considerable amount of under-utilization of industrial capacity. If the economies of scale to be expected from regional integration are important anywhere in the world, they must be important in Central America: even the largest of these countries has a total income equivalent to only one-twentieth or so of that of Greater London.

The establishment of the Committee for Economic Co-operation in 1951 was followed by a lengthy process of study and negotiation, with the aid of the ECLA Secretariat. It can be said, in fact, that of all the programmes for economic integration thus far developed in various parts of the world—including Europe—the Central American programme had by far the best advance preparation in terms of background analysis and documentation. An immense amount of study was devoted not merely to the elaboration of agreements for intra-regional free trade and a common external tariff (including the working out of a uniform customs nomenclature) but also to such subjects as: (*a*) the problem of integrated industrial development; (*b*) special questions arising in agriculture, livestock, and fisheries; (*c*) the development of a regional infrastructure, including transport and communications (especially adequate roads) and the co-ordination of electric power systems; (*d*) weights, measures, and statistical co-ordination; (*e*) social aspects of economic integration, notably the demographic and housing implications of the programme; (*f*) fiscal aspects, including the effect of a programme of regional free trade on government revenues.

[2] West Africa is an equally compelling example.

The Early Treaties

These studies provided the basis for the drafting of a Multilateral Treaty on Free Trade and Central American Economic Integration and an Agreement on the Régime for Central American Integration Industries. These two instruments were signed in Tegucigalpa on 10 June 1958 and were subsequently ratified in all countries except Costa Rica.[3]

The Multilateral Treaty provided for trade among participating countries in some 200 commodities to be freed from all restrictions at once. Further agreements were to add new commodities to the list and provide for a common external tariff, so as to achieve a customs union in not more than ten years.

The 200 commodities covered by immediate liberalization consisted largely of items not yet produced in Central America, so that few were actually traded within the region at the time: this contrasts with the Treaty of Montevideo, where the emphasis is on the liberalization of existing trade. The Central American integration programme was thus essentially directed in the first instance towards the creation of new industries in the region rather than towards the encouragement of competition among existing industries. A more gradual process of transition was envisaged for other products, notably the most important consumer goods produced in the region, such as rice, coffee, textiles, clothing, shoes, cement, soap, tobacco products, and beer.

Of crucial importance in the Central American programme was the special agreement on industrial integration. The objectives of the agreement were twofold: 'to encourage and promote the establishment of new industries and the specialization and expansion of existing industries within the framework of Central American economic integration' and to ensure that this would be done 'on a reciprocal and equitable basis in order that each and every Central American State may progressively derive economic advantages'.[4]

The scheme was applicable to industries—referred to as 'integration industries'—which needed access to the combined market of the whole area because of the scale requirements of a plant of minimum efficiency. A special Commission was set up to establish what industrial plants should qualify for 'integration industry' treat-

---

[3] The text of the Treaty will be found in *Multilateral Co-operation*, and that of the Agreement on pp. 269–75 below.
[4] Art. I, see below, p. 270.

ment.[5] Action was to be taken, in each case, under an additional protocol signed by governments, and stipulating:

(a) The country or countries in which the industrial plants covered by this Régime are to be initially situated, the minimum capacity of the said plants and the conditions under which additional plants are to be subsequently admitted into the same or other countries;

(b) The quality standards for the products of the said industries and any other requirements that may be deemed convenient for the protection of the consumer;

(c) The regulations that may be advisable as regards the participation of Central American capital in the enterprises owning the plants;

(d) The common Central American tariffs which shall be applied to the products of Central American integration industries; and

(e) Any other provisions designed to ensure the attainment of the objectives of this Agreement.[6]

It was further provided that

In order to promote an equitable distribution of the Central American industrial integration plants, the Contracting States shall not award a second plant to any one country until all of the five Central American countries have each been assigned a plant in conformity with the protocols specified in Article III.[7]

In this way, every country would be assured of benefiting from the programme of industrial development and the danger that all new industries would gravitate to the existing industrial centres would be avoided, at least to some extent.

Thus the Central American programme provided for a much more direct intervention in the distribution of new industries within the region than was contemplated under the Treaty of Montevideo. This aspect of the Central American programme provoked considerable controversy because of the limitation on the free operation of market forces that was implied. Particularly strong criticism came from those who felt that the location of industry within a common market should be determined entirely by free market forces. The reply of the supporters of industrial planning was that if the benefits

---

[5] Previous studies had suggested that the following industries were suitable for such treatment: petroleum refining; fertilizers, insecticides, and fungicides; veterinary, biological, and pharmaceutical products; tyres and inner tubes; paints, varnishes, and dyes; ceramics; glass, plastic, and metal containers; fisheries products; welded tubings; absorbent cotton; timber; and pulp and paper.

[6] Art. III, see below, p. 271.   [7] Transitional Article, see below, p. 275.

of integration were not widely shared among the participating countries, the temptation for the least favoured countries to break away would become irresistible.

Once the 'integration plants' were set up, they were, under the agreement, to enjoy the benefits of free trade within the region. Any other plants in the same industry not qualifying for 'integration' status would benefit only from annual reductions of 10 per cent in the import duties applied to their products: this implied, however, that they likewise would gain free entry to the whole regional market at the end of ten years from the date specified in the protocol establishing the 'integration plant'. Thus the preferential treatment given to the designated 'integration plants' was to be strictly limited in duration.[8]

There followed, on 1 September 1959, the signature of the Central American Agreement on the Equalization of Import Duties and Charges. Under this agreement, the five countries decided to 'set up a Central American import tariff consistent with the integration and economic development requirements of Central America' and 'to equalize import duties and charges within not more than five years from the date on which the present Agreement enters into force'.[9]

At this point a new and unexpected element was introduced into the situation through the signing in February 1960 of an entirely separate integration agreement between El Salvador, Guatemala, and Honduras. External pressure from interests favouring greater freedom for market forces in the integration programme was believed to have played a major role in bringing about the new tripartite agreement. In any case it is significant that the negotiation of the agreement 'was done independently of the Economic Commission for Latin America'.[10]

---

[8] A system basically similar to the above was agreed to at ministerial level between Kenya, Tanganyika, and Uganda in April 1964, at Kampala. The Ministers agreed that certain industries should be scheduled under the territorial Industrial Licensing Acts, and a declaration made in favour of an exclusive license to a firm operating in the agreed territory. Tanganyika was to have exclusive rights to assemble and manufacture Landrovers, radios, and motor vehicle tyres and tubes. Uganda was to have sole rights in the manufacture of bicycles and nitrogenous fertilizers. Kenya was to have similar rights for electric light bulbs (see *Kampala Agreement*, Dar-es-Salaam, Information Service of the United Republic of Tanganyika and Zanzibar, 1964).

[9] Art. I, *Multilateral Co-operation*, p. 11.

[10] ICA, *The Five Central American Economic Integration Agreements*, PAD Prints and Reprints no. 31 (Washington, D.C., 1960), p. 4.

The tripartite treaty had three fundamental differences from the Multilateral Treaty of 1958. First, it was more far-reaching not only in shortening the period of transition to a customs union from ten years to five, but also in introducing internal free trade immediately in all except fifty-six listed commodities: the 1958 treaty had provided for free trade in 200 listed commodities and had made all others subject to negotiation over the period of transition.

The second fundamental difference was the omission from the tripartite treaty of any agreement for co-ordinated industrial development along the lines of the agreement on 'integration industries' mentioned earlier. In other words, the location of industry was to be determined entirely by private enterprise without government interference.

Finally, although the treaty was theoretically open to participation by Costa Rica and Nicaragua, it in fact presented the latter countries with a *fait accompli*, and there was even some uncertainty as to the terms on which such participation might take place.[11]

The divisive effect of the new developments was reflected in a sharply worded statement by the President of Costa Rica, declaring that the new treaty represented 'the worst setback for economic integration Central America has ever experienced'. And the President of Nicaragua asserted that if the United States gave economic aid to the group of three, his country would consider it an act of economic aggression. As *New York Times* reporter Paul Kennedy pointed out at the time, this was considered strong language for a country that, for more than a quarter of a century, had never openly questioned the United States attitude towards Central America.[12]

The General Treaty

Fortunately it proved possible, with the aid of ECLA, to strike a compromise between the objectives of the multilateral and tripartite treaties and in December 1960 a new General Treaty on Central American Economic Integration was signed at Managua.[13]

Under the compromise the accelerated tempo of the tripartite treaty was substantially, though not entirely, accepted, but the idea of co-ordinated industrial development was revived.

[11] According to the ICA (see n. 10), some versions of the tripartite treaty made the accession of Costa Rica and Nicaragua conditional on the acceptance of terms established by the original signatory parties. This clause was, however, absent from the Guatemalan version of the Treaty.

[12] *NYT*, 16 Feb. 1960.   [13] The text of this treaty will be found on pp. 256–69.

The Treaty of Managua provided for immediate free trade in all products originating in the region except for those specially listed: this meant in fact that almost 50 per cent of intra-regional trade was freed at once. Trade in the excluded products was, with some exceptions, to be freed by the end of a period of five years from the date of the treaty's entry into force—that is, by June 1966. The signatories to the treaty also undertook to 'create a customs union' and to adopt a common external tariff as provided in the Agreement of 1959—without, however, specifying the time in which this was to be done.

The Treaty specifically endorsed 'all the provisions' of the 1958 Agreement on the Régime for Central American Integration Industries, discussed above. It also provided for the establishment of a Central American Bank for Economic Integration to serve 'as an instrument for the financing and promotion of a regionally balanced, integrated economic growth'. The concept of 'regional balance' was consistent with the ideas underlying the co-ordinated development of 'integration industries'. The bank's initial capital was $16 million, subscribed equally by the four initial signatories—El Salvador, Guatemala, Honduras, and Nicaragua.[14]

The Treaty of Managua created a Central American Economic Council, composed of the respective Ministers of Economic Affairs, for the purpose of 'integrating the Central American economies and coordinating the economic policy of the Contracting States'. The application and administration of the treaty were entrusted to an Executive Council composed of one member and one alternate representing each Contracting State. A Secretariat, with headquarters in Guatemala City, is headed by a Secretary General appointed by the Economic Council for a period of three years.[15]

[14] Early in 1964 the US Agency for International Development (AID) announced a loan of $10 million to the Central American Bank for Economic Integration (*International Financial News Survey* (IMF), 22 May 1964, p. 171).

[15] A constitutional development of potential importance resulted from a meeting of Foreign Ministers in El Salvador early in 1963 which decided to change the structure of the Organization of Central American States (ODECA). Plans were made for the powers of ODECA to be strengthened by transferring direction from the Secretariat General to an Executive Committee consisting of the Foreign Ministers or their representatives meeting in ordinary session at least four times a month. It was also envisaged that a Central American Legislative Council would be established, consisting of three members designated by each country, and chosen by their respective Congresses: the Council was to be consulted in legislative matters and was to study the possibility of unifying the legislation of the Central American States. Other organs would include the

The Treaty of Managua was ratified quickly by El Salvador, Guatemala, Honduras, and Nicaragua and entered into force in June 1961.

Costa Rica's initial aloofness from the 1960 treaty partly reflected its discontent with the manner in which the earlier tripartite treaty had been negotiated. In addition, however, Costa Rica had long been uncertain about the advantages which it, as the highest-income country in the area, would be likely to gain from association with the other four. Not until July 1962 did it finally accept the provisions of the Treaty of Managua and of the agreement establishing the Central American Bank.

The growth of regional trade in Central America, starting from a very low base, has been remarkably rapid ever since 1956. Trade within the area, amounting to only $8·3 million in 1950, as shown in Table I, reached a level of $95 million in 1964: intra-regional trade by 1964 amounted to over 14 per cent of the total trade of the five countries, as against only 3 per cent in 1950. During the eight years ending in 1964 the average annual rate of growth of intra-trade was more than 25 per cent: although the period of rapid expansion began even before the Multilateral Treaty was signed, it is quite possible that the contacts resulting from the trade studies and negotiations that preceded the signing of the integration treaties contributed to the increase in trade. All the same, it is difficult to tell how far the upsurge in regional trade reflects factors that would have come into play irrespective of the integration programme.

Whatever the reasons for the rapid growth in regional trade, it seems that the Central American integration programme is a going concern. Unlike LAFTA, it does not depend on annual negotiations for the elimination of obstacles to trade. By mid-1965 internal free trade had been established on 85 per cent of tariff items, and many of the remaining items were to be freed by mid-1966. Agreement had also been reached on uniform duties for 98 per cent of the tariff items. However, the remaining items represented about 30 per cent

Central American Economic Council, the Central American Cultural and Educational Council, and the Council for the Defence of Central America (see *Comercio Exterior*, Jan. 1963, pp. 41–42). A draft agreement concerning payments arrangements and a Central American cheque, drafted at San José in June 1963, provided in Article 11 that the design on the cheque should contain the emblem of the 'Federal Republic of Central America' (*Suplemento al Boletín Quincenal*, July 1963, p. 210).

TABLE I

Trade of Central America

(*Millions of dollars; percentage*)

	Total exports	Intra-trade	% of intra-trade
1950	278	8·3	3·0
1951	326	9·7	3·0
1952	359	10·3	2·9
1953	383	11·4	3·0
1954	406	13·4	3·3
1955	416	12·8	3·1
1956	434	13·5	3·1
1957	466	16·6	3·6
1958	448	20·5	4·6
1959	431	28·0	6·5
1960	435	30·3	7·0
1961	436	36·2	8·3
1962	510	47·6	9·3
1963	585	69·4	11·9
1964	648	95·0	14·7

Sources: Comercio Exterior, Mexico, Aug. 1963; United Nations, *Monthly Statistical Bulletin*; ECLA, *Survey, 1964* (E/CN.12/711), i. 71, Table 11–38.

of total imports and between 25 and 45 per cent of total customs revenue, depending on the country; and the completion of the customs union was not expected until 1970.[16]

At the same time some progress has been made in economic policy co-ordination among the Central American countries, and it has been agreed to undertake co-ordinated programming of economic activity in the region. This implies, in addition to a full programming of public investment, a less extensive planning effort designed to encourage private investment on a regional basis. Provision was made in 1963 for the unification of tax incentives to industry in the region within seven years. Since October 1961 a Central American voluntary clearing system has been in operation, and in 1963 total clearings amount to $52·6 million, or about 80 per cent of the total

[16] See statement by the representative of Guatemala speaking for all Central American countries, UNCTAD, *Proceedings*, ii. 159.

visible intra-trade of Central America.[17] The credit element in the clearing is quite small, and most of the credit extended is available only for short periods—generally one week.[18] The clearing makes it possible to economize on the costs of transfers through United States banks—the traditional method of settlement—and to make more efficient use of convertible exchange reserves.

In August 1963 the Central American Clearing House made an agreement with the Banco de México. Under the agreement the Banco de México opened a line of credit of $5 million and received in return credits of $1 million from the central banks of each of the Central American countries. Thus payments between the six countries could now be settled in their respective currencies; and the first formal link was established between Central America and a member of LAFTA.

In March 1963 the economic integration of Central America was a major subject of discussion at a meeting at San José, Costa Rica, between the Presidents of the Central American countries and of Panama together with President Kennedy of the United States. The meeting ended with the issuing of the Declaration of Central America, in which the Central American heads of state pledged unity in their efforts to accelerate the establishment of a customs and monetary union and the adoption of common fiscal, economic, and social policies. In the same document the President of the United States offered the wholehearted support of the United States government to the governments of the region and to regional institutions in these endeavours. To facilitate greater technical and financial assistance, President Kennedy proposed a fund for the development of regional projects, to which the United States would immediately contribute sizeable resources. The Central American Bank for Economic Integration was designated as trustee of this fund. The Presidents of the Central American countries and Panama also agreed to take steps to strengthen the private business sector and to establish promotion agencies to attract foreign capital. The heads of state further undertook to link Central America with Panama through a special agreement.

[17] Although participation in the clearing is voluntary, exchange restrictions imposed in El Salvador and Guatemala in effect make it necessary for the payments of these countries to be routed through the clearing, and the figure for 1963 must be interpreted in this light.

[18] F. A. G. Keesing and P. J. Brand, 'Possible Role of a Clearing House in the Latin American Regional Market', IMF, *Staff Papers*, Nov. 1963, p. 435.

These decisions were quickly followed, in April 1963, by a special meeting of the Central American Economic Council in Managua, in which the Co-ordinator of the Alliance for Progress and representatives of Panama also participated. Studies were initiated with a view to the establishment of the fund proposed by President Kennedy. It was agreed that the following regional projects needed immediate financing: the stabilization of the price of basic foodstuffs; a regional highway programme involving the construction of some 1,000 miles of roads by 1969; the cadastral survey of Central America; and a regional network of telecommunications. The United States offered a $5 million loan to finance the study of these projects. At the same meeting a representative of Panama conveyed the desire of his government to join the Central American economic integration programme.[19]

Towards the end of 1964 it was announced that agreement had been reached between the United States and the Central American countries on the need for early establishment of the Fund for Central American Economic Integration. Initial resources would consist of $5 million contributed by the Central American countries and $25 million by the United States: these resources would be used to cover requirements for the first twelve to eighteen months following the setting up of the fund. The United States contribution would be made under the most favourable conditions permitted by existing legislation—namely for a period of 40 years, with a 10-year period of grace, and at a rate of interest of 1 per cent per annum for the first 10 years and of $2\frac{1}{2}$ per cent for the remaining period. The fund was to be used exclusively for financing infrastructural projects and other projects of high priority and of obvious region-wide interest: it is not clear whether this wording was intended to exclude price stabilization, as had been contemplated earlier. It was also revealed that participation in the fund by other countries was being considered —notably by Mexico, Venezuela, Western Germany, and Spain.[20]

On 25 February 1964, at a meeting in El Salvador, the presidents of the central banks of the five Central American republics signed an agreement for the establishment of the Central American Monetary Union, aimed at fostering the co-ordination and harmonization of monetary, exchange, and credit policies of the region. The com-

[19] Secretaría Permanente del Tratado General de Integración Económica Centro-americana, *Carta informativa* (Guatemala City), 12 Feb. 1964.
[20] *Comercio Exterior*, Dec. 1964, pp. 850–1.

ponents of the Union were to be the Central American Monetary Council consisting of the central bank presidents, Consultative or Action Committees, and an executive secretariat.[21] Steps towards the establishment of a single currency for the region were envisaged, once the agreement was duly ratified. Ratification by all five countries was in fact completed by 11 March 1964, and under the agreement the Union became operative on 18 March.[22]

Trade Growth and Economic Development

The expansion of Central America's regional trade during the latter 1950s was not accompanied by an acceleration in the overall growth rate of the economy. From 1950 to 1957 the total output of the area rose at an average annual rate of 4·6 per cent, but from 1957 to 1960 the rate dropped to 2·8 per cent, less than the rate of increase of population.

An important adverse factor during the latter period was a sharp deterioration in terms of trade that caused the purchasing power of exports to decline at the rate of 2·1 per cent per annum, despite the fact that export volume was advancing at an average annual rate of 7·1 per cent.

The expansion of the as yet small sector of intra-regional trade could not offset the effect of the deterioration in terms of trade. The integration programme had not yet gathered speed, and industrial development was not on a scale sufficient to give upward momentum to the economy as a whole: the share of industrial production in the total output of the Central American region was at virtually the same low level in 1960 as ten years earlier—namely 12 per cent. Moreover there was no sign as yet of any appreciable change in the structure of manufacturing industry: the traditional types of small-scale manufacture that had provided 80 per cent of the total output of manufacturing industry in 1950 still accounted for as much as 77 per cent in 1960.[23]

From 1960 to 1964 the rate of growth of total output recovered to an average of over 5 per cent, while industrial production advanced at the rate of over 7 per cent per annum. This recovery has been attributed by ECLA to a renewed and vigorous expansion in the purchasing power of exports, combined with the progress made in

---

[21] *Comercio Exterior,* Mar. 1964, p. 183.   [22] Ibid. Apr. 1964.
[23] ECLA, *General Situation and Future Outlook of the Central American Integration Programme* (E/CN.12/666, Feb. 1963), pp. 30–31.

economic integration, and the inflow of external finance. The integration programme helped to broaden the market and stimulate demand in the industrial sector, the increase in production being based largely on more intensive utilization of existing capacity. As a result, exports of manufactures soared at an annual rate of 30 per cent after 1960, amounting by 1963 to $43 million, or two-thirds of total intra-regional trade.[24] This provides a remarkable contrast with the LAFTA countries, whose trade with one another consists overwhelmingly of primary commodities.

There is also beginning to be evidence of the establishment of new types of industry in Central America, although this development is still at a very early stage. Apart from the traditional branches of industry—food, beverage, and tobacco processing, textiles and clothing, and wood products—fertilizer, petroleum-refining, and sodium chloride/insecticide industries have been established. Moreover projects are under way for the manufacture of glass and steel products, welded tubes, and electric lamps.[25]

Important advances have also been made in the co-ordination of agricultural policies, although restrictions still apply to regional trade in most primary commodities for domestic consumption and in traditional export items. Particularly significant is the progress made in aligning producer prices, notably for staple items in Central American consumption.[26]

The Need for a Development Strategy

It would be premature to see in these undoubtedly favourable developments the kind of major structural transformation and reform that will be indispensable in Central America if progress is to be consolidated, and assured for the future. No integration programme, however well conceived, can do much for underdeveloped countries in the long run unless it forms part of an overall strategy for development. Experience suggests that without the requisite measures of land reform, without really purposeful national and regional planning, and without the many other measures needed for harnessing the region's human and material resources, no sustained process of development will be possible.

[24] ECLA, *Survey, 1963*, vol. i (E/CN.12/696), pp. 27–28.
[25] ECLA, *Note by the Secretariat on the Commission's Activities in the Field of Economic Integration* (E/CN.12/C.1/22), Oct. 1964), p. 28.
[26] Ibid. 29 .

The problem is complicated by weaknesses in the Central American integration programme itself. The view seems to have prevailed that the main task was to sweep away the internal barriers to trade, whereupon spontaneous market forces would do the rest. Moreover, too much confidence has been placed in the idea that foreign capital, attracted by the region-wide market, would come in and develop the area. In August 1963 Guatemala adopted new legislation making far-reaching concessions to foreign investors by guaranteeing not merely the free transfer of profits and dividends out of the country, but also the right of such investors to withdraw their capital at any time. Subsequently, the permanent secretariat of the integration programme suggested to the other four Central American governments that they should follow Guatemala's example.[27]

It appears that a substantial proportion of the new manufacturing activities consists of assembly. Foreign companies may be able to gain access to the Central American market by locating the final assembly stage or stages of manufacture at a new plant within the region. But such assembly operations do not necessarily contribute a great deal in terms of value added in Central America, while the cost of imported components and managerial staff may impose a new burden on the balance of payments. Indeed, if the imported components bear a lower tariff than the finished product, the net result may be an increase in Central America's consumption of what may be low priority items from the standpoint of regional development. The danger of unplanned industrial development is that it may increase the external vulnerability of an underdeveloped economy without adding very much to its underlying growth potential.

These considerations must also be borne in mind in evaluating the growth of regional trade. If a significant proportion of the increase in trade is in products only assembled in Central America, the rate of expansion may be exaggerated by figures of exports valued gross. In such circumstances, much of the additional trade may correspond essentially to products manufactured up to the assembly stage outside the area and traded within the area under the new common market arrangements.

The Problem of Joint Industrial Development

Meanwhile the programme for joint industrial development through the establishment of 'integration industries' lags and

[27] *Comercio Exterior*, Jan. 1964, p. 32.

languishes. A Protocol to the 1958 Agreement was signed in January 1963, declaring as 'integration industries' the plants to be established in Nicaragua for the production of caustic soda and chlorinated insecticides, and in Guatemala for the production of rubber tyres and tubes. But this was a quite inadequate result after so many years.[28]

The paucity of action under the industrial agreement contrasts vividly with the rapid progress in the dismantling of trade barriers, and confirms the impression of an integration programme lacking purposeful direction and relying mainly on uncoordinated action by private enterprise, domestic and foreign.

While the slowness in implementing a programme of joint industrial planning must be laid at the door of the Central American countries themselves, part of the difficulty has been the reluctance of major national and international lending agencies to support the idea of 'integration industries'.[29] It is worth while examining the considerations involved at some length, since they are of relevance to the broader Latin American setting as well as to Central America.

Three main arguments have been advanced against the programme of 'integration industries': that it would interfere with the optimum location of industry; that it would impede the establishment of small-scale factories catering to local markets; and that it would encourage monopoly.[30]

In the first place it is contended that strictly industrial considerations based on the principle of comparative advantage would cause new factories to be located in regions providing the best combination of transport and power facilities, trained labour, and ample raw materials and intermediate products. The 'integration industry' approach, on the other hand, would retard industrial efficiency in so

[28] An alternative system has been favoured whereby as soon as an industry produces over one-half of the area's needs, it may qualify for a protective outer tariff. This, however, may not be a very powerful incentive to new industries uncertain of being able to capture one-half of the market in a short space of time.

[29] According to Prof. Mikesell, 'both the Inter-American Development Bank and the Agency for International Development have refused to sanction the use of their funds loaned to the Central American Bank for Economic Integration for loans to firms designated as "integration industries" and, therefore, given preferential treatment within the Central American common market'. See R. F. Mikesell, 'El financiamiento externo e integración latinoamericana', in M. S. Wionczek, ed., *Integración de la América Latina* (1964), pp. 214–15.

[30] See Joseph Pincus, *The Central American Common Market* (Mexico City, Dept. of State, AID, 1962), pp. 102–8. The following discussion draws extensively on the criticisms of 'integration industries' advanced by Pincus.

far as new plants had to be located in countries or areas that were less suitable than the best sites available.

The weakness of this argument lies in the static concept of the principle of comparative advantage that is implied. If, indeed, this static point of view were pressed to its logical conclusion, one would have to say that most of the new plants probably should not be placed anywhere in the less developed areas, but rather in North America or Western Europe. If, on the other hand, the principle of comparative advantage is reinterpreted within a dynamic framework, there is every reason to expect that even those countries that are industrially least developed at the present time will be operating viable industries in the long run.

It is also apparent that concentration of new industries in one or two countries of Central America would quickly cause the common market to break up for lack of any incentive to the less favoured countries to stay in. There is no reason why Honduras should agree to import manufactured goods from El Salvador or Guatemala at prices higher than those at which it could buy them from the United States unless El Salvador and Guatemala are in turn prepared to take manufactures from Honduras. For industrial development is just as indispensable an ingredient in the solution of the economic problems of Honduras as it is in the advancement of El Salvador and Guatemala.

A second objection to the 'integrated industries' programme is that it would be likely to prejudice the development of small-scale factories supplying local markets. For one thing, local investors would have reason to fear competition from regional enterprises and, indeed, there would be a general expectation of higher returns on investment in large-scale operations. These tendencies would be intensified if the Central American Bank developed a regional capital market and publicized the opportunities for investment in regional enterprises; and if the latter enterprises offered greater inducements to skilled labour than the small-scale firms could afford to do.[31]

The reader may find it odd that this objection should be set forth side by side with the emphasis on free market forces operating in accordance with the principle of comparative advantage, noted earlier. For if efficiency is regarded as the principal criterion relevant in taking decisions about the *location* of new industries, why is

[31] Pincus, pp. 103–4.

it not also the main consideration in determining the *size* of these industries?

A much more significant objection to the 'integration industry' approach is that it might tend to create regional monopolies, and it is probably this consideration that has been most influential in the reluctance of national and international financing agencies to aid this approach. Even if economies of scale were achieved by setting up only one plant catering to the whole of the Central American region, what reason is there to believe that the benefits would be passed on to the consumer in the form of lower prices? Might not monopoly profits generate additional demand for luxury imports, while the high prices charged prevented any increase in exports?

It should first be noted that the text-book assumption that a single-firm situation is invariably bad and a multi-firm situation invariably good represents a serious oversimplification of reality. One firm may dominate a market and yet be very go-ahead in discovering and applying new techniques: and in another market there may be a competitive dog-fight so intense that no resources are devoted to research and development because of the general state of uncertainty induced thereby. Quite commonly, in underdeveloped as in developed countries even where there is more than one producer in an industry, the producers may get together and reach understandings about their respective shares of the local market; and the stalemate brought about by such understandings may be even more inimical to technical progress and dynamism than monopoly would be. Thus a doctrinaire approach to the problem of monopoly and competition is not likely to prove even relevant, let alone successful. At the same time, there is no doubt that the creation of new monopolies in Central America could have an adverse effect upon the economy of the region: it was for this reason that the agreement on 'integration industries' provided for the protection of consumers by various means, including the establishment of an inter-governmental commission to supervise the programme. The way was left open for the stipulation of quality standards and possibly even the regulation of prices. Moreover, the special advantages available to the designated 'integration industries' were to be progressively reduced year by year, and eliminated within ten years.[32]

In a region as small as Central America it is almost inevitable that there may not be room in certain industries for more than one or two

[32] Art. IV, see below, p. 271.

F

plants, if full advantage is to be taken of the economies of scale. The answer to this problem is not to hinder the establishment of such plants—nor, as has been done in the motor vehicle industries in several Latin American countries, to permit the squandering of resources on the proliferation of uneconomic plants operating at sub-optimal rates. In the industrially advanced countries the answer to this problem has been sought in the public regulation of monopoly, and this may be one of the best ways of approaching the matter. The public interest can always be safeguarded, in the last resort, through the degree of protection afforded to local monopolies against competition from abroad. In other words, the government can always force the hand of a recalcitrant monopoly by lowering import duties. In due course, moreover, Central America may join the larger LAFTA market, at which time regional industries may have to face a growing measure of competition from other parts of the LAFTA area.

In any case, if there are profitable business opportunities, failure to act along the lines of the 'integration industry' approach will not necessarily prevent the creation of monopolies. It may merely leave the field open for foreign companies to set up the monopolies in question: and it would obviously be much more difficult for Central American governments to control foreign-owned monopolies than those domestically owned. There is, in fact, a fear that the free-trade approach of the Central American integration programme may tend to favour foreign as against domestic enterprise. Towards the end of 1963 the Federation of Central American Chambers of Commerce and Industry passed a resolution calling on the Central American governments to suspend negotiations for the entry of Panama into the regional common market. The reason given was that the admission of Panama would only benefit those United States interests that control the Panamanian economy, to the detriment of business enterprise in the Central American region itself.[33] The sharpness of this resolution clearly reflects the lack of any overall Central Ameri-

[33] *Comercio Exterior*, Dec. 1963, p. 914. Panama is, however, linked to Costa Rica and Nicaragua by a Free Trade Treaty originally signed in August 1961. In March 1963 the three countries agreed on the goods which would be liberalized or given preferential treatment in trade between them. At the request of Panama preferential treatment was accorded only to goods already produced in the area, although provision was made for the addition of other goods by agreement. Provision for exchanges between Costa Rica and Nicaragua covers the goods already agreed upon in connexion with the General Treaty of Economic Integration (see *Boletín Quincenal*, 25 Mar. 1963).

can plan for achieving a fruitful combination of efforts by the public and private sectors and by domestic and foreign enterprise. In the absence of some kind of generally agreed development targets, it is difficult to see how the integration programme can fully succeed in the longer run.

Although some way of achieving inter-governmental agreement on a distribution of industry policy appears indispensable, such agreement cannot be based on a purely political decision. Any such policy would be bound to run into difficulties if it did not take account of all relevant economic considerations. While due allowance should be made for the likelihood that the current money costs of establishing new industries in less developed regions will be much higher than the social costs, there must be a reasonable expectation that in the long run any industry established will be able to stand on its own feet without special subsidy or support. The economic and technical basis for inter-governmental agreements on the distribution of industry should therefore be as solid as modern methods of analysis can make it. If industries are to be sited in locations that are less than optimal, it is essential to know what additional costs will be incurred thereby, and how long it will take for them to become fully competitive. Once these facts are known, informed decisions can be taken at the political level. Such decisions should not, however, be left simply to the pull and push of political pressure, although it would be naïve to imagine that such pressure can be altogether avoided.

There are, perhaps, grounds for a certain optimism regarding the long-run prospects of industries located even in the least advanced regions. Except in industries tied closely to highly specific natural resources that are expensive to ship, the advance of modern technology has greatly reduced the natural advantages of siting manufacturing activities in one place rather than another. By now, the advantages of one site over another are largely man-made rather than nature-made. And if advantages are made by man, they can also be changed by man in accordance with rational and deliberate planning criteria. Such planning is a vital element in any common market among underdeveloped countries, but is thus far largely lacking in Central America.

CHAPTER V

AFTER THE TREATY OF MONTEVIDEO

Trade Negotiations and Trends

As far as tariff-cutting is concerned, the LAFTA countries achieved a certain initial measure of success following the entry of the Treaty of Montevideo into force. The first round of negotiations was held in Montevideo from 24 July to 12 August 1961, the second in Mexico City from 27 August to 21 November 1962, the third in Montevideo again from 5 October to 31 December 1963, and the fourth in Bogotá from 20 October to 11 December 1964.

During the first two rounds of negotiations, a total of 7,593 tariff concessions were made.[1] It was estimated that the tariff reductions averaged about 25 per cent in the first round and 15 per cent in the second—well in excess of the 8 per cent average required under the Treaty. In the next two rounds the number of additional concessions was sharply reduced—655 at the third and 307 at the fourth. The slow-down reflected growing difficulties within LAFTA and the fact that the easy concessions had already been made.

At the end of the third round of negotiations in 1963, the distribution of mutual concessions granted since the signing of the Treaty was as shown in Table II opposite.

Thus over 50 per cent of the concessions during the first three rounds were made by three countries—Ecuador, Brazil, and Argentina. The number of concessions granted is not, however, in itself a measure of the market opportunities afforded to trading partners. Much depends on the significance of the various items in the imports of the member countries, and the extent of the preferences granted on each.[2]

In some cases, moreover, the value of tariff concessions is limited by the application of other restrictions, notably licensing. At the end

---

[1] The figure was obtained by adding together all concessions granted by each LAFTA country to the remaining members as a group.

[2] For a selected tabulation of items subject to preferential treatment within LAFTA, see Table XI, p. 223.

TABLE II

LAFTA: Distribution of Concessions, 31 Dec. 1963

Country*	Cumulative total of tariff concessions granted, 31 Dec. 1963	Percentage distribution
Ecuador	1,677	20·3
Brazil	1,312	15·9
Argentina	1,280	15·5
Chile	864	10·5
Mexico	727	8·8
Colombia	704	8·5
Paraguay	665	8·1
Uruguay	664	8·1
Peru	355	4·3
Total	8,248	100·0

* In descending order of the number of concessions granted.

Source: LAFTA, Standing Executive Committee, *General Appraisal of the Negotiations*, as cited in *Comercio Exterior*, Nov. 1964.

of 1963 Colombia and Mexico required import licenses for 22 per cent and 7 per cent, respectively, of the items on their National Schedules, but were gradually eliminating this requirement in accordance with a LAFTA decision.[3]

In 1963 trade in all products covered by negotiated concessions reached the amounts shown in Table III.

The recovery of regional trade, both absolutely and relatively, following the Treaty of Montevideo undoubtedly reflected in some measure at least the impetus afforded by the Treaty. Trade among LAFTA countries recovered from the low point of $299 million reached in 1961 to $558 million in 1964: the share of such trade in the overall total likewise rose from 6 per cent in 1961 to 10 per cent in 1964.[4]

The rise in trade was, however, unevenly distributed. Argentina, which supplied one-third of LAFTA's intra-regional exports in

[3] *Resoluciones*, 66 (II).
[4] For Latin American countries as a whole, the share of intra-trade in total trade declined from 12·1% in 1953 to 7·1% in 1961 and recovered thereafter to 10·8% in 1964. See Tables VI and VII, pp. 218–19.

TABLE III

Trade in Negotiated Products, 1963

(*Millions of Dollars*)*

Country†	Negotiated products		
	Exports	Imports	Balance
Argentina	179·3	92·5	86·8
Brazil	85·3	147·3	—62·0
Chile	53·3	93·6	—40·2
Peru	49·5	54·1	— 4·6
Mexico	33·2	9·1	24·1
Paraguay	22·0	2·0	20·0
Uruguay	11·5	24·2	—12·8
Ecuador	9·0	4·0	5·0
Colombia	3·4	19·5	—16·2

* All data c.i.f. 'Exports' of each country are recorded as the sum of imports c.i.f.
of negotiated products by all other LAFTA members.
† In descending order of the value of exports.

Source: LAFTA, Standing Executive Committee, *General Appraisal of
the Negotiations*, as cited in *Comercio Exterior*, Nov. 1964.

1961, accounted for nearly one-half of the entire gain in regional exports from 1961 to 1964. Most of the remaining increase was recorded by Brazil, Mexico, Peru, and to a lesser extent Chile. While the remaining countries also achieved export gains, these were very small in absolute terms.

The trade expansion was also unbalanced in the sense that it consisted almost entirely of traditional primary products. In the case of Argentina, for example, nearly 90 per cent of exports to LAFTA countries in 1964 consisted of traditional primary commodities shipped to traditional markets; and a significant proportion of the remainder consisted of traditional commodities supplied to new markets within LAFTA. The share of traditional products from traditional suppliers in Argentina's imports was even higher—96·5 per cent in 1964.[5]

While much of the activity under the Treaty, therefore, did not do more than safeguard channels of trade already in existence, mutual trade concessions were beginning to open up certain new flows of

[5] LAFTA Doc. CEP/Repartido 426/64, pp. 5–7. The commodity composition of
intra-regional trade in 1960–2 is set forth in Table IV below, p. 81.

trade of potential importance. Particularly striking in this respect was the growth of Mexican trade with LAFTA members—almost entirely in products not hitherto traded between Mexico and other Latin American countries.[6]

Characteristic of the sort of collaboration in trade matters that is beginning to develop in Latin America is the fact that when particular countries find themselves compelled to tighten restrictions on imports they seek to exempt trade with other Latin American countries. Colombia, Ecuador, and Mexico, for example, are among the countries that have exempted imports from LAFTA members from certain types of prohibition or licensing applied to other countries.[7] When Brazil introduced an import deposit requirement involving the purchase of 150-day Bank of Brazil notes equivalent to a percentage of the value of desired imports, purchases from LAFTA members were exempted.[8]

On the other hand, it became necessary in May 1963 for the Standing Executive Committee of LAFTA to meet to consider the imposition by Uruguay of a surcharge of 20 per cent on imports, accompanied by the establishment of prior deposits of 200 per cent in respect of certain specified products. The committee considered that the fact that imports from other LAFTA countries were not exempted by Uruguay from the application of these two new measures was contrary to the spirit of the Treaty of Montevideo. The committee also took exception to the fact that Uruguay had failed to communicate in time the list of products in respect of which import duties had been reduced *vis-à-vis* LAFTA countries, as well as the temporary suspension of imports of raw sugar from Brazil and Peru.[9] It was subsequently announced that the government of Uruguay had approved a decree freeing imports from LAFTA countries from the new charges that had been imposed.[10]

While most of the trade among LAFTA countries continues to consist of traditional agricultural and mineral products, and the growth of trade in manufactures has been disappointingly slow, some companies, notably foreign ones, have been alert to the business opportunities afforded by the new regional preferences. For

[6] Mexican exports to LAFTA countries rose from $7·9 million in 1961 to $33·1 million in 1964, while corresponding Mexican imports increased from $4·1 million to $17·3 million (see Table VIII, p. 221).

[7] *Comercio Exterior*, Feb. 1963, p. 79.

[8] The US protested against this discrimination, see ch. ix.

[9] *Boletín Quincenal*, 10 June 1963.   [10] Ibid. 25 June 1963.

example, it was announced in November 1962 that Volkswagen do
Brazil, a subsidiary of the West German company, would shortly
begin shipping spare parts to Volkswagen representatives in Buenos
Aires. In the normal course of events, such trade would not have
been profitable, especially since freight costs between Santos and
Buenos Aires are actually higher than between Western Germany
and the Argentine capital. The interest in using Brazilian-made
parts was stimulated by the preferences that resulted from concessions under the Montevideo Treaty. The same factor was
responsible for a corresponding order for spare parts from Paraguay.[11]

Similarly Sperry Rand of Argentina was enabled to sell electric
razors for the first time in Brazil as a result of a reduction in the import duty from 300 per cent to 6 per cent. A Mexican subsidiary of
duPont producing titanium dioxide, hitherto exclusively for the
domestic market, began to find a new outlet in Chile, and planned to
enlarge the capacity of its plant by 50 per cent so as to be able to sell
to Colombia, Peru, and possibly other LAFTA members.[12]

Numerous other international companies made new dispositions
to take advantage of expanded market opportunities, established
continent-wide sales networks, and in some cases set up new plants
or expanded the capacity of old ones.[13]

The Lack of Dynamism

The question arises why LAFTA has not experienced the same
sort of boom in area trade as has occurred within the EEC. It should
be noted that the Rome Treaty was signed at a time of rapid European
growth. Even prior to the Treaty industrial production in the EEC
countries had been rising at a rate of 8–10 per cent a year, and the
volume of their trade with one another even faster than that. The
treaty was thus signed under the most favourable conditions possible. Although production and trade have continued to rise very
rapidly in the member countries, it is far from clear that this has

---

[11] British Chamber of Commerce in Brazil, *Monthly Bulletin* (Rio de Janeiro),
Nov. 1962, p. 174.
[12] *Comercio Exterior*, Jan. 1963, p. 11.
[13] In *Latin America's Merging Market* (1964), pp. 21–23, Business International
describes the activities of the following companies, *inter alia*, in responding to
the situation brought about by the Montevideo Treaty: IBM, RCA, General
Electric, Philips, Singer, Necchi, Olivetti, Allied Chemical, IBEC, American
Motors, Union Carbide, Krupp, Mannesmann, Ferrostaal, Siemens, Hitachi,
Ishikawajimi.

been due, to any very great extent, to the Treaty of Rome itself. Very different is the climate in which the Treaty of Montevideo has had to operate. Indeed, the objective of economic integration in Latin America has gained widespread acceptance precisely because the existing rate of development both in production and foreign trade is so unsatisfactory. The Treaty of Montevideo was not superimposed on a situation of growth and prosperity, but of slow-down and stagnation. In Western Europe, while the rate of growth has slackened in recent years,[14] it has still remained high enough for people to be satisfied with business prospects and to feel that the Treaty of Rome has, on the whole, brought success. In Latin America, the fact that the Treaty of Montevideo has not suddenly brought about a radical change in the region's economic outlook has led to disappointment and dismay, even though a moment's reflection should have made it clear that the Treaty could never in any case have done any such thing, seeing that intra-regional trade starts from such a low level in relation to total trade and total production.

But there is a second reason for the greater success of Western Europe than of Latin America thus far. For Western Europe the lowering of the inner barriers to trade means returning to a position which had prevailed previously. The barriers to trade among Western European countries which resulted from the Great Depression and the Second World War were an unnatural element in the economy of Western Europe, and the programme of trade liberalization which was begun soon after the end of the Second World War therefore represented a return to something which might be called normalcy. In any case, the channels of trade were all there, ready made, transport facilities were available, and the necessary commercial contacts and relations could easily be resumed. In Latin America, on the other hand, it is a question of creating entirely new channels of trade, entirely new commercial contacts, and entirely new sources of supply and market outlets; of attempting, in many cases, to provide transport facilities between points which have never yet had anything of the kind. To imagine that all this could have changed since June 1961 is to underrate the problem of economic development in Latin America.[15]

[14] Industrial production in the EEC countries rose by about 50% during the seven-year period from 1957 to 1964, as against 75% from 1950 to 1957.
[15] For example, it was estimated that in 1963 Mexican imports *from all sources* of

It must also be conceded, however, that the cuts in tariffs and lowering of other trade barriers in Western Europe were much more significant, even in the early stages, than the corresponding developments in Latin America. The Western European countries were much more drastic in their implementation of the liberalization programme required by the Treaty of Rome than the Latin American countries were. At first sight this may seem surprising, since the average percentage of tariff reduction achieved during the early rounds of negotiation within LAFTA was much higher than the minimum required by the Treaty of Montevideo—namely 8 per cent per annum. But many of the reductions in the early stages were more apparent than real, since frequently the reductions were from legal rates that had never been applied in practice or which at any rate were not being applied at the time the Treaty of Montevideo was signed. This makes it difficult to assess how much genuine lowering of trade barriers there has really been.

There has been growing impatience with the laborious process whereby internal trade barriers are reduced under the Montevideo Treaty. In this respect, LAFTA procedures have been compared unfavourably with those of EEC and EFTA. While internal tariff reductions by the latter two groups proceed across the board according to a predetermined time-table—which can be accelerated but not greatly delayed—similar reductions under the Treaty of Montevideo have to be negotiated item by item, year after year, on a *quid pro quo* basis. It is not surprising, therefore, that the programme has run into growing difficulties.

The advantages of predetermined percentage rates of tariff reduction across the board will be obvious. In the first place, since such a programme is in principle applicable to all products, there is less opportunity and less justification for individual industries to press their governments for special exemptions from import duty concessions. At the same time the automaticity of the reductions on certain fixed dates enables industry to plan ahead and adjust its production and investment plans in the certain knowledge that import

products on which concessions had been granted to LAFTA countries amounted to $103·5 m. But the share of LAFTA countries in such imports was only $8·1 m., or 7·8%, of which fish-meal from Peru alone accounted for $3·6 m. (see *Comercio Exterior*, Jan. 1965, p. 64). It was, however, bound to take time to build up the channels of trade required to take advantage of the new preferential opportunities in the Mexican market—quite apart from the cases in which expansion of existing productive facilities in other LAFTA countries was required.

duties will decline on a region-wide basis. Item-by-item negotiations, on the other hand, invite delay at every level.

It was precisely the difficulty previously experienced in item-by-item negotiations that led to the proposal in GATT for the Kennedy round of tariff reductions, which were to take place across the board with a minimum of exceptions. By the same token, the extraordinary difficulties encountered in getting the Kennedy round started provide a striking illustration of the fact that comprehensiveness and automaticity in reducing trade obstacles can be achieved only where there is a strong political will to this end.

Thus, for example, the EEC refused to enter the Kennedy round unless the United States agreed on special treatment for cases of large tariff disparities. The same objection could perfectly well have been raised *within* EEC by the low-tariff countries—the Benelux countries and Western Germany. The fact that one procedure obtained within EEC and another in relations between EEC and other countries reflects a difference of political will and political objectives.

The contrast between the methods of tariff reduction adopted by the LAFTA and EEC countries is therefore much more than a difference of technique. It reflects on the one hand a difference in the degree of determination to reach the desired goal, which in turn corresponds to a difference in underlying political conditions. On the other hand, it results also from the fact that the release of market forces through tariff reductions will not suffice to bring about accelerated growth in Latin America, and that other forms of co-operative action are therefore also needed.

The reluctance of the member countries of LAFTA to adopt a more adventurous policy in the lowering of tariffs and other trade barriers against their neighbours is in part the result of fears of damaging competition and of imbalance in intra-regional trade and payments. With respect to the first point, the fact that Latin America already has a significant amount of industry has both positive and negative implications for the creation of a common market. On the one hand it does mean that there is already a foundation on which to build an altogether larger and more comprehensive industrial structure. On the other hand, however, the industrial development of Latin America has thus far proceeded within the limitations of existing national markets. Each of the national industries is comfortably oriented towards its own national market and usually fears the consequences of competition from more efficient rivals (actual or potential) in neighbouring countries even more than it is tempted by the prospects of larger market opportunities that the creation of a region-wide common market would bring about.

While it is widely recognized that the protectionist tendencies of inefficient local industries must not be allowed to defeat the whole purpose of economic integration in Latin America, it is also important to distinguish between the problem facing Latin America and that facing the EEC. It is frequently taken for granted that because the EEC places a good deal of emphasis upon the intensification of competition between existing European industries, a similar objective is valid for Latin America also.

But this is to place the emphasis in entirely the wrong place. In Western Europe there is already a massive industry in being, and the main problem is to make it more productive and more efficient. This objective can be secured by creating market conditions in which the more efficient firms will drive the less efficient ones out of business—or at least so the theory goes. There is no doubt a good deal of inefficiency in Latin American industry that could also be removed through the stimulus or incentive of more intense competition. But this is only a small part of the problem—by far the greater problem is how to enlarge Latin American industry out of all recognition, notably through the establishment of entirely new industries in sectors where none at present exist. Doctrinaire emphasis on the need for greater competition will not necessarily contribute anything to the achievement of this broader objective. Indeed there are many cases in which the prospect of competition might well deter new investment, whereas the guarantee of an assured market free from competition would be a powerful incentive. Of course monopoly creates its own problems, and these problems have to be dealt with effectively if the consumer is not to suffer. But free trade is not the only answer, nor necessarily the best answer, to monopoly. As noted in Chapter IV, there is scope for public regulation of monopoly, and governments always retain an ultimate and supremely effective weapon in defence of the public interest—namely a reduction in import duties.

A study of technical progressiveness in British industry by Carter and Williams[16] did not yield the kind of decisive answer that the theorists usually assume in this field. They found that while there

---

[16] C. F. Carter and B. R. Williams, *Investment in Innovation* (London, 1958), p. 142, and *Industry and Technical Progress* (London, 1957), pp. 163–9.

were industries in which competition had indeed acted as a spur to technical efficiency, others had been helped by protection. It has to be borne in mind that the uncertainties created by competition may prevent investment in new technology, especially where projects are likely to yield their fruits only over a long period.

Certainly if one considers which are the most efficient and which the least efficient industries in North America and Western Europe, it is not at all obvious that differences in the extent of competition are of great relevance. Some of the most efficient industries are those in which a high degree of monopoly or market-sharing exists, while the textile and clothing industries are not usually distinguished for their high productivity or efficiency, despite the intense competition that prevails.

All this is in any case of only limited relevance to a situation, such as that prevailing in Latin America, where the problem is primarily the enlargement of the industrial base rather than increasing the efficiency of existing industry.

Above all, the smaller and less developed LAFTA countries are not inclined to allow the location of new industries in Latin America to be determined entirely by market forces operating in an environment of regional free trade. The fear is that all the new industries catering to the regional market will gravitate to the established centres in Argentina, Brazil, and Mexico, and that other LAFTA countries will gain little or nothing from the process—and may even lose through the destruction of their existing industries by more powerful competitors.

Thus for countries like Chile, Colombia, Peru, and Uruguay, as well as for the less developed Ecuador and Paraguay, it is of vital importance to reach understandings with the Big Three on the planned growth of the LAFTA area as a whole, in a way which will enable them to ensure that they obtain their fair share of the benefits of that growth. The absence of an agreed programme of joint development has thus been a major factor—perhaps the most important factor of all—in slowing down the process of tariff-cutting within LAFTA. This may be seen from the difficulties that arose in drawing up the Common Schedule in 1964.

The Problems of a Common Schedule

As noted in Chapter III, the Treaty of Montevideo requires the LAFTA countries to establish a Common Schedule of products on which they collectively agree to eliminate, by 1973, all duties and restrictions affecting trade with one another. The Common Schedule was to be set up in four stages. The first stage required the inclusion in the Common Schedule by the end of 1964 of products accounting for not less than 25 per cent of trade among the LAFTA countries in the first three-year period. This proportion was to rise in successive three-year stages until at the end of the transition period the Common Schedule would consist of products accounting for 'substantially all' intra-trade during the fourth three-year period.[17]

It will be noted that the negotiation of a Common Schedule of free-traded items among LAFTA members tends to enlarge the scope of trade affected by the provisions of the Treaty. Under the rules relating to the establishment of National Schedules, each country undertakes to reduce, and ultimately eliminate, its tariff and non-tariff restrictions only on those goods which it has previously imported from other member countries. No corresponding obligation is assumed in respect of those products not previously imported from other LAFTA countries. The adoption of a Common Schedule, on the other hand, must ultimately imply, at the end of the twelve-year period of transition, that each country will eliminate restrictions not only on those products which have hitherto figured in its own imports, but also on substantially all items which have been traded between any two LAFTA members in the past. In other words, Peru, for example, would have to eliminate restrictions not only on all items appearing in its imports from other LAFTA members, but also on all items figuring in its exports to those members, and indeed on any products traded between, say, Argentina and Brazil.

During their third annual session, the LAFTA countries decided that the first round of triennial negotiations on a Common Schedule should begin in May 1964. They agreed further that the inclusion of products in the Common Schedule would commit all Contracting Parties to the elimination of all import duties and restrictions on such products by 2 June 1973: but that there was no obligation to make any reduction in such duties or restrictions *prior* to that date (except, of course, in so far as the products concerned were included in a particular country's National Schedule).[18] This decision may

---

[17] Treaty of Montevideo, Arts 4 and 7, and Protocol No. 1. See below, pp. 229–30.
[18] *Resoluciones*, 70(III). See below, p. 315.

prove to be a serious source of difficulty since countries may be tempted to postpone duty reductions on items appearing on the Common Schedule, but not on their respective National Schedules, until the very last moment—and then find it politically or otherwise impossible to undertake the sweeping elimination of duties that would then become necessary all at once.

It has already been noted that the inclusion of products in the Common Schedule, once agreed upon, is final, and the concessions granted on these products are irrevocable, except for temporary relief provided under escape clauses. The issues involved in setting up such a Schedule may be illustrated from Table IV, which pro-

TABLE IV

Composition of Trade among LAFTA Countries, 1960–2

(*Percentage of total intra-trade*)

Cereals	19·3	Copper	2·4
Wood & wood products	11·4	Cocoa & products	1·7
Coffee, tea, maté, & spices	9·6	Vegetables	1·6
Live animals	8·1	Metalliferous ores & scrap	1·5
Fruit	5·4	Fats & oils	1·4
Cotton, raw	4·6	Wool & hair	1·4
Mineral fuel & oils	4·5	Paper & paper products	1·3
Sugar & sugar products	4·3	Meat	1·3
Iron & steel products	3·6	Other products	16·6
		Total	100·0

Source: Based on LAFTA statistics as cited in Banco Nacional de Comercio Exterior, *Tres años en el camino de la integración*, pp. 84–85.

vided the basic data for the negotiations on this matter that took place in 1964. The great bulk of products traded among LAFTA countries and listed in Table IV are raw or simply-processed primary commodities: even the residual 17 per cent consists mostly of primary commodities and elementary manufactures. If the structure of trade among LAFTA countries remains basically unchanged during the years ahead, the Common Schedule will include little but primary commodities not merely at the end of the first three-year period, but also at the end of six and nine years, when the items listed must account for 50 and 75 per cent, respectively, of products traded. Even at the close of the transition period, the significance of

manufactures in the Common Schedule will be relatively small unless major efforts are made to alter the whole structure of intra-
trade. In the absence of such a shift, the whole purpose of the Treaty
would be frustrated, since nothing would have been done to promote
industrial specialization and exchange on a region-wide basis.

Nor can it be assumed that the inclusion of agricultural products
in the Common Schedule would have any very great significance in
itself. As there are very marked differences in agricultural productivity from country to country it would be idle to expect free trade in
agricultural commodities to be introduced in the near future: this
would undoubtedly mean the destruction or dislocation of agriculture in the low productivity areas, and hence the further impoverishment of peasant populations, which would obviously be intolerable.

It was for this reason that in its document prepared for the first
round of Common Schedule negotiations in 1964,[19] the Standing
Executive Committee of LAFTA referred repeatedly to an issue
never previously raised in the proceedings of LAFTA—the issue of
agreements for the organization of commodity markets.

In analysing prospects for the Common Schedule negotiations,
the Standing Executive Committee of LAFTA made the following
observation:

> Consequently, not only so as to facilitate the elaboration of the
> Common Schedule, but, more fundamentally, in order to calm the fears
> of the agricultural producers of LAFTA and offer the Governments of
> the Contracting Parties the opportunity of studying continuously and
> exhaustively the most suitable methods of organizing agricultural
> markets . . . it appears essential that . . . steps be taken, in sufficient time
> before the end of the transition period, to study and conclude market
> arrangements for certain products.[20]

As we shall see, a common market among underdeveloped countries can scarcely succeed without a large measure of joint industrial
planning. It is equally true, as the Standing Executive Committee of
LAFTA implied in the document under discussion, that regional
agreements, providing for some kind of rational division of labour
within the area and for co-operative planning of production and
trade, are also indispensable in agriculture.

The inclusion of industrial products in the Common Schedule
would be an important factor in giving potential investors the assur-

[19] Text reproduced in *Comercio Exterior*, May 1964, pp. 308–12.
[20] Ibid. p. 309.

ance they need of access to a region-wide market. This assurance does not result from the inclusion of particular items in the National Schedules alone. For one thing, some countries may include certain items in their National Schedules while others do not. More important still is the fact that concessions on items contained in National Schedules may later be withdrawn. Only when an item is included in the Common Schedule do the concessions become irrevocable and only then is the opening up of the region-wide market guaranteed by the end of the transition period.

Thus even though industrial products are of little importance in existing trade among LAFTA countries—and therefore cannot as yet add very much, statistically, to the realization of the target percentages of liberalization—the inclusion of as many industrial items as possible in the Common Schedule is a vital necessity. There should be little difficulty in doing this where the items concerned are not produced in any LAFTA country at the present time: this would ensure that in these cases production would from the very beginning be organized with the needs of the region-wide market in mind.

Where, however, the vested interests of existing industries are affected, relatively few items have been placed even on the National Schedules, and the difficulty of including such items on the Common Schedule is likely to be even greater. A solution to this problem is likely to be possible only within the framework of a general plan for the industrial development of the region as a whole, as will be indicated further below.

One point of some importance for a rational development of industry throughout the region is that enterprises in all LAFTA countries should, as far as possible, be able to gain access to raw materials at competitive prices so that the location of industry is not distorted by arbitrary differences in raw material costs between the various member countries. This implies a need for harmonizing raw material import tariffs among LAFTA countries, and means also that as many raw materials as possible should appear on the Common Schedule, and be traded freely throughout the region. This may raise difficulties in the case of certain agricultural raw materials: in some cases it may be necessary for particular countries to subsidize the prices of high-cost agricultural raw materials so as not to penalize their industrial producers. Such subsidies should, however, be subject to review by the LAFTA countries as a group so as

G

to ensure consistency with Article 52 of the Treaty, which prohibits subsidies that are 'likely to disrupt normal competitive conditions in the Area'. In other words, subsidies may be permissible to offset the effects of artificially high raw material costs and thus, in a sense, restore or maintain 'normal' competitive conditions. Subsidies would *not* be acceptable if they artificially reduced raw material costs in a particular country below the level prevailing in the region in general.

The Common Schedule Negotiations

The difficulties actually encountered in drawing up the first list of products for the Common Schedule proved to be even greater than had been expected. The negotiations began on 26 May 1964 and had still not been brought to a successful conclusion five months later, in October 1964. At this point it was decided to hand the negotiations over to the fourth regular session of the Contracting Parties, and the list was finally approved by all members except Uruguay[21] on 11 December 1964.

The basic reason for the exceptional difficulties associated with the Common Schedule negotiations was the unwillingness of the smaller and less developed LAFTA countries to commit themselves irrevocably to freeing their imports unless corresponding progress were made in other aspects of the integration programme. These countries felt that liberalization of trade should proceed parallel with—and not ahead of—concrete action for the coordination of economic development programmes and policies, the establishment of a common external tariff, and other measures directed towards the integration of the region. There was a feeling that the large countries were gaining most from the liberalization programme and that the balance must be restored by a variety of co-operative measures: it was this view that had been responsible, as we shall see in Chapter VII, for the decision at the third LAFTA session to give a special status to Chile, Colombia, Peru, and Uruguay—Ecuador and Paraguay having already been recognized as less developed countries within the meaning of the Montevideo Treaty.

More specifically, several countries made it clear that their agree-

---

[21] Uruguay also declined to sign the Final Act of the fourth regular session, to which were annexed the resolutions of the session. The other LAFTA members decided to give Uruguay 90 days in which to sign the Common Schedule and the Final Act of the session, and it complied within the time limit laid down.

ment to a Common Schedule would be conditional on adequate arrangements being made regarding: (*a*) institutional arrangements to speed the process of integration; (*b*) trade in agricultural products after the end of the transition period; (*c*) the rules of origin to be applied; (*d*) the margins of preference to be granted; (*e*) the nature and extent of export subsidies or benefits to be permitted; (*f*) the limitation of benefits under complementarity agreements to participants; (*g*) reciprocity of benefits under the liberalization programme.[22]

In addition, the less developed countries insisted that the special concessions accorded to them on items listed in the Common Schedule should be maintained until the end of the transition period in June 1973.

Institutional aspects will be considered in Chapter XI. Equally important were agricultural considerations. Since the bulk of intra-trade in 1960–2 consisted of agricultural products, it was inevitable that the first list of products for the Common Schedule would be heavily weighted on the side of agriculture. Indeed, out of the 25 per cent of regional trade covered by the list ultimately adopted, over 14 per cent was accounted for by the four commodities: coffee, cotton, cacao, and bananas; and a large number of the remaining items were also agricultural.

But could the LAFTA countries afford to allow regional free trade in agricultural products after 1973? If so, they would be the only region in the world adopting such a policy. A prosperous Latin American agriculture will depend on land reform and many other radical changes to raise productivity: free market forces can scarcely be relied on to promote this process and might in fact impede it. The only way forward in agriculture is for countries to plan jointly for a gradual mutual adjustment of production and investment so as to permit a more rational utilization of land resources and distribution of productive activities throughout the region.

There have been a number of resolutions calling for progress along these lines. For example a resolution adopted at the fourth annual session of the LAFTA countries required 'the coordination and harmonization of the policies of the respective Contracting Parties'. To this end the LAFTA countries were to undertake a confrontation of their respective agricultural programmes with a

---

[22] For an exposition of views along these lines, see the statement of the representative of Chile (pp. 279–84 below).

view to co-operation in adjusting them in the light of each country's particular resources and conditions.[23]

But all this still lay in the future: in the meantime the LAFTA countries wanted to be sure that if they included a large number of agricultural items in the Common Schedule, this would not commit them unconditionally to free trade in those items by 1973. They therefore decided, in resolution 97 (IV), to extend the validity of Article 23 of the Montevideo Treaty into the post-transition period. Under this Article, LAFTA countries may, 'as a provisional measure and providing that the customary level of consumption in the importer country is not thereby lowered', impose non-discriminatory restrictions on imports of products[24] likely to cause damage in the domestic market.

This decision did not, of course, take matters a single step further along the path to regional coordination of agricultural production and planning. On the contrary, the effect of the decision was not merely to recognize that no progress had yet been made in this direction, but that there might be little advance to record by the time the transition period ended in 1973. Reasonable and realistic as decision 97 (IV) may have been, it undermined the integrity of the Common Schedule. For in effect it limited the unconditional commitment to the elimination of mutual trade barriers by 1973 to non-agricultural products.

If the structure of trade among LAFTA countries remains essentially what it is now—consisting mainly of agricultural commodities —it may be easy for these countries to put 'substantially all' their traded items into the Common Schedule by 1973, but in view of decision 97 (IV) this will mean very little. If the Common Schedule approach is to have any validity, therefore, it is essential that the whole structure of regional trade should change very rapidly, with industrial items accounting for a growing share of the total. The weakness here, however, is that there is no firm obligation on LAFTA countries to eliminate duties or other restrictions on items not previously traded in the area.

It will thus be apparent that the whole programme of lowering trade barriers could come to a halt if all countries insisted on invoking their full rights under the Treaty and under decision 97 (IV).

---

[23] *Resoluciones*, 100 (IV), Sections I.C.6 and I.C.7.

[24] While Art. 23 does not limit the type of products to which it relates, the resolution extending its applicability refers only to agricultural products.

The main hope is that the intention has been to provide safeguards rather than to put the whole machinery of liberalization into reverse.[25]

A further step taken to pave the way for the adoption of the Common Schedule was to make a whole series of new concessions, at least on paper, to the less developed countries. The period of validity for certain existing special concessions to the less developed countries was extended, and a number of new concessions were granted.[26] An undertaking was given that everything possible would be done to maintain the special margins of preference granted to Ecuador and Paraguay, and to support their applications to the Inter-American Development Bank to obtain financing for their exports of certain products.[27]

In addition, as discussed more fully in Chapter VIII, steps were taken to prevent countries not participating in complementarity agreements from enjoying the benefits of the agreements (as they would normally have been entitled to do under the most-favoured-nation provision of the Treaty) unless they granted appropriate concessions in return.[28]

Decisions were also taken arranging for the study of methods of achieving reciprocity[29] and for the establishment of rules of origin for liberalized goods, giving priority to those listed in the Common Schedule.[30] While a general declaration was made in favour of 'equitable conditions of competition',[31] no specific arrangements regarding export subsidies or benefits had been made up to the end of 1964.

[25] It may be asked why the LAFTA countries bothered to include any agricultural items at all in the Common Schedule if the effect of this was to be immediately undone by allowing restrictions on agricultural imports to continue after 1973. Why did they not simply list non-agricultural products? The answer, of course, is that since under the Montevideo Treaty the list had to contain items accounting for at least 25% of intra-trade in 1960–2, there was no way of avoiding the inclusion of agricultural items, non-agricultural items being of very little consequence in existing trade.

[26] *Resoluciones*, 98 (IV), 107 (IV), 108 (IV). [27] Ibid., 105 (IV), 111 (IV).

[28] Resolution 99 (IV), pp. 324–9 below. The intermediate group of countries (Chile, Colombia, Peru, and Uruguay) gained only part of their objectives under this resolution. They did not succeed in getting agreement to a clause they had proposed, whereby the Standing Executive Committee would have been able to authorize a limited group of LAFTA members to participate in complementarity agreements which would not be open to accession by other LAFTA members for a certain period of time.

[29] *Resoluciones*, 93 (II E). [30] Ibid., 94 (II E).

[31] Ibid., 100 (IV), Preamble.

Potentially the most important decision of all was the agreement that: 'In order to achieve an equitable distribution of the benefits of integration, given the different structures and levels of development of the LAFTA countries, it is necessary that the location of industry should be determined by joint planning'; and that: 'Planning for the location in certain countries of industries catering to the region as a whole implies the adoption of a common policy in the production sector in question'.[32]

As we shall see in Chapter VII, only the adoption of agreed targets for all LAFTA countries, and of joint measures to achieve them, could provide the smaller and weaker countries with the assurances they need to proceed with the trade liberalization programme.

The agreements reached on the various issues discussed above, as well as on the convening of a meeting of Foreign Ministers in 1965,[33] made it possible to break the long deadlock over the Common Schedule. It remained to be seen whether the decisions that had been taken in principle would lead to more effective joint measures by the LAFTA countries in the direction of economic integration. One thing the deadlock had made abundantly clear, however—that any attempt to reduce trade barriers without a parallel advance towards co-ordination of economic programmes and policies was doomed to failure.

Free Trade Area or Customs Union?

Despite the difficulties that the LAFTA countries have had in making adequate progress towards a free-trade area, in any real sense of the term, the inadequacy of the free-trade area concept in certain respects has prompted consideration of the possibility of moving on still further towards a customs union.

Originally, the Latin American countries had even stronger reasons than the EFTA countries for preferring a free-trade area arrangement over a customs union. It will be recalled that the most important difference between the two types of association is that in a customs union the members agree to establish a common tariff against the outside world, while in a free-trade area they do not, and are in fact free to maintain their existing national tariffs if they so wish.

Generally speaking, therefore, countries will choose the free-trade area goal if they attach as much importance to the mainten-

[32] *Resoluciones*, 100 (IV), paras. I.B. 7 and I.B. 9.   [33] See ch. xi.

ance of their trading links with the rest of the world as to the development of trade with their fellow-members in the new economic association. They will prefer a customs union if they place higher priority on the strengthening of trade links with their fellow-members than on maintaining trade relations with non-members.

For Britain the free-trade area concept offered attractions because trade with Western Europe is a smaller proportion of its total trade than is typical of countries on the Continent; and because in a free-trade area it would be possible to preserve the essential fabric of Commonwealth trade and preference.

Like Britain, the Latin American countries trade more extensively outside the region than inside. In fact while Britain does 40 per cent of its trade with Western Europe Latin America's internal trade amounts to less than one-tenth of its total trade. It was thus quite natural for Latin American countries to consider, in the early stages, that they should not do anything to harm the 90 per cent sector of their foreign trade for the sake of a 10 per cent sector, the future of which was in any case very uncertain. They felt that any disturbance of the level of their tariffs against third parties might endanger their whole external trading position, without adequate compensating advantages within the region.

A free-trade area does, however, pose administrative problems that do not arise in a customs union. In particular, while customs posts can ultimately be abolished all along the internal frontiers of a customs union, a constant check has to be maintained in perpetuity on the origin of goods circulating within a free-trade area. For if all goods had unrestricted freedom to move from country to country within a free-trade area, exporters from the outside would obviously have an incentive to send their goods to the member countries with the lowest tariffs, for transhipment to the high-tariff countries. Although LAFTA has made the arrangements necessary for ascertaining and defining the origin of goods traded in Latin America, it will be obvious that such arrangements cannot but invite evasion and smuggling.

But it is not the administrative difficulties that are the principal defect of a free-trade area. Much more important is the fact that no serious measure of economic integration is possible so long as individual member countries remain free to set whatever tariffs they please on imports from the outside world.

For one thing, if the manufacturers of a particular product in one member country have to pay a higher rate of duty on their imports of raw materials than corresponding manufacturers in another member country, the latter obviously acquire an unfair advantage within the regional market. Sooner or later something has to be done to remove this inequality: in other words, the tariffs on imported raw materials have to be harmonized. The same argument can, of course, be applied to other goods needed in the production process, such as fuel, as well as machinery and equipment. Ultimately even the tariffs on food and other consumer goods would have to be harmonized, since inter-country discrepancies would tend to be reflected in wage differentials: other things being equal, manufacturers in high-tariff countries would probably have to pay higher wages than those in low-tariff countries, and this, again, would affect their competitive power in a region-wide market. In short, the very concept of a regional market to which all member countries have equal access implies the ultimate harmonization of customs duties against third parties, so that the location of manufacturing enterprises does not come to depend on chance differences in tariff levels instead of on considerations of productive efficiency.

There is, however, still another factor tending to push national tariffs into line, and that is the need to establish adequate and comparable margins of regional preference throughout the area. A member country with a low average level of tariffs obviously cannot grant as extensive an average margin of preference in favour of its high-tariff neighbour as the latter can—unless, of course, it raises its own tariffs against third parties to the level maintained by that neighbour.

If, for example, the average level of tariffs in country A is 5 per cent and in B 20 per cent, the elimination of tariffs on their mutual trade would leave A enjoying a preferential margin averaging 20 per cent in B's market, while B's preference in A's market was only 5 per cent. In such circumstances B would exert strong pressure on A to raise its average level of tariffs to the extent required to equalize the mutual flow of benefits from a unified market between them.

In practice, of course, tariffs on particular products may differ much more from country to country than the average level of tariffs overall. For example underdeveloped countries often maintain relatively low tariffs on goods that they do not produce for themselves and relatively high tariffs on those that they do. This means that they are in a position to grant substantial preference to their neighbours on the goods that they make at home (and which they are therefore not especially anxious to import) but that they cannot give much if any encouragement to their neighbours on those that they do not manufacture for themselves (and which must therefore be imported in any event).

If this situation were maintained, underdeveloped countries would be able to grant one another significant tariff preferences only in respect of those goods that they are already producing for themselves. In practice this would mean that the members of LAFTA would undertake cut-throat competition in the light industries producing textiles and other non-durable consumer goods, but that no significant mutual advantages could be extended in respect of some of the durable producer and consumer goods not now manufactured in the area, and on which, therefore, tariffs may be low. If this were the effect of the Treaty of Montevideo, operating within the terms of Article XXIV of GATT,[34] it would indeed be most unfortunate. For it would lead to economic and ultimately political conflict between the Latin American countries without helping very much in raising the level of industrial development in the region.

These considerations suggest a need for tariff levels to move towards one another in such a way as to provide adequate regional incentives not only in those industries in which Latin America already has some productive capacity but also in those in which it does not. Where all or most member countries already do some manufacturing for themselves, as for example in the textile or other light industries, the need to harmonize preferential margins leads inevitably to a requirement for a common external tariff to be established in the course of the transitional period.

[34] Article XXIV of GATT requires that the average import duties or other trade controls imposed on third countries by members of a free-trade area must not be higher than, or more restrictive than those prevailing, on the average, prior to the formation of the free-trade area. It is true that compliance with the rules of GATT might be achieved if a country raising its tariff on, say, capital goods reduced its tariff on other goods, thereby maintaining an unchanged average level of protection. The difficulty here is that the products subject to higher tariffs would presumably be those important in the domestic production of the country in question, so that a lowering of protection would be unacceptable. It would scarcely be fair to expect an underdeveloped country to risk damage to its own few industries as the price for being allowed to grant a preference to the industries of another country. This rule of GATT therefore requires modification in its application to underdeveloped countries. A similar problem occurs in relation to customs unions. For the text of Article XXIV of GATT, see below, pp. 225–8.

On the other hand, where particular products are manufactured in only one or two of the member countries, or in none, the need for an adequate margin of regional preference throughout the area will usually imply a raising of tariff rates in some or all of the member countries. And once tariff rates on particular products have in any case to be changed, it is natural to move them to the same level in all countries in the interests of internal non-discrimination.

More generally, the advantages of a customs union over a free-trade area derive essentially from the need to establish the principle of internal non-discrimination throughout the region as a whole. Such non-discrimination means on the one hand that no firm should be penalized through higher duties charged on imports in the country in which it happens to be located; and on the other hand that, in the interests of reciprocity, the margins of regional preference on particular products should be standardized in all member countries—which again implies the need for a common tariff in the long run.

At least two of the resolutions adopted during the second session of the Contracting Parties to the Treaty of Montevideo reflect the beginnings of a shift towards the closer forms of economic integration implied by a customs union as against a free-trade area.

Resolution 53 (II) adopted by the Contracting Parties sets forth a basic interpretation of the Treaty's intentions. It says that the Treaty has as its objective not only the freeing of trade among the signatories, but also the establishment of a 'reasonable' margin of regional preference that would stimulate the gradual substitution of domestic output for imports. The resolution does not seek to define what a 'reasonable' margin of preference might be. Nor does it call for any raising of customs duties against third parties where these are currently too low to afford a significant level of regional preference. It does, however, take a first step towards maintaining the value of such preferences as have in fact been created by the mutual reduction of tariffs under the Treaty through the annual negotiations. For it requires the member countries not to reduce any preference thus established through tariff concessions to third parties or by other means. It thus seeks to guard against the danger that, under pressure from exporters in North America and Western Europe, members of LAFTA may be induced to extend their mutual concessions to third parties. To this extent, it makes a first move against the tariff autonomy implied in the concept of a free-trade area.[35]

In resolution 99 (IV) relating to industrial complementarity agreements,[36] customs union concepts are introduced more directly, so as to provide for equality of treatment throughout the region. The resolution lays down that such agreements may include provision for the harmonization of treatment accorded to imports from third countries, both of products included in the scope of the agreement and of the raw materials and component parts used in their manufacture.[37] The very first of these industrial agreements, covering data processing machines, and signed in July 1962, provided that national restrictions on imports from third countries of the materials and components used in their production should be harmonized as soon as possible. A second agreement, on radio and television valves, signed in February 1964, went further in calling for harmonization of restrictions on imports from third countries not only of materials and components but of valves as well.

All this for the time being implied nothing more than a piecemeal approach: if the procedure described above in respect of valves were followed in every industry, a customs union[38] would ultimately emerge, but only as the combined result of a large number of separate agreements covering all individual industries. It should, however, be noted that tariff harmonization on an industry-by-industry basis has the drawback that it may lead not only to imbalance between industries but also to inequities between countries, depending on which industries happen to suit their local circumstances best. On such a basis, some industries may end up with a very high level of regional preference, others with a much lower level. An integrated approach, on the other hand, would make it possible to try and achieve some sort of balance in the advantages secured by the various countries for the particular industries in which they are actually or potentially interested.

It is therefore not surprising that at their third session, at the end of 1963, the LAFTA countries called, in resolution 75 (III), for

---

[35] *Resoluciones*, 53 (II).
[36] This was an amended version of the text, adopted at the second session, in resolution 48 (II).
[37] See resolution 99 (IV), pp. 324–9 below.
[38] If the industrial complementarity agreements included the food processing industries as well as the industries using agricultural raw materials, the customs union would thereby cover agriculture as well as industry.

certain preliminary work to be done as a basis for studying 'the possibility of establishing a common external tariff'.[39]

Despite the foregoing considerations, the establishment of a common external tariff may be a very long and slow process. This is because the degree of inter-country variation in national tariffs is very great—much greater than that prevailing among the EEC countries. For example, among the illustrative tariffs listed in Appendix Table XI, rates between 150 and 200 per cent *ad valorem* are quite common in Argentina, whereas the highest tariff listed for Mexico (excluding bauxite) is 28 per cent. Consequently the problem of harmonization between Argentina and Mexico may be immense, and of a completely different order of magnitude from the corresponding problem faced in the EEC as between, say, Italy and Belgium. The problem is even greater when one takes into account the multiplicity of non-tariff devices for controlling imports in Latin America, including import surcharges, advance deposits, and quantitative restrictions, as well as the rapid shifts that constantly take place in the relative overvaluation or undervaluation of currencies.[40]

It is therefore one thing to recognize the advantages of a customs union over a free-trade area and quite another to reach agreement on the common external tariff to be applied. It will clearly be necessary to approach the problem of harmonization with a good deal of patience and circumspection. The approach would be considerably facilitated if progressive steps could be taken to replace non-tariff restrictions by tariffs; and, in the countries with abnormally high tariffs, it would be desirable, when any opportunity occurs for adjusting exchange rates, to do this in such a way that the average level of tariffs may be greatly reduced, without detriment to the industries concerned. If, in addition, excess protection (in the sense of duty rates higher than those needed to give the desired degree of protection) could be gradually eliminated, the problem would be further eased.

A Latin American Common Market

Although the Latin American countries have not yet accepted the idea of a common external tariff, there is already active discussion of the possibility of moving even beyond the customs union stage, to-

---

[39] See resolution 75 (III), pp. 320–2 below.
[40] For a further discussion of these shifts, see ch. ix.

wards the organization of a 'common market'. Indeed, the preamble to the Treaty of Montevideo voices the determination of the Latin American governments to 'persevere in their efforts to establish, gradually and progressively, a Latin American common market'; and Article 54 of the Treaty requires the participating countries to 'make every effort to direct their policies with a view to creating conditions favourable to the establishment of a Latin American common market'.

The term 'common market' has not been given a precise meaning in the literature on economic integration. The generally accepted definitions of 'customs union' and 'free-trade area' are those to be found in Article XXIV of GATT:[41] but this article contains no reference to the term 'common market'.

While no agreed definition exists, it appears that in Latin American usage the idea of a 'common market' is quite similar to, though not identical with, that of an 'economic union' as understood in Europe and North America.[42] In addition to possessing all the properties of a customs union, an economic union removes all obstacles to the free internal movement of labour and capital, coordinates the economic, financial, and social policies of the participating governments, and operates as a single unit in economic relations with third countries. It may or may not adopt a single currency, and establish a common central bank.

The Secretariat of ECLA has listed the following requirements of a common market:

(i) The abolition of all mutual barriers to imports and the establishment of fair conditions of competition within the market.

(ii) Alignment of trade and tariff policies towards third countries.

(iii) Adoption of 'realistic' exchange rates.

(iv) Harmonization of fiscal and social policies.

(v) Establishment of rules and procedures to govern trade in agricultural commodities.

---

[41] See below, p. 227.

[42] In Europe and North America the term 'common market' is used rather loosely to convey the idea of an area in which there are no artificial barriers to the free movement of goods or services. A 'common market' may be quite limited in terms of commodity coverage. The European Coal and Steel Community, for example, maintains a 'common market' in coal and steel products only. This does not appear to correspond to Latin American usage.

(vi) Creation of an adequate network of internal transport and communications.

(vii) Measures to strengthen Latin American enterprise, including a standardization of legislation dealing with foreign investment.

(viii) Institutional arrangements sufficiently powerful to

(*a*) take effective action for the promotion of the economic development of the LAFTA area as a whole;

(*b*) encourage regional specialization and complementarity within the area;

(*c*) ensure an equitable distribution of benefits among participating countries.[43]

Some comment is, perhaps, called for on the general policy orientation implied in a shift from a free-trade area to a customs union or economic union in Latin America. It might be held by some critics that such a shift would imply an 'inward-looking' bias in the development of the region, since it would signify a lesser concern with the region's trade with the rest of the world, and a correspondingly greater concern with the development of intra-regional trade.

It has become commonplace in contemporary discussion of economic unions to say that such unions ought to be 'outward-looking' and not 'inward-looking'. Indeed, the term 'inward-looking' has become synonymous with everything that is evil in a regional economic association. Now there is no doubt that this judgement has a certain validity when applied, say, to the regional groupings in Europe. For example, in so far as the EEC follows unnecessarily protectionist policies in agriculture or other sectors, it damages both itself and the other countries of the world with which it trades. But it would be quite absurd to transfer this line of thinking automatically to economic unions among underdeveloped countries. For the trouble with underdeveloped countries is precisely that they are already too 'outward-looking', in the sense that they are much too oriented towards their trade with the industrially developed countries and too little concerned with their own domestic

---

[43] ECLA, *Note by the Secretariat on the Commission's Activities in the Field of Economic Integration*, p. 9. The points set out in this document have been partially rearranged above.

development. They would therefore do well to look inwards to their own development needs to a far greater extent than has been the case hitherto, and there is no reason for them to be ashamed of this or to subordinate their own requirements to the trade objectives of the industrially developed countries. For LAFTA a more coherent 'inward-looking' policy would be a step forward rather than backwards, given the present economic circumstances of the Latin American region.

This is not to say, of course, that Latin American trade with the rest of the world is a matter of no consequence, or that it can be ignored in devising a regional economic policy for the continent. Any such idea would fly in the face of the obvious fact that nine-tenths of Latin America's trade is still carried on with North America and Western Europe, and is likely to be for some time. What does emerge, however, is that the notions of 'inward-looking' and 'outward-looking' unions, so frequently discussed in the context of European economic integration, are subject to serious qualification when applied in the context of Latin America. Here, on the contrary, there is a presumption that joint economic development behind a common barrier of regional protection would be in the interests of Latin America as a whole, and ultimately of the rest of the world as well. For a more prosperous and more rapidly growing Latin America is bound to be a more active trading partner for the rest of the world than a Latin America beset by the economic stagnation and retrogression of recent years.

Closely linked with the general economic strategy to be followed by the Latin American countries is the question of a common commercial policy *vis-à-vis* the rest of the world. Resolutions 56 (II) and 75 (III) adopted at the second and third annual conferences of the LAFTA countries provided for meetings and studies concerning the elaboration of common economic and commercial policies in the various member countries as well as for the exchange of information and study of commercial policy matters of mutual concern. These resolutions, though full of good intentions, do not indicate any great advance thus far towards drawing up a common commercial policy in Latin America. This is, perhaps, not surprising since progress on this front, even in the dynamic EEC, has also been quite slow. And although theoretically the Commission of the EEC ought to be taking over responsibility for commercial policy from the national governments, in practice the Commission remains very de-

pendent upon the acquiescence of the member countries in anything it may do: this situation is likely to persist, especially if the
French concept of 'Europe des patries' is generally accepted throughout the Community. The difficulty of concerting economic and
commercial policies is therefore likely to be even greater in Latin
America, where the political forces for unity appear to be much
weaker than in Western Europe.

Thus developments following the Treaty of Montevideo revealed
conflicting tendencies in LAFTA. On the one hand there was a
recognition that LAFTA had not gone far enough on the road to integration—that efforts were needed to reduce disparities in external
tariffs and make progress in the direction of common margins of
preference, common economic, fiscal, and commercial policies,
joint planning, and stronger central institutions. On the other hand,
LAFTA was experiencing difficulty in achieving even the limited
goals of tariff disarmament envisaged in the Treaty, and agreement
on the first stage of the Common Schedule was made possible only
by eliminating the unconditional character of the commitment to
free imports of agricultural products by 1973.

In part the difficulties in the tariff negotiations were themselves a
result of the failure to make progress in other directions, so that
certain countries began to argue that further advances in tariff reduction must be conditional on parallel action in other parts of the
integration programme.

The problem also arose, however, to what extent the difficulties
encountered had been created by the Treaty itself, with its attempt
to force the integration objectives of a group of underdeveloped
countries into a GATT framework that had originally been designed with the problems of Western Europe in mind. The concept
of National and Common Schedules was, however, neither fully in
line with GATT—because of their definition primarily in terms of
existing trade—nor responsive to the needs of the LAFTA countries. Indeed, since existing trade was largely in agricultural products, it was obvious from the beginning that a simple lowering of
trade barriers would not be acceptable to the LAFTA countries,
any more than it was to the EEC countries.

The question had, in fact, emerged whether the lowering of trade
barriers should not henceforward concentrate on industrial rather
than agricultural products; and whether the Treaty of Montevideo
should not be revised to this end. In a sense, what the LAFTA

countries need most is to eliminate their mutual tariffs not so much on their existing trade with one another as on *the industrial goods they import from the developed countries*. This would mean the creation of a region-wide protected market designed to promote the manufacture of goods that would displace imports from third countries. In other words, it would transfer the emphasis of the liberalization programme away from trade in agricultural commodities and in the products of traditional industries, and focus on the expansion of Latin American enterprise into new products and new markets. The negotiation of trade barrier reductions along these lines would presumably be much easier than those required under the Treaty. It would also concentrate the effort at the precise point where it could be most beneficial—namely in the establishment of new industries.

Exports of the industrial countries to Latin America would not decline in total as a result of such a reorientation of the LAFTA programme, even if there were a drop in exports of particular goods to the region. Latin America's aggregate imports from the industrial countries will be limited for many years to come not by the volume or structure of domestic demand but by the level of foreign exchange earned, or received as aid: the shortage of external resources is such that LAFTA countries will continue to spend all the foreign exchange they receive, whatever new industries they may set up. A recasting of the Treaty of Montevideo along the lines envisaged above should therefore help LAFTA without damaging the overall interests of third countries.

H

CHAPTER VI

PROBLEMS OF TRANSPORT AND COMMUNICATIONS

IT is remarkable that, unlike the Treaty of Rome, the Montevideo Treaty has nothing to say about the establishment of a common transport policy: it does not even assert that a common policy for transport would be desirable.[1] The omission reflects the exceptional difficulties that have to be overcome in this field, not only because of vested interests within the LAFTA region but also on account of the conflict of interests between Latin America and the big shipping countries.

South America runs some 4,500 miles from north to south and about 3,000 miles from east to west at its widest point. Yet the great bulk of the population lives within 200 miles of the coast: the interior of the continent consists largely of uninhabited mountain, jungle, and desert regions. Since interior communications are relatively poor, more than nine-tenths of the merchandise traded among the countries of Latin America goes by sea.

While inland transport facilities in Latin America are limited, they compare favourably with those available in other underdeveloped areas. Substantial resources are now being allocated to the development and modernization of inland transport in several countries and a number of major projects are under way or contemplated that will assist the growth of regional trade. For example, the Inter-American Development Bank has granted a substantial loan for a road that will cross Uruguay from the Brazilian border to Argentina and link up the national highways of all three countries. An $18·5 million World Bank loan to Uruguay is being used for the rebuilding of the main north–south link with Brazil. Other plans provide for a trans-Andean road to connect Mendoza in Argentina with the Chilean port of Valparaiso, and a huge $200 million high-

[1] In response to a question during GATT's examination of the Montevideo Treaty, the LAFTA countries went so far as to state that it was not intended to give any preferential treatment in respect of invisible trade and credits within LAFTA (see *Resoluciones (Comité)*, p. 199, Question 124).

way system to provide outlets from the hinterland of the Amazon basin to the north and south of the continent. Efforts are also being made to re-equip and modernize the railways. Part of the deficiency in continental transport facilities is made good by the airlines, both domestic and foreign. The number of daily flights between Rio de Janeiro and São Paulo is probably larger than between any other two cities in the world. This is, of course, an exceptional case, but it illustrates the possibilities of air transport in a region of low road and rail density. Mail and telephonic communications are much less satisfactory. Delays in postal service are a tiresome hindrance to business efficiency, while it is normal for telephone calls from one Latin American country to another to be routed via New York—if indeed an adequate connexion can be made at all. In many cases telephone calls even between neighbouring cities in the same country present almost insurmountable difficulties.

The Cost of Maritime Transport

By far the most important problems are those affecting maritime transport. The high cost of transport between Latin American ports has seriously impeded the development of area trade: in many cases it is cheaper to ship goods from Europe or North America than between points within the region. For example, the freight rate for lumber shipped from Mexico to Venezuela was $24 per ton in 1963 as compared to $11 from Finland to Venezuela, even though the distance is three times greater. From Buenos Aires to Tampico, Mexico, the ocean freight rate for chemicals was $54 per ton for direct shipment; but if the goods were trans-shipped in New Orleans the rate was only $46, while trans-shipment in Southampton brought down the rate further to $40, despite the tremendous increase in distances involved.[2]

Nor is it simply a question of high costs. Goods shipped from Porto Alegre in Brazil to Montevideo actually reach their destination more quickly if sent via Hamburg, Western Germany. In fact Uruguayan wool is shipped to the United States by way of Hamburg even when there are ships available going directly to New York.[3]

There are several reasons for the high cost of maritime transport

[2] Business International, *Latin America's Merging Market*, p. 29.
[3] Enrique Angulo, 'El transporte y el comercio interlatinoamericano', in M. Wionczek, ed., *Integración de América Latina* (1964), p. 186.

in Latin America. For one thing, the volume of traffic is in any case too low to permit regular, frequent, and stable services on an economic basis. Thus transport tends to be organized bilaterally, with all the disadvantages that this implies, especially where the traffic is seriously unbalanced. For example, in 1963 Argentina's exports to Chile were valued f.o.b. at $41·5 million while imports, c.i.f., amounted to only $17·2 million; corresponding trade exchanges with Peru were valued at $36 million and $9·2 million respectively. In the same year Brazil's imports from Mexico amounted to $17·9 million while the value of exports was only $1·4 million. Underutilization of shipping capacity in one direction inevitably tends to drive up freight costs.

Another major factor in high costs is the poor condition of the ports: according to a study by the OAS more than two-thirds of the cost of transport is incurred in the handling of cargo, and here one encounters all the problems of unsatisfactory and poorly maintained equipment, an inadequate labour force, and frequent labour disputes. At the same time operations are seriously obstructed by a maze of port formalities and documentation, leading to intense congestion of both trucks and vessels in the ports. According to the OAS, moreover, the situation is growing worse rather than better.[4]

The third main factor affecting maritime transport costs in Latin America is the monopolistic position of the conferences. Only four Latin American shipping lines are represented in international shipping conferences, which are dominated by foreign companies. It is not possible to determine precisely how the monopolistic power of the conferences is reflected in the fixing of freight rates because of difficulty in obtaining any information on this matter. The secrecy of conference operations naturally prompts the greatest misgivings about their impact on the Latin American economy.

Evidence presented to the Joint Economic Committee of the United States Congress has revealed that it costs more to ship United States exports to South America, Africa, and India than to ship comparable products to the same ports from Western European countries and Japan. A sampling of rates on forty export commodities showed that the average rate per ton-mile from the United States was 85 per cent higher than the rates from European ports to the same ports of destination. The Joint Economic Committee concluded that in part this situation had been caused by the fact that

[4] *Informe sobre actividades portuarias,* doc. 18-E, 10 July 1962.

rates are commonly made in concert by shipping conferences chiefly controlled by European lines, many of which also serve competitive sources of supply in their home countries.[5]

The Committee also came to the following striking conclusion:

There is evidence which suggests that the major steamship lines of the world may have divided up trade markets. A conference, a pool, a rate agreement are not necessarily separate and unrelated, but might well be parts of a complicated structure affecting the entire ocean freight market. However, the extent of possible market division is not known. Whether a conscious plan has been adopted by some lines calling for worldwide cargo distribution also is not known.[6]

If a country as powerful as the United States is subject to certain types of rate discrimination, it is a not unreasonable presumption that developing countries may be having the same experience. A study of ocean shipping and freight rates was undertaken for the United Nations Conference on Trade and Development as a preliminary step in assembling the data and information required for the exploration of this difficult field. The first conclusion of the study was that

High priority should be given by developing countries to measures for the provision of 'countervailing power', through the creation or strengthening of negotiation machinery, on a national or regional basis, between shipping conferences and representative shippers' and traders' associations of developing countries; such machinery, for ventilating and remedying complaints, would be entrusted with consultative functions in all matters related to conference rates and practices.[7]

The second recommendation emerging from the Conference study was that developing countries should continue efforts towards the development of merchant marines, preferably on the basis of regional arrangements, and taking into account the priority and productivity of investment in this field compared with other alternatives. It was also considered that developed countries should be prepared to accept a reasonable degree of flag discrimination or other protective practices by developing countries, so as to foster the growth of national shipping lines.

[5] US Congress, Joint Economic Committee, *Discriminatory Ocean Freight Rates and the Balance of Payments*, Report (1965), pp. 3–4 and 18–19.
[6] Ibid. p. 6.
[7] UNCTAD, *Ocean Shipping and Freight Rates and Developing Countries*. By the Economist Intelligence Unit (E/CONF.46/27, Jan. 1964), p. 238.

Action by LAFTA

LAFTA has been slow to act in this field. Transport questions did not figure prominently at the first annual conference of the LAFTA countries, and not until mid-1962 did these questions begin to get the consideration they deserved, at a meeting of transport experts convened by LAFTA. This was followed by the establishment of an intergovernmental Advisory Committee on Transport, under the Standing Executive Committee, to assist in promoting the integration of sea and river transport, and of the Latin American Association of Shipowners, to co-operate in this task.

Sustained efforts have been made towards the adoption of a general agreement on maritime, river, and lake transport. While LAFTA members are united on the need for preferential treatment of Latin American shipping lines in intra-regional trade, differences have occurred on the degree of bilateralism that should be accepted.

At the meeting of transport experts in July 1962, referred to above, a proposal by four countries (Brazil, Chile, Mexico, and Uruguay) had favoured a completely bilateral distribution of traffic. Each LAFTA member should, it was felt, have the right to reserve to itself the transport of 50 per cent of cargo carried in trade with another member, and should have first option on any portion of its partner's share that the latter did not carry. Other members of LAFTA would receive preference over non-members, but only in respect of that portion of bilateral trade not in fact transported by the trading partners concerned.

The difficulties raised by this proposal were pointed out by the Secretariat of ECLA. Such a system would involve misuse or under-utilization of available shipping capacity, especially since it would lead to the fragmentation of a volume of cargo already insufficient for the economic operation of frequent and regular regional services. Only if the preferential system were applied in favour of the shipping companies of the region *as a whole* would these companies have an incentive to extend their shipping routes along the entire coast of Latin America, and thereby benefit from economies of scale.[8]

After considerable further discussion, a compromise formula was submitted in a draft agreement adopted by the Advisory Committee on Transport in April 1964. It was proposed that each member of

[8] ECLA, *Realizaciones y perspectivas en el proceso del mercado regional* (E/CN.12/668, May 1963), p. 45.

LAFTA should be entitled to reserve to itself up to 40 per cent of the bilateral transport of freight carried in area trade. The remainder, together with any portion of bilateral quotas not in fact utilized, should be divided between the shipping lines of other LAFTA members, and of non-members giving preferential service to LAFTA countries.[9]

This arrangement would be some improvement on strict bilateralism, since it would enable regional shipping lines maintaining long-range services to carry cargo between intermediate ports. It would also maintain an element of competition with non-member shipping lines. The draft agreement was to enter into force on ratification by five countries.

The Reaction of Big Shipping

The prospects of ratification were, however, slim. Apart from differences among the Latin American countries themselves as to the manner of implementing a system of 'cargo preference', intense pressure against the whole proposal was brought to bear by the shipping companies of North America and Western Europe. Ideas regarding the economic development of underdeveloped countries that have by now come to be accepted quite widely in the governmental and business circles of the industrial countries have still scarcely penetrated the anachronistic outlook of shipping circles. And while many of the shipping companies in the developed countries benefit directly or indirectly from government subsidies and protection of their markets, they see no inconsistency in enlisting government support against similar practices in underdeveloped countries designed to promote the expansion of the latter's own meagre resources in this field.

In September 1964 the Standing Executive Committee of LAFTA published a communication indicating that the United States had registered a protest with the Colombian government in connexion with LAFTA integration plans for maritime transport.[10] The United States, it was said, considered that the participation of the Gran Colombian Merchant Marine in the proposed shipping agreement under LAFTA would contravene the most-favoured-nation clause applying to sea navigation contained in the Treaty of 1864 between Colombia and the United States. In its reply, the

[9] ECLA, *Survey, 1963* (E/CN.12/696/Add. 1, July 1964), p. 119.
[10] *Boletín Quincenal*, 25 Sept. 1964.

Colombian government took the position that the integration of merchant fleets of LAFTA countries was entirely in accordance with clause 11 of Title III of the Charter of Punta del Este, subscribed to by the United States as well as by the Latin American countries. This clause supported the idea of including the transport and communications systems of Latin America in the integration process, and recognized the need to encourage the establishment of multi-national enterprises to this end.[11]

Resistance by the industrially advanced countries to the development of national merchant marines in underdeveloped countries appears, in fact, to go beyond opposition to mutual preferential arrangements such as are envisaged in LAFTA. It seems that the leading shipping nations are even opposing measures for the protection of national shipping in the underdeveloped countries. For example, strong protests were made by the governments of Belgium, Britain, Italy, Norway, and Sweden against a decree by the government of Uruguay in June 1963 under which partial exemption from certain import charges was granted in respect of merchandise imported in Uruguayan ships; and in September 1964 the United States announced its intention of levying an equalization fee on goods exported to Uruguay in the ships of that country.[12]

The Uruguayan newspaper *La Mañana* (30 November 1964) pointed out editorially that the partial exemption from import charges was part of a 'timid programme of encouragement for our very modest, not to say impoverished, merchant marine'. Uruguay spends $30 million annually on freight, but its own ships earn only 4 per cent of the total amount spent for exports, 1 per cent for imports of dry goods, and 19 per cent for imports of liquid products. The earnings of the three Uruguayan ships plying to the United States could not (said *La Mañana*) make a significant difference to the income of the big shipping lines of the latter country.

La Mañana added that Uruguay was only doing what the United States itself had been doing since 1935, despite the protests of the European shipping lines. The Uruguayan decree was, it said, in the

[11] Inter-American Economic and Social Council. Special Meeting at the Ministerial Level (Punta del Este, Uruguay, 1961), *Alliance for Progress: Official Documents*, OEA/Ser. H/XII. 1 (English), (Washington, D.C., 1961), p. 19.

[12] *Comercio Exterior*, Oct. 1964, pp. 676–7, 727; *NYT*, 3 Dec. 1964. A similar equalization fee was ordered against Ecuador's shipping in 1959 when Ecuador assessed charges against United States shipping similar to those imposed by Uruguay in 1963. Ecuador thereupon cancelled its charges.

spirit of United States shipping legislation of 1935 and 1954, and of the energetic programme of cargo preference and subsidies developed under that legislation.[13]

A few weeks later it was announced that the United States had suspended application of the equalization fee on being informed that the government of Uruguay was preparing a new law to assist the country's merchant marine without discriminating against United States shipping.[14]

On the whole, the need for protection of infant industries in underdeveloped countries has, by now, become fairly well recognized and accepted in the industrial countries. Efforts to prevent the building up of merchant marines in underdeveloped countries under protection are therefore not typical of the more enlightened attitudes prevailing in the industrial countries at the present time.

It is possible, and perhaps even likely, that the established shipping companies are correct in asserting that for many of the underdeveloped countries the creation of national merchant marines could not be an economic proposition, at any rate for some time to come. The force of this contention is not, however, strengthened by pressure or reprisals against underdeveloped countries introducing measures to protect their shipping—particularly when one bears in mind the extensive protectionist and discriminatory practices affecting shipping in the industrial countries themselves. Moreover, the steadfast refusal thus far to make available the minimum of essential data required for an objective evaluation of the operations of the established shipping lines has led to the impression, rightly or wrongly, that the latter have a great deal to hide.

As indicated by the prompt Uruguayan withdrawal, the Latin American countries may be forced to exercise some caution in the face of the fierce resistance of the shipping lines of the developed

[13] According to the report of the Joint Economic Committee of the United States Congress referred to (n. 5, p. 103), US taxpayers are paying more than $350 m. a year in direct subsidies to 15 American steamship lines, excluding the excess cost of preferential cargo routing (p. 7 of report).

[14] *Boletín Quincenal*, 10 Jan. 1965, pp. 11–12. Although Uruguay had been accused of discrimination, the decree of June 1963 treated all foreign shipping companies alike. The decree was designed to protect Uruguayan shipping against all foreign competition, and this is not normally regarded, under such international agreements as the General Agreement on Tariffs and Trade, as discrimination. The term 'flag discrimination', which *inter alia* is applied to the protection of domestic shipping companies along the lines attempted by Uruguay, thus goes beyond GATT usage.

countries, with strong governmental backing. The Latin American countries dare not overlook the fact of their dependence on the major shipping lines for the transport of the bulk of their exports and imports. There is an obvious need, however, for a mobilization of national opinion in the developed countries, as well as of international opinion, to induce the shipping companies to reconsider their policies towards underdeveloped countries.

At all events, transport and communications are among the areas in which a concerted effort by the LAFTA countries is most needed, and where joint projects might be most feasible. Such projects might well include the establishment of co-operative shipping, air, and road transport enterprises, in addition to the joint building of international railway, highway, and communications systems. Such projects would, moreover, seem to be ideally suited for financing by the international lending agencies.

CHAPTER VII

SPECIAL DISPENSATIONS

The Less Developed Countries

To their credit, the Latin American countries have recognized from the very beginning of the common market programme that the advancement of the least developed areas within the region could not be left simply to market forces operating within a framework of regional free trade and *laissez-faire*. Thus the Treaty of Montevideo made provision for special privileges and advantages to be granted to those countries which were likely to fall behind even further if their economies were opened up as fully to the forces of regional free trade as those of the more developed countries in the region.

The special 'advantages' envisaged by the Treaty of Montevideo have in fact been granted to Paraguay and Ecuador; and Bolivia has been declared eligible for them if it joins the Association. The Paraguayan representative warned a LAFTA conference in July 1961 that unless his country obtained reasonable concessions from the other members, the free-trade area would become a dangerous experiment for the economy and finances of Paraguay. The loss of customs revenue on the freed imports, he said, could have serious consequences in itself: Paraguay is far ahead of all other member countries in the share of its total trade that is carried on with the LAFTA area—nearly one-third in 1964.

In response to the Paraguayan case, LAFTA agreed in September 1961 to authorize participating countries to free their imports of primary and industrial products from Paraguay of all duties and restrictions for a period of nine years beginning on 1 January 1962.[1] Paraguay was to present a list of products on which it was seeking such concessions, from which the other countries might exclude any items the liberalization of which might involve them in serious damage. The future of these special privileges was to be reviewed by the Contracting Parties during the eighth year from 1 January 1962.

[1] *Resoluciones*, 12 (I).

Similar treatment was subsequently extended to Ecuador for a period of eight years beginning 1 January 1963.[2]

Despite these arrangements, Ecuador and Paraguay did not obtain the benefits they had expected from the Treaty, and during the course of 1963 their dissatisfaction became acute. On 4 September 1963 the Minister of Commerce and Banking of Ecuador issued a general report on the problem in which he stated, *inter alia*:

Ecuador will demand [at the third annual session of the Contracting Parties] the full application of Article 32 of the Treaty of Montevideo [providing for special measures favouring the less developed countries] and in the event that this demand is rejected, the Government military junta will take the necessary action, through the Ministry of Commerce and Banking, with the firmness and resolution that the progress and future of the country require.[3]

There was no doubt that Ecuador intended to withdraw from LAFTA if its basic demands were not satisfied.

The three fundamental reasons for Ecuador's dissatisfaction were that the favourable treatment expected under the Treaty had not materialized: that the export balance with other LAFTA countries had declined sharply in the first half of 1963, imports having risen considerably while exports were stagnant; and that no aid had been received from the major LAFTA countries, particularly for the establishment of new industries in Ecuador. As regards the larger rise in imports than exports in the first half of 1963, Ecuador pointed out that while it had received special concessions on only 323 tariff items,[4] many of them of scant significance, it had itself made concessions on no less than 1,701 items.

Similar discontent with progress made was voiced by the Central Bank of Paraguay in a report on developments in 1962. The bank pointed out that the fine intentions of the participating countries had not been translated into concrete action. Brazil and Mexico had liberalized long lists of items, but most of these were agricultural and it would take time for private enterprise in Paraguay to begin to produce them for export. Paraguay's major market, Argentina, was

[2] *Resoluciones*, 38 (II).   [3] *Comercio Exterior*, Sept. 1963, p. 634.
[4] Under resolution 38 (II), mentioned above. In addition, of course, all concessions granted to other LAFTA countries in the normal course of negotiations were extended to Ecuador under the most-favoured-nation provision of Art. 18 of the Montevideo Treaty.

the least willing to grant concessions of immediate interest, for example on wood products.

In an attempt to deal with the causes of dissatisfaction in Ecuador and Paraguay, the members of LAFTA adopted, at their third annual session in 1963, a 'Plan of Operations and Special Measures' for encouraging the development of these countries. These measures were to include the supply of machinery, equipment, and other essential items needed for infrastructure and technical training; the opening of lines of credit for the import by Ecuador and Paraguay of various types of development goods from the LAFTA area; and the creation of a fund to supplement the resources of development banks in the two countries for supplying working capital to projects of interest to the LAFTA area as a whole. Technical assistance was also to be given to Ecuador and Paraguay in a number of fields, including the study of markets and identification of industries that might be located in these countries.

The Standing Executive Committee was instructed to study and approve joint approaches to the international lending agencies in support of requests for financial and technical aid presented to these agencies by the less developed countries. Authority was, moreover, given to the committee to study and report on any requests submitted by Ecuador or Paraguay for maintaining, for a definite period, the margins of preference on particular products resulting from the special liberalization of imports from these two countries referred to above.[5]

Steps have also been taken to ease the burden of the less developed countries in liberalizing their imports from other LAFTA members. At the third annual session of LAFTA, Ecuador claimed that it had already gone so far in the liberalization of imports during the

---

[5] See resolution 74 (III), pp. 318–20 below. Under resolutions 12 (I) and 38 (II), as noted earlier, authority had been given to LAFTA countries to free their imports of certain products from Ecuador and Paraguay of all restrictions. In so far as duties were maintained on imports from other countries, Ecuador and Paraguay would thereby enjoy preferential treatment not merely *vis-à-vis* non-LAFTA countries, but even in relation to other LAFTA exporters of the same products. However, resolutions 12 (I) and 38 (II) also stated that the advantages thus conferred on Ecuador and Paraguay should not prevent the importing countries concerned from negotiating concessions on the same products with other LAFTA members. Thus the value of the preferences to Ecuador and Paraguay could be progressively diminished; under resolution 74 (III), the Standing Executive Committee was therefore to consider the possibility of maintaining preferential margins favouring these two countries for some definite period. This was finally agreed to by the LAFTA countries at their fourth annual session, in resolution 111 (IV), as indicated below.

first two rounds of negotiations that it would face considerable difficulties in undertaking any further major freeing of imports. It
therefore asked for a special dispensation in accordance with
Article 32 (*b*) of the Treaty of Montevideo, which provides that a less
developed country may be authorized 'to implement the programme
for the reduction of duties, charges and other restrictions under
more favourable conditions, specially agreed upon'.

After considering the matter, the LAFTA countries decided to
authorize Ecuador to undertake such liberalization of its imports in
1963 'as its economic circumstances and development plans would
permit'. Authority was also granted to Ecuador to continue this procedure in 1964 and 1965 if, in its judgement, conditions still required special treatment of this type; in that case Ecuador should
report accordingly to the Standing Executive Committee and present documentary evidence to justify its decision. It was further
agreed that at the end of the period of special treatment, Ecuador
should enter into negotiations with a view to fulfilling its obligations under the Treaty within the time laid down in Article 2—that
is, within twelve years from the date of the Treaty's entry into force.
In other words, Ecuador was granted a postponement of its obligations, but this will have to be offset by a speeding up of its liberalization programme later on. Ecuador accepted these arrangements as a
solution of its immediate problem, but it remains to be seen whether
it will really be able to accelerate its rate of liberalization later on,
once having slowed it down.[6]

The LAFTA countries also authorized Ecuador to introduce
measures to protect domestic output of certain products already included in the liberalization programme. Such measures might remain in force for up to five years, so long as this did not involve over-
stepping the terminal date of the special eight-year period referred
to above—namely 1 January 1971.[7]

---

[6] *Resoluciones*, 72 (III). Ecuador had in fact hoped that the period for completing
the liberalization of imports would be extended, in the case of the less developed
countries, from 12 to 18 years.

[7] This action was taken in accordance with Art. 32 (*d*) of the Treaty of Montevideo.
Under this article, the Contracting Parties may authorize a less developed
country to apply, temporarily, non-discriminatory measures to protect the
domestic output of products included in the liberalization programme which are
of vital importance to its economic development, provided that this does not
entail a decrease in its 'customary consumption'. The commodities specified
in the case of Ecuador included certain chemicals, certain iron and steel products,
and agricultural machinery and implements (see *Resoluciones*, 73 (III)).

Finally, the Standing Executive Committee was requested to study measures for the implementation of various provisions of Article 32 of the Montevideo Treaty, notably the identification of industries that could be located in the less developed countries and could supply the requirements not only of these countries but of their LAFTA partners as well; and the lowering of trade barriers by LAFTA countries that would be required to provide adequate export markets for any industries thus established in the less developed countries.[8]

Further concessions were made to Ecuador and Paraguay at the fourth annual session of the LAFTA countries. The period of validity of certain of the concessions already granted was extended to the end of the transition period—mid-1973.[9] LAFTA countries were authorized to give special concessions to Ecuador and Paraguay in respect of particular manufactured items of which they could show exportable surpluses.[10] Steps were taken to prevent any reduction in the margins of preference accorded to Ecuador and Paraguay on the concessions made to them.[11] Finally, efforts were to be made to create special credit facilities for imports from these two countries[12] and support was to be given to applications by them to the Inter-American Development Bank for the financing of their exports.[13]

It will be apparent that the decisions described above go some way, at least on paper, towards establishing the necessary preconditions for encouraging the development of the less developed countries. How adequate or effective the programme will be remains to be seen. LAFTA has called for the identification of industries to be located in the less developed countries, but no firm provision has been made to ensure that such industries are, in fact, established. Economic and technical aid has been promised for them, but no clear commitment has been given thus far on the amount of funds or resources to be contributed by the LAFTA countries themselves. The period of special advantages for Ecuador and Paraguay is envisaged as ending in 1973, after which these countries are presumably expected to be able to hold their own against any other Latin American country. Yet there is no reason to suppose that the gap between per capita incomes in Ecuador and Paraguay and the more

[8] Resolution 74 (III), paras (*b*) 3 (i) and (ii), see below, p. 320.
[9] Ibid. 98 (IV).   [10] Ibid. 107 (IV).   [11] Ibid. 111 (IV).
[12] Ibid. 108 (IV).   [13] Ibid. 105 (IV).

advanced LAFTA members will, by 1973, have been narrowed to the point at which they could engage in unhampered free trade with them. Some observers would say that Ecuador and Paraguay will have done well if the income gap has not widened by 1973.

It would seem that the concessions made to Ecuador and Paraguay by LAFTA may be less generous than those given to Greece by the EEC countries. The agreement governing Greece's association with the EEC provides for a twelve-year period of transition to a customs union, ending in 1973, whereas the EEC countries themselves plan to eliminate their mutual tariffs by 1967. Moreover, for products on a special list, including almost all industrial articles produced in Greece, a transitional period of twenty-two years is provided. And, until 1973, Greece may impose new duties or increase existing ones on up to 10 per cent of goods imported from the EEC, in order to foster industrial development: these duties may be maintained up to the end of the twenty-two-year transition period.[14]

Thus the treatment of Greece by the EEC countries involves a definite easing of the terms of the Treaty of Rome, because this country is at a lower level of development than the other members of the Community. In particular, it was granted exemptions lasting well beyond the end of the transition period under the Treaty.

In the case of LAFTA, on the other hand, it has been specifically stated that the special advantages accorded to Ecuador and Paraguay do not constitute an exception to the general provisions of the Montevideo Treaty. Consequently, Ecuador and Paraguay 'shall, in common with the other Contracting Parties, enjoy all the rights and be subject to all the obligations emanating from the Treaty'.[15] One such obligation is to fulfil all treaty requirements by the end of the transition period, and thus to give up the right to all special concessions at that time. It could be argued that Ecuador should not receive less favourable treatment from its LAFTA partners than Greece does from the EEC. The same goes for Paraguay, where income per head is substantially lower even than in Ecuador.

At any rate, the special advantages given to Ecuador and Paraguay had not encouraged Bolivia to join LAFTA by the end of 1964, although it had often announced its intention of doing so. Bolivia had participated in the discussions and negotiations leading up to

[14] *International Financial News Survey* (IMF), 21 Apr. 1961.
[15] *Resoluciones*, 17 (I), Explanatory Notes. See below, p. 314.

the drafting of the Treaty of Montevideo, and a place for Bolivia as a founding member was kept open by the other signatories. The reason given by the Bolivian government for not acceding immediately to the Treaty was that most of Bolivia's exports go to countries outside Latin America and that Bolivia is able to buy better and cheaper manufactured products in North America and Western Europe than it can in Latin America. In other words, Bolivia objected to subsidizing industry in Argentina, Brazil, or Mexico through having to pay higher prices for imports from these countries than it would if it imported comparable products from the industrially developed countries.

The Bolivian dilemma is a genuine one. On the one hand, no doubt Bolivia would like to play its part in the evolution of a prosperous Latin American economy and contribute to the success of the enterprise launched by the Treaty of Montevideo. On the other hand, Bolivia is much too poor a country to be able to sacrifice the living standards of its people to regional ideals, however lofty. If Bolivia is to pay high prices for imports of manufactures from Argentina, Brazil, or Mexico, there must be some *quid pro quo*. There must be some assurance for Bolivia that a beginning will be made in the industrial development of the country.

Again, it is by no means clear that the special concessions granted by the LAFTA countries would be sufficient to persuade private industry to locate new plants in Ecuador or Paraguay rather than in one of the more highly developed industrial centres elsewhere in Latin America. It is not unlikely that the specially favourable treatment given to imports from Ecuador and Paraguay would encourage their export trade in traditional products, but would not greatly advance their industrial development. On the whole, industrialists considering the location of new plants are likely to attach more importance to such questions as the availability of skilled labour; access to fuels, raw materials, and intermediate products; proximity to other industries, to engineering and repair facilities and to major markets; and the general level of development of the area as a whole, than to the particular advantages that Ecuador and Paraguay have been granted by the other participating countries in LAFTA. If this assessment is correct, Bolivian hesitation is well founded.

The real solution to the problem of Ecuador, Paraguay, and presumably of Bolivia, therefore, is an agreed programme for the region as a whole in which these countries would be able to see their

I

way forward in terms of the economic development of their countries. This brings us back once again to the problem of joint planning. Without a carefully thought out joint plan of economic and industrial development for the region as a whole, agreed to by all the participating countries, and implemented by them through concrete action including subsidies to the less developed areas, great uncertainty is bound to persist as to whether countries like Bolivia, Ecuador, and Paraguay are really getting their share of any benefits that the opening up of the regional market may bring. And if private enterprise does not respond to the incentives, subsidies, and other advantages offered to establishments in the less developed areas, the case for public enterprise will be inescapable.

The Intermediate Countries

A basic assumption of the Treaty of Montevideo was that apart from certain special cases—such as Bolivia, Ecuador, and Paraguay —all members of the free-trade area should be treated alike, and that their trade with one another should be conducted in accordance with the most-favoured-nation principle, as provided in Article 18. This basic assumption came under attack in the course of 1963, and was finally discarded by the LAFTA countries at their third annual meeting at the end of the year.

The attack was led by Uruguay. Early in 1963 the Chamber of Industries of Uruguay sent a note to the government, pointing out that, in the third year of operation of the Treaty of Montevideo, the Uruguayan deficit with the rest of the LAFTA area was continuing; in 1962 Uruguay's imports from other LAFTA members amounted to $34 million while exports were valued at only $8 million. The Chamber of Industries also pointed out that the structure of exports had not changed significantly in the direction of including a larger proportion of manufactured products. The Chamber therefore concluded that Uruguay should take steps to balance its trade with the rest of the LAFTA area. It was suggested that Uruguay should negotiate special treatment for itself for a reasonable period until such time as its economy should be able to overcome the difficulties resulting from the smallness of its domestic market and its large trade deficit.[16] Such treatment might consist in certain countries admitting certain exports from Uruguay without extending

---

[16] It should be noted that in 1962 Uruguay's deficit with the LAFTA area amounted to $26 m., compared with a total trade deficit of $77 m.

parallel treatment to similar exports from other LAFTA members, for some adequate period. This, of course, would mean the suspension of Article 18 of the Treaty of Montevideo, providing for most-favoured-nation treatment within the LAFTA area. The Chamber of Industries note added that unless Uruguay could obtain some solution along these lines, it should seek relief in the escape clauses laid down in Chapter II of the Treaty and impose import restrictions over a period sufficient to restore its balance of trade with the region.

By October 1963, at the third annual session of LAFTA, Chile, Colombia, and Peru had joined Uruguay in demanding recognition of the fact that even though their level of development was higher than that of Bolivia, Ecuador, and Paraguay, it certainly could not be compared with that of Argentina, Brazil, and Mexico. Speaking on behalf of the intermediate group of four countries, at the third session, the Uruguayan representative argued strongly for joint regional planning, and said that countries like his own could not afford to allow the location of industry in Latin America to be settled simply by the forces of the market. 'It is obvious', he added, 'that the Free-Trade Area must bring equal benefits to all its members if we want it to achieve prosperity and stability.'[17]

The heart of the Uruguayan case was that while allowance had been made in the Treaty of Montevideo for the special problems of countries at an early stage of economic development, no such arrangements existed for the countries which, although enjoying a certain degree of development, were not yet able to stand up on equal terms to the economic power of the larger countries in LAFTA. The middle group of countries had relatively small domestic markets, and their industrial development was much less advanced and diversified than that of the leading countries in the region. Consequently, more flexible procedures were needed in their case.

To this end, Uruguay invoked the reciprocity provisions of the Treaty.[18] The liberalization of trade thus far had not, according to Uruguay, brought comparable benefits to all LAFTA members: those countries that were running substantial deficits in LAFTA would find it very difficult to grant further trade concessions to other members under the liberalization programme, unless the reci-

---

[17] *Comercio Exterior*, Nov. 1963, pp. 799–800.
[18] Arts 10–13, see below, p. 231.

procity provisions of the Treaty were fully implemented. Such implementation would have to involve not merely ensuring the equivalence of mutual tariff reductions, narrowly considered, but a parallel expansion of export markets for all countries.

'The method of tariff reductions is totally useless, taken by itself', the representative of Uruguay told the LAFTA session, 'since it only deals with a secondary aspect of the basic problems that have to be resolved.' The real problems, he said, were: to provide for regional planning in its widest sense, and for the unification of monetary, financial, and foreign trade policies of LAFTA members; to introduce adequate flexibility in the application of the Treaty so as to take account of the different levels of economic development of various member countries; and to establish a Council of Ministers to consider outstanding problems of regional integration at the highest level.

Following a discussion of these matters, the LAFTA members agreed[19] that special collective measures were required to stimulate the economies of the middle group of countries (Chile, Colombia, Peru, and Uruguay), as well as of the less developed group (Ecuador and Paraguay). No specific action was proposed as yet, but the Standing Executive Committee was instructed to give priority to this question in its programme of work and that of its subsidiary bodies (including the Advisory Committee on Industrial Development). Moreover, special mention was made of the need to ensure 'effective participation' of both the intermediate and less developed groups in complementarity agreements.[20]

Thus the intermediate group had clearly won its demand for a special status, although the significance of that status had yet to be spelled out. No doubt a failure to make this concession would have placed the entire future of LAFTA in even greater peril than a failure to meet the complaints advanced by Ecuador and Paraguay. And yet the acceptance of a new group of privileged countries with-

---

[19] See resolution 71 (III), pp. 316–18 below.

[20] Resolution 71 (III) mentions particularly the possibility of applying the principles established in para. 3 (*b*) of resolution 48 (II) and para. 8 (*c*) of resolution 49 (II). The former provides that in connexion with complementarity agreements in particular industrial sectors, the rate of liberalization might be different for different countries and products. The latter provides that application of the rules relating to the determination of the origin of products may be deferred for a certain period in order to give producers unable to satisfy the rules immediately time in which to make the necessary adjustments.

in LAFTA may prove to be a source of great difficulty and friction in the future.

It should be noted that the new group is not 'intermediate' in terms of average income: if the LAFTA countries are listed in order of per capita income, Uruguay and Chile follow Argentina at levels significantly higher than those of Mexico and Brazil. On the other hand, the group does appear to have had adverse experience in the development of regional trade. It will be seen from Appendix Table VIII that the imports of Chile, Colombia, and Peru rose appreciably more than exports from 1960 to 1963, so that the balance of trade deteriorated significantly. While the regional balance of Uruguay was actually better in 1963 than in 1960, there was a sharp increase in imports and in the trade deficit in 1964.

The principal gains were made by Argentina and Mexico. Much less satisfactory was the situation of Brazil, where exports to the LAFTA group were actually lower in 1963 than in 1960, while imports were up by more than one-half, with serious consequences for the balance of trade. Many industrialists in Brazil consequently complained that the Treaty of Montevideo had been having unfavourable effects on Brazilian trade and called for 'reciprocity of benefits'.[21]

If, therefore, Ecuador and Paraguay could justify a case for special tariff treatment in terms of the level of their economic development, the intermediate group in terms of the absolute size of their national markets, and Brazil in terms of a failure to achieve 'reciprocity of benefits' the only countries left carrying out the Treaty in full would be Argentina and Mexico. And one might well ask how long these two would be able to go on reducing their tariffs and other restrictions on imports, if their exports began to be affected by their trading partners pursuing less liberal policies.

Once again we are led back to the proposition that it is only through agreement upon, and implementation of, a coherent regional plan of development that all these various special interests can be reconciled—if they can be reconciled at all. No process that consists merely in the reduction or elimination of the barriers to trade can be sensitively adjusted to the needs of the less developed countries, the intermediate group, and the Big Three, all simultaneously. Indeed, tariffs, by their very nature, are not a sensitive

[21] See *Journal Visão* (Brazil), 10 May 1963, as cited in *Comercio Exterior*, June 1963, pp. 399–400.

instrument even of a national development policy, let alone of a policy that would seek to differentiate between various types of country. Tariff disarmament must be seen as one of the tools—but by no means the only one—to be used in building new large-scale industries catering to the needs of the region as a whole, and located in accordance with the requirements of efficiency—it being understood that such requirements include an adequate rate of growth not merely of the LAFTA area generally, but of its component parts as well.

Given the rate of development of the LAFTA area as a whole, there is some critical rate of expansion for each of the participating countries below which these countries would not consider it worthwhile to remain members of the group. It is therefore idle to maintain that the LAFTA countries should abandon their internal trade restrictions and let the chips fall where they may. Area trade restrictions can be reduced only within the framework of a regional plan. And only on the basis of such a plan can the needs of all the various types of member country be even partially satisfied. In the absence of clear and practical agreements on a suitable division of labour among the member countries, LAFTA may well founder on the obstacles and complications thrown up by the demands of sectional interests throughout the area, and by the claims of the intermediate and less developed groups for special treatment.

CHAPTER VIII

INTEGRATION AND PLANNING

The Need for Joint Planning

The fact that the Treaty of Montevideo was drawn up with the intention of complying with the rules of GATT relating to free-trade areas has, perhaps, focused too much attention on the reduction of trade barriers and too little on other forms of co-operation, particularly in the field of joint development planning.

The difficulty facing the LAFTA countries is that the release of market forces through the reduction of regional trade barriers cannot be relied on to bring about the economic development of Latin America. If, indeed, the free play of market forces were the key to economic development, we should not now be faced with the problem of underdevelopment over the greater part of the earth's surface.

It is true that it was private enterprise, operating through the market system, that provided the motive power for the development of the industrially advanced countries of North America and Western Europe. But the very success of market forces in these countries made it more difficult for comparable development to take place elsewhere. So long as trade was relatively unimpeded by restrictions, the competitive capacity of established industries in the advanced countries was bound to be a formidable deterrent to industrial development anywhere else. Thus the free market system developed the world unevenly, concentrating industry and technical progress in limited areas of the globe. The gap in living standards between industrial and non-industrial areas that resulted from this process has widened persistently during the past century, and there can no longer be any serious expectation that spontaneous forces of the market-place could do much to arrest this tendency, much less reverse it.

Underdeveloped countries cannot therefore be content to depend upon private enterprise alone for the future development of their economies. In a period of growing understanding of the nature of the development process, of increasing government sophistication in employing the tools of economic policy, and of a greater willingness, even in the industrially advanced countries, to make use of planning techniques, the underdeveloped countries are keen to promote development through deliberate and rationally determined planning. They cannot afford the risks of haphazard development: time is short and their peoples grow impatient. If science has brought man to the threshold of the exploration of space, it is intolerable that the majority of humanity still cannot be guaranteed decent provision of food, clothing, and shelter.

By the same token, the Latin American countries cannot rely upon free trade even within the region to bring about the rate and distribution of economic progress that they seek. Market forces will tend to concentrate development in the richer areas of the continent, bypassing the poorer areas. Balanced and harmonious development of the region as a whole is, however, indispensable if the loyalty to LAFTA of all member countries is to be maintained. And harmonious development can in turn be ensured only through concerted planning efforts based on agreement among the participating countries.

Consequently, if there are grounds for concern about the rate of progress thus far in implementing the objectives of the Treaty of Montevideo, they are to be found not merely in the sphere of the reduction of restrictions on trade, but perhaps even more in the lack of any serious approach to joint development planning.

In retrospect, it was probably unfortunate that the programme for regional development in Latin America had to be forced into the rigid GATT mould for free-trade areas. The Latin American countries themselves had originally hoped to introduce a partial system of preferential arrangements to foster trade with one another. But they were informed that this would raise difficulties in GATT.[1] They were thus compelled to put up for GATT approval something that at any rate looked like a free-trade area. And ever since then, the programme of regional integration continues to be judged by the artificial standards set by Article XXIV of GATT.[2] Yet this article, drafted originally with the situation of Western Europe in mind,[3] has much less relevance to the circumstances and problems of underdeveloped countries.

---

[1] See ECLA, *The Latin American Common Market*, pp. 94–97, 100–2.
[2] See below, pp. 225–8.
[3] See Clair Wilcox, *A Charter for World Trade* (N.Y., 1949), p. 71.

Unfortunately this fact was not generally recognized, especially in the developed countries, when the Treaty of Montevideo was being drafted in 1959. At that time the view of the major Western European countries and the United States was that Latin American countries were not likely to benefit very much from any attempt to set up a common market—for reasons drawn from orthodox economics that have already been discussed in Chapter II; but that if these countries insisted on going ahead with an integration programme, that programme should conform to the maximum extent possible to Article XXIV of GATT. In particular, the Latin American countries would be expected to adopt a clear 'plan and schedule' for the elimination of all tariff and non-tariff restrictions on 'substantially all' their trade with one another; the scope of the programme should be comprehensive in terms of commodities, and all restrictions on intra-trade should be eliminated, and not merely reduced. Moreover, all this should take place within a reasonable number of years, and not be protracted over an indefinite period of time.

The views of the developed countries have changed significantly since 1959, as we have seen. Unable or unwilling to throw their own markets open to exports of manufactures from the underdeveloped countries, they have begun to see hitherto unrecognized merits in the idea of underdeveloped countries trading more extensively with one another. And wishing to encourage such trade, they are now less inclined to insist on all the rigours of GATT. Consequently, partial preferential arrangements among underdeveloped countries were unanimously endorsed by the United Nations Conference on Trade and Development in June 1964, and it was also agreed that the rules governing world trade would have to be adjusted to make this possible.[4]

As was pointed out by a committee of experts convened by the OAS in connexion with the Alliance for Progress,

. . . the diversity of circumstances and the vested interests [in Latin America] are of such a magnitude that total and immediate integration of the region cannot be accomplished quickly. Instead, integration will have to be gradual, both in scope and in intensity.

Furthermore, partial integration or a series of agreements on partial

---

[4] UNCTAD, *Proceedings*, i. 41 f., Final Act. Annex A. III. 8, sections III and IV (*b*).

integration, whether by economic sectors or by groups of countries, or by a combination of both, is not incompatible with progress toward over-all integration of the area, particularly if a certain coordination of national development plans can be achieved. Perhaps this is the fastest way of advancing toward over-all integration. . . . [5]

Clearly this is a far cry from any approach to the economic development of the Latin American region that would be based on the rules of GATT or the free-trade incentive alone. The committee went on to devote a special chapter to the coordination of national development plans. It suggested a periodic confrontation of such plans in order to determine that they were complementary, and called for regular examination of the extent to which targets for the Latin American region as a whole were being attained in the various sectors of the economy. The objective would be to establish criteria for priorities in investment, to influence the location of new industries, and to promote mutually consistent adjustments in national plans. [6]

It stands to reason, however, that regional planning can only begin once there is a firm foundation of national planning. However much one may deplore the obvious tendency of national planners to confine themselves to perspectives dictated by domestic market conditions and to overlook the possibilities for fruitful co-operation with other countries, the fact remains that it would be quite impossible for any meaningful planning for Latin America as a whole to take place without being rooted in the national plans drawn up and implemented by each of the Latin American countries individually.

There has been much talk of planning in Latin America, but very little as yet in the way of action. The studies that have been made by the Secretariat of ECLA are very well known in this respect, and have created a characteristic line and style that have attracted attention all over the world. And while ten years ago the idea of planning in the underdeveloped countries was considered controversial, to say the least, the preparation of an adequate development plan is beginning to be regarded as an indispensable prerequisite in securing economic aid. Thus, for example, under the Alliance for Pro-

[5] OAS, *Latin American Economic Integration* (Washington, D.C., 1961), p. 3. The members of the group included Javier Márquez (Chairman), Emilio Barreto, Jorge Franco Holguín, Alberto Fuentes Mohr, Bert Hoselitz, Flavian Levine Bawden, Raymond Mikesell, Manuel San Miguel, and Gerson Augusto da Silva.

[6] Ibid. pp. 14–16, 26.

gress, participating Latin American countries were called upon to formulate long-term development programmes, if possible within eighteen months of the signing of the Charter of Punta del Este on 17 August 1961. In response to this requirement, most Latin American countries prepared national development programmes, and this was potentially an important step forward on their part. It would be idle to pretend, however, that the adoption of a national development programme by a government in itself indicates that economic planning has begun or is even about to begin. Quite apart from the question whether, in some cases, the elaboration of such programmes was undertaken merely in order to document a case for foreign aid, it must inevitably take time before the machinery of planning can be established and blueprints are translated into specific action whether by governments or private individuals.

If planning has yet to take concrete form in the domestic economies of the various Latin American countries, it stands to reason that region-wide planning, in any comprehensive sense of the term, lies still further in the future. A first meeting of industrial development planners in the various member countries was held in 1963 and was intended to lay the groundwork for future action by exchanging information, studying past trends and future prospects, and confronting production targets with the trend of future demand in the LAFTA countries as a whole. The agenda of the meeting also included an examination of the possibility of adjusting national targets in the light of regional needs and of coordinating policy measures so as to stimulate and direct public and private investment with a view to balanced economic development throughout the region. These ideas all pointed in the right direction, but once again concrete action still lies in the future, and many difficulties will have to be overcome, both at the technical and political levels, before one can really say that effective procedures have been devised for joint regional planning in Latin America as a whole. Yet in the absence of such measures purposeful action to knit together the Latin American economy may be unduly delayed.

Joint Industrial Planning

Reduction of tariffs and other trade restrictions is one of the two main paths to a common market laid down by the Treaty of Montevideo: the other route lies through complementarity agreements, involving the planned joint development of specific industries.

The underlying concept here is that the economic integration of Latin America may be approached on an industry-by-industry basis. The immediate objective is to create region-wide markets for the products of particular industries by eliminating regional trade barriers affecting these products and promoting a planned division of labour across national frontiers between the firms producing them. Gradually, as the number of complementarity agreements increases, the integrated sector of the economy will grow; and this process will, it is hoped, react upon and reinforce the cognate movement towards the elimination of trade obstacles across the board.

Various types of complementarity arrangement can be envisaged, depending on the particular circumstances of each industry. In some cases inter-country specialization might be organized vertically, in others horizontally. In the former type of situation, each member country might maintain or establish a fully integrated industry, comprising all stages of a particular manufacturing process from raw material to finished product. Specialization would be secured through an agreement whereby each firm would undertake to concentrate on a limited number of products, instead of manufacturing the entire range. Countries would satisfy their needs partly from domestic production and partly through trade with their neighbours: each of the specialized firms would thus gain the advantages of access to a region-wide market. Moreover, there would be provision for continuous consultation on the market outlook and supply prospects for the industry, and the mutual adjustment of investment plans so as to avoid overlap and duplication.

In cases of horizontal specialization, on the other hand, various stages of a particular industrial process might be located in different countries. Each country might, for example, specialize in the production of certain components, while assembly plants for the finishing stages might be set up in several countries, using both domestically produced and imported components. Each of the participating countries would, in other words, export some components and import others, while all would do at least some types of assembling. Here again the advantages of access to a region-wide market would become available to the manufacturers of components, and investment plans would need to be dovetailed in such a way as to ensure a balance between productive capacity at the assembly stages and the supply of raw materials and components.

Reality is, of course, much more complex than either of the two hypothetical situations described above. In practice, elements of both vertical and horizontal specialization are likely to be needed. In some of the larger countries, moreover, the size of domestic markets may warrant a relatively broad range of industrial activities being located close to those markets, whereas industries in the smaller countries may have to be somewhat more specialized if they are to benefit from the advantages of catering to the region as a whole.

The basic rules governing complementarity agreements were laid down by the LAFTA Conference at its second annual session, and subsequently revised at the fourth session.[7] An agreement of this type is designed to establish a programme of 'sectoral integration' through the liberalization of trade in the complementary products of a particular industrial sector. It may also provide for harmonization of treatment accorded to imports from third countries. Such harmonization may be applied not only to products directly covered by the agreement—so as to standardize preferential margins throughout the LAFTA region—but also to raw materials and components—so that manufacturers in one LAFTA country should not gain an advantage simply by paying lower tariffs on imports of raw materials and components than their competitors elsewhere in the region. The agreement may also arrange for co-ordination of governmental programmes and incentives designed to facilitate industrial complementarity, and for special advantages for less developed countries.

While agreements may be entered into by as few as two member countries, they should, under the rules laid down, be such as to facilitate the inclusion of other LAFTA members. Moreover, negotiations must always be open to all LAFTA members, and the intention to conclude an agreement must be notified to the Standing Executive Committee, which must in turn advise all member countries accordingly. Negotiations must not start until forty-five days after the Standing Executive Committee has been notified, and a further delay of up to sixty days may be imposed at the request of any member country, except that the Standing Committee is authorized to reduce or eliminate these time intervals.

The agreements take the form of protocols subscribed to by the respective countries; and the Standing Committee is required to pronounce on their compatibility with the Treaty within thirty days. Any such agreements enter into force only after they have been

[7] Resolutions 48 (II) and 99 (IV). For the latter, see below, pp. 324–9.

declared consistent with the principles and objectives of the Treaty: they must remain open to accession by all LAFTA countries.

Countries participating in complementarity agreements must report periodically on progress to the Standing Executive Committee, which must in turn report to the regular annual Conference of LAFTA. At the request of any country participating in an agreement, measures may be taken to deal with anomalous situations arising in the course of implementation of the agreements, notably where one or more LAFTA countries, whether participants or not, adopt measures tending to disturb the normal functioning of an agreement.

Following the definition of the content and purpose of complementarity agreements laid down at the second annual session of LAFTA, a meeting of industrial development planners was held in Lima in April 1963 to lay the groundwork for future joint action. The meeting made a number of recommendations for the coordination of national development plans, the promotion of industries on the basis of access to region-wide markets, and the encouragement of a harmonious and balanced development of the region as a whole. But the recommendations did not go beyond generalities.

Prior to this, in November 1962, a meeting representative of the principal industrial associations of the LAFTA countries, held in Mexico City, had decided to establish the Association of Latin American Industrialists. The objectives of the Association were to coordinate the views of national industrial associations on the economic integration of Latin America, to evolve a common policy for promoting industrial complementarity and co-operation, and to maintain contact with LAFTA countries on questions of mutual concern.[8]

Meanwhile, numerous meetings were taking place at which government officials and business men were exploring the possibilities of regional co-operation in particular industries or branches of industries. Moreover, in addition to the groups organized on a multilateral basis, including representation from all or most LAFTA countries, many bilateral groups were meeting from time to time. For example, during the visit of a mixed mission of government officials and business men from Argentina to Mexico in September 1963, seventeen working groups were established, each

[8] *Comercio Exterior*, Jan. 1963, p. 32.

dealing with the affairs of a particular industry, with a view to studying the possibility of complementary activities.[9]

By the end of 1964, there was remarkably little to show for all this activity. Some limited success had been achieved as a result of the tariff reduction programme as noted earlier in Chapter V. So far as complementarity agreements were concerned, there was very little to report. Progress in developing large-scale industries on the basis of access to region-wide markets was conspicuous by its absence, as were agreements for specialization as between similar industries operating in the various member countries. Industrial meetings were leading nowhere, and were often being used by business men largely to ensure the maintenance of the *status quo* and avoid any disturbance to the existing pattern of production and demand, based on the segregation of national markets into watertight compartments.

Complementarity Agreements

Only two complementarity agreements were in force at the end of 1964, both of them in relatively unimportant industries, and both of them resulting from initiatives of foreign rather than Latin American enterprise.

The first agreement, signed in July 1962 by Argentina, Brazil, Chile, and Uruguay, dealt with data processing machines and certain carefully defined materials and components required for their production or operation. It provided for the elimination of import duties and other restrictions on products of LAFTA origin and for the unification of duties on imports of materials and components from third countries. The agreement was the result of a suggestion by IBM to the governments concerned that, if duties were eliminated between them, it would build plants in Argentina and Brazil and arrange for another United States company to license the manufacture of the business forms needed for the machines by a Chilean paper producer. On the other hand, machines would qualify under the agreement as being of LAFTA origin even if all parts and components were imported from third countries.[10] Indeed, a special paragraph of the agreement provided that participating governments should not impose 'prohibitions or restrictions with equivalent effect' on imports from third countries of components, spare

[9] Ibid. Oct. 1963, p. 717.
[10] Business International, *Latin America's Merging Market*, pp. 12, 16.

parts, accessories, and other materials, as well as of complementary units used in manufacturing or operating the machines in question.[11]

It is difficult to judge the significance of an agreement of this sort without knowing how it will be operated in practice and developed over time. In certain circumstances it could provide a means whereby a foreign company could take advantage of the opportunities offered by a multi-country market and escape high tariffs on finished products by the simple device of introducing all materials and components from parent company plants for local processing and assembly within the LAFTA region. Agreements such as the one described can bring substantial benefit to Latin America only if they ensure a progressive increase in the degree of fabrication within the region and a reduction in the imported components. This would mean elimination of the special paragraph referred to above, which may obstruct development along these lines.

A second agreement, signed in February 1964 by Argentina, Brazil, Chile, Mexico, and Uruguay, dealt with valves for radio and television sets as well as their parts and components. This agreement likewise provided for the elimination of import duties and other restrictions on products of LAFTA origin, and for the unification of duties on imports from third countries. Certain types of valves were initially excluded from the scope of the agreement by individual participating countries, but these exceptions were to be progressively eliminated over a period of six years. Unlike the first complementarity agreement discussed above, the agreement on valves did not contain any clause designed to prevent the imposition of restrictions on imports of materials, parts, and components from third countries. On the contrary, the agreement sought to avoid imports of this sort by laying down various requirements tending to encourage production within the region. Moreover, there were certain provisions, not contained in the agreement on data processing machines, to deal with cases of damage to domestic industries and to maintain regional margins of preference against imports from third countries.[12] The establishment of a Special Committee was considered necessary to administer the agreement; and the duties of the committee were to include the consideration of cases in which

---

[11] 'Acuerdo de complementación sobre máquinas de estadística y análogas de cartulinas perforadas', Art. 7, para. 2, *Tres años*, p. 76.

[12] 'Acuerdo de complementación sobre válvulas electrónicas', Arts 7, 8, and 12, *Tres años*, pp. 77–78.

governments might seek suspension of the agreement because of injury to home production resulting from its operation. These provisions highlight the different kind of situation that obtains where the manufacture of products covered by a complementarity agreement is already in full swing in the region, as compared with the position where production has yet to be started, as in the case of data processing equipment.

Caution is essential in drawing general conclusions from only two complementarity agreements.[13] The fact that it has been found so difficult to draw up such agreements is, however, itself worthy of note. The potential advantage of complementarity agreements is that it may prove easier in the first instance to plan inter-country coordination of production and investment within certain selected industrial sectors than for the economy as a whole. At the same time the rate of reduction of trade barriers may be much faster for individual industrial products than for trade in general. As the number of such agreements increases, the scope of planned industrial coordination would likewise grow, with trade liberalization advancing in step. The difficulty in getting a programme of this sort started appears to reflect the lack of a drive at the governmental level capable of overcoming the reluctance of Latin American manufacturers to disturb the traditional rules of the game, and break out of the vicious circle of low output, high costs, and a high degree of national protection and restrictionism.

A second point to be noted is the narrowness of the sectors with which both agreements are concerned. The prototype of complementarity agreements is the Treaty of Paris, which established the European Coal and Steel Community; but that Treaty dealt with a very substantial sector of the economy of the six European countries concerned. It would take literally hundreds of complementarity agreements as narrowly based as the first two LAFTA ones to cover a major part of the Latin American economy. Any effort to coordinate such a large number of agreements and ensure coherence and consistency between them would be likely to founder in a morass of administrative confusion.

[13] In August 1964 it was announced that a draft complementarity agreement covering the glass industry had been prepared by industrialists from Argentina, Brazil, Chile, Colombia, Peru, and Uruguay, and that approaches were to be made to the governments of these countries to initiate the action required for the adoption of this agreement. Efforts were also to be made to obtain the cooperation of Mexican producers. See *Boletín Quincenal*, 10 Sept. 1964, p. 287.

K

The agreements themselves are defective, moreover, in failing to provide clearly for planned expansion, specialization, and diversification of the respective industries, and for the mutual confrontation and adjustment of investment plans in the various countries. The two agreements appear at first sight to leave the development of the industries to market forces operating within the specific environment created. To this extent, they provide little gain as compared with across-the-board methods of tariff reduction. In practice, however, the lack of any provision for an industrial plan, and for coordinated inter-country investment programmes may abandon the process of development not so much to free market forces as to the big foreign companies that dominate the particular industries concerned.[14]

The obvious danger is that intra-industry agreements might prove to be little more than government-sponsored arrangements for parcelling out the Latin American market, whether among foreign or domestic entrepreneurs. And it may not be easy to tell, from the mere wording of the agreements themselves, whether they are intended to be a means of expanding output and lowering costs and prices through specialization and exchange; or whether they are envisaged as instruments for maintaining the existing segregation of national markets, and reinforcing the position of the dominant suppliers in each market. The industrial development of Latin America is not likely to be furthered by the organization of private regional cartels; this was not the purpose intended for the complementarity agreements.

The lack of a coherent plan for industrial expansion throughout the region may account for the limited degree of participation in the two complementarity agreements, the other countries being unable to see any advantage in opening up their own markets unless there is some intention of developing their production too.

Complementarity agreements that cover a very narrow industrial sector cannot, in the nature of the case, always ensure the participation of every single LAFTA member in productive operations. Only if such agreements cover a sufficiently broad sector, and contain special provisions for planned development and investment coordination throughout the region, will the smaller and less developed countries have an interest in participating in every agreement. And

[14] International Business Machines, Radio Corporation of America, General Electric, and Philips. See *Tres años*, p. 6.

unless virtually all LAFTA members do participate in all agreements, conflicts of interest are bound to arise and it may be exceedingly difficult to secure a reasonable balancing of advantages gained and obligations incurred over the field of industry as a whole.

This is the basic shortcoming of industrial complementarity agreements—that an exact balance of advantages and disadvantages cannot be struck for each country for each industry. It is inevitable that certain countries will gain more than others under one agreement and less under another. What is important is to achieve reciprocity overall, so that the same countries—the most powerful ones—are not the winners every time: this is not an easy task in any event, but the prospect of success would be virtually nil if there were hundreds of agreements, each covering a minute sector and each having less than two-thirds of the LAFTA members participating.

Another difficulty lies in the definition of eligibility of products in connexion with complementarity agreements. If the value added to imported components and materials is very small, as in the case of simple assembly operations, inclusion of the product concerned in a complementarity agreement may simply provide a means for foreign companies to escape heavy duties on finished goods. Moreover, one may consider an imaginary case in which, say, Brazil manufactures a certain product with a very low import content, protecting the industry concerned with a high tariff. If Brazil agrees to a complementarity arrangement with Peru without specifying a fairly low maximum import content for both countries, it runs the risk that a United States or European firm will establish assembly operations in Peru and take over not only the Peruvian market but the Brazilian market as well.

On the other hand, the smaller and less developed countries may have grounds for complaint if Argentina, Brazil, and Mexico do specify a low maximum import content. For in that case they may have little or no hope of ever achieving a foothold in a great many industries of vital importance for them, simply because it may be impossible to reach the required degree of domestic content at a single jump. The small countries are entitled to argue that, in many industries, assembly operations may be the best way of beginning, and that this is in fact what happened in the bigger countries at an earlier stage.

The reconciliation of these divergent interests cannot be achieved by purely legal rules or automatic devices, because such rules and devices cannot distinguish a *bona fide* build-up of industrial capacity from small beginnings from the undermining of regional protection through simple assembly of imported components. Since questions of judgement are involved, planning machinery is again required, operating in accordance with regionally accepted criteria.

Because of the inability of LAFTA to solve all these various problems, not only did vested interests succeed in preventing any liberalization of trade in the products of the light industries during the early years of the Montevideo Treaty, but the uncoordinated proliferation and duplication of new capacity proceeded apace in the durable goods industries.

The Automobile Industry

Particularly remarkable was the chaotic situation that developed in the automobile industry. The extraordinary multiplication of excess capacity in this industry—at heavy cost to the countries concerned—has already been discussed at some length in Chapter II. Sixty firms were engaged in manufacturing for a regional market that could have been supplied much more efficiently by half a dozen or less. In 1963, in Argentina and Brazil alone, forty-two different types of passenger cars were being produced and thirty-three different types of truck.[15]

Despite all this, it has proved quite impossible to bring about region-wide co-operation in the development of the industry. The most that could be done was to arrange a modest amount of bilateral co-operation, notably between Chile and its powerful neighbours, Argentina and Brazil. In line with a previous joint declaration by the Presidents of Brazil and Chile in April 1963, a Joint Commission of representatives of the two countries met in July 1963 and worked out a programme of co-operation for their automobile industries. The Chilean side declared its intention of promoting the manufacture in Chile of certain types of vehicle, selected from among the types already produced in Brazil. Chile would import parts and components from Brazil for use in such manufacture. In return Brazil would import from Chile, to the extent that supplies were available, parts and components 'which will permit the exchange to be balanced'. In addition, the Brazilian industry would assist in the

---

[15] *Boletín Quincenal*, 10 Sept. 1963, p. 296.

development of the Chilean industry: mixed companies drawing capital from both countries would be set up for this purpose.

Since it would obviously take time for the Chilean industry to reach the point at which it could balance its transactions with the Brazilian industry, it was agreed that for a maximum period of three years trade should be balanced by Chile supplying less highly fabricated products linked to the automobile industry. Such products should form a declining proportion of Chilean exports, so as to maintain the required stimulus to the Chilean industry.

The Joint Commission recognized that the success of the programme would depend on the negotiation of reductions in trade barriers affecting the products in question through the normal machinery provided by the Montevideo Treaty. It was also stated that the joint understanding between the two countries, once it became definitive, should be open to participation by all LAFTA members. In the commission's view, however, serious problems were raised by the need, under the most-favoured-nation provisions of the Montevideo Treaty, to extend the benefits of import liberalization under complementarity agreements to all LAFTA members, whether they were participating in the agreements or not. The commission recommended that the advantages secured under such agreements should be limited strictly to the countries signing them.[16]

Here, then, is a further dilemma inherent in complementarity agreements. For a variety of reasons, it may be impossible to secure universal participation in an agreement, and the question arises whether a lack of interest in one or two countries should prevent the others from going ahead. And if they do go ahead, should all countries benefit from measures of import liberalization adopted by only some of them? If the most-favoured-nation provision were retained in an unconditional form, many complementarity agreements would never see the light of day, because any large-scale producer staying out of an agreement might gain additional markets without having to make corresponding concessions. On the other hand, if the Joint Commission's proposal were followed, there would be a danger of 'cliques' or sub-groups arising within the LAFTA region, creating new sources of friction and dissension. The solution to this problem adopted at the fourth annual LAFTA Conference was to retain the most-favoured-nation provisions of Article 18 of the Treaty, but

[16] *Comercio Exterior*, Aug. 1963.

on a conditional basis; so that countries not participating in a complementarity agreement would be entitled to benefit from a freeing of trade under the agreement only if they granted 'adequate compensation'.[17]

Immediately following the adoption of the joint understanding between Brazil and Chile, a similar programme of joint development was established between Argentina and Chile in August 1963. As in the case of the agreement with Brazil, Chile was to take steps to promote the import of automobile components from Argentina for assembly; and Argentina, in return, was to arrange to purchase parts and components in Chile for use in its own assembly lines. Trade was to be balanced as far as possible, Chile supplying, if necessary, products at a lower level of fabrication but required at some stage of car manufacture. The Argentine industry was to help in the development of the Chilean industry. Chile was to arrange for Argentina to be admitted to membership of the Joint Commission established by Brazil and Chile to organize co-operation in the automobile industry. And the agreement was to remain open for accession by other LAFTA countries.

These arrangements were followed in November 1963 by a meeting of government officials and business men of all three countries, which adopted several recommendations subsequently endorsed by Uruguay. The recommendations included the establishment of a permanent advisory committee to LAFTA on the automobile industry; strict rules for defining country-of-origin; discouragement of new automobile plants; measures to avoid competition from imports from third countries, harmonize trade laws and tax rules, and ease international payments; and a complementarity agreement to be signed by all LAFTA members.

There was little prospect that these provisions would commend themselves to other LAFTA countries. Towards the end of 1964 for example, it was reported that, though so much excess capacity had already been created elsewhere in the region, about $22 million would be invested in Peru in 1964-6 by 'at least' fourteen foreign motor-vehicle manufacturing companies, for the establishment of assembly plants.[18] It hardly seemed likely, under these conditions, that Peru would be interested in joining any agreement involving discouragement of new automobile plants.

[17] Resolution 99 (IV), Art. 21, see below, p. 328.
[18] *NYT*, 30 Nov. 1964.

The Lack of Progress

It will be apparent that the programme of industrial agreements had achieved very little by the end of 1964 and there was a danger of complete breakdown. In this respect, experience in LAFTA was closely following that in Central America, where the special régime of industrial integration had been pushed aside. The two main reasons for the failure were, as in Central America, the intrinsic difficulty of getting countries to dovetail their programmes of industrial development; and the reluctance of national and international lending agencies to invest substantial funds in industrial projects, especially where they suspected that such projects might involve the creation of local monopolies.[19]

It may well be that the success or failure of LAFTA may ultimately come to depend not on the extent to which the tariff provisions of the Treaty of Montevideo are implemented, but on the amount of new industry established on the basis of assured access to the entire LAFTA market. This simply cannot be done without a large measure of intergovernmental agreement on the distribution and location of the new industries.

In some cases intergovernmental agreements along these lines, accompanied by the dismantling of regional trade barriers, may suffice to prompt entrepreneurs to invest in the new industries required, within the zones laid down in the agreements. In other instances, especially where the chosen site is in a less developed area, additional incentives may be needed in the form of subsidies, direct or indirect; or, alternatively, a public enterprise may have to be established, as noted earlier.

Even where no special incentive is needed, there is a case for controlling the number of firms established in the first instance, so as to avoid the sort of proliferation of excess capacity that has taken place in the motor-car industry in Latin America. Where subsidies or other incentives are provided, it is essential to introduce some limitations, for a predetermined period, on the number of new firms in order not to dilute and perhaps negate the effect of such incentives. It goes without saying that countries agreeing to forego certain types of industry in exchange for reciprocal concessions by their neighbours would be required to take effective action in implementing such agreements.

[19] See also the discussion of this matter in the Central American context in ch. iv.

Any resulting monopoly should, of course, be subject to public control as well as to scrutiny by an appropriate organ of LAFTA. There are many effective ways of exercising such control—including, if necessary, the progressive reduction of duties on imports from third countries so as to force down excessive profits. Moreover, the special advantages given to the pioneer firm or firms should be limited in duration. But it would be a mistake to weaken the investment incentive resulting from prospective access to a region-wide market through doctrinaire insistence on the need for a competitive market to be created. Where, of course, the market is sufficiently large to permit a considerable number of firms to be set up and to operate at an optimum scale of output, there is no reason to restrict them to less than this number. Where, however, the market is large enough for only a handful of firms, or less, operating at optimum efficiency, scarce resources should not be squandered on the creation of excess capacity.

It cannot, incidentally, be assumed that a competitive situation is necessarily secured by the mere establishment of some minimum number of firms. On the contrary, the typical market situation in Latin America, as in other underdeveloped areas, is oligopoly—whereby the market is shared by the various producing firms by open or tacit agreement among them: it is precisely the fear that LAFTA would disrupt the stability of these arrangements that has caused much of the Latin American business community to resist the movement towards a common market.

However this may be, there can be little doubt that a considerable impetus could be given to the integration programmes in Latin America if national and international lending agencies would set aside substantial funds for use in financing joint industrial projects, involving agreement by participating countries to open up region-wide markets for the manufactures to be produced.

The Nature of Joint Planning

It was noted earlier that even national planning is in its infancy in the Latin American countries. What, then, would it be reasonable to expect by way of joint or regional planning?

Experience in other regions unfortunately gives only limited guidance in this respect. Not until October 1962, nearly five years after the Rome Treaty had gone into effect, did the Commission of the European Economic Community propose a measure of joint 'programming' and this immediately ran into stiff opposition from the Federal Republic of Germany. The objections raised were partly political—the Commission's proposal was held to imply a bias in favour of a single central authority for the Community instead of the federal concept implicit in the Rome Treaty. The economic objections advanced were that liberalism provided a more efficient system than planning, that economic forecasting had proved notoriously unreliable, that economic quantification failed to allow sufficiently for the human factor, and that planning tended to be biased against foreign trade, which was not under the control of the planners.

A subsequent restatement of the Commission's position in July 1963 in terms of the need to concert a medium-term economic policy for the Community as a whole appears to have narrowed the differences with the Federal Republic, but experience along these lines is quite limited thus far.

In any case, the objectives of Western European and Latin American planning are quite different, and this in itself makes any comparison exceedingly difficult. EEC 'programming' is concerned mainly with problems of business cycle control, and the dovetailing of national short- and medium-term economic policies so that countries keep in step. The reason for this is that as the barriers to trade come down and countries become increasingly dependent on one another, if any one country moves seriously out of line in its economic policy, this is almost immediately reflected in pressures on the balance of payments. This type of growing mutual inter-dependence has been experienced throughout the industrially developed group of countries in recent years, but it is likely to be particularly marked among members of the EEC as their internal tariff barriers disappear.

As Professor Hallstein has pointed out, it would be false to conclude from this that the EEC Commission favours a planned economy. All that the Commission is advocating is the coordination of government intervention in each of the EEC economies.[20]

Indeed, the net effect of such coordination could well be a reduction in the degree of initiative of national planning without any offsetting increase in Community planning, especially if the objections of the Federal Republic of Germany (and presumably of

[20] *Bulletin of the European Economic Community* (Brussels), Jan. 1963, English ed., p. 11.

France as well) to any centralizing tendencies are maintained. In Professor Hallstein's view only part of existing government intervention in the economy could be maintained under a Community régime, while part would have to be abolished. 'In any case', he has said, 'such intervention would become entirely a matter for the Community, as Community policy came to supersede the policy of individual states.'[21]

If certain types of intervention in the economy are to be undertaken by the Community or not at all, the extent of such intervention will, of course, depend on the possibility of reaching an identity of views among the Community members as to the policies to be followed and the specific measures to be adopted. The record of EEC efforts to achieve common policies, especially in agriculture, suggests that the difficulties involved should not be underestimated, and that in many cases action may be prevented or at least greatly delayed by stalemated negotiations.[22]

Quite different is the problem facing Latin America. Here the need is not for less planning but more. Moreover, such planning should aim at something much more fundamental than the short- or medium-term regulation of economic momentum—namely a complete transformation in the whole structure of the economy. Even the most radical of the Western European national plans has not sought far-reaching structural changes—mainly, no doubt, because the existing structure of production provided a sufficiently good foundation on which to build. Thus any comparison between Western European and Latin American planning requirements is bound to be of rather limited value.

Comecon experience is in one sense more relevant, in another less so. The Comecon countries are certainly faced with the problem of profound structural change and have tackled it with considerable vigour. Their experience of joint construction of major projects in the fields of power, transport, and communications, of joint investment, of joint enterprises, and of planned industrial specialization may well be of great interest for Latin America. The difficulties that have been encountered in reconciling divergent national interests in this regard, and in promoting a more rapid growth of the less

[21] *Bulletin of the European Economic Community* (Brussels), Jan. 1963, English ed., p. 11.

[22] For a more detailed discussion of the significance of the Rome Treaty for government planning and intervention, see the author's *Trade Blocs and Common Markets*, pp. 79–82.

developed member countries in Comecon may likewise have relevance to the Latin American situation. But differences in the stage and concept of planning, and above all the fact that the bulk of the Latin American economy is in the hands of private enterprise, make it necessary to be cautious in translating the experience of the one area into the context of the other.

Consistent Targets

For present purposes, the concept of planning relevant in the Latin American context may be defined as the drawing up of an interrelated and consistent set of targets for the economy embodying the structural changes required, and the application of measures to bring about the achievement of these targets. Many Latin American countries have initiated the first stage of the planning process, but relatively few, if any, have yet taken effective action to direct or influence the economy to move towards the goals desired.

The establishment of internal consistency between various targets is usually held to involve the construction of a generalized picture of the economy as a whole in which present and future demands upon various types of resources, physical and financial, are matched with available supplies, anticipated and actual. Any prospective financial imbalance will then indicate the need for corrective fiscal or monetary action; while any prospective imbalance between the bill of goods demanded and that supplied will point to the need for adjustment partly through the promotion of new investment in the directions required and partly through imports and exports; the latter in turn must also be brought into balance by direct or indirect measures, except in so far as there are compensating capital flows of a long-term nature.

Moreover, if government action is to be purposeful and effective, enough must be known about the dynamic inter-relationships of the economy to permit an assessment to be made of the changes that will occur over time as the various policy goals are approached.

The construction of such a generalized dynamic picture or model is not easy to achieve even in a fully developed economy with an abundance of reliable statistical data. In underdeveloped countries the problem is a much more difficult one, and in many instances unacceptable delays would arise if the initiation of planning were to depend on the completion of a fully coherent model of development of the economy as a whole. In many of these countries, for example, the volume of agricultural output in any year may be known only within an order of error of 5–10 per cent or more either way. Data on other sectors may be equally unreliable. Consequently, while the planner must always be sensitive to what he has been able to learn or guess of the broad inter-relationships in the economy, he cannot afford to be a purist, insisting on complete information as an indispensable condition of effective planning. If it is plain that the targets for a particular economy must include the development of, say, half a dozen known strategic sectors, it would be an error to wait upon the elaboration of a fully consistent set of goals for all sectors within a comprehensive framework. It would be much better to begin immediately by setting targets for the strategic sectors and by adopting the measures required for their achievement. This should not prevent work on more thorough-going lines from being initiated.

If the drawing up of a comprehensive plan for a single country presents serious problems, it will be apparent how much more difficult the same task would be for an entire region. Here one encounters all the conceptual and statistical problems that must be faced in every component country, compounded by such obstacles as the incomparability of data from country to country. Even the compilation of simple gross-product figures for Latin America as a whole poses immense difficulties, reflected in continuous and radical revisions of the available series.[23]

Strategic Sectors

Thus there are great difficulties in drawing up, in the immediate future, a complete set of targets for Latin America as a whole that could be fully reconciled with global estimates of the growth of the overall supply and use of financial and physical resources for the entire region. This does not mean, however, that joint planning is impossible. It means only that the construction of a fully integrated model of the Latin American economy lies some way in the future.

---

[23] The very concept of summing the gross products of a number of countries raises baffling problems, since the result obtained depends on whether or not a common set of prices is used to value the various outputs, or categories of income or expenditure, in the countries concerned. If each country's own prices are used, the meaning of the aggregate is far from clear, and its usefulness for planning purposes may be in doubt. If a common set of prices is used, the answer may be one thing in terms of Mexican prices and another in terms of Argentinian; there is no 'ideal' or 'correct' set of prices for this purpose. The choice of exchange rates also raises great difficulties.

What is nevertheless clear even now is that certain strategic sectors of the Latin American economy must be expanded by very large factors if a tolerable rate of growth of total production and consumption is to be secured. It will not be possible to be precise about the sectoral rates of expansion required until the various economic inter-relationships for the region have been much more thoroughly analysed than they have been thus far. But for immediate purposes it is sufficient to know what the general orders of magnitude are likely to be. There is more to be lost by waiting for refinements in the data than by setting the targets too low or too high at this stage.

Projections published by the Secretariat of ECLA in 1959, prior to the Montevideo Treaty, had already indicated the enormous increases in demand for certain kinds of goods that would occur by 1975 if Latin America's per capita rate of growth were to be maintained at an average level of 2·7 per cent per annum. For example, the demand for machinery and equipment was considered likely to increase about fourfold. Even if two-fifths of total import expenditures in 1975 were allocated to machinery and equipment (as against one-third at the time the projections were made), it was estimated that production of capital goods in the region would have to rise twenty-seven-fold (from $200 million to $5,400 million at 1950 prices) corresponding to an average annual rate of increase of 18 per cent.[24]

What is important in these projections is not the exact figures but the order of magnitude of the problem that they indicate. No matter what alternative assumptions one makes about overall rates of growth, ratios of investment to output, shares of import expenditure allocated to investment goods, and so forth, it is quite clear that Latin American production of machinery and equipment will have to advance by *some very large factor*. Planning of this sector could therefore begin on this basis, without waiting for greater precision or for a fully consistent set of targets for the economy as a whole.

More recently a Joint Programme has been set up in the ECLA Secretariat, with the added sponsorship of the Inter-American Development Bank and the Latin American Institute for Economic and Social Planning, to explore the possibilities of regional integration in a number of industries: steel making, capital goods, chemi-

[24] ECLA, *The Latin American Common Market*, pp. 71–72.

cals, pulp and paper, non-ferrous metals, textiles, and agricultural requisites (machinery, seed, fertilizer, pesticides).[25]

The studies are intended to serve as a basis for investment proposals in manufacturing activities of importance for regional integration, without the need for general complementarity agreements covering the industries concerned. Proposals along these lines may be submitted for the consideration of the Inter-American Development Bank for promotion and financing. Other studies are to deal with transport and communications.

Thus joint planning may be envisaged as taking place at three levels, involving different sorts of co-operation and different degrees of mutual commitment by governments. At the simplest level, specific projects for new investment in regional industries may be promoted and financed without the full apparatus of a complementarity agreement. The minimum requirement here, presumably, is that enough countries should open their markets to the new industries thus established to make it possible to operate them at an efficient scale of production. If, in addition, countries can agree to co-operate in identifying obvious inconsistencies or inadequacies in their investment programmes in particular industrial sectors, so much the better.

At the second level, still within the context of a single industry, member countries may adopt complementarity agreements embodying more formal and comprehensive arrangements regarding the manner in which the future demand of member countries is to be satisfied from existing or new capacity, including provision for inter-country specialization, market access, margins of preference, consistent patterns of investment and investment incentives, and so forth.

At the third and most sophisticated level, governments may agree to set both industrial and overall growth targets for the region as a whole, as well as for each member country, within a consistent general framework of perspective planning for a gradual process of integration.

The most practical approach to regional planning by LAFTA countries may thus be through a phased programme of gradually expanding scope. Such a programme might begin with primary emphasis on limited joint industrial projects. It would move step by

[25] ECLA, *Note by the Secretariat on the Commission's Activities in the Field of Economic Integration*, pp. 14 f.

step towards comprehensive agreements covering entire industrial sectors. Finally, these individual agreements would themselves have to be brought together within the framework of an integrated plan for the region as a whole: at that point the full machinery of regional planning would be needed, and with it a new approach to the institutional requirements of the Association, as will be seen in Chapter XI.

CHAPTER IX

THE PRINCIPLE OF RECIPROCITY AND THE PAYMENTS SYSTEM

The Principle of Reciprocity

Among the most difficult problems that have arisen in the development of economic co-operation in Latin America have been those of providing mutually satisfactory incentives for all participating countries, and of making adequate payments arrangements to facilitate the growth in regional trade. As will become evident in the course of the discussion, these two problems are closely linked.

First, as regards reciprocity of incentives or benefits, we have already had to deal with some of the most important aspects of this matter in examining the issues raised by the less developed and intermediate groups of countries in LAFTA in Chapter VII. We shall now recapitulate the findings of that chapter in a more general setting.

One general observation may be made by way of introduction. Free trade tends to bring about unequal rates of development in whatever area or region it applies. And just as, in the past, worldwide free trade led to great and growing inequality between continents, so now would intra-regional free trade be likely to lead to, or intensify, corresponding inequality between countries. Yet if the cohesiveness of a regional trading arrangement is to be maintained or strengthened, it is *vital* that all participating countries should gain from the arrangement more than they could have gained without it; and *highly desirable* that any inequality in gains by various member countries should be held within reasonably narrow limits. More specifically, the problem of reciprocity is that of ensuring that all countries participating in a common market receive benefits from such participation commensurate with the concessions they make.

It must be recognized at the outset that there is rarely any objective way of measuring precisely the advantages that one country may obtain from an international agreement as compared with those obtained by another. This is just as true of any procedure for establishing a common market between a group of countries as of the bilateral agreements which governments conclude with one another from time to time. No country can be entirely certain when it enters into negotiations with other countries for mutual tariff reductions that the gains it will achieve in terms of additional markets will be exactly equivalent to the concessions it makes. The most that can be done within the framework of a common market is to create incentives for all countries, so that each country will consider the possible gains sufficient to justify the concessions it makes, and to make provision for avoiding excessive disequilibrium in the advantages achieved by any one country or group of countries.

The need for reciprocity is particularly important because in granting one another mutual trade preferences, the countries participating in a common market deliberately forego the advantages of being able to buy from the cheapest possible sources available anywhere. It makes sense for a country to grant preferential treatment to its neighbour if it receives preferential treatment in return. If, say, Colombia undertakes to buy a particular product in Brazil instead of getting it more cheaply from suppliers in the United States, it is only natural that Colombia should ask for reciprocity in return.

In other words, in so far as a Latin American country shifts its source of supply to another Latin American country, particularly for manufactured goods, it may well be bringing about, in effect, a deterioration in its own terms of trade. Indeed it is tacitly subsidizing the manufacturing industry of the supplying country by the amount of the difference between the price paid to that country and the world market price.

One might ask why it should be necessary to make special arrangements for reciprocity within the framework of LAFTA if no such arrangements have proved necessary in the EEC. It would, however, be a mistake to imagine that because there is no explicit doctrine of reciprocity in the Treaty of Rome no such concept is implied. So long as all countries appear to be benefiting from the implementation of the Rome Treaty, no difficulties will arise. But if it began to appear that one country or another was getting an undue share of the advantages, there is no doubt that the problem of reciprocity would have to be tackled in one way or another. Indeed the conflict over the role of agriculture in the EEC is in fact, if not in principle, a conflict over reciprocity. It was a tacit assumption of the

L

Treaty of Rome that if Western Germany gained access to an enlarged market for the products of its industries, France would obtain corresponding benefits for the output of its farming communities.

During the early years of the EEC, this basic pattern of reciprocity was not in fact achieved. While tariffs came down on industrial products, and Western Germany did very well with its exports of manufactures to other members of the Community, little or no progress was made in securing agreement on a common agricultural policy which would create new outlets for the output of French agriculture. The matter came to a head just before the end of the first four-year stage of the transition period, at which time the unanimous agreement of the member governments was required for the formal transition to the second stage to begin. The French government issued a warning in June 1961 that it might use its powers under the Rome Treaty to delay the opening of the second stage of the Common Market arrangements at the beginning of 1962 unless significant progress were made in the application of a common agricultural policy. As the French Minister of Agriculture remarked at the time, each of the EEC countries was interpreting the Treaty of Rome after its own fashion, and increasing use was being made of the escape clauses of the treaty to avoid compliance with its terms.[1] In the end a compromise was reached which permitted passage to the second stage of the transitional period to take place. In 1964 there was a further crisis when France let it be known that it regarded the entire future of the EEC as dependent upon an agreement by the members to establish a common price for grain at a level substantially below the price ruling in Western Germany. Not until Western Germany abandoned its resistance to such an agreement was it possible to make progress in other important areas of the integration programme.

Thus while the principle of reciprocity does not receive formal recognition in the Treaty of Rome as it does in the Treaty of Montevideo, it is in fact just as important an element in the development of the EEC as it is likely to be in the context of Latin America. That is not to say that it will be easy to achieve such reciprocity in Latin America, particularly if market forces were to be left free to determine the distribution and location of industry. Within the EEC, the countries are sufficiently close to one another in level of income and

[1] *The Times*, 15 June 1961.

of economic development for each one of them to feel that it is likely to gain from the merger. Within groups of underdeveloped countries, on the other hand, one can hardly expect market forces, operating freely, to lead to mutually beneficial results for all countries. The dispersion of per capita incomes and levels of development in Latin America is very much greater than in Western Europe. Countries like Bolivia, Ecuador, and Paraguay are bound, as we have seen, to be concerned at the possibility that a complete freeing of their trade with such powerful neighbours as Argentina, Brazil, and Mexico might be disastrous for them. There are good grounds for believing that uncontrolled free trade among any group of underdeveloped countries would lead to the more advanced countries enriching themselves at the expense of the more backward ones.

This does not mean, of course, that a sound development policy inevitably requires the equalization of growth rates throughout the area considered. It may well be that for any area regarded as a single unit, the most efficient way of developing may lie through deliberately unequal rates of growth in various districts, and an intentional concentration of effort in the richer and more advanced regions. This may apply particularly where one starts from a very low level of development and encounters major indivisibilities, especially in outlays for social overhead investment.

Such a policy can, however, apply only to politically unified areas. It is not likely to be politically acceptable in an economic union, which cannot be regarded as a single unit for all purposes. Any one government can adopt policies which, while beneficial for the country as a whole—and leading to ultimate advancement for every part of the country—nevertheless leave particular areas within the country behind, at any rate in the short run. But no government could possibly defend itself before its people if it allowed its own national interests to be submerged and compromised by the policies of an economic union of which it was a member, even where such policies were of demonstrable advantage to all other members of the union. Thus an economic union must study the interests of its constituent parts to an extent not required of a unified country. And where such a union is formed in the absence of strong federal loyalties among the mass of the people, the individual countries are likely to try and limit, as far as they can, the extent of any damage to their national interests caused by a powerful and perhaps zealous central authority.

The Treaty of Montevideo does not indicate at all clearly how reciprocity should be achieved within a Latin American common market, although there is a broad indication that export gains should be of a similar order of magnitude from country to country. Studies that had led up to the Treaty had made fairly specific proposals to this end. For example, a Working Group of prominent personalities from the United States and Latin America convened by ECLA in February 1959 had made the following recommendations regarding reciprocal benefits in a common market:

> For the success of the common market it is important that all the member countries should have the opportunity of expanding their exports at the same time as they take action to reduce their duties, taxes and other restrictions on imports. To this end, member countries, which, as a result of the facilities granted to them, increase their exports to the common market without a proportionate increase in their imports, should accelerate the rate at which they reduce their duties, taxes and other restrictions.[2]

Giving its reasons for this recommendation, the Working Group referred to the possibility that reduction or abolition of customs duties and other taxes and restrictions might bring substantially greater benefits to some members of the common market than to others. These greater benefits would probably be reflected in a persistent tendency for the former countries to export more to the latter than they imported from them. In the Working Group's view, countries in this position should increase the rate of reduction of their duties and other taxes and restrictions in order to promote their imports 'and so offer the others greater opportunities of participating adequately in the reciprocal trade benefits of the common market'.[3]

It was the view of the ECLA Secretariat that if measures along these lines proved inadequate, countries with persistent import surpluses should be entitled to reduce their duties and restrictions at a slower rate.[4]

Reciprocity and the Treaty of Montevideo

These views of the Working Group and of the ECLA Secretariat did not fully prevail in the drafting of the Treaty of Montevideo. The Treaty states, in Article 10, that negotiations among the Con-

---

[2] *Multilateral Co-operation*, pp. 48–49.   [3] Ibid. pp. 55–56.
[4] See, e.g., ibid. p. 102.

tracting Parties should be 'based on reciprocity of concessions'; and Article 13 provides that: 'The reciprocity mentioned in article 10 refers to the expected growth in the flow of trade between each Contracting Party and the others as a whole, in the products included in the liberalization programme and those which may subsequently be added.'

It remains unclear, however, whether the Treaty categorically requires a commensurate growth of exports and imports of all participating countries, although it may be open to countries to interpret it in this way.

Additional support for the principle of reciprocity may also be derived from Article 11, which provides that

If, as a result of the concessions granted, significant and persistent disadvantages are created in respect of trade between one Contracting Party and the others as a whole in the products included in the liberalization programme, the Contracting Parties shall, at the request of the Contracting Party affected, consider steps to remedy those disadvantages with a view to the adoption of suitable, non-restrictive measures designed to promote trade at the highest possible levels.

This is a substantially weaker provision than that recommended by the Working Group—namely that countries experiencing a greater rise in exports than in imports should accelerate the liberalization of their imports.

The reason why the principle of reciprocity was not given clearer expression in the Treaty of Montevideo is that it ran counter to conventional thinking about world trade.[5] According to orthodox theories, it is quite wrong to envisage a regional balancing of accounts in Latin America; and the only valid principle of reci-

---

[5] It is noteworthy that opposition to the principle of reciprocity seems to come primarily from the banking community, national and international, rather than from private enterprise as a whole. Mention has already been made of the emphasis placed by industrialists in some of the Latin American countries on the need for reciprocity in trade relations within LAFTA. Even in the United States, however, support for the principle of reciprocity has been voiced by some of those favouring the greatest possible expansion of domestic and foreign private enterprise in Latin America. For example, in his study for the National Planning Association, Frank Brandenburg proposes that foreign corporations should take the initiative 'in designing workable arrangements based on compensating reciprocity of trade, a fundamental principle of LAFTA—arrangements that in turn promise to expedite progress toward integration'. (See Frank Brandenburg, *The Development of Latin American Private Enterprise* (Washington, D.C., National Planning Association, 1964)).

procity is that which applies to the whole of a country's trade, not to its trade with a particular region. Why, it is asked, should each and every Latin American country be made to balance its accounts with the rest of the region? A particular country might be in surplus with the other Latin American countries, and need the proceeds of that surplus to pay for its deficit with the rest of the world. It would be a hardship for such a country to balance its trade with Latin America, because that would imply a corresponding need to balance its trade with the other countries as well—which, in practice, would have to be done through a curtailment of imports from the rest of the world.

It is striking that precisely the same criticisms had been voiced prior to the establishment of the European Payments Union. There too the particular mechanism adopted tended to encourage intra-regional balancing of accounts by compelling debtors to pay increasing proportions of gold or convertible currency as their cumulative deficits with other members increased. Moreover, creditors within the EPU received no more than 50 per cent of gold or convertible currency in respect of their surpluses even when such surpluses exceeded the pre-agreed quotas. Thus debtors within the Union had a direct incentive to reduce their regional deficits, and creditors their regional surpluses.

Moreover, the proposal for differential rates of liberalization by debtor and creditor countries, which has also provoked criticism in the Latin American context, was likewise fortified by experience in Western Europe. During the 1950s, chronic creditor countries such as Western Germany were frequently requested to accelerate their liberalization of quota restrictions, while debtor countries were often allowed to slow down their liberalization temporarily. Yet there is no doubt that the system worked very well, and did not ultimately prevent a return to convertibility.

In other words, the principle of reciprocity—the principle that all countries should make roughly comparable gains from the liberalization of trade among them—was implemented continuously in Western Europe during the early postwar years and is still being implemented to a considerable extent even now within the Common Market: the fact that the principle is not referred to by name cannot obscure the essential facts that indicate its implied acceptance.

It is true that there has thus far been no pressure upon countries within the EEC to achieve a precise intra-regional balancing of accounts. This, however, is a reflection of the strength of their balance of payments positions to date. Even so, as we have seen, there is a general implied understanding that all members of the EEC are entitled to expect that their exports will grow roughly parallel with their imports.

The greater emphasis placed on this principle in the Latin American context results naturally from two basic considerations. First, the weakness of Latin American balance of payments positions compels the countries in the region to do everything they can to avoid new pressures on their limited exchange reserves. Secondly, as we have seen, goods obtained from other Latin American countries are likely to be more expensive, in many cases, than those available from other sources.

Conventional objections to the principle of reciprocity are based on a highly simplified model of the world economy in which every country serves its own best interests by buying in the cheapest market and selling in the dearest. Obviously it would be pure coincidence if a particular country's purchases and sales in a given region balanced out exactly, given that the only criterion for such transactions was that they occurred in the most advantageous markets.

But if buying in the cheapest market and selling in the dearest held the key to the trade problems of underdeveloped countries— or even of Western Europe, for that matter—there would be no need for regional integration. The establishment of customs unions and free-trade areas, whether among developed or underdeveloped countries, is designed quite deliberately to prevent the flows of trade from being determined by price relationships prevailing in a completely free market. The idea is rather that a focusing of trade flows within an integrated region, insulated to a greater or lesser extent from the outside world, would lead to a dynamic growth of output and income within the region to an extent that could not otherwise be achieved.

In terms of the reasoning of this study, a severalfold increase in intra-regional trade in Latin America would bring great benefits to the participating countries whether the resulting trade was balanced or unbalanced. And if the only way of getting countries to co-operate in stepping up their trade with one another is to assure them of a roughly equivalent expansion of exports and imports, that is certainly not too great a price to pay for the opening up of new opportunities for regional specialization and exchange. Even for those Latin American countries now able to realize a net surplus of convertible currency from their transactions with the rest of the region, it would be better, in the long run, to accept the prospect of balance *at a much higher level of trade* than to persist with the present limited flows of trade, even though they do yield a surplus.

In other words, the present surplus countries must decide for themselves whether or not they wish to participate in an expansion of intra-regional trade on a basis of reciprocity. The choice they face is not between balanced and unbalanced regional trade, but between unbalanced trade at the present level and balanced trade at a higher level. The surplus countries must decide which they prefer— an active regional trade balance or a larger volume of trade.

It is, no doubt, natural for the surplus countries to seek to maintain the channels whereby they are presently able to earn a surplus of exchange for the purchase of goods in North America or Western Europe. But such arrangements are precarious at best. From a long-run point of view it would be better for these countries to play their part in encouraging the growth of new sources of supply within the region itself, and thereby create new markets for their own exportable goods. In that event, the way in which trade balanced out would be much less important than the overall expansion of the economy that it would generate.

Thus the Latin American countries cannot rest content with a passive policy of simply allowing the intra-regional balances to take whatever form they may, irrespective of the effect on the willingness of participating countries to liberalize their trade further. If something like the principle of reciprocity were not followed, for every case of a surplus country increasing its export balance with the region, there would be at least one other country which, in all probability, would decide to withdraw from the liberalization process either temporarily or permanently.

The error made by the critics of the principle of reciprocity lies in viewing the Latin American economic problem in static terms— in terms of the optimum use of existing resources; whereas the real need is to seek and expand the opportunities for dynamic growth. The objective should be to create maximum incentives for the establishment of new industries in Latin America, and such incentives will be all the greater the larger are the markets available. The important thing is to ensure that the industries producing, say, iron and steel, pulp and paper, and petrochemicals will be constructed and adapted in line with the requirements of region-wide markets and not on the assumption of narrow national markets.

But no individual Latin American country would have any incentive to shift its existing source of supply for many industrial products away from North America or Western Europe and in favour of its Latin American neighbours if it did not receive a corresponding advantage in return. This fact lies at the heart of the difference of view between orthodox thinking, with its refusal to consider anything but the aggregate balance of payments, and the modern view, which emphasizes the need for reciprocal incentives if a Latin American common market is to achieve its development objectives. It is a question of free trade versus economic development—that is the crux of the problem of reciprocity.

The Payments Problem

Our second major problem, closely linked with the first, results from the fact that no adequate system of regional payments has been established. While the Secretariat of ECLA has supported the idea of special arrangements for intra-regional payments involving a system of reciprocal credits, the International Monetary Fund has seen great difficulties, especially as regards the latter feature; and Latin American governments have been unwilling to flout IMF views because IMF goodwill is frequently a prerequisite for access to the financial resources not only of the IMF itself but of other national and international agencies. The Latin American governments have appealed repeatedly to ECLA and the IMF to try and achieve a meeting of minds; and a special resolution, adopted at the same time as the Treaty of Montevideo was signed, asked that studies of methods to facilitate the financing of transactions among Latin American countries be continued by ECLA, the IMF, and the OAS.[6] Little if any success has attended these efforts, because of policy differences that are fundamental. Yet there is no doubt that the failure to settle this question has seriously obstructed the progress of economic integration in Latin America.

It has to be borne in mind that the reduction or removal of restrictions on trade within any group of countries is apt to lead to all sorts of unexpected trade flows, responding to the new business opportunities. While countries may seek to secure equivalence be-

[6] *Multilateral Co-operation*, Resolution I, pp. 69–70.

tween the concessions that they grant and those that they receive, any precise forecast of the overall effects of the bargain is, in the nature of the case, impossible. Thus countries always face the risk that their imports may rise more than their exports by virtue of concessions given and received, and this in turn may lead to sharp swings in balances of payments.[7] Now if the Latin American countries had large foreign exchange reserves, they could use these reserves to meet any deficits arising from the freeing of trade with their neighbours, and simultaneously adopt whatever measures might be needed to restore equilibrium in the balance of payments. The reserves would thus enable them to tide over the period of disequilibrium.

But most Latin American countries have very low foreign exchange reserves and are likely to hesitate about any significant freeing of imports from their neighbours unless they have some assurance of at least short-term accommodation to deal with unexpected deficits. When Western Europe was confronted with an analogous problem in easing its quantitative import controls in 1950, it set up the European Payments Union to deal with it.

The Analogy of the European Payments Union

The European Payments Union was a mechanism through which participating countries undertook to clear their balances with one another on a multilateral non-discriminating basis within the group. To this end, each Union member granted to the rest of the group, and itself received from the group, automatic multilateral credit facilities that permitted the financing of temporary disequilibria in the regional balances of payments of members. In other words, if, in the process of liberalizing restrictions on trade, certain EPU members found their imports rising more than their exports, they knew they could count on an automatic line of credit from the Union, up to a certain level, that would give them a breathing space in which to take action to restore equilibrium, without excessive

---

[7] It is true that trade among Latin American countries is likely to remain, for some time at least, a small fraction of their total trade. But this does not mean that the trade *balances* generated by transactions within the region might not be very large in relation to total trade balances. For example, although the trade of Uruguay with the LAFTA area accounted for only 12% of its total trade, it was estimated that in 1962, 1963, and the first eight months of 1964, Uruguay's deficit with LAFTA countries amounted to $59·3 m., equivalent to 86% of the total deficit with all countries. See *Comercio Exterior*, Dec. 1964, p. 844.

drawings upon their limited reserves of gold or convertible currencies.

In setting their course towards a common market, the Latin American countries likewise need some assurance that they will not, as a result of trade liberalization, suddenly be faced with large balance of payments deficits, leading to heavy inroads upon their limited reserves. Does a payments union represent a way out for them, as for the Western European countries in the 1950s?

Those who believe that it does not contend that there is no analogy between the position of Western Europe in 1950 and of Latin America in 1965. In 1950 Western European currencies were inconvertible and trade was moving in restricted bilateral channels. For countries in such a situation, a payments union may have represented a step forward, a move in the direction of convertibility.[8] But for Latin American countries, whose currencies are for the most part already convertible, a payments union would, it is argued, be a step backwards. For in so far as such a union places automatic credit facilities at the disposal of members, it relieves deficit countries of the need to settle their accounts in convertible currency—to the extent of the credit thus made available.

The implication here, of course, is that the Latin American countries are in a stronger balance of payments position now than the Western European countries were almost throughout the 1950s— since the latter did not restore currency convertibility until 1958. Yet this seems a paradoxical view to hold. If Western Europe delayed its return to convertibility so long, it was not because it was less well prepared for that goal than Latin America, but because it was not willing to sacrifice other economic objectives such as full employment and a sustained rate of economic expansion. For Latin America likewise the question arises whether financial orthodoxy is to be placed ahead of the goal of economic development.

In any case, the Latin American countries have been able to maintain convertibility only by applying very severe restrictions on

---

[8] Although orthodox attitudes to the EPU have mellowed somewhat in retrospect, they were severely critical at the time: orthodox views were as opposed to the EPU in 1950 as they are to any similar arrangement for underdeveloped countries now. The fact that the EPU was nevertheless established in 1950 was due to the support it received from US officials administering the Marshall Plan, who understood that Western Europe was not yet ready for the far-reaching discipline of full convertibility. No comparable support has yet emerged in the similar situation now facing the underdeveloped countries in LAFTA.

trade, and by resorting to heavy exchange surcharges and prior deposit systems. Under such conditions currency convertibility is little more than a formality: the form is there without the substance. Even orthodox economics does not view convertibility as an end in itself but as a means to the fullest international division of labour; and trade and payments restrictions required to sustain convertibility are just as disruptive of the international division of labour as the maintenance of inconvertibility of currencies. It is therefore not at all obvious that for countries like Argentina and Chile the preservation of a precarious convertibility is to be preferred to the liberalization of regional trade and payments within the framework of a payments union.

The fact is that for many underdeveloped countries the reduction of restrictions on trade with one another is incompatible with full payment in convertible currency. If Latin American countries were to pay wholly in dollars for their imports from other countries in the area, they would find themselves compelled to maintain restrictions upon trade with one another not less severe than those which they employ on trade with the rest of the world. In other words, given the present foreign exchange position in Latin America, the conduct of intra-regional payments on the basis of complete settlement in gold or dollars would obstruct the whole purpose of a common market by making the liberalization of trade much more difficult than it need be.

Indeed, the decline in trade among the Latin American countries during the later 1950s, which was analysed in Chapter II, was due in large measure to the return to convertibility of a number of South American countries and the consequential termination of their bilateral payments arrangements. For as these arrangements were, one after the other, allowed to lapse, the margins of credit that they had provided were no longer available to facilitate trade among the countries concerned. One example was the drop in Brazilian lumber exports to Argentina, which went hand in hand with a reduction of Brazilian wheat imports from Argentina. The disappearance of bilateral credit facilities also depressed certain trade flows in agricultural commodities which follow a marked seasonal pattern: the concentration of heavy obligations in convertible currency at certain periods of the year created impossible difficulties for countries struggling with the problem of inadequate international reserves.[9]

[9] See Keesing and Brand in IMF, *Staff Papers*, x/3 (Nov. 1963).

A second reason advanced for not following the EPU model is that while in Western Europe in the 1950s intra-regional trade accounted for some 40 per cent of total trade, in Latin America the corresponding proportion is of the order of only 10 per cent. As Professor Mikesell has put it, since intra-regional trade is such a small proportion of the total trade of Latin America, 'a special currency mechanism for intra-regional trade scarcely seems to be warranted'.[10]

But if a special currency mechanism would help to promote intra-regional trade, does it matter that only a small proportion of total trade is intra-regional? If, further, it is agreed that a rapid expansion of intra-regional trade is indispensable for Latin America in the longer run, is not now the time to begin, using the most effective instruments available? And if intra-regional trade preferences are considered acceptable to this end, why not intra-regional preference in payments as well, the latter being simply a complement and reinforcement of the former?

A third consideration to be taken into account is that the credit advanced within a payments union would not necessarily be provided by those best able to afford it. It might so happen that the surplus countries within the union were the poorest, which would therefore be required to give credit to the richer ones rather than the other way round. In other words the configuration of surpluses and deficits within a payments union may not yield a suitable basis for decisions as to which countries should be giving credit and which receiving it. This may not have created serious problems in the EPU, but it might well do so in Latin America, where inter-country differences in levels of income and development are much greater.

One of the assumptions on which a payments union is founded is that, over a period of years, the position of each member will average out at something reasonably close to a zero balance with the other members, taken together. Thus the short-period positions of union members are expected to fluctuate on both sides of the break-even point, while cumulative surpluses and deficits over extended periods are expected to be small. Moreover, in accordance with the principle of reciprocity discussed earlier, trade policies, including particularly the rate of liberalization of imports, would presumably

[10] Raymond F. Mikesell, *Latin American Regional Markets and U.S. Policy* (Committee for a National Trade Policy, Conference on Trade Policy, Jan. 1960 (mimeo.)), p. 4.

be adjusted so as to secure a parallel rise in the regional exports and imports of all participating countries.

If countries were successful in achieving this kind of uniform and concerted upward movement in their regional exports and imports, there would be no grounds for fearing that the weaker members of the group might be called upon to finance excessive credits to other members for any extended period. It must be recognized, however, that the practical difficulties may be quite serious, and that suitable arrangements would be required to protect the weaker countries against undue burdens, even over short periods. This could be done through prior agreement on situations in which the payments union itself might grant special credit facilities outside the scope of normal settlements. Such situations might include not only cases in which a relatively less developed country was running persistent surpluses with the union, but also instances of particularly severe balance of payments disequilibrium resulting from trade liberalization. To the extent that such arrangements involved the union itself in a temporary excess of gold or dollar payments over gold receipts, there would be a need for a capital fund of suitable size to draw on: the EPU began its operations with a fund of $350 million, but a Latin American payments union would probably be able to function successfully with a lower level of liquid resources.

We now come to the last and perhaps most decisive objection to a Latin American payments union. Mr Pierre-Paul Schweitzer, Managing Director of the IMF, has defined the general problem of international liquidity in a strikingly concise passage:

The goals of international financial stability and world economic growth would not be served if countries could finance external deficits for prolonged periods without having to deal with the factors which were causing the deficits. On the other hand, an adequate supply of international liquidity is necessary to spare countries from having to make precipitate changes in their financial and economic policies because an insufficiency of reserves allowed them no time to make orderly adjustments.[11]

The question is—granted that a Latin American payments union would aim to provide additional liquidity along the lines of the second part of Mr Schweitzer's statement, would it also satisfy the requirements of the first part?

[11] Address to National Foreign Trade Convention, New York, 16 Nov. 1964 (*International Financial News Survey* (IMF), 4 Dec. 1964, p. 444).

The Problem of Automatic Credits

The conventional answer is that it would not. The heart of the case against a payments union is that it is undesirable for deficit countries to have access to automatic credits of the type available in a payments union, since this may encourage delay in the adoption of the necessary corrective fiscal or monetary measures, which are likely to be unpopular. Disciplined monetary behaviour requires domestic monetary stability combined with full payment in gold or convertible currencies for external deficits incurred. If, in cases of balance of payments difficulty, credit is needed, such credit is available from the IMF, which will make the required advances on a discretionary basis, once it is satisfied that steps adequate to deal with current difficulties have been taken, and that such advances do not encourage unsound monetary expansion. Alternatively, any central bank is free to negotiate for credits from other central banks, again on a discretionary basis. But since the opportuneness of advancing credits to a country in balance of payments difficulties must depend on the circumstances of each particular case, automaticity should, on this view, be avoided at all costs.

Now the case against automaticity would be a very strong one if the proposal were for automatic credits of indefinite amounts. In fact, however, the total credit available could be limited under pre-agreed quota arrangements. Moreover, as in the case of the EPU, it would be easy to devise systems in which deficit countries would be required to pay increasing proportions of gold and receive decreasing proportions of credit as their cumulative deficits grew; and, once the credit ceiling was passed, a deficit country could be required to finance additional deficits fully in gold or convertible currency.

When the EPU began its operations in the middle of 1950, settlements were effected as to 40 per cent in gold and 60 per cent in credit up to the quota limit, determined for each country on the basis of its trade with other participants. However, the 40/60 ratio was an average. The actual ratio was on a sliding scale, which depended on the overall cumulative debit or credit balance of each country. Up to a level equivalent to 20 per cent of the pre-agreed quotas, the net balances of individual countries with all other participants were covered entirely by credit. Once a country's cumulative net deficit exceeded 20 per cent of its quota, however, gradually increasing proportions of gold and decreasing proportions of credit were employed in settling additional debit balances.[12] By the time the fifth 20 per cent tranche of the quota was reached, debtor countries had to settle as much as 80 per cent of additional deficits in gold and only 20 per cent in credit. And if the cumulative net deficit went on to exceed the quota, settlements had to be fully in gold.

The advantage of this sliding-scale arrangement was that while it provided liberal credit facilities so long as cumulative deficits remained within normal limits, it gave every incentive to debtor countries not to abuse these facilities, and to make any necessary adjustments if their cumulative deficits became too large. The system gave a breathing space to debtor countries, and assured them that their reserves of convertible currency would not be drawn upon simply because of seasonal or other short-term fluctuations in their trade, or because of unexpectedly large inflows of imports associated with rapid trade liberalization. But the debtor countries were not relieved of the necessity, ultimately, to take whatever steps might be required to deal with more fundamental external imbalance. As time went on the EPU countries were able to harden settlements within the Union progressively, so that larger proportions of gold or dollars were required for settlements and smaller proportions of credit. By this means a gradual transition to full convertibility was brought about.

[12] In the early stages of the EPU's evolution, monthly deficits and surpluses were settled in the following proportions:

Percentage of quota	Deficit		Surplus	
	Gold	Credit	Gold	Credit
First 20 per cent	—	100	—	100
Second 20 per cent	20	80	50	50
Third 20 per cent	40	60	50	50
Fourth 20 per cent	60	40	50	50
Fifth 20 per cent	80	20	50	50
100 per cent	40	60	40	60

It will be seen that all settlements to creditors above the first 20 per cent of the quota were at the standard rate of 50 per cent gold and 50 per cent credit. This is because while increasing proportions of gold settlement were designed to restrain deficit countries from adding to their cumulative debits, it was necessary to avoid offering creditors a symmetrical incentive—namely the incentive to earn hard currency from their Union partners. Indeed, settlements to creditors even beyond quota limits were in practice effected only as to 50 per cent in gold and 50 per cent in credit, despite the fact that corresponding debtors had to pay 100 per cent in gold. This procedure was designed to induce possible creditor countries to limit their surpluses in the area—whether by accelerating the rate of liberalization of their imports, stepping up domestic expansion, or by other means.

Automaticity is not unknown even in the IMF's own operations: every member country has automatic access to finance in the first tranche of its IMF quota. The first tranche corresponds to each country's gold subscription: countries would obviously not have agreed to the subscription if they had not been assured of unconditional access to at least that amount of finance.

But once automaticity is accepted up to a certain point, the problem becomes one of degree rather than of principle. It is arguable, for example, that automatic access to IMF resources for some way beyond the first tranche could be conceded without detriment to the needs of monetary discipline; for many countries the first tranche of the IMF quota is too small to give adequate leeway in the event of a sharp, albeit temporary, swing in the balance of payments.

Naturally, there is room for honest differences of opinion as to how far automatic access to external finance should go—and this is just as true of the operations of the IMF as of a Latin American payments union. Some would no doubt contend that the 40/60 gold/credit ratio of the EPU would be too 'soft' for Latin America today, others that it would be too 'hard'. One could imagine a reasoned examination being made of the points that could be advanced on both sides of this question, leading to some kind of common-sense resolution of the issue.

The trouble is, however, that the discussion of payments arrangements in Latin America has never reached this stage: it has thus far proceeded not in terms of *how much* automaticity could be conceded without detriment to monetary stability, but of whether any automaticity should be tolerated at all. In effect, the extreme position has prevailed that automatic access to significant amounts of credit would be undesirable, no matter what the conditions governing such credit might be, and irrespective of whether a view as restrictive as this might seriously deter the liberalization of imports.

Opposition to special payments arrangements for Latin America has been based on the assumption that any such arrangements would involve the abandonment of financial discipline and responsibility. As we have seen, however, it is possible to make such arrangements as 'hard' as one pleases. But discipline should be combined with flexibility, so that countries may gain the confidence they need to bring about radical reductions in their trade restrictions. This they will do only if they are secure in the knowledge that

M

adequate arrangements have been made to absorb the short-term effects of any consequential upsurge in imports, so that they are not forced into a corner in which they would have to choose between renewed trade restrictions and the abandonment of domestic development programmes relying upon imported goods.

The Exchange Rate Problem

In Chapter III we examined the problems that arose in Venezuela because at the existing rate of exchange virtually the only exportable commodities were petroleum and iron ore. Equally, or perhaps even more important are the strains in the system of regional trade and payments caused by persistent changes in the relative rates of increase of domestic prices and exchange rates. Differential rates of inflation in the member countries of a customs union or free-trade area tend to cause difficulties in so far as the exports of countries with slowly rising prices tend to expand faster than those of countries with rapidly advancing prices; and this leads to balance of payments surpluses for the former and deficits for the latter.

If exchange rates varied in such a way as to offset exactly inter-country differences in rates of inflation, no pressure on balances of payments would be experienced. But since exchange rates do not necessarily follow rates of inflation at all closely, relative costs and prices, expressed in any common unit of currency, may fluctuate within quite wide limits.

On the basis of some calculations of purchasing power parities by ECLA, the LAFTA Secretariat has prepared estimates of month-to-month changes in 'parity exchange rates', defined as the exchange rates that equate the internal and external purchasing power of the respective currencies.[13] These parity rates have then been compared with the actual exchange rates in force to give a measure of undervaluation or overvaluation.[14] Table V seeks to show the maximum degree of overvaluation and undervaluation ex-

---

[13] If, for example, a given bundle of goods costs 100 units of currency in country A and 200 units in country B, the parity exchange rate is defined as 1 A-unit to 2 B-units.

[14] For example, in the case referred to in the preceding footnote, if the actual exchange rate were 1 A-unit to 3 B-units, the currency of A would be regarded as overvalued. See LAFTA, *Influencia de los tipos de cambio en las corrientes comerciales entre los paises de la ALALC*, document ALALC/CAM/I/di 5, 8 May 1964.

perienced by each country listed during the four-year period from
the beginning of 1960 to the beginning of 1964. Negative signs indicate overvaluation, positive signs undervaluation: in Chile, however, the currency is shown as overvalued throughout the period,
and the entry in the second column, with a negative sign, indicates
the minimum degree of overvaluation during the period.

TABLE V

Maximum Extent of Overvaluation and Undervaluation,
1960–3

(*Percentage*)

Country*	Maximum degree of		Range
	Overvaluation	*Undervaluation*	
Brazil	−25·0	+41·4	66·4
Uruguay	−26·8	+27·0	53·8
Argentina	−19·9	+23·1	43·0
Colombia	−23·5	+12·2	35·7
Peru	−15·8	+12·0	27·8
Chile	−38·5	−10·9†	27·6
Ecuador	−14·6	+ 4·7	19·3

* In descending order of the range between the maximum degree of overvaluation and undervaluation.
† Minimum degree of overvaluation.

Source: LAFTA, *Influencia de los tipos de cambio.*

The important feature of Table V in the present context lies not
in the *absolute* figures of maximum over- and undervaluation, which
are open to serious objection, but in the range between the two
figures, shown in the third column;[15] the latter indicates the extent
to which the movement in exchange rates failed to keep pace with
the rate of increase in domestic prices—the former now running
ahead of the latter, now lagging behind.

It will be obvious how disruptive such fluctuation in the degree of

---

[15] There are serious conceptual and statistical objections to estimates of 'true'
exchange rates on the basis of purchasing power parities. For a discussion of
the general issues involved, the interested reader may refer to Paul A. Samuel-
son, 'Theoretical Notes on Trade Problems', *Review of Economics and Statistics*
(Cambridge, Mass.), xlvi/2 (May 1964) and Bela Balassa, 'The Purchasing-
Power Parity Doctrine: a Reappraisal', *Journal of Political Economy* (Univ. of
Chicago), lxxii/6 (Dec. 1964).

overvaluation or undervaluation would be of any serious attempt at the liberalization of trade within the region. The entire benefit supposed to be derived by the LAFTA countries from the application of tariff reductions by any one of them could easily be offset or more than offset by a tendency of the latter country's exchange rate to depreciate faster than its prices were rising; moreover the latter country might well be deemed to be gaining an unfair advantage for its exports at the expense of its neighbours.

EEC Views

Although fluctuations to the extent shown in Table V are not as common in other regions as in Latin America, the basic difficulty involved is by no means unknown in Western Europe. During the Italian balance of payments crisis of 1964 Karl Blessing, President of the West German Bundesbank, stated that the differential development of cost and price levels in the various EEC member countries had been causing difficulties threatening to hold up the integration process. As long as certain countries made use of 'their sovereign right to indulge in inflation', other countries were compelled to follow suit to some extent in accepting such inflation. Even reductions in customs duties might be fully or partially overridden by depreciation in the value of money. Nevertheless he asserted that the EEC is predicated on fixed exchange rates: what was needed for the economic and political integration of Europe was a revival of the type of monetary stability that had prevailed under the Pax Britannica before the First World War.[16]

What Blessing was saying here, in effect, was that under the Treaty of Rome countries had agreed to forego independent exchange rate policies. For Article 107 of the Treaty requires each member state to treat its exchange rate policy 'as a matter of common interest'; and there is provision for counter-measures by other members if devaluation by any one country is considered likely to lead to difficulties for its neighbours and distort the 'conditions of competition'.

Commenting subsequently on a report by German experts recommending a system of flexible exchange rates, the EEC Commission took the position that: 'Under the terms of the Treaty of Rome, the conditions for an internal market are to be established in the area of the Community. Flexible exchange rates between the

[16] *The Times*, 29 June 1964, p. 16.

member states are not compatible with the conditions for such an internal market.'[17]

The Commission went on to illustrate this proposition from the common agricultural policy of the Community: for example, the Council of Ministers decision of 15 December 1964 setting common prices for cereals in terms of units of account clearly precluded fluctuating exchange rates.

The Commission drew the conclusion that it would be necessary to change over from the existing system of rigid exchange rates 'to a system under which exchange rates between member states are in principle invariable, i.e. change over to a Community monetary union'.[18]

Exchange Rates in LAFTA

The Treaty of Montevideo is much less direct and categorical than the Treaty of Rome in its approach to the exchange rate problem. Article 52 states in part that: 'No Contracting Party shall promote its exports by means of subsidies or other measures likely to disrupt normal competitive conditions in the area.' Evidently exchange rate changes may in certain circumstances be regarded as coming under the heading of 'other measures'.

The main point of substance, however, is that while exchange rate adjustments may cause at least as much disturbance in LAFTA as in EEC or EFTA, it might be exceedingly difficult to introduce the idea of 'common interest' in relation to exchange rates in any concrete way. So long as divergences in price movements among Latin American countries remain as great as they were during the early years of LAFTA, a régime of fixed exchange rates is out of the question. Blessing and the Commission were able to envisage such a régime for the EEC because in their view there were methods other than exchange rate adjustments—fiscal and monetary contraction, for example—available for correcting a tendency for prices to rise too rapidly in any one EEC country. Such methods can be effective, however, only where inter-country differences in price movements are relatively small, and develop only gradually over time. The magnitude and speed of differential price movements in Latin America have been such as to leave exchange rate changes as

---

[17] *Europe: Common Market/Euratom Bulletin* (Luxembourg), 14 Jan. 1965, as cited in *International Financial News Survey* (IMF), 29 Jan. 1965.
[18] Ibid.

the only method of adjustment that could be both effective and prompt.

The lack of any simple criterion for determining the degree of overvaluation or undervaluation of a currency is also a serious obstacle to establishing the 'common interest' in exchange rate relationships. Any attempt by a group of countries to agree on a modification of the exchange rate of one of them would be likely to lead to seriously protracted discussion, in the course of which the country concerned might well be subjected to unbearable pressure on its balance of payments, especially if news of the discussion leaked out and gave rise to exchange speculation. From the latter standpoint, it is not easy to imagine a member country even of the EEC being prepared to submit to any prolonged discussion by other members of its intention to adjust its exchange rate (so long as such adjustment remains possible).

But if exchange rates can be shifted wholly or mainly at the discretion of the individual member country, without any effective means of establishing the 'common interest', what protection is there against the nullification of tariff concessions through currency devaluation, or the creation of undue advantages for exporters by the same means?

It is easy enough to say that countries should consult and seek to reach an understanding as to what their common fiscal, monetary, exchange rate, and other policies should be. But this is a counsel of perfection for the long term—such understandings will take much time to work out and implement.

Some protection no doubt lies in the fact that any country modifying its exchange rate may have to defend its action before other LAFTA members, and risk retaliation of one kind or another if such action is considered to be in violation of Article 52. But while extreme cases of excessive devaluation may be readily identified, it may be much less easy to prove moderate overdevaluation, simply because the conceptual difficulties involved in assessing what the 'true' exchange rate should be are probably insurmountable.[19]

[19] The problem of the 'true' rate is even more difficult to solve for an underdeveloped than for a developed country because the exchange rate appropriate for the bulk of primary commodity exports is not usually the same as that which would make exports of other products competitive in world markets—which may be more relevant for intra-regional trade in Latin America. See the discussion of the position of Venezuela in ch. iii.

What one may have to fall back on once again is the principle of reciprocity. Any country that manages to get an excessively large share of the benefits of the common market—as reflected in a substantially greater growth of exports than of imports—should expect to be asked to speed up the rate of liberalization of its imports. And this would apply whether the origin of the excessive benefits gained was an undue lowering of exchange rates, application of export subsidies, or any other relevant factor.

The adoption of such an indirect way out does not, of course, preclude serious efforts to reach general agreement on exchange rate policies; it does, however, recognize that indirect methods may be needed where direct methods fail.

Other Payments Problems

It will already have become apparent that important difficulties are apt to arise for LAFTA countries from the fact that the right to discriminate in trade, under the free-trade area provisions of GATT, does not carry with it the right to discriminate in payments. These difficulties may be illustrated by a minor but significant incident involving the governments of Brazil and the United States in 1962. Because of its LAFTA commitments, Brazil had decided not to extend to members of LAFTA restrictions which it had imposed on imports to protect the balance of payments. Specifically, imports originating in member countries of LAFTA were exempted from a requirement to purchase 150-day Bank of Brazil notes equivalent to a percentage of the value of desired imports.

The United States protested against this measure in notes handed to the Brazilian government in March and July 1962.[20] While the United States government recognized that Brazil's exchange restrictions were of a temporary character, and part of a stabilization programme, it nevertheless considered that measures introduced for balance of payments reasons should be applied on a non-discriminatory basis. From a United States point of view, the matter had become particularly urgent with respect to exports of sulphur, which, owing to the discriminatory requirement, were being supplanted in the Brazilian market by shipments from Mexico. The problem was resolved when, on 14 January 1963, Brazil exempted sulphur from the import deposit requirement.

[20] *Boletín Quincenal*, 10 Dec. 1962, p. 389.

If the United States interpretation of the rules of IMF and GATT is correct, as it seems to be, LAFTA countries are precluded from employing exchange restrictions in a manner which would favour their trade with one another. Thus an important weapon for encouraging intra-regional trade would be denied to them.

Moreover, this doctrine might logically be taken a step further to prevent LAFTA members in balance of payments difficulties from applying quantitative import restrictions in a manner designed to favour imports from other LAFTA countries. Such a view would, in effect, challenge Article 24 of the Treaty of Montevideo under which specific authorization by the Contracting Parties is required for a member to extend measures to protect the balance of payments so as to limit intra-zonal trade in products included in the liberalization programme. Indeed, the same article requires the Contracting Parties to try and prevent any restrictions imposed by a member because of balance of payments difficulties from affecting intra-zonal trade in liberalized products.[21]

Direct questions on this matter were addressed to the LAFTA countries during GATT's examination of the Treaty of Montevideo. If Article 24 of the Treaty were to be interpreted as meaning that measures to protect the balance of payments of LAFTA members might include discriminatory restrictions on imports from third countries, how could this be reconciled with the obligations of LAFTA members under GATT and the Article of Agreement of the International Monetary Fund? The latter instruments require that restrictive measures to protect the balance of payments should be applied in a non-discriminatory manner.

The LAFTA countries replied that they saw no conflict between Article 24 of the Treaty and the obligations assumed in GATT and the IMF, since it was of the very essence of a free-trade area to eliminate all restrictions on trade within the area.[22] While LAFTA members thus made their interpretation of the Treaty clear, it is far from obvious to what extent they would be able to act on the basis of

[21] There is a similar, albeit much vaguer, provision in the Treaty of Rome. For example Art. 108, para. 2 (*b*) envisages that in certain circumstances member countries may be authorized to protect their balances of payments by imposing quantitative restrictions on imports from third countries. Similarly Art. 109 allows that in the event of a sudden crisis in the balance of payments, a member state may provisionally take the necessary measures of safeguard, which should 'cause the least possible disturbance in the functioning of the Common Market'.

[22] See *Resoluciones (Comité)*, p. 141, Question 14, p. 173.

that interpretation in the event of strong opposition from third countries.[23]

At the same time, there are good reasons for third countries to take a constructive attitude on this matter. The Latin American countries are particularly subject to balance of payments difficulties for reasons discussed earlier—the growing structural gap between export earnings and import needs, and the vulnerability of their export commodities to price declines. If every time they run into balance of payments troubles they are to be compelled to reimpose restrictions on trade and payments with one another as well as with the rest of the world, it will become impossible for them to create the security of market access which is indispensable if entrepreneurs are to undertake new investments catering to the regional market as a whole. If third countries were to insist that Article 24 of the Treaty of Montevideo must be set aside and non-discrimination prevail, they would be gravely impeding the construction of a Latin American common market.[24]

In practice it appears that some latitude has been given to the LAFTA countries *de facto* and that no effort has been made to enforce the letter of GATT and IMF law in all cases. The IMF has reported without comment the exemptions granted by LAFTA countries to one another concerning the application of import surcharges, advance deposits, and other restrictive practices.[25]

A secondary payments problem of some importance arises from the fact that the ability of exporters in industrial countries to offer attractive credit terms gives them a big competitive advantage, frequently outweighing the margins of preference available within LAFTA. In many cases Latin American importers might prefer to pay substantially higher prices for imports from industrial countries

[23] When the United Kingdom imposed a 15% surcharge on certain imports in October 1964, it did not seek to exempt its EFTA partners from that surcharge. The government did, however, consider compensating its EFTA partners by an accelerated reduction of import duties under the Stockholm Convention. This idea, however, had to be discarded as a result of strong opposition from third countries upon whom the United Kingdom was relying for financial support. Similarly, insistence by the LAFTA countries on invoking Art. 24 of the Treaty of Montevideo at a time of balance of payments crisis might well add to their difficulties in mobilizing financial resources abroad.

[24] The gain to third countries from non-discriminatory application of import and exchange restrictions by LAFTA members would in any case be small, since intra-regional imports account for only one-tenth of total LAFTA imports.

[25] IMF, *Fifteenth Annual Report on Exchange Restrictions* (Washington, D.C., 1964).

supplied on generous terms of credit rather than buy cheaper goods in other Latin American countries for cash. It has been estimated that at the going interest rate in some Latin American countries, 12-month or 18-month credit terms at nominal cost might well compensate for a price difference of 30 per cent or more.[26]

In the light of this problem, and of the problem of Latin American export finance generally, the Inter-American Development Bank prepared a study proposing the establishment of a regional credit system for Latin America with the objective, *inter alia*, of improving the competitive position of Latin American exports *vis-à-vis* those coming from the industrially developed countries.

Under the IADB proposal, the regional system would consist of both national elements and a regional organism. The basic function of the national organs would be to arrange, directly or through the commercial banking system, finance for exporters, through the discounting of credit instruments associated with the exports of goods which, in accordance with regionally agreed criteria, would be suitable for medium-term financing. The national organ would in turn have the right to re-finance, with the regional agency, a substantial part of the credit which it had supplied to the exporter. The national organ would be a public or semi-public institution—possibly the central bank or a national foreign-trade bank, empowered to give straight guarantees in accordance with the requirements of IADB. The regional organ would establish general standards in this field, and would seek to mobilize international financial resources for its re-financing operations. The IADB subsequently decided to introduce a pilot project along these lines from the beginning of 1964. There is a clear need for substantial resources to be made available for this sort of purpose.

The preceding discussion has revealed several areas in which a careful reconsideration of orthodox financial principles and practices is urgently needed; but nowhere is this more evident than in the field of payments arrangements. Some evolution of thinking has already taken place since the Treaty of Montevideo was signed, and there appears to be support for the idea of Latin American payments arrangements on the lines of the Central American clearing house referred to in Chapter IV. Such arrangements would include machinery for intra-regional compensations, but would not provide a significant source of credit. The danger of this type of approach is

[26] Keesing and Brand, in IMF, *Staff Papers*, x/3 (Nov. 1963), p. 422.

that, while it would achieve some economies in the use of external currencies, it would not do anything to meet the need for a system of mutual credits, as discussed earlier in this chapter. It might therefore have the effect of diverting attention from the more basic issue and thereby postpone a serious reappraisal of the whole matter. At a time when radical measures to step up the pace of trade liberalization are being sought, it is important to make use of the powerful leverage that could be obtained from a regional system of mutual credits, reinforced and sustained by a central fund of financial resources along EPU lines. With such a system in being, one major source of opposition to the lowering of trade barriers would be removed, and it would be reasonable to expect LAFTA countries to go much further in trade liberalization than they have been prepared to do hitherto.

CHAPTER X

THE ROLE OF FOREIGN ENTERPRISE

Latin American Attitudes

There is a widespread view in North America and Western Europe that one of the primary purposes of any regional common market in the underdeveloped areas would be to attract foreign capital. The available evidence does not make it possible to reach firm conclusions as to how far foreign private capital has in fact responded to any expected enlargement of Latin American markets. Preliminary data do not appear to suggest a major upsurge in capital inflow into Latin America following the Treaty of Montevideo.[1] On the other hand, most of the international companies having substantial interests in Latin America are represented at LAFTA headquarters in Montevideo and are following developments there carefully. Accustomed to thinking in international terms, they appear to be much more alive to the significance of a lowering of trade barriers in the region than Latin American industrialists, most of whom have been in the habit of thinking only in terms of their own domestic markets, and who frequently lack the confidence to venture out into unknown areas beyond national frontiers. It is no doubt partly

---

[1] Total direct investment inflow (including undistributed earnings of subsidiaries) into Latin America, excluding Cuba, appears to have declined from an average annual rate of $853 m. in 1956–60 to $320 m. in 1960–2 (see ECLA, *Survey, 1963*, vol. iii (E/CN.12/696/Add.2), Table IX–26). This drop, however, was attributable to the net outflow of capital from Venezuela accompanying the virtual cessation of new investment by the petroleum companies after 1960 and the transfer of part of their reserves to their parent bodies. Excluding Venezuela as well as Cuba, the inflow averaged $543 m. in 1956–60 and $460 m. in 1960–2. This latter decline does not, however, appear to be fully consistent with the reported increase in direct investment outflow from the USA to Latin America, excluding Venezuela and Cuba, from an annual average of $289 m. in 1956–60 to $403 m. in 1960–2: if both sets of data were valid and comparable, this would imply a sharp decline in new investment in Latin America by European countries and Japan. It is not clear that such a decline has in fact taken place. The significance of these magnitudes in the Latin American setting may be judged from the fact that total gross fixed investment in Latin America in 1960 was estimated at $10 billion.

for this reason that foreign companies appear to have been much quicker to make use of complementarity agreements under the Treaty of Montevideo.

There is no doubt that foreign enterprise could play—and in some sectors is playing—an invaluable role in the development of Latin America, as of other underdeveloped regions. Foreign capital has the experience, the resources, the managerial skills, the technical knowhow, the ability to 'think big' and, indeed, to act big. It would lighten the burden of development immensely if the underdeveloped countries had abundant access to the facilities that could be made available by foreign private capital, on terms that could be regarded as satisfactory to both sides.

Why, then, is it that foreign capital has such a bad name in Latin America? How is it that a group of eminent consultants jointly appointed in 1961 by ECLA and the OAS, after making careful inquiries throughout the region, came to the conclusion that public opinion in Latin America 'has little more than a latent prejudice against foreign interests'?[2]

Why is it that Dr Placido García Reynoso, speaking for the Mexican government in May 1961, felt compelled to state that: 'Public opinion in my country is showing a profound and growing anxiety over the dangers that unrestricted foreign investment would involve for the Latin American Free Trade Association'?[3] And what accounts for the extraordinarily sharp tone of President Betancourt of Venezuela—a firm ally of the United States—in saying that: 'The United States must give up the glorification of "free enterprise" '?[4]

Similar views have been expressed by another eminent friend of the United States—Alberto Lleras Camargo, former President of Colombia, and a man of considerable influence in Latin America in no way associated with the Left or hostile to private enterprise. Lleras strongly urged that the Alliance for Progress should not take on the character of a campaign for capitalism and free enterprise.

In the shade of capitalism and free enterprise the United States has grown in power and justice. But in Latin America it has happened not infrequently that the very same system has led to the amassing of odious

---

[2] *Foreign Private Investment in the Latin American Free-Trade Area* (UN Sales No. 60.II.G.5), p. 2.
[3] *Comercio Exterior*, May 1961, p. 283. [4] *Life* (Span. ed.), 5 Sept. 1960, p. 19.

and infamous concentrations of capital and of means of production. This type of capitalism owns vast land areas—certainly the best land; it scarcely pays any taxes; it controls agricultural and industrial credit; and there is no law or power in the state that can stand against its monolithic advance.[5]

President Kennedy was among those who recognized and understood the factors that have shaped Latin American views on the part to be played by private capital in the future development of the continent. In 1958, as a Senator, he had pointed out that '[Latin Americans] resent our insisting upon a larger role for their private enterprise, which cannot cope with many of their problems, or a larger role for our private investors, who have limited their interests almost entirely to extractive industries and to only five countries (Brazil, Cuba, Mexico, Venezuela, and Chile).'[6]

It will be obvious that neither President Kennedy nor the Latin American statesmen cited above were opposed to the co-operation of private foreign capital in the economic development of Latin America—quite the contrary. If they drew attention to the difficulties that have arisen, it was not because they wanted to see the flow of foreign capital come to an end, but rather to demonstrate the need for reconsidering its role and method of functioning.

Throughout the discussion that follows, it will be taken for granted that the basic need for an expanded flow of foreign private capital to Latin America, under mutually satisfactory conditions, is not in question. For a country at an early stage of development, foreign investment may make it possible to finance urgently needed imports of machinery and equipment that could not otherwise be paid for,[7] in addition to introducing vital new growing-points for

---

[5] *Comercio Exterior*, Feb. 1963, p. 102.

[6] John F. Kennedy, *The Strategy of Peace*, ed. by Allan Nevins (N.Y., 1960), p. 139.

[7] It should not, however, be assumed that the overall balance of payments effect of foreign investment is necessarily favourable for the recipient country. For example, according to the Chairman of Imperial Chemical Industries, an examination of the direct and indirect effects of overseas investment by ICI from 1950 to 1965 established 'that receipts for the exports of equipment from the United Kingdom, for materials exported from this country for consumption in overseas plants, for technical aid, fees, royalties, and dividends and interest attributable to this investment overseas, actually exceed double the amount we have invested in these overseas undertakings. The reasons are manifold. For example, we do not in all cases put up the whole cost of the plants to be erected overseas, local capital making up the difference. In such a case there is an im-

the further expansion of the economy as a whole. If, however, the potential role of foreign private capital is to be realized, it is essential to face, fairly and squarely, the issues that have prompted the reservations quoted above.

We may note first that foreign capital generally concentrated in the past on the development of those sectors of the Latin American economy that were needed for serving the import requirements of the industrially advanced countries of Europe and North America. The bulk of foreign capital thus went into minerals, plantation agriculture, and the transport and power facilities supporting them; the object was to develop cheap exportable supplies of such commodities as sugar, bananas, non-ferrous metals, and petroleum. There was no attempt to create a balanced or rounded Latin American economy, and the growth of the export sector was not matched by corresponding progress in the domestic economy. There was, in fact, no reason to expect foreign enterprise to be interested in a balanced development of Latin America as such, except in so far as balanced development offered profitable business opportunities: for a variety of reasons, such opportunities were rather limited until comparatively recently.

Particular resentment was caused by the creation of enclaves for the extraction and shipment overseas of mineral wealth. These enclaves were, and often still are, virtually a kingdom within a kingdom, self-contained and self-sufficient. The employment provided is relatively small, and the best posts are occupied by expatriates. There is little or no dissemination of skills or techniques to the rest of the economy: the broader impact on the economy is largely confined to the payment of royalties and taxes to the government—and even here, as we shall see in a moment, such payment may fall short of the amount to which the government is entitled. As Dr Prebisch has said:

These enclaves of the past, which are still with us, must either change of themselves or give way to domestic enterprise. The days when foreign

---

mediate gain to Britain's balance of payments if the remittance to Britain for the plant erected overseas exceeds the remittance from Britain for our share of the capital cost. Again, the supply by us of materials needed by an overseas plant can in a fairly short time exceed the capital cost of that plant. There are also other indirect exports which follow a decision to erect a plant overseas, such as the supply of the product in question for a number of years until the overseas plant is in full production' (*The Times*, 2 Apr. 1965).

enterprise came in to do what Latin America could not are definitely over. We need the outside world to help us to cultivate our own ability, so that the population as a whole can be brought to share in the process of development. Thus, the foreign enterprise must be a nucleus for the dissemination of technology, as it already is in some cases.[8]

There is thus a widespread feeling in Latin America that while the help of foreign enterprise is needed for the establishment of new industries employing advanced techniques, profits that arise simply from the extraction of non-renewable natural resources should remain in Latin America. It is for reasons of this sort that some of the larger and stronger underdeveloped countries such as Brazil and Mexico have sought to curtail or eliminate the operations of the international oil companies on their territory. There is also a desire that raw materials and minerals should be processed in the countries of origin, and not shipped off to parent plants in North America or Western Europe for processing.[9]

While foreign private enterprise could not be blamed for the one-sided development of the Latin American economy, it could be and was blamed for the way in which it conducted its affairs. As Professor Alexander has pointed out, foreign companies frequently behaved as if they, and not the nation's citizens, were the sovereign power in the Latin American countries in which they operated.[10]

If a government resisted their demands, they would intrigue with opposition factions to secure its overthrow. They would bribe both government officials and private persons to do their will, and by this and other means would gain unfair advantages for themselves over local enterprise. Clarence B. Randall, president of the Inland Steel Company and former adviser to President Eisenhower, has stated that such practices still continue.[11] They are not, of course, by any means confined to foreign enterprise: local standards, established under the prevailing system of business oligarchy, are frequently no

[8] Prebisch, *Towards a Dynamic Development Policy*, p. 54.
[9] Part of the difficulty here, of course, is the fact that the industrial countries maintain relatively high tariffs on imports of processed goods, while admitting the raw commodities duty free.
[10] Robert Alexander, *Today's Latin America* (N.Y., 1962), p. 5.
[11] *NYT*, 7 Jan. 1962. The cost of bribes to some of the major international companies operating in Latin America is believed to amount to between 5 and 10% of their gross sales in the area.

better. It is simply that foreign enterprise usually has larger resources at its disposal.

A major problem for countries seeking to collect taxes from local branches or subsidiaries of international companies is to ascertain the 'true profit' gained from the operations in question. International companies may reduce or even eliminate tax liabilities to countries in which they have invested by setting artificially low export prices for local products, thereby shifting profits from firms located in the exporting countries concerned to other associated companies elsewhere. The rationale of such shifting does not necessarily arise from any desire to defraud the countries in question. If tax rates on company profits were the same all over the world, no incentive to shift profits would exist. It is because there are 'tax havens' where profits are taxed at nominal rates, or not at all, that such an incentive arises. The result is that international concerns establish holding companies in the tax haven countries, to which as large a proportion of profits as possible is transferred. The underdeveloped countries are not, of course, alone in suffering from this practice, as is indicated by the amendments introduced into the tax legislation of the United States in an effort to prevent losses of tax revenue sustained in this way.

Conflicts of Interest

Even where foreign companies behave with the utmost decorum, not seeking to acquire unfair advantages over local enterprise or escape their fair burden of taxation, serious difficulties may arise because of a conflict of interest. This is especially likely where a parent company establishes branches or subsidiaries abroad, or buys up existing productive facilities in other countries. The interests of the company as a whole may not coincide with those of any particular plant located in a given country. The production policy followed in a particular branch or subsidiary may differ considerably from the policy that would be followed if the plant or plants concerned were independently owned and controlled.

In addition, there are cases where the national policies of particular investing countries have infringed upon governmental policies in the recipient countries. A study for the Canadian-American Committee by Professor Kingman Brewster, Provost of Yale, has shown the manner in which United States law may be projected beyond its borders and affect the conduct of business in

N

Canada.[12] For example, United States anti-trust legislation favours the conduct of foreign operations through wholly owned branches: 'the less complete the U.S. parent's control, and the greater the foreign participation, the easier it may be to claim that any co-operation is a conspiracy in restraint of trade'.[13] This, together with tax advantages favouring branch operation in certain cases, may go counter to any policy in the recipient country tending to encourage substantial equity participation by the residents of that country.

Tax considerations may also deter exports of a foreign facility of a United States firm if that firm seeks to qualify for a United States tax reduction as a Western Hemisphere Trade Corporation: it will lose this advantage if substantial operations are conducted beyond the limits of the western hemisphere.

United States anti-trust legislation may extend its reach to foreign arrangements in so far as the latter affect United States imports, exports, or domestic competition. It may be argued that it is just as much in the interests of other countries as of the United States that cartel activities should be broken up. The point is, however, that anti-trust policies differ from country to country, and that, as Brewster points out, the resentment engendered by extra-territorial jurisdiction 'is a fact of international political life. It is especially acute when the intruder is a neighbor whose economic dominance is already of powerful proportions.'[14]

Finally, Brewster shows how United States policies relating to trade with such countries as China may prevail in the behaviour of United States foreign branches and subsidiaries rather than the policies of the countries in which they are situated. While there may be no conflict as regards political attitudes and policies, 'Canada's non-recognition policy [towards China] is more tentative and tempered by a willingness to permit private exchanges and trade'.[15] Thus the instances in which firms in Canada turn down orders because of the obligations of their parent companies in the United States are apt to cause resentment in Canada.

It is the possible conflict between national and foreign interests that has caused widespread misgivings about the influx of foreign investment even in a number of the developed countries such as

---

[12] Kingman Brewster, Jr, *Law and United States Business in Canada* (Washington and Montreal, Canadian American Committee Sponsored by National Planning Assoc. (USA) and Private Planning Assoc. of Canada, 1960).
[13] Ibid. p. 7.   [14] Ibid. p. 22.   [15] Ibid. p. 26.

Australia, New Zealand, Britain, France, and Western Germany—in addition to Canada. In Canada, the Royal Commission on Canada's Economic Prospects noted that:

> In the course of the Commission's hearings, concern was expressed over the extent to which our productive resources are controlled by non-residents, mostly Americans. Many Canadians are worried about such a large degree of economic decision-making being in the hands of non-residents or in the hands of Canadian companies controlled by non-residents. This concern has arisen because of the concentration of foreign ownership in certain industries, because of the fact that most of it is centered in one country, the United States, and because most of it is in the form of equities which, in the ordinary course of events, are never likely to be repatriated.[16]

In September 1964 the Government of Canada introduced a bill into Parliament that would restrict future foreign ownership of Canadian banks and insurance companies to a maximum ceiling of 25 per cent.[17]

For similar reasons, legislation was presented in New Zealand in 1964 which, while seeking to promote overseas investment in that country, would avoid the danger of 'economic colonization'. At a manufacturers' conference at Auckland in 1960, many speakers had expressed views about the dangers that New Zealand faced if it opened its doors to unrestricted overseas capital investment. To meet these fears the Finance Minister announced that new taxes would be imposed on income from foreign investment and that the government would set up a new authority with wide powers over foreign investment and take-over bids. There were bound to be enterprises, he said, where retention of New Zealand control over domestic concerns was more likely to serve the public interest.[18]

Foreign ownership of a country's industries may have a particularly important effect on the export capacity of those industries—quite apart from the special factors noted above in the case of United States companies. In many cases companies with worldwide interests set up facilities in underdeveloped countries that are intended to cater to the home market only: exports may be virtually prohibited so as not to encroach upon the sales of the parent company, or of other associated companies.

[16] Canada. Royal Commission on Canada's Economic Prospects, *Final Report*, *November 1957* (Ottawa, 1958), pp. 389–90.
[17] *NYT*, 24 Sept. 1964, p. 57.   [18] *The Times*, 10 July 1964.

International companies may also buy up existing facilities with the same objective in view. British car sales to the United States used to be dominated by Ford of Britain and by Vauxhall. In 1960 the Ford Motor Company of the United States bought out all other shareholders in Ford of Britain. This was followed by a sharp decline in the range and number of British-made Ford cars imported into the United States. Similarly, British-made Vauxhall cars are no longer marketed in the United States: instead, General Motors imports the West German Opel.[19]

It is probable, moreover, that the exports of British Ford and Vauxhall to third markets are likewise determined by the overall policies and interests of the parent companies in the United States, taking into account their various holdings in other European countries—and not simply by the interests of Britain.

Similar considerations prompted France to try to persuade the EEC to examine the possibility and desirability of imposing some limitation on foreign investment in the Community. In France itself restrictions on foreign investment were tightened early in 1965, particularly in cases involving the acquisition of French companies.[20] Even in Western Germany, perhaps the strongest supporter of the free movement of capital, anxiety about United States investment was sufficiently widespread for Dr Hermann J. Abs of the Deutsche Bank to propose the creation of a records centre for foreign investment.[21]

It should not be taken for granted, of course, that the interests of an international company, taken as a whole, will invariably lead to priority being accorded to the output of the parent company, at the expense of branches or subsidiaries. There is, for example, a strong impression in the United States that in many cases the operations of affiliated companies overseas have led to a curtailment in the export sales of parent companies, and this is believed to have been a contributing factor in the balance of payments problem of the United States. The fundamental point at issue, however, is not the manner in which international companies have taken specific decisions in specific cases. What is involved is the underlying point of principle as to whether decisions affecting output and employment in a particular country should be taken by an international company on the basis of considerations that go beyond the interests of that country.

[19] *The Times*, 17 Apr. 1964.　　[20] Ibid. 22 Jan. 1965.
[21] *The Economist*, 13 Feb. 1965, p. 710.

It does appear that Latin American governments are less inclined than formerly to permit foreign ownership and control of strategic sectors of the economy, and this may have been a factor in inducing them to enter business enterprise themselves. In his study for the National Planning Association entitled *The Development of Latin American Private Enterprise*, Frank Brandenburg found that the government's share of ownership in the thirty largest companies in each of six Latin American countries was 62·4 per cent, on the average, while the share of domestic private capital was 21·2 per cent, and of foreign private capital 16·4 per cent.[22]

These proportions are impressive, though not, perhaps, quite as remarkable as they may appear at first sight. Almost all of the enterprises wholly or mainly owned by the governments of the six Latin American countries analysed are to be found in the fields of banking, utilities, or mineral extraction. Such enterprises are often publicly owned in Western European countries as well. If these types of business operation are excluded, virtually the whole of the remainder (including smaller establishments) are owned by private enterprise, domestic or foreign. Indeed it is estimated that of the *total* volume of economic activity in Latin America 70 per cent is in private hands, while 30 per cent is controlled by governments. Thus the scope for private enterprise, especially in manufacturing industry, remains immense.

The Political Dilemma

It would be misleading to deduce from the foregoing that the somewhat uneven record of private capital in the past development of Latin America can necessarily be projected into the future. Just as private capital has come to take a more enlightened view of its relationship with labour in the industrially advanced countries than it did before the Second World War, so also are there many business men, big and small, who now see the economic development of Latin America, as well as Africa and Asia, in broader and more responsible terms than in the past.

Even so, and with the best will in the world, such men find themselves faced by a basic dilemma. For private capital investment in developing countries depends not only upon prospective profit opportunities, but also upon safety and security. In January 1963 a report entitled *Proposals to Improve the Flow of U.S. Private*

[22] For detail by countries, see Table XII, p. 224.

Investment to Latin America was presented to the United States government by the Commerce Committee for the Alliance for Progress (known as COMAP), a group of twenty-five prominent business men under the chairmanship of Mr J. Peter Grace. The report pointed out that: 'Latin America is a continent in political and social ferment and this is just as truly a deterrent to private investment as are the purely economic and financial obstacles.'[23]

It is not in the least improper or unnatural that private investors should seek a certain minimum of security for their resources, or that they should see in 'political and social ferment' a potential menace to their holdings. As the COMAP report indicates, investors are bound to be concerned at the possibility of 'massive expropriations', of 'the creeping erosion of investment values through the effect of plunging currency depreciation on working capital', and of 'socialistic solutions of economic problems'.[24]

But Latin America is struggling to free itself from the stranglehold of traditional social and political forces that are hostile to progress and enterprise of any kind, whether private or public. There is a growing recognition that economic development in Latin America is indissociably linked to political and social change—this, indeed, was one of the assumptions underlying President Kennedy's original concept of the Alliance for Progress. As he pointed out:

Now, as never before, hundreds of millions of men and women—who had formerly believed that stoic resignation in the face of hunger and disease and darkness was the best one could do—have come alive with a new sense that the means are at hand with which to make for themselves a better life.

If the title deeds of history applied, it is we, the American people, who should be marching at the head of this world-wide revolution, counseling it, helping it to come to a healthy fruition. For whenever a local patriot emerges in Asia, the Middle East, Africa, or Latin America to give form and focus to the forces of ferment, he most often quotes the great watchwords we once proclaimed to the world: the watchwords of personal and national liberty, of the natural equality of all souls, of the dignity of labor, of economic development broadly shared.[25]

Now political change cannot be engineered with the same precision as the production of a transistor radio. Nowhere in the world

[23] Commerce Committee for the Alliance for Progress, *Proposals to Improve the Flow of U.S. Private Investment to Latin America* (US Dept. of Commerce, 1963), p. 4.
[24] Ibid. p. 4. [25] Kennedy, *Strategy of Peace*, pp. 5–6.

have major transformations in the structure of government and society been brought about without 'political and social ferment'.

And it is in the very nature of such ferment that it brings together people of widely differing opinions, ranging from Right to Left, who co-operate for the achievement of immediate political objectives without necessarily stopping to iron out their differences on long-run goals. It is inevitable, therefore, that there should be what COMAP calls 'socialistic' elements in such movements alongside more conventional ideas.

It is a remarkable feature of the COMAP report that nowhere is the need for political and social change in Latin America even mentioned, let alone considered. Indeed, the report notes that the younger business leaders of Latin America are puzzled by what they regard as a tendency 'to export socialistic ideas to Latin America'.[26] It may come as a surprise to some to learn that Latin American business leaders are worried about the importation of 'socialistic ideas' from the United States. The only sense that can be made of this strange phenomenon is that they fear that, in supporting ideas of political change and social reform, the United States may have been making common cause with forces in Latin America that do not necessarily have the interests of private enterprise at heart.

Particularly striking is COMAP's finding that there was uncertainty in Latin America regarding the significance of Alliance for Progress policies with regard to land reform and tax reform; and that this uncertainty might well be discouraging to foreign investors and to local private enterprise.[27] COMAP therefore seems to have been inclined to favour some modification or playing down of the reform issue; it argued, for example, that 'in many instances the call for tax reform in Latin America is more truly a call for more efficient and modern tax administration and collection'.[28]

It is not that private enterprise is necessarily against land reform or tax reform. Most private entrepreneurs of the younger school probably recognize that the political and economic power of the old-style landlords must be broken or at least greatly reduced if Latin America is to move ahead. Nor are they against tax reform: those of them that do pay their fair share of taxes in Latin America are aware that the burden falls more heavily upon them because of the many who escape.

But their sympathies are divided because of a realization that

[26] COMAP report, p. 9.   [27] Ibid. pp. 11–12.   [28] Ibid. p. 12.

among those who shout loudest for land reform and tax reform there
are many who are not particularly friendly to private capital—and
especially to foreign private capital.

And thereby hangs the dilemma facing the Alliance for Progress
and any similar movement that seeks to harness social reform and
private enterprise side by side. Granted that no one can foresee the
precise form that radical movements will take, or the goals that they
will ultimately seek, should one take the risk of supporting them, in
the knowledge that the resulting 'political and social ferment' may
be a powerful deterrent to private enterprise? Or should one play
safe, preferring the security of the *status quo* to the uncertainties of
political change, in the knowledge that the climate of social stagnation and decay will, if it persists, in the long run stifle private
initiative no less?

If there is a solution to this dilemma, it has not yet been found;
and it is because men like Betancourt and Lleras Camargo fear the
consequences of treating social reform and private enterprise as
though they were equally important objectives that they have so
emphatically counselled caution in this vital area of the politics of
economic development in Latin America.

Foreign Capital and the Economies of Scale

It is frequently taken for granted that foreign enterprise, accustomed to large-scale operations, would take advantage of every
opportunity to establish plants of optimum size in the underdeveloped countries; and that their incentive to do so would be
much greater if they could count on free access to region-wide
markets such as those of the LAFTA countries.

As we saw in Chapter II the fragmentation of Latin American
industries into an excessive number of units, all operating below
optimum capacity, has usually been attributed to the economic isolation of the twenty republics, each one trying to be self-sufficient
and maintaining high tariffs or other restrictions against its
neighbours.

But however valid this reasoning may be in explaining the
duplication of capacity from country to country, or in the region as a
whole, it cannot throw any light on the extensive duplication of
capacity *within individual countries*, where the market for industrial
products is not divided up by tariffs or other restrictions.

We have already referred to the multiplication of automobile

plants in Argentina and Brazil to an extent far beyond their needs.
While the governments of these and other Latin American producing countries must shoulder much of the responsibility for the
chaotic state of the industry, there is no doubt that the automobile
firms themselves deliberately built up capacity in each individual
country in the certain knowledge that since others were doing the
same, the rate of utilization would be extremely low and hence costs
very high. The excessive cost of operations would in turn make it
necessary to maintain a high level of protection, open or concealed,
and the industry would be dragged into the well-known vicious
circle of low output, high costs, and inflated protection.

There appears, in fact, to be an unwritten law among at any rate
some of the major international companies that they should seek to
acquire a stake in all the larger primary-producing countries that
would roughly reflect their general position in world markets. It is
not merely a question of prestige for them, but of safeguarding sales
and profits. If, as country after country in the underdeveloped world
began to go in for the manufacture of automobiles, only General
Motors were to establish a plant in each of them, on the grounds
that one such plant could produce all their needs, obviously the sales
of other companies would very soon be adversely affected. This the
latter try to avoid by setting up their own new plants in underdeveloped countries, in the hope of sharing whatever profits can be
made there with the aid of extensive protection of one kind or
another.

It is noteworthy that the multiplication of excess capacity by
foreign enterprise has been characteristic not only of underdeveloped countries, but of such countries as Canada. For example, Professor English has pointed out that in the early days of the production of television sets in Canada, virtually every significant American manufacturer established a Canadian branch, some twenty in
all, in total neglect of market prospects in relation to economies of
scale. English concludes that 'the existence of foreign, especially
American, ownership makes possible a structure of Canadian industry which involves, paradoxically, the duplication of under-
sized production facilities and therefore an important misuse of
resources'.[29]

It cannot therefore be taken for granted, as it usually is, that free

[29] 'The Pervasive Effects of Government Policy', in T. N. Brewis and others,
Canadian Economic Policy (Toronto, 1961), pp. 24–25.

market forces would spontaneously ensure the achievement of the economies of scale and specialization if only Latin American governments would arrange for private enterprise to have unrestricted access to the whole of the Latin American market. If free market forces are unable to prevent the duplication of capacity within a single country, they may be equally unable to do so within a customs union or free-trade area.

Problems of Incentives and Location

We have already referred to the work of the group of consultants appointed by ECLA and OAS in 1961 to inquire into the problems likely to arise in the field of foreign investment as a result of the establishment of LAFTA. The group found that during the discussions that had preceded the signing of the Treaty of Montevideo, fears had been expressed in many quarters on two important points: first, that the creation of a free-trade area might result in the member governments being drawn into a competitive race to attract foreign capital through the granting of special incentives which, in the long run, would not only result in serious revenue losses to the governments concerned, but might lead to the uneconomic location of industries, with consequent adverse effects on productivity. Secondly, there was widespread concern in industrial circles that the market expansion resulting from the creation of a free-trade area would lead to severe and damaging competition from new and modern plants set up by powerful foreign interests.[30]

As regards the question of incentives, it must be borne in mind that while the establishment of LAFTA has no doubt given the matter additional urgency, the problem antedated the Treaty of Montevideo. Underdeveloped countries anxious to interest foreign capital in the development of domestic resources have frequently been prepared to give lavish incentives, ranging from tax holidays of five years and upwards to special privileges for duty-free imports of plant, equipment, and raw materials. In many cases foreign enterprise has been given even more favourable treatment than domestic —to the obvious detriment of the latter. Moreover, foreign companies have frequently taken advantage of the situation to play one country off against another so as to increase the incentive benefits obtained. In this process, much revenue has been lost to the countries concerned, often over a long period of years.

[30] *Foreign Private Investment*, p. 1.

There are no doubt many cases in which incentive systems have brought about the results desired. But it is not always the countries that provide the largest incentives that receive the greatest inflows of foreign capital. During the ten-year period from 1951 to 1960, Argentina, Brazil, and Mexico obtained 70 per cent of the inflow of direct investment into all Latin American countries other than Cuba and Venezuela,[31] and it cannot be said that these three countries were the most liberal in their treatment of foreign investment.

Private entrepreneurs are likely to determine the location of new enterprises primarily on the basis of such factors as availability of labour, power, raw materials, and transport facilities, and access to markets. Only where these factors are fairly evenly balanced as between two possible locations would government-provided incentives normally be decisive in settling the outcome. The ECLA/OAS consultants found that in the case of Brazil, for example, success in attracting capital to particular incentive areas had been rather limited, whereas capital flows into the southern States had been substantial despite tax and other obstacles: this was because of the much more favourable economic conditions in the south.[32]

This is a conclusion of considerable importance for the less developed countries in LAFTA. Unable to provide facilities for production as advantageous as those available in the more developed countries, they are not likely to attract much industry simply by using special incentive systems, as they are entitled to do under Article 32 of the Treaty of Montevideo. A study for United States business men by Business International has suggested that since 'the most important factor in locating a plant is nearness to the buyers and the suppliers', the most promising sites for new industries to be established by foreign firms would be 'the Buenos Aires–Montevideo–São Paulo–Rio de Janeiro complex, and the Mexico–Colombia arc'.[33]

Direct action to attract enterprise to less obviously attractive areas may therefore often be necessary in many cases, within the framework of concerted regional planning, as discussed in Chapter VIII. And where private enterprise will not accept the risks of investing in countries like Ecuador and Paraguay, even when it knows

[31] ECLA, *External Financing in the Economic Development of Latin America* (E/CN.12/649, Apr. 1963), Table III.
[32] *Foreign Private Investment*, p. 7.
[33] Business International, *Latin America's Merging Market*, p. 33.

that the regional plan has allocated certain industries to these countries and these alone, it may be essential for public enterprises to be set up to do the job. Moreover, other countries should not, at the very least, use incentive systems to try and thwart the accepted regional plan for allocation of industries; on the contrary, it would be desirable for them to prohibit the establishment of competitive facilities, at any rate during an initial period. This would imply, in effect, the adoption of some agreed distribution of industry policy, perhaps along the lines of the system of integration industries originally worked out in Central America but subsequently allowed to fall into disuse, as described in Chapter IV.

The LAFTA countries are, however, no closer to the adoption of such a system than the Central American countries. Indeed, great difficulties have been encountered even in securing a common code for the treatment of private foreign capital in the LAFTA area. The ECLA/OAS consultants found in 1960 that the wide variety of policies and attitudes among the countries forming LAFTA, and the possibility of strong competition for United States private capital from Europe and Africa, made it extremely difficult to draft a common code which would be liberal enough to satisfy the needs of some countries and restrictive enough to meet the views of others.[34] A report to the first session of the Advisory Committee on Monetary Questions, held in May 1964, showed the situation to be unchanged in this respect. As the report pointed out, countries inclined to adopt restrictive policies towards foreign investment would be likely to accuse the more liberal member countries of stimulating unfair competition; while the latter would no doubt retort that there was nothing to prevent the former from taking the same steps to encourage the inflow of foreign capital as they themselves had done.[35]

The Impact on Domestic Enterprise

There is also not much indication of a willingness on the part of LAFTA countries to take concerted action to prevent foreign capital from damaging or inhibiting domestic enterprise. The sort of situation that may develop has been described in the report to the Advisory Committee on Monetary Questions mentioned above.

[34] *Foreign Private Investment*, p. 7.
[35] *Armonización de los tratamientos aplicados a las inversiones privadas extranjeras en los países de la ALALC;* see *Tres años*, p. 32.

The report suggests that a good deal of foreign capital will no doubt flow into types of production not now undertaken in the region: while this would limit the possibilities of friction between domestic and foreign capital, it would not remove the need for a harmonization of the policies of LAFTA members, if only so as to avoid the uneconomic location of new enterprises.

Mention was made earlier of the potentially strategic importance of complementarity agreements as a means of industrial planning on a region-wide basis, and as a first step towards more generalized regional planning. But it was foreign rather than domestic private enterprise that was the first to seize the opportunities offered. Up to the end of 1964 complementarity agreements had been negotiated on only two products—data processing machines and electronic valves: Latin American output of these is almost entirely in the hands of foreign-owned companies.[36] Likewise the pressure for a complementarity agreement in the automobile industry (including the proposed discouragement of new plants) would, if successful, lead to a consolidation of the position of foreign-owned enterprises.

The fact that thus far only foreign companies have managed to benefit from complementarity agreements does not, of course, mean that Latin American companies could not have made similar use of this instrument for their own ends: if they have not done so, they have only themselves to blame.

Of greater immediate (though not necessarily long-term) concern is the situation in industries where domestic requirements are currently satisfied from domestic production, and the respective countries seek to have the products of such industries included in the Common Schedule. The danger here is that the resulting guaranteed access to a region-wide market would prompt other member countries to offer special concessions to foreign enterprise to come in and take over the market. The danger may be particularly great where existing indigenous industries were originally set up some time ago, and have fallen behind in technique or quality. While action is no doubt required to stimulate greater efficiency in such industries, it would not be in the general interest to allow foreign enterprise to come in without further ado. As noted earlier, the problem in Latin America is to create new factory capacity and new employment—not to destroy that which already exists. The virtues

[36] See ch. viii.

of competition cannot be evaluated in the same way in an under-developed region such as Latin America as in a developed region such as North America or Western Europe.

There are, of course, many cases in which Latin American companies are completely lacking in enterprise, and are content to operate in a restrictionist and oligarchic environment where the needs of the consumer can be almost totally neglected, because of extremely high tariffs or prohibitions on imported goods. Where this is the case, and where companies show no sign of being prepared to plough back profits for the improvement of efficiency and for investment in new plant and equipment, governments may have to contemplate a graduated series of steps ranging from persuasion and exhortation to sharp reductions in import duties. In some obviously intractable cases, it may be considered desirable to welcome foreign enterprise into the industry, but obviously this is an extreme measure; on the whole, in a situation of overall shortage of productive capacity, it is better that foreign resources should have the effect of supplementing domestic capacity rather than of competing with it. This would also tend to minimize friction between domestic and foreign capital.

The report to the Advisory Committee on Monetary Questions notes further that there seems to be no chance at present that LAFTA members would agree on the sectors from which foreign capital should be excluded in all countries: interests vary from country to country, depending on whether domestic enterprise has already established itself in a particular industry, or whether a country had hoped to attract foreign enterprise with the prospect of access to a region-wide market. The only immediate possibility, apparently, is that countries might undertake not to introduce new incentives to foreign enterprise in those industries whose products are included in the Common Schedule. An alternative suggestion made is that countries should agree not to introduce new incentives more far-reaching than those already available in the countries that go furthest in this respect.[37]

One possible solution frequently advocated in dealing with the problem of conflict between foreign and domestic enterprise is the establishment of joint ventures, preferably with foreign holdings in the minority. It appears that there have been a growing number of joint ventures in Latin America in recent years: a compilation pub-

[37] See ch. viii.

lished in Brazil in 1958 listed 1,496 such enterprises.[38] These enterprises accounted for somewhat more than 20 per cent of total direct foreign investment in Brazil. In Mexico 11 per cent of all new direct foreign investments during 1950–7 were in joint ventures. An overwhelming proportion of such investments (94 per cent in the case of Mexico) were in firms in which foreign interests had majority control.[39]

It appears that while joint ventures are growing in importance, they still account for only a fraction of total foreign investment; and that, within this fraction, the proportion of domestic participation remains extremely low. This is not surprising, since it is not difficult to understand the desire of foreign investors to retain control over their capital. The very factors that prompt governments in underdeveloped countries to favour joint ventures with majority domestic control are likely to be viewed with misgivings by the foreign investor. For what is the primary need for majority domestic control, if not to ensure that domestic interests shall, in case of conflict, prevail over foreign interests?[40] But it is precisely this that the foreign investor must, in the nature of things, seek to avoid.[41]

To sum up the discussion thus far, if the Latin American countries could concert their policies with respect to foreign investment, they could probably make very effective use of the capital resources and skills that foreign enterprise is introducing and will introduce into the area. Their inability thus far to achieve such common policies exposes them to serious difficulties and dangers in relation to foreign capital. For one thing, the mere fact that the treatment of foreign capital varies from country to country gives foreign enterprise many opportunities for gaining special advantages in particular countries—to the detriment of the region as a whole.

Even more important, however, is the fact that, in the absence of a firm regional policy of the LAFTA countries themselves, some of the most profitable business opportunities may be seized by foreign rather than domestic enterprise, and, in some cases, even existing

[38] José Garrido Torres and Denio Nogueira, *Joint International Business Ventures in Brazil* (N.Y., 1959).

[39] George Kalmanoff and Benjamin Retchkiman, *Joint International Business Ventures in Mexico* (N.Y., 1959), p. 29.

[40] There may, of course, be other reasons for preferring majority domestic control, such as the reduction in the proportion of profits remitted abroad. But such reasons are of secondary significance.

[41] Mention was made earlier in this chapter of special factors militating against United States participation in joint ventures.

Latin American industries may be endangered. This would be a serious matter for the Latin American economy, even if one were sure that foreign enterprise was in all cases going to operate with the greatest possible efficiency and at the lowest possible level of costs that existing conditions and the size of the regional market made possible. In fact, however, foreign enterprise has shown a tendency in some cases to establish redundant capacity and operate suboptimal facilities even within single countries; and the resulting inefficiency may occasionally be compounded by the unwillingness of parent companies to permit exports from Latin American countries, for fear of encroaching upon parent sales.

For all these reasons it will be apparent that the effective utilization of foreign capital can be ensured only through co-operation with domestic public and private capital. And this in turn can be undertaken satisfactorily only within the framework that would be provided by regional investment plans for the principal Latin American industries, representing a synthesis and harmonization of all the respective national industrial plans. By planning co-operation with foreign enterprise, the LAFTA countries can ensure that while foreign capital achieves reasonable security and a fair return, the main gains from regional integration stay within the region, and help to provide resources for still further expansion.

This presupposes a greater measure of regional solidarity and sense of common purpose than has emerged thus far. Inter-country differences in the treatment of foreign capital are not simply a matter of ideology, although this has some bearing. Nor are they entirely a question of the comparative strength of domestic industrial enterprise in the various countries—although obviously the fact that domestic industry is relatively more powerful in Argentina, Brazil, and Mexico than in some of the other countries has a major influence on the attitudes of these countries towards foreign capital. If the task of harmonizing policies towards foreign enterprise is to be tackled successfully by the LAFTA countries, they will need to become more conscious than they are now of the relationship between their own individual national interests and those of the LAFTA area generally; and there will need to be a recognition that the case for allowing foreign capital into a particular sector of the economy of a country cannot be judged in terms of the interests of that country alone, but only in terms that give due weight to the interests of other LAFTA countries and of the region as a whole. By the same token, the smaller LAFTA countries cannot be expected to resist foreign offers to set up industries in competition with those of Argentina, Brazil, and Mexico, unless the latter show themselves ready to fall in with the principle of reciprocity, as discussed above, and to assist in the establishment of new industries in the smaller or less developed countries.

A Latin American Development Corporation

Many of the Latin American countries have established national development corporations or development banks that engage in the promotion of developmental enterprise and provide financial, technical, and other resources to this end. Such banks and corporations may be particularly helpful in overcoming the competitive disadvantages facing Latin American enterprise by virtue of the overwhelmingly superior financial resources and technical and managerial skills available to the big international companies.

By analogy, it has been suggested that a Latin American Development Corporation is needed to deal with the problems that are arising in the field of integration. According to Dr Prebisch, such a corporation should give systematic support to Latin American enterprise in three main areas: searching out opportunities for cooperation and specialization through complementarity agreements; developing export industries, especially in the less developed countries and in countries not benefiting from an adequate growth of their exports under the Treaty; and in facilitating adjustments, including redeployment of labour, made necessary by growing intraregional competition.[42]

Strong support for the idea of a 'promotion mechanism' was also voiced by a Committee of Experts convened by the OAS in preparation for the Punta del Este Conference. The committee called for an intensive programme of investment promotion involving a direct search for the new investment opportunities that would arise from the integration of markets. It considered that efforts should also be made to train local entrepreneurs and technicians so that they could compete on terms of equality with foreign private enterprise.

While much help could be given by existing institutions, including the Inter-American Development Bank, the committee saw a

---

[42] Raúl Prebisch, 'El Mercado común constituye una de las grandes reformas estructurales de América Latina', *Revista de Ciências Econômicas* (São Paulo), June 1962.

o

need for 'an institutional mechanism' that would give its exclusive attention to the preparation of projects of multi-national interest. Such projects would include:

(a) Infrastructure investments related to two or more countries;

(b) Establishment of new industries for supplying integrated markets, including the channelling of technical assistance to Latin American entrepreneurs;

(c) Transformation of existing industries with a view to their expansion, modernization or change of production structure, with a view to equipping them to meet the effects of new competition arising from the reduction of trade restrictions;

(d) Location in more than one country of the production of the various elements of complex industries;

(e) Increase or diversification of agricultural production for supplying the regional market by means of a more effective use of resources, according to the principle of comparative advantage,[43] and

(f) Utilization of natural resources from adjacent areas in two or more countries.[44]

The fact that nothing has so far been done about these ideas reflects the general inadequacy of the forward momentum of LAFTA and particularly the failure to see that for Latin America reductions in trade barriers are only a part—possibly not even the most important part—of a programme of regional economic co-operation and development.

---

[43] The committee was a little less careful than usual in thus suggesting that the principle of comparative advantage is directly applicable to what is, to a very considerable extent, a subsistence economy. Undoubtedly, however, regional integration could, under favourable conditions, lead to 'a more effective use of resources' in Latin American agriculture.

[44] OAS, *Latin American Economic Integration*, pp. 21–23.

CHAPTER XI

INSTITUTIONAL REQUIREMENTS

Weaknesses of LAFTA Institutions

The institutions created by the Treaty of Montevideo were never intended to provide a dynamic centre of decision-making for the LAFTA area as a whole on problems of economic integration. Yet the joint planning and joint development activities envisaged in the preceding chapters would appear to require much more powerful central institutions than those established by the Treaty.

The Montevideo Treaty institutions carry far less weight than the corresponding institutions of the EEC, and do not have the level or stature they would need to press effectively for inter-governmental agreement on common plans and policies. The Standing Executive Committee of LAFTA, for example, does not have the power of decision and action that the Council of Ministers of the EEC has. Nor can the Secretariat of LAFTA be compared in strength, prestige, or influence with the EEC Commission. The central organs of LAFTA, as established under the Montevideo Treaty, have much more in common with those of EFTA than with those of the EEC. The analogy is a significant one. EFTA is primarily a mutual tariff-cutting association, whereas EEC has the much more far-reaching objectives of economic and ultimately political integration. LAFTA institutions, like those of EFTA, were originally conceived as simply watching over the reduction of trade barriers.

It was not long, however, before countries began to realize that tariff-cutting would not take Latin America very far. The need for harmonizing the economic policies of LAFTA members and for jointly planning the integrated development of the LAFTA area became increasingly evident.[1] With it came the recognition that if governments were to agree on significant adjustments to national policies and programmes in the interests of regional integration, the issues would have to be explored carefully at the working level, and then presented for decision at the highest political level. The diffi-

[1] See discussions of the Common Schedule in ch. v.

culty about the early evolution of LAFTA institutions was that
while abundant provision was made for examination of problems
at the working level, the means for translating any conclusions
reached into action were totally inadequate.

Industrial and Functional Groups

An extraordinary number and variety of meetings were convened
during the early years of LAFTA to discuss integration questions.
While the practical significance of all these meetings is not easy to
evaluate, there can be no doubt of the beneficial effect of the many
personal, professional, business, and official contacts that have been
established across national frontiers. It must be remembered that,
traditionally, the Latin American countries have had much closer
relations with North America and Western Europe than with one
another. One should not underestimate the barrier to regional co-
operation that results quite simply from lack of familiarity of the
Latin American peoples with one another.

Meetings under LAFTA auspices at the working level may be
broadly classified into those exploring the possibilities of co-
ordinated development in specific industries, and those concerned
with certain types of integration problems. Among the former are
groups dealing with the following industries: agricultural machinery; automobiles and parts; chemicals; construction equipment;
electrical equipment; electronic equipment; engineering products;
food products; iron and steel; machine tools; mining machinery;
paper and pulp; printing machinery; railway equipment; refrigera-
tor equipment; rubber products; shipping; textile machinery;
textiles; wood products.

The groups dealing with the above sectors of Latin American
industry are usually composed of representatives of governments
and of the industries concerned. In addition, however, many meetings have been organized by private enterprise alone, and an
Association of Latin American Industrialists coordinates business
interests in dealing with problems of regional integration in Latin
America.

Despite the tremendous amount of activity indicated by the
many meetings of all these various industrial groups, concrete
results were rather meagre in the early stages. Little was achieved
by way of coordination of industrial plans or policies, and agreements on a rational division of labour in agriculture and industry

were, with certain minor exceptions, conspicuous by their absence. In so far as the meetings of industry representatives have achieved anything at all, their effect has been largely to ratify the *status quo*. Little progress has been made in planning industrial growth, taking into account the needs and resources of the Latin American continent as a whole. As we have seen, countries are still creating new industrial capacity without any regard to the capacities that already exist elsewhere in the region or to the opportunities for specialization and exchange.

Alongside the industrial groups, the Standing Executive Committee of LAFTA initially set up permanent Advisory Committees of government experts to consider problems in the following fields: statistics; transport; definition of origin; industrial development; customs questions; customs nomenclature;[2] monetary questions; agricultural questions.

At their fourth session in 1964, the LAFTA countries began to strengthen this machinery by establishing a permanent Council on Financial and Monetary Policy, composed of presidents of central banks and similar institutions: the Advisory Committee on Monetary Questions was henceforward to report to this council and assist it in its work. At the same session the Standing Executive Committee was given authority to set up similar high-level Councils for Commercial Policy,[3] Agricultural Policy, Industrial Development, and Transport and Communications.

This effort to raise the level at which inter-country examination of LAFTA problems was taking place reflected a partial recognition of the inadequacy of the institutional arrangements that had been made under the Treaty of Montevideo. While the various committees listed above had been doing a certain amount of useful technical work, a serious shortcoming was that the results of their labours were not being regularly examined at a high enough level to stimulate prompt and effective action. Indeed, there was no machinery within LAFTA carrying sufficient weight with the national governments on a continuing basis. The result was a growing log-jam of undecided issues and paralysis of action within LAFTA.

[2] The Advisory Committee on Customs Nomenclature is a subsidiary organ of the Advisory Committee on Customs Questions.

[3] It was also recommended that an Advisory Committee on Commercial Policy should be created, taking over the functions of the existing Advisory Committee on Customs Questions (see *Resoluciones*, 101 (IV)).

Strengthening LAFTA Machinery

There is therefore a need for a considerable strengthening of the Standing Executive Committee of LAFTA, which may have to meet at ministerial level at frequent intervals: this would be tantamount to the establishment of a governing Council of Ministers along the lines of the EEC. Governments would thus be made more aware of the effect of their national policies upon other member countries, and would be compelled to examine more seriously, and at a higher level, the problems of policy coordination and joint planning. This in turn would no doubt enhance the effectiveness of, and lend added importance to, the various advisory and industrial bodies operating under the direction of the Executive Committee.

Raising the level of the Standing Executive Committee would have immediate consequences for the Secretariat, which would have to assume correspondingly greater responsibilities. It has even been suggested that an organ analogous to the EEC Commission should be created. It would thus consist of outstanding men nominated by the member governments, but enjoying a large measure of independence by virtue of being collectively responsible to the member countries as a whole rather than individually to their respective governments. The advantage of such an organ, endowed with a substantial freedom of action, is that it could exercise dynamic leadership without having to be unduly concerned about the vested interests in each country, as any body of ministers or government representatives is bound to be.

The Supranational Approach

How well prepared are the Latin American countries for the possible supranational implications of institutional proposals such as these? It would seem that there has been much less concrete consideration of the need for supranational institutions in Latin America than in Western Europe—and even the EEC countries have not all accepted the idea that the Community institutions have a supranational character.

Yet influential voices have been raised in Latin America in support of the supranational approach. On 6 January 1965 the President of Chile, Eduardo Frei, wrote a letter[4] expressing the view

[4] For the full text, see below, pp. 279–84.

... that the time has come to create an efficacious set of institutions capable of spurring on the formation of the Latin American common market.... At this very moment, in international conferences and parliaments convened by the countries of other continents which have set significant examples in this respect, it is the Governments, through their highest representatives, that are daily committing themselves to undertake the tasks entailed, because there is no other possible way of carrying them out.... [The institutional machinery] of the Montevideo Treaty has manifestly proved insufficient and inadequate. The object-lessons afforded by other similar processes show us how necessary it is that such institutions should incorporate certain supra-national elements.

Strong support for the idea of supranational institutions had already been voiced previously by Dr Felipe Herrera, president of the Inter-American Development Bank. He had gone so far as to call for the political as well as economic integration of Latin America, and for the creation of the institutions required to that end—namely, a Latin American Parliament, an Inter-American Court of Justice, and an Organization for Economic Co-operation and Development.[5]

As Dr Herrera sees it, a Latin American Parliament should be set up with sufficient powers to approve agreements regarding joint action on a region-wide basis—agreements that at the present time have to go through the laborious process of national ratification, and therefore tend to get lost in national archives. A step in this direction was taken in December 1964, when a conference of Latin American parliamentarians in Lima decided on the establishment of a permanent 'Latin American Parliament', to work for the creation of a regional economic community. The new body, modelled on the European Assembly at Strasbourg, was to consist of national parliamentary delegations chosen on a multi-party basis by participating countries.[6]

In addition to a Latin American Parliament, Dr Herrera considers it important to set up an Inter-American Court of Justice. This would help in settling not only commercial or contractual disputes arising in the relations among the various American states,[7]

[5] Address to the Colombian Association of Economists, in Bogotá, 12 June 1964, as reported in the Supplement to *Boletín Quincenal*, Aug. 1964.
[6] Countries represented at the parliamentary conference in Lima were Argentina, Brazil, Chile, Colombia, Costa Rica, El Salvador, Guatemala, Nicaragua, Paraguay, Peru, Uruguay, and Venezuela. Mexico was represented by observers (see *NYT*, 13 Dec. 1964).
[7] It will be noted that while Dr Herrera speaks of a *Latin American* Parliament, he

but also more serious conflicts. The latter may be the result of the failure of a particular country to implement regional agreements or obligations, or may involve damage to certain countries caused by the economic policies of others.

Finally, Dr Herrera sees a need for an Organization for Economic Co-operation and Development equipped both politically and technically to direct and coordinate the measures required for a policy of regional economic co-operation. He considers the establishment of CIAP (the Inter-American Committee for the Alliance for Progress) as a step in the right direction. But he regards it as important to formulate a regional policy not only on internal matters but also regarding relations with other 'geo-economic blocs'. Any institutional machinery created for this purpose would have to be able to direct the process of planning and development accordingly—and this means that it would have to be a supranational body charged with the responsibility for realizing a definite programme of integration. This in turn, says Herrera, implies the need for a philosophy or ideology of integration that will demonstrate that there is no conflict between the interests of national and regional development—in other words, a philosophy of continental nationalism.

This does, perhaps, underrate the chances of conflict between national and regional interests—previous chapters have shown the many ways in which such conflict may arise. Would a board of outstanding technicians be able to find purely technical solutions for cases of conflict? It may be doubted whether it could, since the solutions to political problems are usually themselves political, not technical. As in the case of the EEC, it would almost inevitably fall to a representative Council of Ministers to resolve major questions of conflict.

Moreover, there are dangers in the irresponsibility of a board of technocrats when placed in an ill-defined relationship to the member countries. Ideally, such a board should be responsible to some kind of Latin American Parliament, as envisaged by Dr Herrera. Unfortunately, the parliamentary system has not been outstandingly successful in Latin America even at the national level. Nor does

refers to an *Inter-American* Court of Justice for *American* states, and to an Organization for Economic Co-operation and Development. (My italics—S.D.). Moreover, the subsequent reference to relations with other 'geo-economic' blocs appears to suggest certain forms of western hemisphere economic co-operation alongside or in conjunction with the economic integration of Latin America.

experience in the EEC suggest that it is very easy to set up an effective regional parliament.

Thus the chances that a board of technocrats, modelled on the EEC Commission, could succeed in the Latin American context would depend very much on the calibre and outlook of the men chosen, and on their ability to respond to the needs and aspirations of the Latin American peoples without any effective institutional method of calling them to account for their actions. Latin America certainly does not lack distinguished men of affairs capable of giving the right kind of leadership, but would these be the men who would be chosen under current conditions?

Above all, would such a board be operating in a political situation broadly favourable to its efforts, or would it find its initiatives continually blocked by nationalist or separatist tendencies among the governments? Even in the much more favourable setting of the EEC, the initiatives of the Commission have been fruitful where they have coincided with the broad direction of governmental thinking but have come to very little where they have run up against entrenched national positions. The Commission's influence may be enhanced when the third stage of the EEC transition period is reached and (in theory) individual national vetos in the Council of Ministers are no longer possible. But this is a matter for speculation, and in any case, there is no disposition in LAFTA at present for individual countries to agree to forego the veto either now or in the future.

Everything therefore comes back to the extent of the political will of the Latin American countries to succeed—the will to take the difficult decisions required for a significant degree of policy co-ordination and joint planning. If there were such a will, which is not yet certain, the necessary institutional arrangements could readily be devised, taking into account both European and Latin American experience. Without the political will to take these difficult decisions, no amount of institutional inventiveness could save LAFTA.

The Need for High-level Decisions

This issue was placed firmly before the LAFTA countries by Raúl Prebisch in the course of his inaugural address to their second annual meeting in August 1962. He made it clear that in his view major political decisions were needed at the highest level to give momentum and vitality to the integration process. The decisions to be taken should include the adoption of quantitative targets so as to bring down the average level of mutual tariffs to 15 per cent[8] and eliminate all other regional trade restrictions within twelve years; the negotiation of a series of complementarity agreements, especially for dynamic industries, accompanied by the provision of special incentives in the form of tax benefits, technical assistance, and long-term financing for industries established under the agreements; the implementation of the principle of reciprocity in such a way as to assure all LAFTA countries that if the complementarity agreements and duty reductions did not provide equality of benefits, supplementary measures would be adopted that would do so; and the creation of a promotional organ to plan and organize the studies required and prepare projects of region-wide interest, to which adequate financial resources (which he estimated at $500 million) should be devoted, with help from the United States and other industrial countries.[9]

In response to Dr Prebisch's appeal for joint action at the highest political level, the Presidents of Brazil and Chile signed a joint declaration in April 1963 calling for a meeting of Foreign Ministers of the LAFTA countries to give a new political impetus to the programme of regional co-operation. The declaration went quite far in proposing permanent consultative machinery among LAFTA countries at the level of Foreign Ministers—a move which would have created an institution analogous to the powerful Council of Ministers of the EEC. The two Presidents also suggested that steps be taken to harmonize national development, tariff, and commercial policies, establish regional payments arrangements, and speed up the reduction of trade barriers.

Although the joint declaration by Brazil and Chile quickly received support from the governments of Argentina, Paraguay, and Peru, the proposed meeting of Foreign Ministers was repeatedly postponed because of the inability of the LAFTA countries to agree on the specific steps that needed to be taken. This in turn reflected the difficulty of reconciling the various national objectives of each member country with the overall interests of the region as a whole.

[8] Duties on agricultural commodities and the products of 'existing industries developing at the natural rate of growth' should, he considered, be lowered to a maximum of 30%; and duties on the products of 'dynamic industries' to 10%.

[9] The above summary of Dr Prebisch's views is based on his *Towards a Dynamic Development Policy*, pp. 89–101.

We shall have occasion to return to this most basic of all problems confronting economic unions towards the end of this study.

It was not until December 1964 that agreement was finally reached to convene during 1965 a meeting of Foreign Ministers, accompanied where appropriate by ministers in charge of LAFTA affairs. The principal objective of the meeting was to 'adopt the political solutions necessary for giving impetus to the process of economic integration and complementation of the Contracting Parties'.[10]

The difficult and protracted negotiations that had preceded the adoption of a Common Schedule in December 1964[11] were not an auspicious prelude to the projected ministerial meeting. Profound differences of opinion had emerged on all phases of the integration programme—the pace of liberalization, the question of reciprocity, the coordination of economic and commercial policies (including the problem of setting up a common external tariff), the harmonization of development plans and policies, and the elaboration of a regional payments system and common policies for transport. Above all, there was as yet no agreement on the strengthening of LAFTA institutions through such measures as the establishment of permanent machinery at Foreign Minister level, capable of acting promptly and effectively. Recommendations on many of these matters were put forward by four distinguished Latin Americans in a report entitled 'Proposals for the Creation of the Latin American Common Market' prepared in response to the initiative of President Frei, referred to above.[12]

It remained to be seen whether, with the aid of this report, the ministers would be able to achieve a breakthrough on at least some of these vital issues, thus allowing LAFTA to gather new energies for the next stage of its struggle for integration.

[10] *Resoluciones*, 112 (IV). It was proposed that the meeting should be held at some time between 1 April and 31 August 1965.
[11] See ch. v.   [12] Text on pp. 284–310 below.

CHAPTER XII

CONCLUSION: NATIONALISM OR CONTINENTALISM?

The Nature of the Problem

By the end of 1964, LAFTA was facing a profound crisis in its affairs and there appeared to be no easy solution to the underlying problems involved.

The main outward symptom of the crisis was the extraordinarily tense and prolonged negotiations that had marked the effort to draw up the first Common Schedule, covering only 25 per cent of the trade among the LAFTA countries during the previous three years, as discussed in Chapter V. If so much difficulty was experienced in finding a common list of items, accounting for 25 per cent of existing trade, that all countries could undertake to liberalize—not immediately but by 1973—what was likely to be the subsequent prospect of increasing the coverage of the Schedule to 50 per cent, 75 per cent, and, in the end, to substantially all trade within the region? While the immediate difficulties were overcome, or evaded, in a more fundamental sense the crisis seemed likely to continue for some considerable time.

The picture was not entirely a dark one. The entry into force of the Treaty of Montevideo had been followed by a relatively rapid expansion in trade among LAFTA countries, at a rate averaging about 20 per cent per annum; and the six-year decline in regional trade from 1955 to 1961 was fully made good by 1964. At the same time there was a growing sense of regional interdependence and solidarity which was no longer confined to economists and intellectuals but was gaining ground among political and business leaders as well.

There was no doubt, however, of the growing difficulties facing the LAFTA countries in maintaining forward momentum. Nearly one-half of the gain in regional trade from 1961 to 1964 had accrued to Argentina alone, while some of the smaller countries appeared to be adding much more to their imports than their exports. In addition, by far the major part of the expansion was in the traditionally traded primary commodities: there was a serious lack of dynamism when it came to the industrial products on which the success of the integration programme really depended.

Some were inclined to see the main problem as arising from the cumbersome process whereby annual negotiations are required for bringing about reductions in trade barriers. Moreover, the negotiations are on an item-by-item basis—precisely the type of procedure that GATT has found ineffective and which it has been trying to replace by linear, or across-the-board, tariff reductions of 50 per cent in connexion with the Kennedy round.

However, the fact that GATT has found the item-by-item approach ineffective does not mean that it has had greater success with the linear method. On the contrary, immense difficulties have been experienced because of disagreement between the EEC and other GATT members about the treatment of trade in agricultural products and on account of disparities between the tariff structures of various countries. Thus there is no magic about any particular method of tariff reduction; stalemated negotiations are just as possible with the automatic as with the item-by-item approach. Countries will agree on automatic across-the-board methods only if it is clear to every one of them that such methods are advantageous, and if there is a strong political will on all sides to reduce tariff barriers.

Across-the-board methods of tariff reduction have achieved major successes only in the EEC and EFTA, and these are the examples to which some observers believe that LAFTA should conform. In September 1964 a Special Committee of high-level experts recommended that the governments of LAFTA countries examine the possibility of replacing the existing arrangements for tariff negotiations by others embodying a greater degree of automaticity:[1] and it was no doubt the EEC and EFTA precedents that the Special Committee had in mind in making this proposal.

One can readily agree that automaticity, if attainable, would lead to more rapid tariff disarmament in LAFTA: this is too obvious to need labouring. But to stress automaticity as the answer to current difficulties is to mistake form for substance. The problem is precisely that the underlying conditions necessary for automatic methods to work smoothly have not yet been created.

[1] *Boletín Quincenal*, 25 Sept. 1964.

For one thing, automatic methods can be applied only where there is a presumption that such methods will lead to comparable benefits for all countries. While the Western European countries are sufficiently close to one another in levels of per capita income and production for such a presumption to provide a workable basis for action, the same cannot be said for Latin America. The adoption of automatic methods in Latin America, coupled with reliance on the spontaneous reaction of market forces to changes in tariff and quota restrictions, would be likely to benefit the strong as against the weak, and the industrially more advanced as against the industrially less developed. As a matter of fact, even in Western Europe, the process of automatic dismantling of tariffs is likely to continue to its final goal only if other steps, of a non-automatic character, are taken to solve the problems of agriculture side by side with those of industry. Highlighting this fact was the warning given by France on 21 October 1964 that it would withdraw from the EEC 'if the agricultural market was not organised in the way that had been agreed'.[2] The agreement on a common price for grain that was reached two months later was thus an indispensable prerequisite for the continuation of the EEC tariff reduction programme, despite the 'automaticity' of that programme.

Now the problems of agriculture in Western Europe have this much in common with the general problems of both agriculture and industry in Latin America—that they cannot be solved exclusively through automatic arrangements operating alongside market forces. The modernization of agriculture in Western Europe is to be handled with direct support from governments, and the same goes for economic development generally in Latin America. In both cases the need is for national and regional planning for the most effective utilization of resources in meeting future demands.

Even the stronger countries in LAFTA might well have reason to fear automaticity in the reduction of trade barriers. For while the industries of Argentina, Brazil, and Mexico may be able to cope with competition from indigenous enterprise in the other LAFTA countries, they are bound to feel much less comfortable about the possibility of competition from international companies setting up branches or subsidiaries in, say, Chile or Peru with a view to taking over region-wide markets.

Thus all the LAFTA countries, large or small, may well feel that

2 *The Times,* 22 Oct. 1964.

the exercise of judgement and discretion in the reduction of trade barriers is indispensable, and that automaticity can be achieved only as part of a comprehensive programme of regional development.

Additional difficulties have resulted from the concentration of the Treaty of Montevideo on the liberalization of existing trade—apparently in an effort at partial compliance with the unduly rigid rules of GATT. Since existing trade is predominantly in agricultural commodities, the LAFTA countries were faced, under the Treaty, with the need to do something that neither the EEC nor EFTA had been prepared to do—namely, to free their agricultural trade with one another. This was even more difficult for Latin American than for European countries. And it is therefore not surprising that, while adopting the first list of products—largely agricultural—for the Common Schedule, the LAFTA countries acted simultaneously to do away with the unconditional character of the commitment by prolonging the right to impose restrictions on agricultural imports beyond the end of the transition period in 1973.

This particular difficulty would not, of course, have arisen had the Treaty emphasized the liberalization not of *existing* trade but of trade in industrial goods, which was the type of trade that was most essential for the success of the integration programme. In effect, what the LAFTA countries needed most was *to eliminate their mutual restrictions on goods imported from third countries rather than on the goods currently imported from one another.* In other words, they needed to create incentives for LAFTA industries to displace manufactured imports from third countries. Here were markets that could be tapped without causing internal dislocation of either agriculture or industry. Nor would the third countries concerned have anything to fear as regards their total exports to Latin America; for the LAFTA countries would certainly continue spending all the foreign exchange they earned, even though the structure of imports from third countries would no doubt shift.

All these changes would, however, have to occur within a framework of action generally agreed among the LAFTA countries: they could not be left to spontaneous forces operating through automatic reductions in trade barriers.

National and Regional Planning

The real question in Latin America, therefore, is this. Have the peoples and their governments reached the stage at which they are prepared to undertake both national and co-operative planning of Latin American development? Are they ready to plan their own national development? And assuming that they are, will they be prepared to try and dovetail their national plans with those of other countries so as to achieve consistent overall targets for the region as a whole?

This is not a matter of trying to produce a detailed blueprint for the entire area of Latin America—obviously an impracticable objective at the present time—but rather of fixing the main lines and proportions of Latin American growth during the coming five or ten years, and the place of each individual country in the overall picture.

Even this objective could be approached step by step, through a phased programme of gradually expanding scope, as suggested in Chapter VIII. A beginning could be made by developing specific projects for investment in new infrastructural and industrial facilities of interest to two or more countries. This could be accompanied by comparative exploration of investment plans with a view to identifying obvious gaps or inconsistencies. On the basis of experience gained, efforts could be made to move towards agreements by groups of countries covering a limited number of key industries. Only after considerable success had been achieved along these lines would it be possible, perhaps, to move on to more far-reaching measures of joint planning covering the economy as a whole.

External as well as internal resources should be mobilized to this end. National and international lending agencies should be prepared to offer active encouragement to these efforts by making large-scale funds available for inter-country projects. Such funds should not be confined, as in the past, largely to agriculture and infrastructure; important as these sectors are, it is in the field of industry that the greatest benefits of regional co-operation are likely to be obtained. The disposition to leave industrial development to unaided private initiative tends to limit the effectiveness of national and international aid programmes. At the same time support should be given to inter-country agreements on industrial location and distribution: where such agreements appear to involve the establishment of industrial monopolies in the first instance, the emphasis could well be on adequate regulation and control rather than on competition for its own sake, at any rate if the existing regional market is small in relation to the output of a single optimum-sized firm.

Once adequate provision had been made for each member country of LAFTA to participate fairly in the new co-operative industrial investment programmes, and once it became clear that aid-giving countries were determined to render strong financial support to such programmes, solutions to many other LAFTA problems would fall quickly into place. Countries would have less reluctance in introducing more vigorous and even automatic methods of tariff-cutting if they knew the targets that the LAFTA trade programme was designed to achieve, and were satisfied with the active steps being taken by LAFTA countries as a whole to promote new industries and new investment within the territory of each member. The introduction of a regional payments system, including mutual credit arrangements designed to absorb unforeseen swings in balances of payments, might also help to move the liberalization programme forward more quickly.

Similarly, the possibility of achieving a more rational division of labour in agriculture in Latin America depends on the creation of a framework assuring to each country the viability of its agricultural economy. It is no use expecting Latin American countries to be prepared to do what countries even in the industrially advanced countries are not ready to do—namely, to expose their domestic agriculture to unbridled foreign competition. By the end of the century Latin American countries will need all the food they can produce for a population totalling 600 million; and it would be the height of folly for them to permit an influx of food imports on a scale that might force land out of cultivation now which will obviously need to be exploited later on. Even from a short-term point of view, moreover, no Latin American country could afford to risk the further impoverishment of its peasantry.

For all these reasons, any reorientation and rationalization of Latin American agriculture depends just as much on region-wide planning for a rational division of labour as does a coherent programme of industrial development and specialization.

By the same token, the problems of reciprocity, of harmonizing economic and commercial policies, of agreeing on a common external tariff, and, above all, of stepping up the rates of growth of the less developed countries could be handled much more smoothly, and with far less dislocation to the forward momentum of the inte-

P

gration programme, if LAFTA countries were committed, jointly as well as separately, to the achievement of definite regional and national targets for production and trade.

Of course, it may be unrealistic to talk of regional planning in Latin America at a time when even national planning cannot be said to have a very firm foundation in most countries of the region. But if regional planning is unrealistic for Latin America, so also is a common market in the area unrealistic. For it is scarcely conceivable that the Latin American countries—particularly the smaller and weaker ones among them—could afford to allow the forces of regional free trade to determine the distribution of regional gains from integration in an unplanned manner. For them it is plan or die.

Some would contend, not without reason, that joint planning in the manner indicated above could not take place in a political vacuum; and that an indispensable prerequisite for any particular degree of economic co-operation is a corresponding degree of political co-operation. Indeed, political co-operation is sometimes seen as the all-embracing solution to the difficulties experienced in achieving economic co-operation.

Nationalism or Continentalism?

It is, unfortunately, not quite so easy to dispose of the conflict between national and regional interests as the foregoing implies: political co-operation may not be enough. Indeed, almost all the difficulties faced by regional groupings, whether in Europe or Latin America, may be reduced, ultimately, to the one fundamental difficulty that underlies them all—namely, how to reconcile the divergent interests of the various members of the groupings in the absence of *political unity*. Within any one country economic disparities between regions do not normally create major obstacles to the overall process of development because there is tacit acceptance of the view that the interests of the community as a whole take priority over those of any one section.[3] But if a number of independent

---

[3] It should be noted, however, that even in a unified state, there is conflict between local and national interests. Such conflicts arise whenever, for example, resources are employed in such a way as to ensure the maximum growth of the national economy as a whole, notwithstanding a lag in particular regions or localities. What is true is that an individual district in a politically unified country may more readily accept such a lag than an independent member country participating in a customs union or free-trade area. Even within a single country, however, there is a limit to the extent of the lag that any one region can be expected to endure without protest or agitation.

countries join together in a grouping, the benefits enjoyed by each must be broadly comparable. As we have already noted, no government could be expected to justify its participation in such a grouping before its own people by saying that their interests could legitimately be sacrificed to those of the group as a whole.

Seen in these terms, the most important obstacle to regional integration is the strength of the forces of nationalism, which make it essential to secure rough justice in the distribution of gains and losses. Methods may be devised for achieving this objective, but it cannot be said that the path to success in this matter is always readily identifiable.

It is difficult to tell how strong are the forces of regional solidarity: many would say that they are exceedingly weak in Latin America. This is, perhaps, not surprising when one recalls that the fragmentation of the region goes back to colonial times.

It is true that the struggle for independence revived regional concepts for a time, and that the great Bolívar assembled the Congress of Panama in 1826 to seek the political, economic, and juridical unity of the continent. But when the creator of Gran Colombia reflected on his deathbed that he had merely 'ploughed the sea', he was doubtless thinking of the disintegration of Latin America into small 'independent' republics reproducing the bureaucratic lines of demarcation that the ineptitude of the Spanish monarchy had imposed.[4]

This fragmentation of Latin America was consolidated and reinforced by the pattern of its economic development. The growth of food and raw material producing activities catering to the needs of the industrially developed countries meant that the ties of Latin American countries to one another became much weaker than those to Europe and North America. The inflow of foreign capital tended to bring about similar results, creating many new industrial and commercial links to parent enterprises located outside Latin America, but very few connexions between one Latin American country and another.

The forces binding Latin American countries to Europe were a source of political and cultural weakness and disunity that has often been the subject of comment by Latin American writers. Thus in the course of a series of 'Meditations' on nationalism, published in

---

[4] See Antenor Orrego, 'El nacionalismo continental y la unidad de Indoamerica', *Examen* (Mexico City), Nov.–Dec. 1959.

1924, the celebrated Argentinian writer Ricardo Rojas observed that while his country had become politically independent in 1810, it had continued to be 'una colonia de otras metropolis'—a colony of other metropolitan powers. It had been colonized by the men, the capital, and the ideas of Europe, and was completely lacking in a culture of its own.[5]

Similar sentiments were expressed by the Brazilian writer Graça Aranha, an aristocrat from an old family of northern Brazil. In *Canaan*, he puts the following words into the mouth of a young lawyer:

You gentlemen speak of independence, but I don't see it. Brazil is, and always has been, a colony. Our regime is not a free one. We are a protectorate. . . . Tell me: where is our financial independence? What is the real money that dominates us? Where is our gold? What is the use of our miserable paper currency if it isn't to buy English pounds? Where is our public property? What little we have is mortgaged. The customs revenues are in the hands of the English. We have no ships. We have no railroads either; they are all in the hands of the foreigners. Is it, or is it not, a colonial regime disguised with the name of free nation?[6]

While dependence on the industrially advanced countries has tended to perpetuate the barriers between the underdeveloped nations—and this is just as true of Africa and Asia as of Latin America—the growing reaction against such dependence is not necessarily accompanied by efforts at integration or reintegration. Indeed, the attempts of the Latin American peoples to shake off the last vestiges of colonial or semi-colonial dependence are frequently associated with a resurgence of national feeling and patriotism rather than of continentalism.

Contemporary patterns of nationalism in Latin America are greatly influenced by widespread aspirations for a better life and swifter economic progress. Nationalistic sentiments have been continually invoked by the rising middle classes as they have sought to take over the reins of power from the old order; the close association of the traditional élite with foreign interests has always been an obvious target for attack. Labour interests have likewise frequently found themselves in conflict with foreign companies.

[5] Ricardo Rojas, *La guerra de las naciones* (Buenos Aires, 1924), pp. 109–11, 274–5.
[6] Graça Aranha, *Canaan* (tr. from the Portuguese by Mariano Joaquin Lorente, Boston, 1920), pp. 196–7, as cited in Gilberto Freyre, *New World in the Tropics* (N.Y., 1959), p. 221.

The new nationalism has therefore given rise to strong protectionism as a means of securing economic independence and freedom from foreign domination. Programmes of economic development have been conceived in nationalistic and protectionist terms, and economic progress has been identified with self-sufficiency— the ability of a country to stand on its own feet and rely exclusively on its own resources.

A complementary element in Latin American nationalism is the belief that the interests of the state must take precedence over all private interests, since only the state can interpret and defend the interests of the nation as a whole. These ideas of state and nation do not, of course, blend readily with concepts of regional or continental solidarity.

The extent of national unity in the Latin American countries is naturally limited by the lack of homogeneity among the people— what do the Indians in their mountain settlements have in common with the inhabitants of the low-lying areas and towns? But heterogeneity of populations is at least as great an obstacle to regional unity as to national cohesion: the fact that there are many social groups in Latin America that do not have any strong community of interest with their neighbours does not in the least imply that they would have any greater sense of identification with Latin America as a whole.

While nationalism remains a most powerful factor in Latin American regional politics, it is possible to discern the simultaneous growth of continentalism, or what Orrego, Herrera, and others have called 'continental nationalism'. As Latin America looks outwards to the other regions and sees the emergence of vast new political and economic power blocs, it begins to gain a greater sense of the factors and interests that unite it.

This growing sense of Latin American solidarity in a world of giant countries and regions was given pointed expression in an address by the President of Uruguay to a conference of LAFTA countries in July 1961. In the President's words:

The formation of a European common market and EFTA constitutes a state of near-war against Latin American exports. Therefore, we must reply to one integration with another one; to one increase of acquisitive power by internal enrichment by another; to inter-European co-operation by inter-Latin American co-operation.[7]

[7] *Observer,* 30 July 1961.

No region, however, can find its sense of identity and purpose solely in reaction against the interests and ambitions of other regions. In a more positive vein, Victor Raúl Haya de la Torre has written of a 'continental spirit' and 'continental aspiration' of Latin America. For him Latin America is the *patria grande*, of which each state is an inseparable and interdependent part: the greatest patriotism for any Latin American in relation to the country of his birth is to uphold its essential solidarity with the continent as a whole.[8] Other writers in all parts of Latin America have rediscovered in recent years the cultural bonds that unite the region and have sought to reawaken sentiments of continental nationalism.

It cannot be taken for granted that the movement towards continental nationalism in Latin America will prove strong enough to modify, in a short period, the ideas of national sovereignty that have hitherto formed a fundamental part of the ideology of the forward-looking social groups in the region. It is not simply a matter of the willingness of national governments to co-operate with one another. More serious is the fact that the promotion of economic development calls for considerable government initiative in many directions. Mounting social pressures are bound to make any dynamic government reluctant to postpone action until its programmes and policies have been dovetailed with those of other, possibly less vigorous, governments. There is an undeniable danger that insistence on a regional approach, and on the harmonization of economic development plans, could paralyse government thinking and action and, indeed, provide a convenient justification for doing nothing. Even if all governments were equally anxious to promote the development of their countries, the process of reaching intergovernmental agreement not merely on whether to do certain things but on how to do them would inevitably be a long and arduous one. It would be dangerous to underestimate the political difficulties involved in securing prompt joint action by a group of independent governments, even if they all act with the best will in the world. The utmost political ingenuity will be required in working out forms and procedures for intergovernmental co-operation that will make it possible to advance on a regional level without holding back progress nationally.

The fact that national and regional progress have thus far been reconciled in Western Europe does not necessarily provide guid-

<hr />

[8] 'Problemas de la América Latina', *Cuadernos* (Paris), July–Aug. 1959.

ance for Latin America. For both EEC and EFTA have emphasized the release of market forces within a broad region of free trade, whereas—if the argument of the foregoing chapters is correct—similar action cannot be equally effective in an underdeveloped region such as Latin America. If economic development in Latin America depends largely on adequate planning and programming, and if national plans and programmes must be shaped into a coherent regional whole, the effectiveness of inter-governmental cooperation becomes a much more crucial factor than it is even in Western Europe. In other words, the evolution of a more powerful institutional structure for LAFTA appears to be indispensable.

It should be emphasized, finally, that regional integration can succeed only within a general context of political and social change in Latin America. Economic progress in Latin America depends on much more than the lowering of the barriers to trade within the area: reductions of tariffs and other obstacles to trade would be meaningless without far-reaching reforms in land tenure and tax structure, and without an improvement in the distribution of income sufficient to persuade the mass of the population that they too may enjoy the fruits of economic advancement. Latin America cannot establish a common market that has any meaning in the midst of economic and social stagnation. In the absence of such reforms, the Treaty of Montevideo and the procedures that it has set in motion are bound to remain sterile and unproductive. On the other hand, given the political will to undertake all the political, social, and economic changes that are required if economic development in Latin America is to make more rapid headway, economic integration can provide a powerful reinforcement of other measures by releasing the dynamic forces of regional specialization and exchange. Economic integration will not give Latin America an easy road to higher living standards or render unnecessary the painful adjustments that the political and social circumstances of the region have shown to be necessary. It can increase the power of the economic forces of development, once those forces are well and truly mobilized. It can never substitute for them.

APPENDIX I: TABLES

TABLE VI

Trade among Latin American Countries*

($ million)

Year	Exports to Latin America		Share of intra-exports in total exports of world to Latin America %
	From world	From Latin America	
1950	5,130	540	10·5
1951	7,130	670	9·4
1952	6,460	610	9·4
1953	6,010	730	12·1
1954	6,820	710	10·4
1955	6,920	770	11·1
1956	7,380	670	9·1
1957	8,730	760	8·7
1958	8,160	760	9·3
1959	7,540	720	9·5
1960	7,820	690	8·8
1961	8,130	580	7·1
1962	8,100	660	8·1
1963	7,990	750	9·4
1964	9,060	980	10·8

* While the data in Table VI relate to the trade of all Latin American countries, subsequent tables concern only LAFTA member countries. It will be seen that while the exports of LAFTA countries to one another totalled $355 m. in 1962, intra-regional exports of Latin America as a whole amounted to $660 m. The main elements of the difference between the two figures are the intra-trade of Central America ($50 m.) and the regional exports of Venezuela—largely of petroleum ($185 m.).

Source: UN, *Monthly Bulletin of Statistics.*

TABLE VII

Total Trade among LAFTA Countries

($ *million; exports f.o.b., imports c.i.f.*)

Year	Trade among LAFTA countries				Share of intra-trade in total trade of LAFTA countries (%)
	Exports	Imports	Total	Index (1952=100)	
1952	359	449	808	100	8·4
1953	509	525	1,034	128	11·3
1954	495	539	1,034	128	10·3
1955	508	574	1,082	134	11·0
1956	358	408	766	95	7·6
1957	396	441	837	104	8·1
1958	374	403	777	96	8·2
1959	324	355	679	84	7·2
1960	340	375	715	89	6·9
1961	299	360	659	82	6·0
1962	354	420	774	96	7·0
1963	425	525	950	118	8·4
1964	558	646	1,203	149	10·1

Source: LAFTA Documents CEP/Repartido 376/64 and CEP/Repartido 472.

TABLE VIII

Trade among LAFTA Countries

($ *million; exports f.o.b., imports c.i.f.*)

	Exports	Imports	Balance
Argentina			
1950	136·1	103·2	32·9
1955	190·1	192·2	− 2·1
1960	162·5	106·6	55·9
1961	100·0	126·0	−26·0
1962	141·4	103·2	38·2
1963	185·0	101·6	83·4
1964	218·4	170·8	47·6

Appendix I

TABLE VIII (*cont.*)

Trade among LAFTA Countries

	Exports	Imports	Balance
Brazil			
1950	106·7	134·9	−28·2
1955	145·2	194·7	−49·5
1960	86·4	108·3	−21·9
1961	95·2	45·2	50·0
1962	75·8	128·6	−52·8
1963	76·0	163·9	−87·9
1964	132·8	168·0	−35·2
Chile			
1950	38·5	45·0	− 6·5
1955	58·0	83·2	−25·2
1960	30·2	81·9	−51·7
1961	34·8	94·5	−59·7
1962	39·4	80·5	−41·1
1963	49·3	120·0	−70·7
1964	54·5	128·9	−74·4
Colombia			
1950	1·1	17·1	−16·0
1955	3·0	12·3	− 9·3
1960	4·8	6·3	− 1·5
1961	6·1	10·2	− 4·1
1962	7·3	12·5	− 5·2
1963	6·1	21·4	−15·3
1964	10·9	33·1	−22·2
Ecuador			
1950	11·5	1·2	10·3
1955	8·6	6·3	2·3
1960	4·7	3·3	1·4
1961	7·5	4·1	3·4
1962	6·1	3·9	2·2
1963	8·0	5·2	2·8
1964	13·3	8·0	5·3

TABLE VIII (*cont.*)
Trade among LAFTA Countries

	Exports	Imports	Balance
Mexico			
1950	5·9	1·3	4·6
1955	5·0	1·5	3·5
1960	5·7	3·6	2·1
1961	7·9	4·1	3·8
1962	16·7	6·1	10·6
1963	25·9	10·8	15·1
1964	34·0	17·3	16·7
Paraguay			
1950	5·1	1·2	3·9
1955	17·0	13·2	3·8
1960	8·9	8·6	0·3
1961	9·9	9·8	0·1
1962	10·9	6·0	4·9
1963	10·7	8·4	2·3
1964	14·8	11·6	3·2
Peru			
1950	51·3	14·6	36·7
1955	49·9	23·2	26·7
1960	33·4	27·5	5·9
1961	31·5	31·8	− 0·3
1962	48·8	45·2	3·6
1963	49·1	62·0	−12·9
1964	63·8	58·9	4·9
Uruguay			
1950	6·4	33·5	−27·1
1955	31·4	47·0	−15·6
1960	3·4	28·9	−25·5
1961	5·8	34·5	−28·7
1962	8·0	34·0	−26·0
1963	15·0	31·8	−16·8
1964	15·0	49·3	−34·3

Source: As for Table VII, p. 219.

TABLE IX

Shares in Total Trade among LAFTA Countries

(*Percentage*)

Country*	1959–61	1962	1963	1964
Argentina	36·0	31·6	30·2	32·3
Brazil	25·7	26·4	25·2	25·0
Chile	16·3	15·4	17·8	15·2
Peru	9·3	12·1	11·7	10·2
Uruguay	5·2	5·4	4·9	5·3
Paraguay	2·6	2·2	2·1	2·2
Colombia	1·9	2·6	2·9	3·7
Mexico	1·5	3·0	3·9	4·3
Ecuador	1·5	1·3	1·3	1·8
Total	100·0	100·0	100·0	100·0

* In descending order of shares in 1959–61.

Source: As for Table VII, p. 219.

TABLE X

Shares of Trade with LAFTA Countries in Total Trade

(*Percentage*)

Country*	1959–61	1962	1963	1964
Paraguay	26·9	23·1	26·2	29·5
Chile	11·2	11·4	14·4	14·9
Argentina	10·9	9·5	12·2	15·7
Uruguay	10·0	10·9	13·7	17·2
Peru	8·0	8·7	10·1	9·8
Brazil	6·4	7·6	8·3	11·2
Ecuador	4·9	4·6	5·1	7·9
Colombia	1·4	2·0	2·9	4·1
Mexico	0·5	1·1	1·8	2·1
Total, LAFTA countries	6·7	7·0	8·4	10·0

* In descending order of shares in 1959–61.

Source: As for Table VII, p. 219.

TABLE XI

Selected Import Duties in Argentina, Brazil, and Mexico, 1963

(Percentages ad valorem)

Commodity	Argentina		Brazil		Mexico	
	Third country	LAFTA	Third country	LAFTA	Third country	LAFTA
Powdered milk	195	45	42	27	18	9
Fishmeal	195	2	9	2	18	6
Bauxite	12	2	37	7	83	0
Tartaric acid	188	103	22	7	15	0
Casein	195	2	37	7	6	0
Wood pulp (sulphate)	29	2	27	2	23	0
Alpaca	175	2	47	7	11	0
Raw cotton	43	3	67	37	9	0
Steel bars	43	2	57	14	—	—
Hydraulic jacks	198	103	87	77	28	18
Lathes	43–153	2–77	37–67	27–37	15	0
Tabulating machines	23	6	27	7	9	0

Source: LAFTA, *Lista consolidada de concesiones, 1963,* as cited in Business International, *Latin America's Merging Market* (N.Y., 1964), pp. 50–51.

TABLE XII

Ownership of the Thirty* Largest Business Enterprises in Latin American Countries

(*Percentage*)

Country	Proportion owned by		
	Government	Domestic private capital	Foreign private capital
Argentina	61·3	20·5	18·2
Brazil	59·1	20·0	20·9
Chile	43·2	10·6	46·2
Colombia†	54·1	39·1	6·1
Mexico	82·2	13·9	3·9
Venezuela†	74·0	22·9	3·1
Total above‡	62·4	21·2	16·4

* Argentina, 29; Brazil, 32; Colombia, 32.
† Excluding petroleum companies.
‡ Unweighted average.

Source: Brandenburg, *Development of Latin American Enterprise.*

APPENDIX II: TEXTS

A. *Article XXIV of GATT*

Territorial Application—Frontier Traffic—Customs Unions and Free-trade Areas

1. The provisions of this Agreement shall apply to the metropolitan customs territories of the contracting parties and to any other customs territories in respect of which this Agreement has been accepted under Article XXVI or is being applied under Article XXXIII or pursuant to the Protocol of Provisional Application. Each such customs territory shall, exclusively for the purposes of the territorial application of this Agreement, be treated as though it were a contracting party; *Provided* that the provisions of this paragraph shall not be construed to create any rights or obligations as between two or more customs territories in respect of which this Agreement has been accepted under Article XXVI or is being applied under Article XXXIII or pursuant to the Protocol of Provisional Application by a single contracting party.

2. For the purposes of this Agreement a customs territory shall be understood to mean any territory with respect to which separate tariffs or other regulations of commerce are maintained for a substantial part of the trade of such territory with other territories.

3. The provisions of this Agreement shall not be construed to prevent:

(a) advantages accorded by any contracting party to adjacent countries in order to facilitate frontier traffic;

(b) advantages accorded to the trade with the Free Territory of Trieste by countries contiguous to that territory, provided that such advantages are not in conflict with the Treaties of Peace arising out the the Second World War.

4. The contracting parties recognize the desirability of increasing freedom of trade by the development, through voluntary agreements, of closer integration between the economies of the countries parties to such agreements. They also recognize that the purpose of a customs union or of a free-trade area should be to facilitate trade between the constituent territories and not to raise barriers to the trade of other contracting parties with such territories.

5. Accordingly, the provisions of this Agreement shall not prevent, as between the territories of contracting parties, the formation of a customs union or of a free-trade area or the adoption of an interim agreement

necessary for the formation of a customs union or of a free-trade area; *Provided* that:

(*a*)   with respect to a customs union, or an interim agreement leading to the formation of a customs union, the duties and other regulations of commerce imposed at the institution of any such union or interim agreement in respect of trade with contracting parties not parties to such union or agreement shall not on the whole be higher or more restrictive than the general incidence of the duties and regulations of commerce applicable in the constituent territories prior to the formation of such union or the adoption of such interim agreement, as the case may be;

(*b*)   with respect to a free-trade area, or an interim agreement leading to the formation of a free-trade area, the duties and other regulations of commerce maintained in each of the constituent territories and applicable at the formation of such free-trade area or the adoption of such interim agreement to the trade of contracting parties not included in such area or not parties to such agreement shall not be higher or more restrictive than the corresponding duties and other regulations of commerce existing in the same constituent territories prior to the formation of the free-trade area, or interim agreement, as the case may be; and

(*c*)   any interim agreement referred to in sub-paragraphs (*a*) and (*b*) shall include a plan and schedule for the formation of such a customs union or of such a free-trade area within a reasonable length of time.

6. If, in fulfilling the requirements of sub-paragraph 5 (*a*), a contracting party proposes to increase any rate of duty inconsistently with the provisions of Article II, the procedure set forth in Article XXVIII shall apply. In providing for compensatory adjustment, due account shall be taken of the compensation already afforded by the reductions brought about in the corresponding duty of the other constituents of the union.

7. (*a*) Any contracting party deciding to enter into a customs union or free-trade area, or an interim agreement leading to the formation of such a union or area, shall promptly notify the CONTRACTING PARTIES and shall make available to them such information regarding the proposed union or area as will enable them to make such reports and recommendations to contracting parties as they may deem appropriate.

(*b*) If, after having studied the plan and schedule included in an interim agreement referred to in paragraph 5 in consultation with the parties to that agreement and taking due account of the information made available in accordance with the provisions of sub-paragraph (*a*), the CONTRACTING PARTIES find that such agreement is not likely to result in the formation of a customs union or of a free-trade area within the period contemplated by the parties to the agreement or that such period is not a reasonable one, the CONTRACTING PARTIES shall make recommendations to the parties to the agreement. The parties shall not maintain or put into force, as the case may be, such agreement if they are not prepared to modify it in accordance with these recommendations.

(*c*) Any substantial change in the plan or schedule referred to in paragraph 5 (*c*) shall be communicated to the CONTRACTING PARTIES, which may request the contracting parties concerned to consult with them if the change seems likely to jeopardize or delay unduly the formation of the customs union or of the free-trade area.

8. For the purposes of this Agreement:

(*a*) A customs union shall be understood to mean the substitution of a single customs territory for two or more customs territories, so that
  (i) duties and other restrictive regulations of commerce (except, where necessary, those permitted under Articles XI, XII, XIII, XIV, XV and XX) are eliminated with respect to substantially all the trade between the constituent territories of the union or at least with respect to substantially all the trade in products originating in such territories, and,
  (ii) subject to the provisions of paragraph 9, substantially the same duties and other regulations of commerce are applied by each of the members of the union to the trade of territories not included in the union;

(*b*) A free-trade area shall be understood to mean a group of two or more customs territories in which the duties and other restrictive regulations of commerce (except, where necessary, those permitted under Articles XI, XII, XIII, XIV, XV and XX) are eliminated on substantially all the trade between the constituent territories in products originating in such territories.

9. The preferences referred to in paragraph 2 of Article I shall not be affected by the formation of a customs union or of a free-trade area but may be eliminated or adjusted by means of negotiations with contracting parties affected. This procedure of negotiations with affected contracting parties shall, in particular, apply to the elimination of preferences required to conform with the provisions of paragraph 8 (*a*) (i) and paragraph 8 (*b*).

10. The CONTRACTING PARTIES may by a two-thirds majority approve proposals which do not fully comply with the requirements of paragraphs 5 to 9 inclusive, provided that such proposals lead to the formation of a customs union or a free-trade area in the sense of this Article.

Q

11. Taking into account the exceptional circumstances arising out of the establishment of India and Pakistan as independent States and recognizing the fact that they have long constituted an economic unit, the contracting parties agree that the provisions of this Agreement shall not prevent the two countries from entering into special arrangements with respect to the trade between them, pending the establishment of their mutual trade relations on a definitive basis.

12. Each contracting party shall take such reasonable measures as may be available to it to ensure observance of the provisions of this Agreement by the regional and local governments and authorities within its territory.

B. *Treaty Establishing a Free-Trade Area and Instituting the Latin American Free-Trade Association* (*Montevideo, 18 February 1960*)

The Governments represented at the Inter-Governmental Conference for the Establishment of a Free-Trade Area among Latin American Countries,

Persuaded that the expansion of present national markets, through the gradual elimination of barriers to intra-regional trade, is a prerequisite if the Latin American countries are to accelerate their economic development process in such a way as to ensure a higher level of living for their peoples,

Aware that economic development should be attained through the maximum utilization of available production factors and the more effective co-ordination of the development programmes of the different production sectors in accordance with norms which take due account of the interests of each and all and which make proper compensation, by means of appropriate measures, for the special situation of countries which are at a relatively less advanced stage of economic development,

Convinced that the strengthening of national economies will contribute to the expansion of trade within Latin America and with the rest of the world,

Sure that, by the adoption of suitable formulae, conditions can be created that will be conducive to the gradual and smooth adaptation of existing productive activities to new patterns of reciprocal trade, and that further incentives will thereby be provided for the improvement and expansion of such trade,

Certain that any action to achieve such ends must take into account the commitments arising out of the international instruments which govern their trade,

Determined to persevere in their efforts to establish, gradually and progressively, a Latin American common market and, hence, to continue collaborating with the Latin American Governments as a whole in the work already initiated for this purpose, and

Motivated by the desire to pool their efforts to achieve the progressive complementarity and integration of their national economies on the basis of an effective reciprocity of benefits, decide to establish a Free-Trade Area and, to that end, to conclude a Treaty instituting the Latin American Free-Trade Association; and have, for this purpose, appointed their plenipotentiaries who have agreed as follows:

CHAPTER I

NAME AND PURPOSE

Article 1

By this Treaty the Contracting Parties establish a Free-Trade Area and institute the Latin American Free-Trade Association (hereinafter referred to as "the Association"), with headquarters in the city of Montevideo (Eastern Republic of Uruguay).

The term "Area", when used in this Treaty, means the combined territories of the Contracting Parties.

CHAPTER II

PROGRAMME FOR TRADE LIBERALIZATION

Article 2

The Free-Trade Area, established under the terms of the present Treaty, shall be brought into full operation within not more than twelve (12) years from the date of the Treaty's entry into force.

Article 3

During the period indicated in article 2, the Contracting Parties shall gradually eliminate, in respect of substantially all their reciprocal trade, such duties, charges and restrictions as may be applied to imports of goods originating in the territory of any Contracting Party.

For the purposes of the present Treaty the term "duties and charges" means customs duties and any other charges of equivalent effect—whether fiscal, monetary or exchange—that are levied on imports.

The provisions of the present article do not apply to fees and similar charges in respect of services rendered.

Article 4

The purpose set forth in article 3 shall be achieved through negotiations to be held from time to time among the Contracting Parties with a view to drawing up:

(*a*) National Schedules specifying the annual reductions in duties, charges and other restrictions which each Contracting Party grants to the other Contracting Parties in accordance with the provisions of article 5; and

(*b*) a Common Schedule listing the products on which the Contracting Parties collectively agree to eliminate duties, charges and other restrictions completely, so far as intra-Area trade is concerned, within the period mentioned in article 2, by complying with the minimum percentages set out in article 7 and through the gradual reduction provided for in article 5.

Article 5

With a view to the preparation of the National Schedules referred to in article 4, sub-paragraph (*a*), each Contracting Party shall annually grant to the other Contracting Parties reductions in duties and charges equivalent to not less than eight (8) per cent of the weighted average applicable to third countries, until they are eliminated in respect of substantially all of its imports from the Area, in accordance with the definitions, methods of calculation, rules and procedures laid down in the Protocol.

For this purpose, duties and charges for third parties shall be deemed to be those in force on 31 December prior to each negotiation.

When the import régime of a Contracting Party contains restrictions of such a kind that the requisite equivalence with the reductions in duties and charges granted by another Contracting Party or other Contracting Parties is unobtainable, the counterpart of these reductions shall be complemented by means of the elimination or relaxation of those restrictions.

Article 6

The National Schedules shall enter into force on 1 January of each year, except that those deriving from the initial negotiations shall enter into force on the date fixed by the Contracting Parties.

Article 7

The Common Schedule shall consist of products which, in terms of the aggregate value of the trade among the Contracting Parties, shall constitute not less than the following percentages, calculated in accordance with the provisions of the Protocol:

Twenty-five (25) per cent during the first three-year period;
Fifty (50) per cent during the second three-year period;
Seventy-five (75) per cent during the third three-year period;
Substantially all of such trade during the fourth three-year period.

Article 8

The inclusion of products in the Common Schedule shall be final and the concessions granted in respect thereof irrevocable.

Concessions granted in respect of products which appear only in the National Schedules may be withdrawn by negotiation among the Contracting Parties and on a basis of adequate compensation.

Article 9

The percentages referred to in articles 5 and 7 shall be calculated on the basis of the average annual value of trade during the three years preceding the year in which each negotiation is effected.

Article 10

The purpose of the negotiations—based on reciprocity of concessions—referred to in article 4 shall be to expand and diversify trade and to promote the progressive complementarity of the economies of the countries in the Area.

In these negotiations the situation of those Contracting Parties whose levels of duties, charges and restrictions differ substantially from those of the other Contracting Parties shall be considered with due fairness.

Article 11

If, as a result of the concessions granted, significant and persistent disadvantages are created in respect of trade between one Contracting Party and the others as a whole in the products included in the liberalization programme, the Contracting Parties shall, at the request of the Contracting Party affected, consider steps to remedy these disadvantages with a view to the adoption of suitable, non-restrictive measures designed to promote trade at the highest possible levels.

Article 12

If, as a result of circumstances other than those referred to in article 11, significant and persistent disadvantages are created in respect of trade in the products included in the liberalization programme, the Contracting Parties shall, at the request of the Contracting Party concerned, make every effort within their power to remedy these disadvantages.

Article 13

The reciprocity mentioned in article 10 refers to the expected growth in the flow of trade between each Contracting Party and the others as a whole, in the products included in the liberalization programme and those which may subsequently be added.

CHAPTER III

EXPANSION OF TRADE AND ECONOMIC COMPLEMENTARITY

Article 14

In order to ensure the continued expansion and diversification of reciprocal trade, the Contracting Parties shall take steps:

(a) To grant one another, while observing the principle of reciprocity, concessions which will ensure that, in the first negotiation, treatment not less favourable than that which existed before the date of entry into force of the present Treaty is accorded to imports from within the Area;

(b) To include in the National Schedules the largest possible number of products in which trade is carried on among the Contracting Parties; and

(c) To add to these Schedules an increasing number of products which are not yet included in reciprocal trade.

Article 15

In order to ensure fair competitive conditions among the Contracting Parties and to facilitate the increasing integration and complementarity of their economies, particularly with regard to industrial production, the Contracting Parties shall make every effort—in keeping with the liberalization objectives of the present Treaty—to reconcile their import and export régimes, as well as the treatment they accord to capital, goods and services from outside the Area.

Article 16

With a view to expediting the process of integration and complementarity referred to in article 15, the Contracting Parties:

(a) Shall endeavour to promote progressively closer co-ordination of the corresponding industrialization policies, and shall sponsor for this purpose agreements among representatives of the economic sectors concerned; and

(b) May negotiate mutual agreements on complementarity by industrial sectors.

Article 17

The complementarity agreements referred to in article 16, subparagraph (b), shall set forth the liberalization programme to be applied to products of the sector concerned and may contain, *inter alia,* clauses designed to reconcile the treatment accorded to raw materials and other components used in the manufacture of these products.

Any Contracting Party concerned with the complementarity programmes shall be free to participate in the negotiation of these agreements.

The results of these negotiations shall, in every case, be embodied in protocols which shall enter into force after the Contracting Parties have decided that they are consistent with the general principles and purposes of the present Treaty.

CHAPTER IV

MOST-FAVOURED-NATION TREATMENT

Article 18

Any advantage, benefit, franchise, immunity or privilege applied by a Contracting Party in respect of a product originating in or intended for consignment to any other country shall be immediately and unconditionally extended to the similar product originating in or intended for consignment to the territory of the other Contracting Parties.

Article 19

The most-favoured-nation treatment referred to in article 18 shall not be applicable to the advantages, benefits, franchises, immunities and privileges already granted or which may be granted by virtue of agreements among Contracting Parties or between Contracting Parties and third countries with a view to facilitating border trade.

Article 20

Capital originating in the Area shall enjoy, in the territory of each Contracting Party, treatment not less favourable than that granted to capital originating in any other country.

CHAPTER V

TREATMENT IN RESPECT OF INTERNAL TAXATION

Article 21

With respect to taxes, rates and other internal duties and charges, products originating in the territory of a Contracting Party shall enjoy, in the territory of another Contracting Party, treatment no less favourable than that accorded to similar national products.

Article 22

Each Contracting Party shall endeavour to ensure that the charges or other domestic measures applied to products included in the liberalization programme which are not produced, or are produced only in small quantities, in its territory, do not nullify or reduce any concession or advantage obtained by any Contracting Party during the negotiations.

If a Contracting Party considers itself injured by virtue of the measures mentioned in the previous paragraph, it may appeal to the competent organs of the Association with a view to having the matter examined and appropriate recommendations made.

CHAPTER VI

SAVING CLAUSES

Article 23

The Contracting Parties may, as a provisional measure and providing that the customary level of consumption in the importer country is not thereby lowered, authorize a Contracting Party to impose non-discriminatory restrictions upon imports of products included in the liberalization programme which originate in the Area, if these products are imported in such quantities or under such conditions that they have, or are liable to have, serious repercussions on specific productive activities of vital importance to the national economy.

Article 24

The Contracting Parties may likewise authorize a Contracting Party which has adopted measures to correct its unfavourable over-all balance of payments to extend these measures, provisionally and without discrimination, to intra-Area trade in the products included in the liberalization programme.

The Contracting Parties shall endeavour to ensure that the imposition of restrictions deriving from the balance-of-payments situation does not affect trade, within the Area, in the products included in the liberalization programme.

Article 25

If the situations referred to in articles 23 and 24 call for immediate action, the Contracting Party concerned may, as an emergency arrangement to be referred to the Contracting Parties, apply the measures provided for in the said articles. The measures adopted must immediately be communicated to the Committee mentioned in article 33, which, if it deems necessary, shall convene a special session of the Conference.

Article 26

Should the measures envisaged in this chapter be prolonged for more than one year, the Committee shall propose to the Conference, referred to in article 33, either *ex officio* or at the request of any of the Contracting Parties, the immediate initiation of negotiations with a view to eliminating the restrictions adopted.

The present article does not affect the provisions of article 8.

CHAPTER VII

SPECIAL PROVISIONS CONCERNING AGRICULTURE

Article 27

The Contracting Parties shall seek to co-ordinate their agricultural development and agricultural commodity trade policies, with a view to securing the most efficient utilization of their natural resources, raising the standard of living of the rural population, and guaranteeing normal supplies to consumers, without disorganizing the regular productive activities of each Contracting Party.

Article 28

Providing that no lowering of its customary consumption or increase in anti-economic production is involved, a Contracting Party may apply, within the period mentioned in article 2, and in respect of trade in agricultural commodities of substantial importance to its economy that are included in the liberalization programme, appropriate non-discriminatory measures designed to:

(*a*) Limit imports to the amount required to meet the deficit in internal production; and

(*b*) Equalize the prices of the imported and domestic product.

The Contracting Party which decides to apply these measures shall inform the other Contracting Parties before it puts them into effect.

Article 29

During the period prescribed in article 2 an attempt shall be made to expand intra-Area trade in agricultural commodities by such means as agreements among the Contracting Parties designed to cover deficits in domestic production.

For this purpose, the Contracting Parties shall give priority, under normal competitive conditions, to products originating in the territories of the other Contracting Parties, due consideration being given to the traditional flows of intra-Area trade.

Should such agreements be concluded among two or more Contracting Parties, the other Contracting Parties shall be notified before the agreements enter into force.

Article 30

The measures provided for in this chapter shall not be applied for the purpose of incorporating, in the production of agricultural commodities, resources which imply a reduction in the average level of productivity existing on the date on which the present Treaty enters into force.

Article 31

If a Contracting Party considers itself injured by a reduction of its exports attributable to the lowering of the usual consumption level of the importer country as a result of the measures referred to in article 28 and/or an anti-economic increase in the production referred to in the previous article, it may appeal to the competent organs of the Association to study the situation and, if necessary, to make recommendations for the adoption of appropriate measures to be applied in accordance with article 12.

CHAPTER VIII

MEASURES IN FAVOUR OF COUNTRIES AT A RELATIVELY LESS ADVANCED STAGE OF ECONOMIC DEVELOPMENT

Article 32

The Contracting Parties, recognizing that fulfilment of the purpose of the present Treaty will be facilitated by the economic growth of the countries in the Area that are at a relatively less advanced stage of economic development, shall take steps to create conditions conducive to such growth.

To this end, the Contracting Parties may:

(a) Authorize a Contracting Party to grant to another Contracting Party which is at a relatively less advanced stage of economic development within the Area, as long as necessary and as a temporary measure, for the purposes set out in the present article, advantages not extended to the other Contracting Parties, in order to encourage the introduction or expansion of specific productive activities;

(b) Authorize a Contracting Party at a relatively less advanced stage of economic development within the Area to implement the programme for the reduction of duties, charges and other restrictions under more favourable conditions, specially agreed upon;

(c) Authorize a Contracting Party at a relatively less advanced stage of economic development within the Area to adopt appropriate measures to correct an unfavourable balance of payments, if the case arises;

(d) Authorize a Contracting Party at a relatively less advanced stage of economic development within the Area to apply, if necessary and as a temporary measure, and providing that this does not entail a decrease in its customary consumption, appropriate non-discriminatory measures designed to protect the domestic output of products included in the liberalization programme which are of vital importance to its economic development;

(e) Make collective arrangements in favour of a Contracting Party at a relatively less advanced stage of economic development within the Area with respect to the support and promotion, both inside and outside the Area, of financial or technical measures designed to bring about the expansion of existing productive activities or to encourage new activities, particularly those intended for the industrialization of its raw materials; and

(f) Promote or support, as the case may be, special technical assistance programmes for one or more Contracting Parties, intended to raise, in countries at a relatively less advanced stage of economic development within the Area, productivity levels in specific production sectors.

CHAPTER IX

ORGANS OF THE ASSOCIATION

Article 33

The organs of the Association are the Conference of the Contracting Parties (referred to in this Treaty as "the Conference") and the Standing Executive Committee (referred to in this Treaty as "the Committee").

Article 34

The Conference is the supreme organ of the Association. It shall adopt all decisions in matters requiring joint action on the part of the Contracting Parties, and it shall be empowered, *inter alia:*

(a) To take the necessary steps to carry out the present Treaty and to study the results of its implementation;

(b) To promote the negotiations provided for in article 4 and to assess the results thereof;

(c) To approve the Committee's annual budget and to fix the contributions of each Contracting Party;

(d) To lay down its own rules of procedure and to approve the Committee's rules of procedure;

(e) To elect a Chairman and two Vice-Chairmen for each session;

(f) To appoint the Executive Secretary of the Committee; and

(g) To deal with other business of common interest.

Article 35

The Conference shall be composed of duly accredited representatives of the Contracting Parties. Each delegation shall have one vote.

Article 36

The Conference shall hold: (a) a regular session once a year; and (b) special sessions when convened by the Committee.

At each session the Conference shall decide the place and date of the following regular session.

Article 37

The Conference may not take decisions unless at least two-thirds($\frac{2}{3}$) of the Contracting Parties are present.

Article 38

During the first two years in which the present Treaty is in force, decisions of the Conference shall be adopted when affirmative votes are cast by at least two-thirds ($\frac{2}{3}$) of the Contracting Parties and providing that no negative vote is cast.

The Contracting Parties shall likewise determine the voting system to be adopted after this two-year period.

The affirmative vote of two-thirds ($\frac{2}{3}$) of the Contracting Parties shall be required:

(*a*) To approve the Committee's annual budget;
(*b*) To elect the Chairman and Vice-Chairmen of the Conference, as well as the Executive Secretary; and
(*c*) To fix the time and place of the sessions of the Conference.

Article 39

The Committee is the permanent organ of the Association responsible for supervising the implementation of the provisions of the present Treaty. Its duties and responsibilities shall be, *inter alia:*

(*a*) To convene the Conference;
(*b*) To submit for the approval of the Conference an annual work pro-gramme and the Committee's annual budget estimates;
(*c*) To represent the Association in dealings with third countries and international organs and entities for the purpose of considering matters of common interest. It shall also represent the Association in contracts and other instruments of public and private law;
(*d*) To undertake studies, to suggest measures and to submit to the Conference such recommendations as it deems appropriate for the effective implementation of the Treaty;
(*e*) To submit to the Conference at its regular sessions an annual report on its activities and on the results of the implementation of the present Treaty;
(*f*) To request the technical advice and the co-operation of individuals and of national and international organizations;
(*g*) To take such decisions as may be delegated to it by the Conference; and
(*h*) To undertake the work assigned to it by the Conference.

Article 40

The Committee shall consist of a Permanent Representative of each Contracting Party, who shall have a single vote. Each Representative shall have an Alternate.

Article 41

The Committee shall have a Secretariat headed by an Executive Secretary and comprising technical and administrative personnel. The Executive Secretary, elected by the Conference for a three-year term and re-eligible for similar periods, shall attend the plenary meetings of the Committee without the right to vote. The Executive Secretary shall be the General Secretary of the Conference. His duties shall be, *inter alia:*

(*a*) To organize the work of the Conference and of the Committee;

(*b*) To prepare the Committee's annual budget estimates; and

(*c*) To recruit and engage the technical and administrative staff in accordance with the Committee's rules of procedure.

Article 42

In the performance of their duties, the Executive Secretary and the Secretariat staff shall not seek or receive instructions from any Government or from any other national or international entity. They shall refrain from any action which might reflect on their position as international civil servants.

The Contracting Parties undertake to respect the international character of the responsibilities of the Executive Secretary and of the Secretariat staff and shall refrain from influencing them in any way in the discharge of their responsibilities.

Article 43

In order to facilitate the study of specific problems, the Committee may set up Advisory Commissions composed of representatives of the various sectors of economic activity of each of the Contracting Parties.

Article 44

The Committee shall request, for the organs of the Association, the technical advice of the secretariat of the United Nations Economic Commission for Latin America (ECLA) and of the Inter-American Economic and Social Council (IA-ECOSOC) of the Organization of American States.

Article 45

The Committee shall be constituted sixty days from the entry into force of the present Treaty and shall have its headquarters in the city of Montevideo.

CHAPTER X

JURIDICAL PERSONALITY—IMMUNITIES AND PRIVILEGES

Article 46

The Latin American Free-Trade Association shall possess complete juridical personality and shall, in particular, have the power:

(*a*) To contract;

(*b*) To acquire and dispose of the movable and immovable property it needs for the achievement of its objectives;

(*c*) To institute legal proceedings; and

(*d*) To hold funds in any currency and to transfer them as necessary.

Article 47

The representatives of the Contracting Parties and the international staff and advisers of the Association shall enjoy in the Area such diplomatic and other immunities and privileges as are necessary for the exercise of their functions.

The Contracting Parties undertake to conclude, as soon as possible, an Agreement regulating the provisions of the previous paragraph in which the aforesaid privileges and immunities shall be defined.

The Association shall conclude with the Government of the Eastern Republic of Uruguay an Agreement for the purpose of specifying the privileges and immunities which the Association, its organs and its international staff and advisers shall enjoy.

CHAPTER XI

MISCELLANEOUS PROVISIONS

Article 48

No change introduced by a Contracting Party in its régime of import duties and charges shall imply a level of duties and charges less favourable than that in force before the change for any commodity in respect of which concessions are granted to the other Contracting Parties.

The requirement set out in the previous paragraph shall not apply to the conversion to present worth of the official base value (*aforo*) in respect of customs duties and charges, providing that such conversion corresponds exclusively to the real value of the goods. In such cases, the value shall not include the customs duties and charges levied on the goods.

Article 49

In order to facilitate the implementation of the provisions of the present Treaty, the Contracting Parties shall, as soon as possible:

(*a*) Determine the criteria to be adopted for the purpose of establishing the origin of goods and for classifying them as raw materials, semi-manufactured goods or finished products;

(*b*) Simplify and standardize procedures and formalities relating to reciprocal trade;

(*c*) Prepare a tariff nomenclature to serve as a common basis for the presentation of statistics and for carrying out the negotiations provided for in the present Treaty;

(*d*) Determine what shall be deemed to constitute border trade within the meaning of article 19;

(*e*) Determine the criteria for the purpose of defining "dumping" and other unfair trade practices and the procedures relating thereto.

Article 50

The products imported from the Area by a Contracting Party may not be re-exported save by agreement between the Contracting Parties concerned.

A product shall not be deemed to be a re-export if it has been subjected in the importer country to industrial processing or manufacture, the degree of which shall be determined by the Committee.

Article 51

Products imported or exported by a Contracting Party shall enjoy freedom of transit within the Area and shall only be subject to the payment of the normal rates for services rendered.

Article 52

No Contracting Party shall promote its exports by means of subsidies or other measures likely to disrupt normal competitive conditions in the Area.

An export shall not be deemed to have been subsidized if it is exempted from duties and charges levied on the product or its components when destined for internal consumption, or if it is subject to drawback.

Article 53

No provision of the present Treaty shall be so construed as to constitute an impediment to the adoption and execution of measures relating to:

(*a*) The protection of public morality;

(*b*) The application of security laws and regulations;

(*c*) The control of imports or exports of arms, ammunition and other war equipment and, in exceptional circumstances, of all other military items, in so far as this is compatible with the terms of article 51 and of the treaties on the unrestricted freedom of transit in force among the Contracting Parties;

(*d*) The protection of human, animal and plant life and health;
(*e*) Imports and exports of gold and silver bullion;
(*f*) The protection of the nation's heritage of artistic, historical and archaeological value; and
(*g*) The export, use and consumption of nuclear materials, radioactive products or any other material that may be used in the development or exploitation of nuclear energy.

Article 54

The Contracting Parties shall make every effort to direct their policies with a view to creating conditions favourable to the establishment of a Latin American common market. To that end, the Committee shall undertake studies and consider projects and plans designed to achieve this purpose, and shall endeavour to co-ordinate its work with that of other international organizations.

CHAPTER XII
FINAL PROVISIONS
Article 55

The present Treaty may not be signed with reservations nor shall reservations be admitted at the time of ratification or accession.

Article 56

The present Treaty shall be ratified by the signatory States at the earliest opportunity.

The instruments of ratification shall be deposited with the Government of the Eastern Republic of Uruguay, which shall communicate the date of deposit to the Governments of the signatory and successively acceding States.

Article 57

The present Treaty shall enter into force for the first three ratifying States thirty days after the third instrument of ratification has been deposited; and, for the other signatories, thirty days after the respective instrument of ratification has been deposited, and in the order in which the ratifications are deposited.

The Government of the Eastern Republic of Uruguay shall communicate the date of the entry into force of the present Treaty to the Government of each of the signatory States.

Article 58

Following its entry into force, the present Treaty shall remain open to accession by the other Latin American States, which for this purpose shall deposit the relevant instrument of accession with the Government of the Eastern Republic of Uruguay. The Treaty shall enter into force for the acceding State thirty days after the deposit of the corresponding instrument.

Acceding States shall enter into the negotiations referred to in article 4 at the session of the Conference immediately following the date of deposit of the instrument of accession.

Article 59

Each Contracting Party shall begin to benefit from the concessions already granted to one another by the other Contracting Parties as from the date of entry into force of the reductions in duties and charges and other restrictions negotiated by them on a basis of reciprocity, and after the minimum obligations referred to in article 5, accumulated during the period which has elapsed since the entry into force of the present Treaty, have been carried out.

Article 60

The Contracting Parties may present amendments to the present Treaty, which shall be set out in protocols that shall enter into force upon their ratification by all the Contracting Parties and after the corresponding instruments have been deposited.

Article 61

On the expiry of the twelve-year term starting on the date of entry into force of the present Treaty, the Contracting Parties shall proceed to study the results of the Treaty's implementation and shall initiate the necessary collective negotiations with a view to fulfilling more effectively the purposes of the Treaty, and, if desirable, to adapting it to a new stage of economic integration.

Article 62

The provisions of the present Treaty shall not affect the rights and obligations deriving from agreements signed by any of the Contracting Parties prior to the entry into force of the present Treaty.

However, each Contracting Party shall take the necessary steps to reconcile the provisions of existing agreements with the purposes of the present Treaty.

Article 63

The present Treaty shall be of unlimited duration.

Article 64

A Contracting Party wishing to withdraw from the present Treaty shall inform the other Contracting Parties of its intention at a regular session of the Conference, and shall formally submit the instrument of denunciation at the following regular session.

R

When the formalities of denunciation have been completed, those rights and obligations of the denouncing Government which derive from its status as a Contracting Party shall cease automatically, with the exception of those relating to reductions in duties and charges and other restrictions, received or granted under the liberalization programme, which shall remain in force for a period of five years from the date on which the denunciation becomes formally effective.

The period specified in the preceding paragraph may be shortened if there is sufficient justification, with the consent of the Conference and at the request of the Contracting Party concerned.

Article 65
The present Treaty shall be called the Montevideo Treaty.

In witness thereof the undersigned Plenipotentiaries, having deposited their full powers, found in good and due form, have signed the present Treaty on behalf of their respective Governments.

Done in the city of Montevideo, on the eighteenth day of the month of February in the year one thousand nine hundred and sixty, in one original in the Spanish and one in the Portuguese language, both texts being equally authentic. The Government of the Eastern Republic of Uruguay shall be the depositary of the present Treaty and shall transmit duly certified copies thereof to the Governments of the other signatory and acceding States.

For the Government of the Argentine Republic:
(*Signed*) *Diógenes Taboada*

For the Government of the United States of Brazil:
(*Signed*) *Horacio Lafer*

For the Government of the Republic of Chile:
(*Signed*) *Germán Vergara Donoso*

For the Government of the Republic of the United Mexican States:
(*Signed*) *Manuel Tello*

For the Government of the Republic of Paraguay:
(*Signed*) *Raúl Sapena Pastor*
Pedro Ramón Chamorro

For the Government of Peru:
(*Signed*) *Hernán Bellido*
Gonzalo L. de Aramburu

For the Government of the Eastern Republic of Uruguay:
(*Signed*) *Horacio Martínez Montero*
Mateo Magariños de Mello

Protocol No. 1

ON NORMS AND PROCEDURES FOR NEGOTIATIONS

On the occasion of the signing of the Treaty establishing a free-trade area and instituting the Latin American Free-Trade Association (Montevideo Treaty), the signatories, thereunto duly authorized by their Governments, hereby agree upon the following Protocol:

TITLE I

Calculation of weighted averages

1. For the purposes of article 5 of the Montevideo Treaty, it shall be understood that, as a result of the negotiations for the establishment of the National Schedules, the difference between the weighted average of duties and charges in force for third countries and that which shall be applicable to imports from within the area shall be not less than the product of eight per cent (8%) of the weighted average of duties and charges in force for third countries multiplied by the number of years that have elapsed since the Treaty became effective.

2. The reduction mechanism shall therefore be based on two weighted averages: one corresponding to the average of the duties and charges in force for third countries; and the other to the average of the duties and charges which shall be applicable to imports from within the Area.

3. In order to calculate each of these weighted averages, the total amount that would be represented by the duties and charges on aggregate imports of the goods under consideration shall be divided by the total value of these imports.

4. This calculation will give a percentage (or *ad valorem* figure) for each weighted average. It is the difference between the two averages that shall be not less than the product of the factor $0 \cdot 08$ (or eight per cent) multiplied by the number of years elapsed.

5. The foregoing formula is expressed as follows:

$$t \leqslant T\,(1\text{-}0\cdot08n) \text{ in which}$$

t=weighted average of the duties and charges that shall be applicable to imports from within the area;
T=weighted average of duties and charges in force for third countries;
n=number of years since the Treaty entered into force.

6. In calculating the weighted averages for each of the Contracting Parties, the following shall be taken into account:

(a) Products originating in the territory of the other Contracting Parties and imported from the Area during the preceding three-year period and further products included in the National Schedule concerned as a result of negotiations;

(b) The total value of imports, irrespective of origin, of each of the products referred to in sub-paragraph (a), during the three-year period preceding each negotiation; and

(c) The duties and charges on imports from third countries in force as on 31 December prior to the negotiations, and the duties and charges applicable to imports from within the Area entering into force on 1 January following the negotiations.

7. The Contracting Parties shall be entitled to exclude products of little value from the group referred to in sub-paragraph (a), provided that their aggregate value does not exceed five per cent (5%) of the value of imports from within the Area.

TITLE II

Exchange of information

8. The Contracting Parties shall provide one another, through the Standing Executive Committee, with information as complete as possible on:

(a) National statistics in respect of total imports and exports (value in dollars and volume, by countries both of origin and of destination), production and consumption;

(b) Customs legislation and regulations;

(c) Exchange, monetary, fiscal and administrative legislation, regulations and practices bearing on exports and imports;

(d) International trade treaties and agreements whose provisions relate to the Treaty;

(e) Systems of direct or indirect subsidies on production or exports, including minimum price systems; and

(f) State trading systems.

9. So far as possible, these data shall be permanently available to the Contracting Parties. They shall be specially brought up to date sufficiently in advance of the opening of the annual negotiations.

TITLE III

Negotiation of National Schedules

10. Before 30 June of each year, the Contracting Parties shall make available to one another, through the Standing Executive Committee, the list of products in respect of which they are applying for concessions and,

before 15 August of each year (with the exception of the first year, when the corresponding final date shall be 1 October), the preliminary list of items in favour of which they are prepared to grant concessions.

11. On 1 September of each year (with the exception of the first year, when the corresponding date shall be 1 November), the Contracting Parties shall initiate the negotiation of the concessions to be accorded by each to the others as a whole. The concessions shall be assessed multilaterally, although this shall not preclude the conduct of negotiations by pairs or groups of countries, in accordance with the interest attaching to specific products.

12. Upon the conclusion of this phase of the negotiations, the Standing Executive Committee shall make the calculations referred to in title I of this Protocol and shall inform each Contracting Party, at the earliest possible opportunity, of the percentage whereby its individual concessions reduce the weighted average of the duties and charges in force for imports from within the Area, in relation to the weighted average of duties and charges applicable in the case of third countries.

13. When the concessions negotiated fall short of the corresponding minimum commitment, the negotiations among the Contracting Parties shall be continued, so that the list of reductions of duties and charges and other restrictions to enter into force as from the following 1 January may be simultaneously published by each of the Contracting Parties not later than 1 November of each year.

TITLE IV

Negotiation of the Common Schedule

14. During each three-year period and not later than on 31 May of the third, sixth, ninth and twelfth years from the time of the Treaty's entry into force, the Standing Executive Committee shall supply the Contracting Parties with statistical data on the value and volume of the products traded in the Area during the preceding three-year period, indicating the proportion of aggregate trade which each individually represented.

15. Before 30 June of the third, sixth and ninth years from the time of the Treaty's entry into force, the Contracting Parties shall exchange the lists of products whose inclusion in the Common Schedule they wish to negotiate.

16. The Contracting Parties shall conduct multilateral negotiations to establish, before 30 November in the third, sixth, ninth and twelfth

years, a Common Schedule comprising goods whose value meets the minimum commitments referred to in article 7 of the Treaty.

TITLE V

Special and temporary provisions

17. In the negotiations to which this Protocol refers, consideration shall be given to those cases in which varying levels of duties and charges on certain products create conditions such that producers in the Area are not competing on equitable terms.

18. To this end, steps shall be taken to ensure prior equalization of tariffs or to secure by any other suitable procedure the highest possible degree of effective reciprocity.

IN WITNESS WHEREOF the respective representatives have signed the Protocol.

DONE at the City of Montevideo, on the eighteenth day of the month of February in the year one thousand nine hundred and sixty, in one original in the Spanish and one in the Portuguese language, both texts being equally authentic.

The Government of the Eastern Republic of Uruguay shall act as depositary of the present Protocol and shall send certified true copies thereof to the Governments of the other signatory and acceding countries.

For the Government of the Argentine Republic:
Diógenes Taboada

For the Government of the Republic of the United States of Brazil:
Horacio Lafer

For the Government of the Republic of Chile:
Germán Vergara Donoso

For the Government of the Republic of the United Mexican States:
Manuel Tello

For the Government of the Republic of Paraguay:
Raúl Sapena Pastor
Pedro Ramón Chamorro

For the Government of Peru:
Hernán Bellido
Gonzalo L. de Aramburu

For the Government of the Eastern Republic of Uruguay:
Horacio Martínez Montero
Mateo Magariños de Mello

Protocol No. 2

ON THE ESTABLISHMENT OF A PROVISIONAL COMMITTEE

On the occasion of the signing of the Treaty establishing a free-trade area and instituting the Latin American Free Trade Association (Montevideo Treaty), the signatories, thereunto duly authorized by their Governments, taking into consideration the need to adopt and coordinate measures to facilitate the entry into force of the Treaty, hereby agree as follows:

1. A Provisional Committee shall be set up, composed of one representative of each signatory State. Each representative shall have an alternate.

At its first meeting the Provisional Committee shall elect from among its members one Chairman and two Vice-Chairmen.

2. The terms of reference of the Provisional Committee shall be as follows:

(*a*) To draw up its rules of procedure;

(*b*) To prepare, within sixty days from the date of its inauguration, its work programme, and to establish its budget of expenditure and the contributions to be made by each country;

(*c*) To adopt the measures and prepare the documents necessary for the presentation of the Treaty to the Contracting Parties of the General Agreement on Tariffs and Trade (GATT);

(*d*) To convene and prepare for the first Conference of Contracting Parties;

(*e*) To assemble and prepare the data and statistics required for the first series of negotiations connected with the implementation of the liberalization programme provided for in the Treaty;

(*f*) To carry out or promote studies and research, and to adopt whatsoever measures may be necessary in the common interest during its period of office; and

(*g*) To prepare a preliminary draft agreement on the privileges and immunities referred to in article 47 of the Treaty.

3. In technical matters, the Provisional Committee shall be assisted in an advisory capacity by the United Nations Economic Commission for Latin America (ECLA) and the Inter-American Economic and Social Council (IA-ECOSOC), of the Organization of American States, in accordance with the relevant Protocol.

4. The Provisional Committee shall appoint an Administrative Secretary and other requisite staff.

5. The Provisional Committee shall be inaugurated on 1 April 1960, and its quorum shall be constituted by not less than four members. Up to that date, the Officers of the Inter-Governmental Conference for the Establishment of a Free-Trade Area among Latin American Countries shall continue to discharge their functions, for the sole purpose of establishing the Provisional Committee.

6. The Provisional Committee shall remain in office until the Standing Executive Committee, provided for in article 33 of the Treaty, has been set up.

7. The Provisional Committee shall have its headquarters in the City of Montevideo.

8. The Officers of the above-mentioned Conference are recommended to request the Government of the Eastern Republic of Uruguay to advance the necessary sums to cover the payment of staff salaries and the installation and operational expenses of the Provisional Committee during the first ninety days. These sums shall be subsequently reimbursed by the States signatories of the present Treaty.

9. The Provisional Committee shall approach the signatory Governments with a view to obtaining for the members of its constituent delegations, as well as for its international staff and advisers, such immunities and privileges as may be needful for the performance of their duties.

IN WITNESS WHEREOF the respective representatives have signed the present Protocol.

DONE at the City of Montevideo, on the eighteenth day of the month of February in the year one thousand nine hundred and sixty, in one original in the Spanish and one in the Portuguese language, both texts being equally authentic. The Government of the Eastern Republic of Uruguay shall act as the depositary of the present Protocol and shall send certified true copies thereof to the Governments of the other signatory and acceding countries.

For the Government of the Argentine Republic:
Diógenes Taboada

For the Government of the Republic of the United States of Brazil:
Horacio Lafer

For the Government of the Republic of Chile:
Germán Vergara Donoso

For the Government of the Republic of the United Mexican States:
Manuel Tello

For the Government of the Republic of Paraguay:

> *Raúl Sapena Pastor*
> *Pedro Ramón Chamorro*

For the Government of Peru:

> *Hernán Bellido*
> *Gonzalo L. de Aramburu*

For the Government of the Eastern Republic of Uruguay:

> *Horacio Martínez Montero*
> *Mateo Magariños de Mello*

Protocol No. 3
ON THE COLLABORATION OF THE UNITED NATIONS ECONOMIC COMMISSION FOR LATIN AMERICA (ECLA) AND OF THE INTER-AMERICAN ECONOMIC AND SOCIAL COUNCIL (IA-ECOSOC) OF THE ORGANIZATION OF AMERICAN STATES

On the occasion of the signing of the Treaty establishing a free-trade area and instituting the Latin American Free-Trade Association (Montevideo Treaty), the signatories, thereunto duly authorized by their Governments, hereby agree as follows:

1. With reference to the provisions of article 44 of the Treaty and in view of the fact that the secretariats of ECLA and of IA-ECOSOC have agreed to assist the organs of the Latin American Free-Trade Association with advice on technical matters, a representative of each of the secretariats in question shall attend the meetings of the Standing Executive Commitee of the above-mentioned Association when the business to be discussed is, in the Committee's opinion, of a technical nature.

2. The appointment of the representatives referred to shall be subject to the prior approval of the members of the said Committee.

IN WITNESS WHEREOF the respective representatives have signed the present Protocol.

DONE at the City of Montevideo, on the eighteenth day of the month of February in the year one thousand nine hundred and sixty, in one original in the Spanish and one in the Portuguese language, both texts being equally authentic. The Government of the Eastern Republic of Uruguay shall act as the depositary of the present Protocol and shall send certified true copies thereof to the Governments of the other signatory and acceding countries.

For the Government of the Argentine Republic:

Diógenes Toboada

For the Government of the Republic of the United States of Brazil:

Horacio Lafer

For the Government of the Republic of Chile:

Germán Vergara Donoso

For the Government of the Republic of the United Mexican States:

Manuel Tello

For the Government of the Republic of Paraguay:

Raúl Sapena Pastor
Pedro Ramón Chamorro

For the Government of Peru:

Hernán Bellido
Gonzalo L. de Aramburu

For the Government of the Eastern Republic of Uruguay:

Horacio Martínez Montero
Mateo Magariños de Mello

Protocol No. 4

ON COMMITMENTS TO PURCHASE OR SELL PETROLEUM AND PETROLEUM DERIVATIVES

On the occasion of the signing of the Treaty establishing a free-trade area and instituting the Latin American Free-Trade Association (Montevideo Treaty), the signatories, thereunto duly authorized by their Governments, hereby agree:

To declare that the provisions of the Montevideo Treaty, signed on 18 February 1960, are not applicable to commitments to purchase or sell petroleum and petroleum derivatives resulting from agreements concluded by the signatories of the present Protocol prior to the date of signature of the above-mentioned Treaty.

IN WITNESS WHEREOF the respective representatives have signed the present Protocol.

DONE at the City of Montevideo, on the eighteenth day of the month of February in the year one thousand nine hundred and sixty, in one original in the Spanish and one in the Portuguese language, both texts being equally authentic.

The Government of the Eastern Republic of Uruguay shall act as depositary of the present Protocol and shall send certified true copies thereof to the Governments of the other signatory and acceding countries.

For the Government of the Argentine Republic:
Diógenes Taboada

For the Government of the Republic of the United States of Brazil:
Horacio Lafer

For the Government of the Republic of Chile:
Germán Vergara Donoso

For the Government of the Republic of the United Mexican States:
Manuel Tello

For the Government of the Republic of Paraguay:
Raúl Sapena Pastor
Pedro Ramón Chamorro

For the Government of Peru:
Hernán Bellido
Gonzalo L. de Aramburu

For the Government of the Eastern Republic of Uruguay:
Horacio Martínez Montero
Mateo Magariños de Mello

Protocol No. 5

ON SPECIAL TREATMENT IN FAVOUR OF BOLIVIA AND PARAGUAY

On the occasion of the signing of the Treaty establishing a free-trade area and instituting the Latin American Free-Trade Association (Montevideo Treaty), the signatories, thereunto duly authorized by their Governments, hereby agree:

To declare that Bolivia and Paraguay are at present in a position to invoke in their favour the provisions in the Treaty concerning special treatment for countries at a relatively less advanced stage of economic development within the Free-Trade Area.

IN WITNESS WHEREOF the respective representatives have signed the present Protocol.

DONE at the City of Montevideo, on the eighteenth day of the month of February in the year one thousand nine hundred and sixty, in one original in the Spanish and one in the Portuguese language, both texts being equally authentic.

The Government of the Eastern Republic of Uruguay shall act as depositary of the present Protocol and shall send certified true copies thereof to the Governments of other signatory and acceding countries.

For the Government of the Argentine Republic:
Diógenes Taboada

For the Government of the Republic of the United States of Brazil:
Horacio Lafer

For the Government of the Republic of Chile:
Germán Vergara Donoso

For the Government of the Republic of the United Mexican States:
Manuel Tello

For the Government of the Republic of Paraguay:
Raúl Sapena Pastor
Pedro Ramón Chamorro

For the Government of Peru:
Hernán Bellido
Gonzalo L. de Aramburu

For the Government of the Eastern Republic of Uruguay:
Horacio Martínez Montero
Mateo Magariños de Mello

Resolution I

MEETINGS OF GOVERNMENTAL REPRESENTATIVES OF CENTRAL BANKS

The Inter-Governmental Conference for the Establishment of a Free-Trade Area among Latin American Countries,

In view of the report submitted to the Conference by the Meeting of Governmental Representatives of Central Banks, held at Montevideo in January 1960,

Considering the desirability of continuing the studies on payments and credits to facilitate the financing of intra-Area transactions and therefore the fulfilment of the purposes of the Treaty establishing a Free-Trade Area and instituting the Latin American Free-Trade Association,

Decides:

1. To take note of the above-mentioned report;

2. To request the Provisional Committee to convene informal meetings of governmental experts from the central banks of Argentina, Bolivia, Brazil, Chile, Mexico, Paraguay, Peru and Uruguay, which shall be organized by the secretariat of the United Nations Economic Commission for Latin America (ECLA);

3. To establish that the object of these meetings shall be the continuance of the studies on credits and payments to facilitate the financing of intra-Area transactions and therefore the fulfilment of the purposes of the aforesaid Treaty;

4. To request the United Nations Economic Commission for Latin America (ECLA), the Inter-American Economic and Social Council (IA-ECOSOC) of the Organization of American States and the International Monetary Fund for their advice and technical assistance;

5. To extend the invitation to experts from the central banks of such countries as may have acceded to the said Treaty.

Montevideo, 18 February 1960

For the Government of the Argentine Republic:
Diógenes Taboada

For the Government of the Republic of the United States of Brazil:
Horacio Lafer

For the Government of the Republic of Chile:
Germán Vergara Donoso

For the Government of the Republic of the United Mexican States:
Manuel Tello

For the Government of the Republic of Paraguay:
Raúl Sapena Pastor
Pedro Ramón Chamorro

For the Government of Peru:
Hernán Bellido
Gonzalo L. de Aramburu

For the Government of the Eastern Republic of Uruguay:
Horacio Martínez Montero
Mateo Magariños de Mello

Resolution II
MORATORIUM GRANTED TO BOLIVIA FOR SIGNATURE OF THE TREATY

The Inter-Governmental Conference for the Establishment of a Free-Trade Area among Latin American Countries,

Considering the generous spirit of co-operation displayed by Bolivia in its participation in the negotiations for the conclusion of the Treaty establishing a Free-Trade Area and instituting the Latin American Free-Trade Association.

Mindful of the motives adduced by the delegation of Bolivia to explain why, for reasons of *force majeure*, it is unable to sign the above-mentioned Treaty on the present occasion.

Decides to grant the Government of Bolivia a moratorium of four (4) months during which it will be free to accede to the aforesaid Treaty as a signatory State.

Montevideo, 18 February 1960

For the Government of the Argentine Republic:
Diógenes Taboada

For the Government of the Republic of the United States of Brazil:
Horacio Lafer

For the Government of the Republic of Chile:
Germán Vergara Donoso

For the Government of the Republic of the United Mexican States:
Manuel Tello

For the Government of the Republic of Paraguay:
Raúl Sapena Pastor
Pedro Ramón Chamorro

For the Government of Peru:
Hernán Bellido
Gonzalo L. de Aramburu

For the Government of the Eastern Republic of Uruguay:
Horacio Martínez Montero
Mateo Magariños de Mello

C. General Treaty on Central American Economic Integration
(*Managua, 13 December 1960*)

The Governments of the Republics of Guatemala, El Salvador, Honduras and Nicaragua,

For the purpose of reaffirming their intention to unify the economies of the four countries and jointly to promote the development of Central America in order to improve the living conditions of their peoples,

Mindful of the need to expedite the integration of their economies, consolidate the results so far achieved and lay down the principles on which it should be based in the future,

Having regard to the commitments entered into in the following instruments of economic integration:

Multilateral Treaty on Free Trade and Central American Economic Integration;

Central American Agreement on the Equalization of Import Duties and Charges and its Protocol on the Central American Preferential Tariff; Bilateral treaties on free trade and economic integration signed between Central American Governments; Treaty on Economic Association signed between Guatemala, El Salvador and Honduras,

Have agreed to conclude the present Treaty and for that purpose have appointed as their respective plenipotentiaries:

H.E. The President of the Republic of Guatemala: Mr *Julio Prado García Salas*, Minister for Co-ordinating Central American Integration, and Mr *Alberto Fuentes Mohr*, Head of the Economic Integration Bureau

The H. Junta de Gobierno of the Republic of El Salvador: Mr *Gabriel Piloña Araujo*, Minister for Economic Affairs, and Mr *Abelardo Torres*, Under-Secretary for Economic Affairs

H.E. The President of the Republic of Honduras: Mr *Jorge Bueso Arias*, Minister for Economic and Financial Affairs

H.E. The President of the Republic of Nicaragua: Mr *Juan José Lugo Marenco*, Minister for Economic Affairs

who, having exchanged their respective full powers, found to be in good and due form, have agreed as follows:

CHAPTER I

CENTRAL AMERICAN COMMON MARKET

Article I

The Contracting States agree to establish among themselves a common market which shall be brought into full operation within a period of not more than five years from the date on which the present Treaty enters into force. They further agree to create a customs union in respect of their territories.

Article II

For the purposes of the previous article the Contracting Parties undertake to bring a Central American free-trade area into full operation within a period of five years and to adopt a standard Central American tariff as provided for in the Central American Agreement on the Equalization of Import Duties and Charges.

CHAPTER II

TRADE REGIME

Article III

The Signatory States shall grant each other free-trade treatment in respect of all products originating in their respective territories, save only for the limitations contained in the special régimes referred to in Annex A of the present Treaty.

Consequently, the natural products of the Contracting States and the products manufactured therein shall be exempt from import and export duties including consular fees, and all other taxes, dues and charges levied on imports and exports or charged in respect thereof, whether they be of a national, municipal or any other nature.

The exemptions provided for in this article shall not include charges or fees for lighterage, wharfage, warehousing or handling of goods, or any other charges which may legally be incurred for port, storage or transport services; nor shall they include exchange differentials resulting from the existence of two or more rates of exchange or from other exchange arrangements in any of the Contracting States.

Goods originating in the territory of any of the Signatory States shall be accorded national treatment in all of them and shall be exempt from all quantitative or other restrictions or measures, except for such measures as may be legally applicable in the territories of the Contracting States for reasons of health, security or police control.

Article IV

The Contracting Parties establish special interim régimes in respect of specific products exempting them from the immediate free-trade treatment referred to in article III hereof. These products shall be automatically incorporated into the free-trade régime not later than the end of the fifth year in which the present Treaty is in force, except as specifically provided in Annex A.

The products to which special régimes apply are listed in Annex A and trade in them shall be carried on in conformity with the measures and conditions therein specified. These measures and conditions shall not be amended except by multilateral negotiation in the Executive Council. Annex A is an integral part of this Treaty.

The Signatory States agree that the Protocol on the Central American Preferential Tariff, appended to the Central American Agreement on the Equalization of Import Duties and Charges, shall not apply to trade in the products referred to in the present article for which special régimes are provided.

Article V

Goods enjoying the advantages stipulated in this Treaty shall be designated as such on a customs form, signed by the exporter and containing a declaration of origin. This form shall be produced for checking by the customs officers of the countries of origin and destination, in conformity with Annex B of this Treaty.

If there is doubt as to the origin of an article and the matter has not been settled by bilateral negotiation, any of the Parties affected may request the intervention of the Executive Council to verify the origin of the article concerned. The Council shall not consider goods as originating in one of the Contracting States if they originate or are manufactured in a third country and are only simply assembled, wrapped, packed, cut or diluted in the exporting country.

In the cases mentioned in the previous paragraph, importation of the goods concerned shall not be prohibited provided that a guaranty is given to the importing country in respect of payment of the import duties and other charges to which the goods may be liable. The guaranty shall be either forfeited or refunded, as the case may be, when the matter is finally settled.

The Executive Council shall lay down regulations governing the procedure to be followed in determining the origin of goods.

Article VI

If the goods traded are liable to internal taxes, charges or duties of any kind levied on production, sale, distribution or consumption in any of the signatory countries, the country concerned may levy an equivalent amount on similar goods imported from the other Contracting State, in which case it must also levy at least an equivalent amount for the same respective purposes on similar imports from third countries.

The Contracting Parties agree that the following conditions shall apply to the establishment of internal taxes on consumption:

(*a*) Such taxes may be established in the amount deemed necessary when there is domestic production of the article in question, or when the article is not produced in any of the Signatory States:

(*b*) When the article is not produced in one Signatory State but is produced in any of the others, the former State may not establish taxes on consumption of the article concerned unless the Executive Council so authorizes;

(*c*) If a Contracting Party has established a domestic tax on consumption, and production of the article so taxed is subsequently begun in any of the other Signatory States, but the article is not produced in the State that established the tax, the Executive Council shall, if the State concerned so requests, deal with the case and decide whether the tax is compatible with free trade. The States undertake to abolish these taxes on consumption, in accordance with their legal procedures, on receipt of notification to this effect from the Executive Council.

Article VII

No Signatory State shall establish or maintain regulations on the distribution or retailing of goods originating in another Signatory State when such regulations place, or tend to place, the said goods in an un-

s

favourable position in relation to similar goods of domestic origin or imported from any other country.

Article VIII

Items which, by virtue of the domestic legislation of the Contracting Parties, constitute State monopolies on the date of entry into force of the present Treaty, shall remain subject to the relevant legislation of each country and, if applicable, to the provisions of Annex A of the present Treaty.

Should new monopolies be created or the régime of existing monopolies be changed, the Parties shall enter into consultations for the purpose of placing Central American trade in the items concerned under a special régime.

CHAPTER III

EXPORT SUBSIDIES AND UNFAIR TRADE PRACTICES

Article IX

The Governments of the Signatory States shall not grant customs exemptions or reductions in respect of imports from outside Central America of articles adequately produced in the Contracting States.

If a Signatory State deems itself to be affected by the granting of customs import franchises or by governmental imports not intended for the use of the Government itself or of its agencies, it may submit the matter to the Executive Council for its consideration and ruling.

Article X

The Central Banks of the Signatory States shall co-operate closely in order to prevent any currency speculation that might affect the rates of exchange and to maintain the convertibility of the currencies of the respective countries on a basis which, in normal conditions, shall guarantee the freedom, uniformity and stability of exchange.

Any Signatory State which establishes quantitative restrictions on international monetary transfers shall adopt whatever measures are necessary to ensure that such restrictions do not discriminate against the other States.

Should serious balance-of-payments difficulties arise which affect, or are apt to affect, monetary relations in respect of payments between the Signatory States, the Executive Council, acting of its own accord or at the request of one of the Parties, shall immediately study the problem in co-operation with the Central Banks for the purpose of recommending to the Signatory States a satisfactory solution compatible with the maintenance of the multilateral free-trade régime.

Article XI

No Signatory State shall grant any direct or indirect subsidy favouring the export of goods intended for the territory of the other States, or establish or maintain any system resulting in the sale of such goods for export to any other Contracting State at a price lower than that established for the sale of similar goods on the domestic market, due allowance being made for differences in the conditions and terms of sale and taxation and for any other factors affecting price comparability.

Any measure involving the fixing of, or discrimination in, prices in a Signatory State which is reflected in the establishment of sales prices for specific goods in the other Contracting States at levels lower than those that would result from the normal operation of the market in the exporting country shall be deemed to constitute an indirect export subsidy.

If the importation of goods processed in a Contracting State with raw materials purchased under conditions of monopoly at artificially low prices should threaten existing production in another Signatory State, the Party which considers itself affected shall submit the matter to the consideration of the Executive Council for a ruling as to whether an unfair business practice is in fact involved. The Executive Council shall, within five days of the receipt of the request, either give its ruling or authorize a temporary suspension of free trade, while permitting trade to be carried on subject to the award of a guaranty in the amount of the customs duties. This suspension shall be effective for thirty days, within which period the Executive Council shall announce its final decision. If no ruling is forthcoming within the five days stipulated, the Party concerned may demand a guaranty pending the Executive Council's final decision.

However, tax exemptions of a general nature granted by a Signatory State with a view to encouraging production shall not be deemed to constitute export subsidies.

Similarly, any exemption from internal taxes levied in the exporting State on the production, sale or consumption of goods exported to the territory of another State shall not be deemed to constitute an export subsidy. The differentials resulting from the sale of foreign currency on the free market at a rate of exchange higher than the official rate shall not normally be deemed to be an export subsidy; if one of the Contracting States is in doubt, however, the matter shall be submitted to the Executive Council for its consideration and opinion.

Article XII

As a means of precluding a practice which would be inconsistent with the purposes of this Treaty, each Signatory State shall employ all the legal means at its disposal to prevent the export of goods from its territory to the territories of the other States at a price lower than their normal value, if such export would prejudice or be liable to prejudice the production of the other States or retard the establishment of a national or Central American industry.

Goods shall be deemed to be exported at a price lower than their normal value if their export price is less than:

(a) The comparable price in normal trade conditions of similar goods destined for domestic consumption in the exporting country; or

(b) The highest comparable price of similar goods for export to a third country in normal trade conditions; or

(c) The cost of production of the goods in the country of origin, plus a reasonable amount for sales expenses and profit.

Due allowance shall be made in every case for existing differences in conditions and terms of sale and taxation and for any other factors affecting price comparability.

Article XIII

If a Contracting Party deems that unfair trade practices not covered in article XI exist, it cannot impede trade by a unilateral decision but must bring the matter before the Executive Council so that the latter can decide whether in fact such practices are being resorted to. The Council shall announce its decision within not more than 60 days from the date on which it received the relevant communication.

If any Party deems that there is evidence of unfair trade, it shall request the Executive Council to authorize it to demand a guaranty in the amount of the import duties.

Should the Executive Council fail to give a ruling within eight days, the Party concerned may demand such guaranty pending the Executive Council's final decision.

Article XIV

Once the Executive Council has given its ruling on unfair trade practices, it shall inform the Contracting Parties whether, in conformity with this Treaty, protective measures against such practices should be taken.

CHAPTER IV

TRANSIT AND TRANSPORT

Article XV

Each of the Contracting States shall ensure full freedom of transit through its territory for goods proceeding to or from the other Signatory States as well as for the vehicles transporting these goods.

Such transit shall not be subject to any deduction, discrimination or quantitative restriction. In the event of traffic congestion or other instances of *force majeure*, each Signatory State shall treat the mobilization of consignments intended for its own population and those in transit to the other States on an equitable basis.

Transit operations shall be carried out by the routes prescribed by law for that purpose and shall be subject to the customs and transit laws and regulations applicable in the territory of transit.

Goods in transit shall be exempt from all duties, taxes and other charges of a fiscal, municipal or any other character levied on transit, irrespective of their destination, but may be liable to the charges usually applied for services rendered which shall in no case exceed the cost thereof and thus constitute *de facto* import duties or taxes.

CHAPTER V

CONSTRUCTION ENTERPRISES

Article XVI

The Contracting States shall grant national treatment to enterprises of other Signatory States engaged in the construction of roads, bridges, dams, irrigation systems, electrification, housing and other works intended to further the development of the Central American economic infrastructure.

CHAPTER VI

INDUSTRIAL INTEGRATION

Article XVII

The Contracting Parties hereby endorse all the provisions of the Agreement on the Régime for Central American Integration Industries, and, in order to ensure implementation among themselves as soon as possible, undertake to sign, within a period of not more than six months from the date of entry into force of the present Treaty, additional protocols specifying the industrial plants initially to be covered by the Agreement, the free-trade régime applicable to their products and the other conditions provided for in article III of the Agreement.

CHAPTER VII

CENTRAL AMERICAN BANK FOR ECONOMIC INTEGRATION

Article XVIII

The Signatory States agree to establish the Central American Bank for Economic Integration which shall be a juridical person. The Bank shall act as an instrument for the financing and promotion of a regionally balanced, integrated economic growth. To that end they shall sign the agreement constituting the Bank, which shall remain open for the signature or accession of any other Central American State which may wish to become a member of the Bank.

It is, however, established that members of the Bank may not obtain guaranties or loans from the Bank unless they have previously deposited their instruments of ratification of the following international agreements:

The present Treaty;

Multilateral Treaty on Free Trade and Central American Economic Integration, signed on 10 June 1958;

Agreement on the Régime for Central American Integration Industries, signed on 10 June 1958; and

Central American Agreement on the Equalization of Import Duties and Charges, signed on 1 September 1959, and its *Protocol* signed on the same day as the present Treaty.

CHAPTER VIII

TAX INCENTIVES
TO INDUSTRIAL DEVELOPMENT

Article XIX

The Contracting States, with a view to establishing uniform tax incentives to industrial development, agree to ensure as soon as possible a reasonable equalization of the relevant laws and regulations in force. To that end they shall, within a period of six months from the date of entry into force of the present Treaty, sign a special protocol specifying the amount and type of exemptions, the time limits thereof, the conditions under which they shall be granted, the systems of industrial classification and the principles and procedures governing their application. The Executive Council shall be responsible for co-ordinating the application of the tax incentives to industrial development.

CHAPTER IX

ORGANS

Article XX

The Central American Economic Council, composed of the Ministers of Economic Affairs of the several Contracting Parties, is hereby established for the purpose of integrating the Central American economies and co-ordinating the economic policy of the Contracting States.

The Central American Economic Council shall meet as often as required or at the request of any of the Contracting Parties. It shall examine the work of the Executive Council and adopt such resolutions as it may deem appropriate. The Central American Economic Council shall be the organ responsible for facilitating implementation of the resolutions on economic integration adopted by the Central American Economic Co-operation Committee. It may seek the advice of Central American and international technical organs.

Article XXI

For the purpose of applying and administering the present Treaty and of undertaking all the negotiations and work designed to give practical effect to the Central American economic union, an Executive Council, consisting of one titular official and one alternate appointed by each Contracting Party, is hereby established.

The Executive Council shall meet as often as required, at the request of one of the Contracting Parties or when convened by the Permanent Secretariat, and its resolutions shall be adopted by majority vote. In the event of disagreement, recourse will be had to the Central American Economic Council in order that the latter may give a final ruling.

Before ruling on a matter, the Executive Council shall determine unanimously whether the matter is to be decided by a concurrent vote of all its members or by a simple majority.

Article XXII

The Executive Council shall take such measures as it may deem necessary to ensure fulfilment of the commitments entered into under this Treaty and to settle problems arising from the implementation of its provisions. It may likewise propose to the Governments the signing of such additional multilateral agreements as may be required in order to achieve the purpose of Central American economic integration, including a customs union in respect of their territories.

The Executive Council shall assume, on behalf of the Contracting Parties, the functions assigned to the Central American Trade Commission in the Multilateral Treaty on Free Trade and Central American Economic Integration and the Central American Agreement on the Equalization of Import Duties and Charges, as well as those assigned to the Central American Industrial Integration Commission in the Agreement on the Régime for Central American Integration Industries, as well as the powers and duties of the joint commissions set up under bilateral treaties in force between the Contracting Parties.

Article XXIII

A Permanent Secretariat is hereby instituted, as a juridical person, and shall act as such both for the Central American Economic Council and the Executive Council established under this Treaty.

The Secretariat shall have its seat and headquarters in Guatemala City, capital of the Republic of Guatemala, and shall be headed by a Secretary-

General appointed for a period of three years by the Central American Economic Council. The Secretariat shall establish such departments and sections as may be necessary for the performance of its functions. Its expenses shall be governed by a general budget adopted annually by the Central American Economic Council and each Contracting Party shall contribute annually to its support an amount equivalent to not less than fifty thousand United States dollars (US$50,000), payable in the respective currencies of the Signatory States.

Members of the Secretariat shall enjoy diplomatic immunity. Other diplomatic privileges shall be granted only to the Secretariat and to the Secretary-General.

Article XXIV

The Secretariat shall ensure that this Treaty, the Multilateral Treaty on Free Trade and Central American Economic Integration, the Agreement on the Régime for Central American Integration Industries, the Central American Agreement on the Equalization of Import Duties and Charges, bilateral or multilateral treaties on free trade and economic integration in force between any of the Contracting Parties, and all other agreements relating to Central American economic integration already signed or that may be signed hereafter, the interpretation of which has not been specifically entrusted to another organ, are properly executed among the Contracting Parties.

The Secretariat shall ensure implementation of the resolutions adopted by the Central American Economic Council and the Executive Council established under this Treaty and shall also perform such functions as are assigned to it by the Executive Council. Its regulations shall be approved by the Economic Council.

The Secretariat shall also undertake such work and studies as may be assigned to it by the Executive Council and the Central American Economic Council. In performing these duties, it shall avail itself of the studies and work carried out by other Central American and international organs and shall, where appropriate, enlist their co-operation.

CHAPTER X

GENERAL PROVISIONS

Article XXV

The Signatory States agree not to sign unilaterally with non-Central American countries any new treaties that may affect the principles of Central American economic integration. They further agree to maintain the "Central American exception clause" in any trade agreements they may conclude on the basis of most-favoured-nation treatment with any countries other than the Contracting States.

Article XXVI

The Signatory States agree to settle amicably, in the spirit of this Treaty, and through the Executive Council or the Central American Economic Council, as the case may be, any differences which may arise regarding the interpretation or application of any of its provisions. If agreement cannot be reached, they shall submit the matter to arbitration. For the purpose of constituting the arbitration tribunal, each Contracting Party shall propose to the General Secretariat of the Organization of Central American States the names of three magistrates from its Supreme Court of Justice. From the complete list of candidates, the Secretary-General of the Organization of Central American States and the Government representatives in the Organization shall select, by drawing lots, one arbitrator for each Contracting Party, no two of whom may be nationals of the same State. The award of the arbitration tribunal shall require the concurring votes of not less than three members, and shall have the effect of *res judicata* for all the Contracting Parties so far as it contains any ruling concerning the interpretation or application of the provisions of this Treaty.

Article XXVII

The present Treaty shall, with respect to the Contracting Parties, take precedence over the Multilateral Treaty on Free Trade and Central American Economic Integration and any other bilateral or multilateral free-trade instruments signed between the Contracting Parties; it shall not, however, affect the validity of those agreements.

The provisions of the trade and economic integration agreements referred to in the previous paragraph shall be applied between the respective Contracting Parties in so far as they are not covered in the present Treaty.

Pending ratification of the present Treaty by any of the Contracting Parties, or in the event of its denunciation by any of them, the trade relations of the Party concerned with the other Signatory States shall be governed by the commitments entered into previously under the existing instruments referred to in the preamble of the present Treaty.

Article XXVIII

The Contracting Parties agree to hold consultations in the Executive Council prior to signing any new treaties among themselves which may affect free trade.

The Executive Council shall examine each case and determine the effects that the conclusion of such agreements might produce on the free trade régime established in the present Treaty. On the basis of the Executive Council's examination, the Party which considers itself affected by the conclusion of these new treaties may adopt whatever measures the Council may recommend in order to protect its interests.

Article XXIX

For the purposes of customs regulations relating to free trade, the transit of goods and the application of the Central American Standard Import Tariff, the Contracting Parties shall, within a period of one year from the date of entry into force of the present Treaty, sign special protocols providing for the adoption of a Central American Standard Customs Code and the necessary transport regulations.

CHAPTER XI

FINAL PROVISIONS

Article XXX

This Treaty shall be submitted for ratification in each State in conformity with its respective constitutional or legislative procedures.

The instruments of ratification shall be deposited with the General Secretariat of the Organization of Central American States.

The Treaty shall enter into force, in the case of the first three States to ratify it, eight days following the date of deposit of the third instrument of ratification and, in the case of the States which ratify it subsequently, on the date of deposit of the relevant instrument.

Article XXXI

This Treaty shall remain effective for a period of twenty years from the date of its entry into force and shall be renewable indefinitely.

Upon expiry of the twenty-year period mentioned in the previous paragraph, the Treaty may be denounced by any of the Contracting Parties. Denunciation shall take effect, for the denouncing State, five years after notification, and the Treaty shall remain in force among the other Contracting States so long as at least two of them remain parties thereto.

Article XXXII

The General Secretariat of the Organization of Central American States shall act as depositary of this Treaty and shall send a certified copy thereof to the Ministry of Foreign Affairs of each of the Contracting States and shall also notify them immediately of the deposit of each instrument of ratification as well as of any denunciation which may be made. When the Treaty enters into force, it shall also transmit a certified copy thereof to the Secretary-General of the United Nations for the purposes of registration as set forth in Article 102 of the United Nations Charter.

Article XXXIII

The present Treaty shall remain open for the accession of any Central American State not originally a party thereto.

Provisional article

As soon as the Government of the Republic of Costa Rica formally accedes to the provisions of this Treaty, the organs hereby established shall form part of the Organization of Central American States (OCAS) by an incorporation agreement; and the OCAS shall be reorganized in such a way that the organs established by this Treaty retain all their structural and functional attributes.

IN WITNESS WHEREOF the respective plenipotentiaries have signed the present Treaty in the City of Managua, capital of the Republic of Nicaragua, this thirteenth day of the month of December nineteen hundred and sixty.

For the Government of Guatemala:

Julio Prado García Sala
Minister for Co-ordinating Central American Integration
Alberto Fuentes Mohr
Head of the Economic Integration Bureau

For the Government of El Salvador:

Gabriel Piloña Araujo
Minister of Economic Affairs
Abelardo Torres
Under-Secretary for Economic Affairs

For the Government of Honduras:

Jorge Bueso Arias
Minister of Economic and Financial Affairs

For the Government of Nicaragua:

Juan José Lugo Marenco
Minister of Economic Affairs

D. *Agreement on the Régime for Central American Integration Industries (Tegucigalpa, 10 June 1958)*

The Governments of the Republic of Guatemala, El Salvador, Honduras, Nicaragua and Costa Rica,

Having regard to the objectives of the Central American Economic Integration Programme which was undertaken through the Central American Economic Co-operation Committee and, in particular, to article XXI of the Central American Multilateral Free Trade and Integration Treaty,

Desirous of strengthening the natural and traditional bonds of brotherhood which unite their countries, and of co-operating towards the solution of their common economic problems,

Having as their basic aim the improvement of the living standards of the Central American peoples and the rational use, for that purpose, of their natural resources, and being convinced that, within the economic development programmes of the Central American Isthmus, the integration of their economies offers favourable prospects for the expansion of trade between their countries and for a more rapid industrialization process on the basis of mutual interest,

Have decided to conclude the present Agreement, which prescribes a Régime for Central American Integration Industries, and for that purpose have appointed as their respective plenipotentiaries:

H.E. the President of the Republic of Guatemala: *José Guirola Leal*, Minister of Economic Affairs;

H.E. the President of the Republic of El Salvador: *Alfonso Rochac*, Minister of Economic Affairs;

H.E. the President of the Council of Ministers exercising the powers of the Executive of the Republic of Honduras: *Fernando Villar*, Minister of Economic Affairs and Finance;

H.E. the President of the Republic of Nicaragua: *Enrique Delgado*, Minister of Economic Affairs; and

H.E. the President of the Republic of Costa Rica: *Wilburg Jiménez Castro*, Vice-Minister of Economic Affairs and Finance

who, having exchanged their full powers, found in good and due form, have agreed as follows:

Article I

The Contracting States undertake to encourage and promote the establishment of new industries and the specialization and expansion of existing industries within the framework of Central American economic integration, and agree that the development of the various activities which are or may be included in such a programme shall be effected on a reciprocal and equitable basis in order that each and every Central American State may progressively derive economic advantages.

Article II

The Contracting States declare their interest in the development of industries with access to a common Central American market. These shall be designated Central American integration industries and shall be so declared jointly by the Contracting States, through the agency of the Central American Industrial Integration Commission established in conformity with article VIII of this Agreement.

The Contracting States shall regard as Central American integration industries those industries which, in the judgement of the Central

American Industrial Integration Commission, comprise one or more plants which require access to the Central American market in order to operate under reasonably economic and competitive conditions even at minimum capacity.

Article III

The application of the present Régime to the Central American integration industries is subject to signature by the Contracting States, in respect of each of the said industries, of an additional protocol stipulating:

(a) The country or countries in which the industrial plants covered by this Régime are to be initially situated, the minimum capacity of the said plants and the conditions under which additional plants are to be subsequently admitted into the same or other countries;

(b) The quality standards for the products of the said industries and any other requirements that may be deemed convenient for the protection of the consumer;

(c) The regulations that may be advisable as regards the participation of Central American capital in the enterprises owning the plants;

(d) The common Central American tariffs which shall be applied to the products of Central American integration industries; and

(e) Any other provisions designed to ensure the attainment of the objectives of this Agreement.

Article IV

The products of plants which form part of a Central American integration industry and which are covered by the present Régime, shall enjoy the benefits of free trade between the territories of the Contracting States.

The products of plants which form part of the same industry but which are not covered by the Régime, shall enjoy in the Contracting States successive annual reductions of ten per cent in the applicable uniform Central American tariff, from the date specified in the relevant additional protocol. As from the tenth year, such products shall enjoy the full benefits of free trade.

Except as provided in the preceding paragraph and in any other provisions of this Agreement or of the additional protocols, all trade in commodities produced by the Central American integration industries shall be governed by the provisions of the Central American Multilateral Free Trade and Economic Integration Treaty.

Article V

In conformity with the provisions of article IV of the Central American Multilateral Free Trade and Economic Integration Treaty, the Central American Trade Commission shall give priority consideration to the equalization of the customs duties and other charges levied upon imports of commodities that are similar to or substitutes for the commodities produced by the Central American integration industries covered by the additional protocols to this Agreement, as well as upon imports of raw materials and of the containers necessary for their production and distribution.

Article VI

Since the Contracting States intend to grant to the Central American integration industries ample fiscal incentives, the enterprises owning industrial plants covered by the present Régime shall enjoy, in the territory of the countries where such plants are or may be established, the benefits and exemptions prescribed by the national legislation of the country concerned.

Article VII

Except in cases of emergency, the Governments of the Contracting States shall not grant customs duty exemptions or reductions below the Central American common tariff on any imports from countries outside Central America of goods which are equal or similar to or substitutes for goods manufactured in any of the Central American countries by plants of industrial integration industries, nor shall they apply to such imports preferential exchange rates equivalent to such exemptions or reductions.

The Governments and other State bodies shall also give preference in their official imports to the products of the Central American integration industries.

Article VIII

In order to ensure due application of this Agreement and of the additional protocols, the Contracting States agree to establish a Central American Industrial Integration Commission, to which each of the Contracting States shall appoint a special representative; the Commission shall meet as frequently as its work may require or at the request of any of the Contracting States.

The Commission or any of its members may travel freely in the Contracting States in order to study matters within the Commission's competence in the field, and the authorities of the Contracting States shall provide them with whatever information and facilities may be necessary for the proper discharge of their functions.

The Commission shall have a permanent secretariat which shall be under the responsibility of the General Secretariat of the Organization of Central American States.

The Commission shall adopt its rules of procedure unanimously and shall prescribe the regulations relating to the conduct of matters within its competence, in particular the regulations relating to the conditions and form in which, in each specific case, the views of private enterprise shall be heard.

Article IX

Individuals or bodies corporate desiring the incorporation of a given plant into the present Régime shall present an application to that effect to the Secretariat of the Central American Industrial Integration Commission and accompany it with the required information. When the Secretariat has sufficient information available, it shall advise the Commission of the application. If the Commission finds that the project meets the aims of this Agreement, the application shall be referred for an opinion to the Central American Research Institute for Industry or to any other person or body that the Commission considers competent. Such opinion shall take into account the technological and economic aspects of the project and, in particular, the market prospects, and the costs incurred shall be borne by the interested parties.

The Commission shall decide on the project on the basis of the said opinion, and if it finds the project capable of being realized, shall make whatever recommendations it considers pertinent to the Governments of the Contracting States on the conclusion of the protocol covering the industry concerned and on the conditions to be stipulated.

When the project refers to a plant which forms part of an industry already covered by a protocol, the Commission may, in conformity with the terms of the relevant protocol and of this article, declare that the plant shall be admitted to the benefits of the present Régime and advise to that effect the Governments of the Contracting States.

Article X

The Central American Industrial Integration Commission shall submit an annual report on its activities to the Contracting States.

The Commission shall periodically carry out studies with a view to enabling the Governments to evaluate the results of the application of the present Régime.

The Commission may propose to the Contracting States measures favourable to the development of the Central American integration industries and to the efficient functioning of their plants. The Commission may also propose to the Governments any measures necessary to resolve any problems arising from the application of this Agreement.

Article XI

The Contracting States agree to settle amicably, in the spirit of this Agreement, any differences which may arise in the interpretation or application of any of its provisions or of the additional protocols. If agreement cannot be reached, they shall submit the matter to arbitration. For the purpose of constituting the arbitral tribunal, each Contracting State shall propose to the General Secretariat of the Organization of Central

American States the names of three judges from its Supreme Court of Justice. From the complete list of candidates, the Secretary-General of the Organization of Central American States and the Government representatives in the Organization shall select, by drawing lots, a tribunal composed of five arbitrators, no two of whom may be nationals of the same State. The award of the arbitral tribunal shall require the concurring votes of not less than three members and shall be binding on all the Contracting States so far as it contains any ruling concerning the interpretation or application of the provisions of this Agreement and of the additional protocols.

Article XII

This Agreement shall be submitted for ratification in each Contracting State in conformity with its respective constitutional or legislative procedures.

This Agreement shall come into force on the date of deposit of the last instrument of ratification. It shall remain in force for twenty years and shall be tacitly renewable for successive periods of ten years.

Any Contracting State may withdraw from this Agreement provided that notice of withdrawal is given not later than two years before the date on which the initial or any other subsequent period of validity expires.

If a Contracting State gives notice of withdrawal after the prescribed time limit but before a new period of validity has commenced, such notification shall be valid, but the Agreement shall remain in force for two further years after the beginning of the new period.

In the event of denunciation of this Agreement, the same shall remain in force as regards its additional protocols until the expiry of the latter.

Should a Contracting State denounce this Agreement, the other Contracting States shall determine whether the Agreement shall cease to have effect between all the Contracting States or whether it shall be maintained between such Contracting States as have not denounced it.

The additional protocols to this Agreement shall be approved in conformity with the constitutional or legislative procedures of each country.

Article XIII

The General Secretariat of the Organization of Central American States shall act as depository of this Agreement and shall send a certified copy thereof to the Ministry of Foreign Affairs of each of the Contracting States. It shall also notify the Contracting States of the deposit of the relevant instruments of ratification as well as of any denunciation which may occur within the prescribed time-limit. When the Agreement comes into force, it shall also transmit a certified copy thereof to the Secretary-General of the United Nations, for registration in conformity with Article 102 of the United Nations Charter.

Transitional Article

In order to promote an equitable distribution of the Central American industrial integration plants, the Contracting States shall not award a second plant to any one country until all of the five Central American countries have each been assigned a plant in conformity with the protocols specified in article III.

IN WITNESS WHEREOF the respective plenipotentiaries have signed this Agreement.

DONE in the city of Tegucigalpa, D.C., capital of the Republic of Honduras, on 10 June 1958.

For the Government of Guatemala:

With a reservation regarding article XI of this Treaty, in accordance with the provisions of paragraph 3, sub-paragraph (*b*) of article 149 of the Constitution of the Republic.

José Guirola Leal
Minister of Economic Affairs

For the Government of El Salvador:

Alfonso Rochac
Minister of Economic Affairs

For the Government of Honduras:

Fernando Villar
Minister of Economic Affairs and Finance

For the Government of Nicaragua:

Enrique Delgado
Minister of Economic Affairs

For the Government of Costa Rica:

Wilburg Jiménez Castro
Vice-Minister of Economic Affairs and Finance

E. Statement Presented by the Delegation of Chile to the Second Special Session of the Conference of LAFTA at Montevideo in May 1964[1]

At the outset of the negotiations for the first stage of the Common Schedule, following three years of operation of the Treaty of Montevideo, the delegation of Chile considers that the moment has arrived for the Contracting Parties to undertake a retrospective examination of develop-

[1] As reprinted in *Comercio Exterior*, June 1964, pp. 385–6. The translations of this statement, and of the resolutions that follow, were made by the author, and have no official standing.

T

ments thus far, so as to obtain a realistic evaluation of the situation that has been reached. This evaluation should indicate whether the expectations in view when the Treaty was signed have been realized, or, if this is not the case, whether there is a reasonable possibility of realizing these expectations in the future.

The present negotiations ought to be taking place in the midst of a profound change in the economies of the Contracting Parties as a result of the application of the Treaty of Montevideo, which is the instrument selected for promoting development by means of integration.

The Chilean delegation considers that by now we ought to be complying fully with the Treaty of Montevideo, not only as a means of liberalizing reciprocal trade but also as an effective mechanism for regional integration.

The Treaty of Montevideo envisages two types of process for achieving the goals proposed. One is the liberalization of reciprocal trade through negotiations, leading to the establishment of National Schedules and the Common Schedule. The second process is of greater significance, involving as it does the coordination of policies for agricultural and industrial development, the elaboration of a Common External Tariff, and the coordination of national rules relating to capital and services, all this being designed to lead to the creation of a common market taking due account of the individual characteristics of our countries.

In order to bring about integration, the Treaty laid down the rules governing the first of the above processes—the programme of liberalization. At the same time the Treaty gave the Contracting Parties a mandate to establish and apply the other procedures required to the same end.

We must recognize that up to the present time we have preferred to limit ourselves to making use of the liberalization process, lacking the imagination and the will to carry out the mandate mentioned above.

We are certain that the delay in giving content to this fundamental undertaking is causing grave difficulties in the process of liberalization, and, which is even worse, is threatening to frustrate completely the hopes of development inscribed in the Treaty of Montevideo.

In the course of the three annual negotiations completed to date, 8,247 concessions have been made, representing a volume of trade several times greater than the customary flow of commerce between the Contracting Parties. Moreover, the reductions in duties listed in the National Schedules far surpass the minimum requirements of the Treaty, amounting thus far to a cumulative total of 24 per cent: this percentage was exceeded by all member countries even by the end of the first round of negotiations.

Thus, from the point of view of the programme of liberalization, it may be stated emphatically that the goals we have sought have been achieved with a degree of success that had never been anticipated, and it might be supposed that this success would have been reflected in each one of our economies.

Nevertheless, the reality is different.

The increase in intra-regional exports, although it has reached an average annual rate of 20 per cent, corresponds to an expansion of not more than 1 per cent of the total exports of our countries, and of hardly 0·1 per cent of the gross product of the area. In other words, the impact of the programme of liberalization on the growth of the region has been insignificant. Moreover, the increase in trade has taken place chiefly in traditional products, that is to say, in raw materials or foodstuffs, which in some cases merely reflects a diversion of trade from third countries to the region.

At the same time there is reason for concern about the momentum of the annual negotiations, since in the first two rounds 7,600 concessions were granted, while in the third round the new concessions added to the National Schedules did not exceed 9 per cent of those listed previously.

This fact reveals the growing rigidity which in present circumstances may be seen in the development of new opportunities for trade. It should cause us to watch carefully the results of future negotiations, in which, unless there is a substantial change, such rigidity will be the dominant note.

The restricted character of the lists presented by the Contracting Parties in connexion with the establishment of the Common Schedule is a clear confirmation of the above-mentioned tendencies.

For these reasons, the delegation of Chile wishes to repeat on this occasion, as on previous occasions since the meeting in Mexico in 1962, its conviction concerning the absolute necessity of making a definite beginning in the process of economic integration, carrying out the mandate of the Treaty. This means that the Contracting Parties should make the maximum efforts to direct their economic policies in such a way as to bring about the creation of a Latin American common market.

It is urgent that concrete machinery be established to coordinate development programmes and economic policies and to set up a Common External Tariff.

We should give the highest priority to ensuring, as a matter decisive for the future of the Association, that the programme of economic integration agreed to by the Contracting Parties in Resolution 75 (III) takes account of the full extent of the structural problems of the region and provides an adequate solution for them.

Chile attaches exceptional importance to the ideas and proposals mentioned above, and firmly believes that the ultimate success or failure of the Association, and of every one of our countries in its pursuit of development, will depend on the decisiveness and urgency with which action is taken upon them.

In the view of the government of Chile, the decisions to be taken on these matters call for the political endorsement of all the Contracting Parties at the highest level if they are to have any reality.

Chile approaches the first negotiation of the Common Schedule fully conscious of the considerable delay that has occurred in fulfilling the mandate of integration laid down by the Treaty. It is faced with numerous problems having a particular bearing on the establishment of the Common Schedule and which persist without being either defined or resolved. And trade with the region is taking a form increasingly unfavourable to Chile.

As regards the last point, it may be noted that while Chilean imports from the Area averaged $70 million during the period 1957–61, in the first two years of the programme of liberalization, imports rose to $100 million, advancing further to $120 million in 1963. On the other hand Chilean exports to the Area grew over the same period from $34 million to only $44 million. Thus the average annual deficit in trade with the Area, which had amounted to $36 million during the period 1957–61, increased to $56 million, on the average, in 1962–63, and reached $71 million last year.

Detailed analysis of Chilean trade also shows a growing adverse balance with all countries of the region except Brazil, which last year made heavy purchases of copper: these purchases were of no significance for the Chilean economy, since they involved a product that can easily be sold in the world market.

Moreover, while Chilean imports are becoming more diversified, and are including purchases previously made in third countries even of highly fabricated products, Chilean exports continued to consist of the same products as before, their composition being even less favourable since primary products now form the preponderant items.

We believe that the situation of Chile, which we have outlined, is substantially similar to that of the majority of the Contracting Parties.

This should not be a source of discouragement but on the contrary should enable us to appreciate the real state of affairs in plain terms and should prompt us to adopt the measures now required.

Finally, in order to facilitate the task of the Conference, the delegation of Chile has submitted for the consideration of the Contracting Parties its point of view on some of the problems which, in its judgement, it is essential to resolve in order to be able to approach the task of negotiating the Common Schedule. Failure to solve these problems would have a major and directly adverse effect on the fulfilment of the programme of liberalization laid down in the Treaty of Montevideo, and, in concrete terms, would limit the possibility of including products in the Common Schedule.

We consider it indispensable that there should be a decision that the inclusion of products in the Common Schedule should be tied to a provision for marks of origin, establishing the conditions under which products are to be regarded as originating in the region; that the treatment to be applied to trade in agricultural products at the end of the programme of liberalization should be determined; that full recognition should be given to the concept of the margin of preference in favour of the Area in respect of the products to be liberalized definitively by virtue of the Common Schedule; that precise rules should be adopted regarding the measures which countries may employ to favour their export products so as to avoid excessive benefits that may gravely disturb the normal conditions of competition in the Area; and, finally, we consider it of fundamental importance to determine precisely the scope of the concept of reciprocity inspiring the Treaty of Montevideo, not only so as to regulate expectations generated by the annual negotiations, but even more so to give orientation to the drawing up of the Common Schedule in which there must likewise be an equilibrium of benefits and obligations of all Parties.

In summary, the position of Chile at the present Conference is necessarily determined by the facts of the situation confronting the Area and, more particularly, by the gravity of the problems which have been outlined and to the solution of which Chile will, as always, apply its maximum efforts.

F. *Letter from the President of Chile*

Santiago, 6 January 1965

Mr Raúl Prebisch,
Mr José Antonio Mayobre,
Mr Felipe Herrera, and
Mr Carlos Sanz de Santa María,
Santiago

Gentlemen,

My recent conversations with Mr Raúl Prebisch on economic integration, together with those I have held with you on other occasions, have strengthened my conviction that the time has come to create an efficacious set of institutions capable of spurring on the formation of the Latin American common market and enabling an undertaking of such supreme importance for the peoples of our region to be placed on a sound footing.

The numerous diagnoses of Latin America's situation reflect the marked inability of many of these countries to programme their economic and social development at the national level, in a world in which the rational utilization of technology and production units calls for vast resources and very broad markets.

Those of us who have assumed the responsibilities of government are confronted with the imperative necessity of easing the painful tension progressively created by the incongruity between the growing numbers of the needy, and the tremendous scientific, technical and economic advances of the last few decades, which have been concentrated in the industrialized centres. Can we continue to organize the development of our economies in watertight compartments, condemning our region to see its position steadily deteriorate, and neglect to pool the efforts of kindred peoples, indisseverably linked by geography and culture alike, in face of other huge aggregates whose progress is redoubled precisely by virtue of their spirit of unity?

I believe it is vitally essential to achieve and consolidate such a union. This affirmation reflects not merely my personal view, but a feeling that is becoming increasingly widespread in Latin America, both inside and outside government circles.

Unquestionably, any process of such importance calls for top-level policy decisions. In no region where changes of this kind have been brought about have they been left in the hands of power groups, however worthy. And at this very moment, in international conferences and parliaments convened by the countries of other continents which have set significant examples in this respect, it is the Governments, through their highest representatives, that are daily committing themselves to undertake the tasks entailed, because there is no other possible way of carrying them out. But it is likewise my belief that formulas based on thorough and impartial studies are a prerequisite for effective action at this level; and herein lies the *raison d'être* of the present letter. Its purpose is to invite you to submit your views on these matters to the Latin American Governments. Your experience in the organizations under your direction, your personal authority and the knowledge you have shown of the problems of our hemisphere will indubitably help to ensure that your words command attention throughout the whole continent.

As I had an opportunity of stressing in my inaugural statements, the integration of Latin America must inevitably supersede outdated patterns if we are to keep in the van of creative thought, of scientific experiment and of technical efficiency; at the same time, it is an essential requisite for economic development and an effective means of increasing the human dignity of our peoples.

But the advance towards economic integration has become slow and cumbersome. The possibilities of making further headway under the present system of minutely detailed tariff negotiations would seem to be exhausted. This is not the way to promote substantial inter-Latin American trade flows or to prepare ourselves for the ineluctable task of competing on world markets. Does the trouble lie in organic defects in the Montevideo Treaty, or in inefficient use of its instruments?

The negotiations recently concluded in Bogotá show how awkward it is to operate machinery that is not under the control of a higher authority, and, it would seem, simply follows the more or less automatic procedures agreed upon years ago, thus betraying a want of dynamic force.

From another angle, would the mere reduction or elimination of customs tariffs suffice to promote the reasonably expeditious integration of certain industries of key importance for the development of Latin America? I refer mainly to steel-making and to the petrochemical, pulp and paper, capital goods, motor-vehicle and other metal transforming industries, although this list must by no means be considered definitive. Is it conceivable that the integration of these and other dynamic industries (which could not otherwise attain the high productivity, the cost levels and the standards of quality that will enable our peoples to improve their working and living conditions) can be achieved without conscious and deliberate action on the part of Governments, accompanied by similar concerted efforts at the level of private enterprise?

The same question arises in relation to the agricultural sector. There, too, should not an attempt be made to devise complementarity agreements which will encourage more efficient use of the land combined with a more liberal supply of food for our peoples and raw materials for our industries—all this with due regard, of course, to the need for promoting agrarian reforms in the individual countries concerned?

In the Latin America of today, no-one disputes the idea that all countries, large, medium-sized and small alike, must have a fair share in the advantages of industrialization. The former system of trading manufactures against primary commodities, the perpetuation of former mistakes and injustices, can no longer be tolerated. Trade in industrial goods and trade in primary commodities must both be developed within the far-reaching process of Latin American integration. How can this proper balance be struck? Are the instruments of the Treaty adequate for the purpose? How can it be ensured that the less developed countries do not lag behind on the road to industrialization and to equitable trade in manufactured goods? Would sufficient funds be available for measures of technical and financial co-operation to be applied to that end?

In this respect, the Inter-American Development Bank would unquestionably have to act as the bank for integration, to quote Mr. Felipe Herrera himself: not only in order to buttress the weak points in the whole process, but with a view to an enlightened promotional effort. This is particularly important in connexion with the key industries to which I referred above; our countries' own enterprise must be strengthened, so that it can gradually make up its technical and financial leeway in relation to foreign enterprise. Otherwise, certain disequilibria would be aggravated, and new ones might emerge, which would seriously handicap progress towards the common market.

Furthermore, I hold that a resolute advance towards this major objective will be impossible unless safeguards are provided against possible distortions deriving from the reduction or elimination of tariffs and other restrictions. Chronic unemployment, not only of labour but also of land and capital, must be prevented at all costs, by the adoption of appropriate measures to permit interim adjustments. What would you propose in this connexion?

Since the scope of the Montevideo Treaty is strictly confined to trade proper, it does not cover that aspect of the problem which relates to payments and credits in Latin American trade. Can a progressive integration system work well in default of agreements in this field?

The Central American countries have made much more determined progress than the rest of Latin America in these respects. There the common market is a *fait accompli*. A Central American economic unit is in process of formation, and one necessary step will be to discuss with our Central American neighbours ways and means of facilitating the incorporation of this unit into the whole Latin American integration area, through the establishment of differential treatments appropriate to the various stages of economic development reached. To judge from your experience, would it be advisable to aim at the conclusion of sub-regional agreements in other areas, with a view to subsequent fusion as a regional whole? At the same time, the other Latin American countries that have not yet joined in the gradual integration process would have to be drawn in.

This list of problems with which I am deeply concerned, as I know you are too, makes no claim to be exhaustive. I am sure you can map out a much more comprehensive picture. But I cannot omit to mention institutional machinery. That of the Montevideo Treaty has manifestly proved insufficient and inadequate. The object-lessons afforded by other similar processes show us how necessary it is that such institutions should incorporate certain supra-national elements.

As evidence of our determination to attain the objectives indicated, a few days ago I submitted to the National Congress a project for the reform of the constitution whose provisions include legal authorization to co-operate in the creation of Latin American organs with supra-national powers.

I should also like to suggest, in the institutional context, that the labour force should be assigned a definite share in the integration movement, together with entrepreneurial activities, whether individual or co-operative. A broad basis of popular support is an indispensable requisite for the integration of Latin America, as for the whole process of structural reform, which would be doomed to failure if it were confined to official circles of a financial or technical character, however competent they might be.

I am convinced, like you, that the economic integration of Latin America is one of the essential means of solving the serious problem of the external bottleneck which at present impedes the acceleration of our countries' rate of economic and social development. Similarly, it is of the greatest importance to expand our trade with the developed countries and to secure our industrial exports an advantageous foothold in their markets, as well as to exploit the considerable potential represented by trade with the socialist countries and with other developing regions. All this was confirmed at the Geneva Conference; and it is in a spirit of pragmatic realism that we must be prepared to play our part in the new institutions required for the pursuance of a herculean labour on which only the merest beginning has been made. But—and herein lies the crux of our problem—we cannot carry our full weight in these and other institutions, or take advantage of them to secure the adoption of all the decisions we want the great industrial centres to agree to, unless we give proof of our ability to achieve, boldly and wisely, what is clearly within our reach— the economic integration of Latin America.

My only aim in writing to you is to get results. I want to take as sober an attitude as possible, without putting forward suggestions or plans on my own behalf.

I have long given thought to ways and means of dealing with these problems. I realize that any rash step might be more of a hindrance than a help. I realize, too, the undesirability of being over-precipitate, or advancing ideas of our own, at the risk of making it appear that a nation or a Government was taking steps and decisions that exceeded its prerogatives, or that might be detrimental to others.

Hence my idea that a proposal formulated by impartial technical experts, exempt from political or national commitments, would do away with all difficulties and mistrust, and would enable us to devote positive and creative study to the whole problem, solely in the interests of the objective pursued, to which, in our eyes, the future of the Latin American nations is linked. If we fail, let us not then complain of crying in the wilderness when we try to secure for our peoples the share in world trade to which they are justly entitled.

I venture to say that the existing situation, in my opinion, cannot last. It is doing great harm, and may add to the sense of frustration which at various levels has already been too long endured.

Moreover, time cannot be allowed to slip by with impunity. Delay is creating obstacles to future action and aggravating disequilibria, and there are many who wonder whether nowadays integration is not just another subject for meetings and speeches, and whether it would not be preferable to decide how the region's foreign trade can best be organized in terms of other markets, if, through our own incapacity, that of Latin America is not integrated.

I hope that you and our other three mutual friends will be good enough to consider my suggestion, in the certainty that my Government, and unquestionably the other Latin American Governments likewise, will once again be ready to listen to views that have the weight of your authority behind them.

Please accept my cordial thanks in anticipation.

Sincerely yours,

Eduardo Frei
President of the Republic of Chile

G. *Proposals for the Creation of the Latin American Common Market*[1]

I. THE NEED FOR A GREAT ECONOMIC BASE

Community of Effort

Latin America is failing to face resolutely a course of events which is jeopardizing the pace and the very meaning of its economic and social development and shaking its political life to its foundations.

Never before have we seen such a population explosion; nor has the very legitimate desire of our peoples for a better life been so strikingly expressed. But neither have we witnessed, until recently, the enormous possibilities that modern technology can offer for the eradication of poverty and its accompanying evils.

We have understood these possibilities. We admire the stupendous rise in the living levels of the long-industrialized countries. And we have been impressed by the experience of others which have, within a short time, gathered great economic momentum in their recent development. From both these categories of countries, the technological revolution is striving to spread out to the rest of the world. We are awaiting impatiently what this revolution has to bring us in order to fulfil that desire for a better life, but perhaps we have not perceived the many and complex aspects of what this process inevitably requires.

If we remain disunited, we shall not be able, in our desire to reap the full benefits of contemporary technology, to meet such requirements, among them the need for great economic bases: 95 per cent of the industrial output of the more advanced countries is produced within large

[1] Published on 15 April 1965 by Mr Felipe Herrera, President of the Inter-American Development Bank, Mr Carlos Sanz de Santamaría, Chairman of the Inter-American Committee for the Alliance for Progress, Mr José Antonio Mayobre, Executive Secretary of the Economic Commission for Latin America, and Mr Raúl Prebisch, Secretary-General of UNCTAD in response to the letter contained in Appendix F.

markets which, even though each of them has immense and varied resources, reach out further in a constant search for more trade.

Our countries, nevertheless, attempt to develop in an area arbitrarily
divided into numerous watertight compartments with very little inter-
communication. By thus dispersing their efforts in isolated action, these
countries cannot carry the weight they should in a world where, in
addition to the countries that were already large, vast economic blocs
have emerged. The full advantages of industrialization will not be
secured if the Latin American countries, thus thrown back on themselves, persist in trying to produce every type of goods and doing, within
their own frontiers, everything that the others are doing within theirs.

This mutual isolation is not confined to the economy: it applies to a
wide range of activities. Scientific and technological research, and the
training of complex skills in these fields, are very haphazard because of
the limited range and dispersal of effort. And so far as culture is concerned
creative activity suffers and languishes because of the same limitations of
national horizons. Moreover, incapacity to combine resources has been
partly responsible for these countries being so far unable to acquire those
powerful technical media of expression and dissemination which are
available to others. Accordingly there have prevailed in Latin America
certain outside elements of dubious value which not only fail to contribute
to the enrichment of the common cultural heritage but are also incompatible with the purpose of enhancing our native values and moulding
the true image of our personality.

Technology will be of ever greater influence in our time. We must
adapt it to the realities of our own situation and resolutely master it, if
we are not to subordinate the essence of our existence and our brotherly
relationship to it. We shall not succeed in this if we continue to use up our
strength in isolated effort.

We must learn to work together; we must form the community of
Latin American peoples. Up to now we have been unable to undertake
this great task to any meaningful extent, because we have not been able
completely to escape from the pattern in which our development began
in the nineteenth century. Thus separated one from another, without
active relationships closely binding them together, each of our countries
in those days was attracted, in isolation, towards the world's major
economic, political and cultural centres. We lived in the reflection of
those centres, and this has had a far-reaching effect not only on Latin
America's past but also on its present. Many features of this pattern continue to exist; we must rid ourselves of them, given the facts of the world's
evolution and the growing tensions within our own process of development.

In order to overcome these and other obstacles which stand in the way
of Latin America's development, we must combine our forces and har-

ness them to the achievement of major common objectives. It is not enough for us merely to respond to the requirements of technology, or to work together to create a great economic base and widen our cultural, scientific and technological horizon. Our action in this sense must also be for the purpose of securing greater political influence internationally.

In this context, a new historical dimension is emerging—the dimension of the developing world. Despite the striking differences that distinguish us from other regions, we have a series of common denominators which inevitably spur us to common endeavours, without detriment to the personality of each of us. We have already set out on this road, and must continue along it with tenacity of purpose. We should try, not to set ourselves up against the major centres in sterile and fruitless competition, but to secure better understanding with them, to strengthen our capacity for effective negotiation so as to place the policy of international co-operation on a new basis.

The extraordinary prosperity of the advanced countries and the opulence which some of them are attaining should open a broad path towards this new policy of international co-operation. This is a matter of urgency. Markets for the traditional export of our primary commodities are shrinking and closing, without new ones being offered for our manufactures. The trend towards imbalance in foreign trade is placing a serious brake on the economic development of many of our countries. And deterioration of the terms of trade is materially reducing the positive contribution of international financial resources to our development.

It is not enough to identify the problems or to talk about the attitude of the major countries towards the lot of the smaller. We must organize our common action in order to secure a constructive response from the former in all fields—in trade, finance and our primary commodities in regard to which a sound policy to uphold values and expand markets is urgently required.

A lesson for all this can be drawn from the United Nations Conference on Trade and Development, held at Geneva in 1964, and from the preparatory meetings of our countries, held at Brasilia and Altagracia. Without joint action we can make no headway towards solving these grave problems at the international level. The more we co-ordinate our own efforts at this level, the better Latin America will be able to help this action to develop effectively and responsibly—a process that is not incompatible with, but on the contrary strengthens, the regional action defined in the Charter of Punta del Este.

The policy of Latin American integration, regional action and, in general, international co-operation are not alternatives to reforms in our own economic and social structure. Such reforms are inevitable. They are already going forward and must acquire great scope in the vast movement to modernize our countries. But it will be much less difficult to cope with this Herculean task in an economy that is growing at a faster pace, with all the inspiration of a bold and clear-sighted policy of integration and of continental and international co-operation. This policy must be applied concurrently with and not after such reforms if we are to avoid frustrations fraught with dangerous consequences.

The Need for Political Decisions

All of these changes require major political decisions at different levels. Conscious of this pressing need, President Frei has urged the authors of this document to offer suggestions for accelerating Latin American economic integration.

We share the concern of the Chilean President. We also associate ourselves with his desire to further a process that has already begun. The Latin American Free Trade Association, established at Montevideo at the beginning of 1960, is a very important step towards the common endeavour, as is also—and from an earlier date—the happy initiative of the Central American countries.

The Central American nations are proceeding resolutely towards the formation of the common market, under favourable conditions of which their Governments took advantage with laudable determination.

The same is not true as regards the broader trend towards Latin American economic integration. What has been done until now, while important, is not enough. We are still far from achieving the goal that the same Latin American countries set themselves, in August 1961, in the Charter of Punta del Este. There our countries undertook to work during this decade, which is already so far advanced, in order: "To strengthen existing agreements on economic integration, with a view to the ultimate fulfilment of aspirations for a Latin American common market that will expand and diversify trade among the Latin American countries and thus contribute to the economic growth of the region".

The integration objectives are not being fulfilled at the pace required by the magnitude of the problem. The practical obstacles are great but not insuperable.

The slow pace of integration is not, of course, due to the Montevideo Treaty itself, but to the fact that no general integration policy has yet been formulated that clearly and distinctly establishes the desired objectives, the methods to be used, or the time required to attain these objectives, and because not all of the countries of the area have acceded to the Treaty.

The Treaty has placed in the hands of Governments the preferential instrument necessary for applying the trade measures required by this general integration policy. Hitherto it has only been used in limited commodity-by-commodity negotiations, and although this initial experience has been very useful and instructive, it is now becoming imperative to pass on to a new stage of commitments that will lead to a common market in the form described below.

Other instruments are also available: the Inter-American Development Bank, which has been defined as the "bank of integration", will have to participate on a major scale in the promotion and financing of sectoral integration agreements and of other multinational or national programmes that are in keeping with the needs of over-all integration policy. The Inter-American Committee for the Alliance for Progress and the Panel of Nine, in view of their important functions as regards Latin American development and the co-ordination of its financing, must make a major contribution towards ensuring that national plans, in their pertinent aspects, follow the lines just mentioned. In short, the machinery already available must be fully utilized.

Other important steps are also indispensable. Agreements to supplement the Montevideo Treaty are necessary: instruments are required for the programming and promotion of investments at the regional level; a compensatory payments and reciprocal credit system is lacking; it is necessary to define more precisely, in the light of experience, the principle of reciprocity, special treatment for the relatively less developed countries, procedures to correct the dislocations that could emerge from the liberation of intra-regional trade, and the fundamental role of the Latin American entrepreneur in the over-all context of the common market.

This general integration policy cannot be carried out without an institutional system which has the powers and resources essential for its independent functioning.

While, for understandable reasons, the proposals presented here respond to the need for a general integration policy that will give a powerful impetus to the constructive work initiated in LAFTA, they are not limited to the geographical area of LAFTA. On the contrary, they are also based on the need to extend this policy to Latin America as a whole. It would therefore be advisable, in addition to seeking the incorporation of other non-member countries, to negotiate the integration of the Central American Common Market in the whole system as a single economic entity. It would thus have to be granted the advantages advocated here in favour of the relatively less developed countries. The fact that Central America is moving more rapidly towards a common market is not an obstacle but rather an advantage as regards implementing the general policy of integration. It would likewise be an advantage if other Latin American countries were to decide on general or specific objectives in order to advance rapidly towards this goal within the framework of the Latin American Common Market.

In this great movement we need the fullest support of our peoples, the active and resolute participation of workers and entrepreneurs, of technicians and researchers, in short, of the Latin American people at all levels.

The idea of a Latin American Parliament is already becoming a reality. It could be an efficient means of giving integration the broad base of popular support that is so essential for its vigorous advance.

The common market that will take shape as integration policy proceeds does not imply that a country should neglect its own development efforts. These efforts remain the prerogative of each country, and to direct them properly will be its individual responsibility. Nevertheless, the common market will provide a favourable environment for national development efforts to be made with the maximum use of our productive resources, thanks to the direct or indirect effects of reciprocal trade and to the possibility of increasing exports to other countries within the system, always provided that imports from the others grow at the same time.

Hence there is no incompatibility between the common market and national development. On the contrary, the common market is one of the means—and certainly a very powerful one—of carrying out a design that is shared by us all, namely, the achievement of vigorous national development. It is a common design in that the national aspect harmoniously expands to cover the entire range of our countries. If our history and our feelings are not sufficient by themselves to demonstrate this, there are inescapable events creating a growing sense of community, of a genuine Latin American community, which, in addition to its vital intrinsic importance, will enable us to guide our relations with the other developing countries and the great industrial centres along the proper lines.

Industrialization, Exports, and the Common Market

Even when conceived in its broadest terms, integration is only one aspect of a vast effort to reform and modernize methods of production and the economic and social structure of the Latin American countries.

This must be done in the face of the serious and growing social tensions in our countries, tensions which largely derive from the lack of internal integration, from rapid demographic growth, from the progressively more conspicuous and disturbing presence, in our countrysides and towns, of swarms of people in occasional employment with precarious incomes who are denied the opportunities for a progressively better life that are offered by modern technology. These problems tend to become worse before they are solved and offer clear proof of the present inadequate dynamism of the Latin American economy to absorb, at rising income levels, the steadily increasing human potential.

It is imperative to incorporate this impressive potential into economic activities of higher productivity. Within this process, industry must play a role of the utmost importance, together with services that grow with general economic development, because, the more technology penetrates into the backward agricultural sector and the outdated marketing of its products, and the more that primitive forms of production disappear, the greater must be the part played by modern industry—and services—in absorbing the surplus manpower which is no longer necessary in those activities where technology is making inroads.

All of this requires considerable capital, which stands in clear contrast to the scarcity of available resources. And here we really touch on the core of our problem, because we are wasting a considerable amount of capital which, if properly employed, would enable growth to be expedited and thereby greatly increase the volume of goods available for Latin American consumption and investment.

We are producing much less than we are capable of, because of the present fragmentation of what should be a large market. It is well known that a large market, the great economic base, is indispensable if production is to be efficient and low-cost, even in the most densely populated countries of Latin America. This need is evident both for reasons deriving from productive technology and for other reasons connected with the process of competition.

Modern technology requires large-scale plant; it requires a division of labour, and a specialization that often is not feasible within the narrow limits of national markets. Latin American industrialization is far from having met this requirement. Within each country all kinds of industries have been, and continue to be, established regardless of their economic viability. Moreover, if we continue industrializing in watertight compartments, this evil will tend to grow worse instead of being remedied. But, since it is not possible to interrupt the establishment of new plants while awaiting a new integration policy that is slow in taking shape, the need to formulate such a policy becomes progressively more urgent.

To understand the importance of these considerations, it is sufficient to cite some figures which indicate the order of magnitude of the problem in the iron and steel industry. If a rational integration programme were to be brought into existence, it has been calculated that, of the probable increase in output of some 15 million tons of iron and steel by 1975, savings of some $3,700 million could be made as regards the investments required if each producing country continued making, by itself, all the items for its own consumption. This would represent an annual saving in direct production costs of more than $400 million by 1975, i.e., a considerable proportion of the total steel cost by that date.[2]

The considerations regarding competition are also very important because it is closely related to the private-enterprise system. In our countries, the scale of competition is usually small or non-existent owing to

[2] Estimates based on studies by the secretariats of ECLA, IDB and the Latin American Institute of Economic and Social Planning.

the high barrier of tariffs and restrictions behind which industrialization has developed. This situation conspires against technical progress and greater productivity. And even in those plants that could attain an adequate scale, especially in the larger countries of Latin America, the small extent of competition—or the lack of it—frequently leads to inadequate utilization of capital and the other productive resources. Moreover, the establishment of new plants, added to those already producing the same items, does not usually stimulate competition but frequently leads to tacit or explicit understandings that, far from lowering costs and prices, often raises them arbitrarily.

Close communication between markets in a single economic area is essential for industry to feel itself continuously spurred on by competition among the Latin American countries. From the point of view of economic viability, this process will have two main effects. Firstly, it will lead to sectoral complementarity or integration agreements, especially in the major import-substitution industries. To a large extent, products that are now imported from the rest of the world would be replaced by others of Latin American origin in intra-regional trade. Secondly, competition will give a powerful impetus to the modernization and readjustment of existing industries.

Of course, the great differences in productivity between our countries and the technically more advanced industrial centres make it necessary to continue protecting our industries. Nevertheless, it will be necessary gradually to reduce this protection, as productivity increases and as the persistent tendency to external disequilibrium prevailing in Latin America is gradually corrected. But, are there any reasons for not promoting active competition among our countries through tariff reductions and the elimination of restrictions?

The reduction of industrial costs, obtained through complementarity and integration agreements and by the effects of reciprocal competition, would further the other objective that must be achieved at the international level, in order to help, together with import substitution, to correct the phenomenon of disequilibrium just mentioned. This objective is an increase in our industrial exports to the major centres. Even if we can achieve rational import substitution—and it is not rational today—we shall still have to continue importing a growing quantity of goods, particularly all those that cannot be produced economically within the common market. Our imports, especially of capital goods, of intermediate products, and of new consumer items, will have to go on growing intensively even though there will be continuous changes in their composition.

We can only obtain these industrial goods in adequate quantities if we export other goods, also of industrial origin, to the major centres. It will

U

not be possible to rely upon primary commodities, since exports of them generally tend to grow slowly whereas the demand for industrial imports tends to develop at a relatively faster pace.

But how are we to increase our exports of manufactures on a large scale if our costs continue to be high? At the above-mentioned Geneva Conference, we strongly urged the major centres to change their trade policy towards the developing countries and we asked them to grant tariff preferences for our manufactured goods. Nevertheless this by itself will not be sufficient for our industrial exports to expand to the extent required. Inevitably we must cut our production costs in order to take advantage of these preferences and be capable of existing without them when the period for which they have been granted has expired. This brings us to another of the decisive reasons for creating a common market.

Imports of certain manufactures from developing countries will certainly require adjustments in the industrial structure of the major centres.

Similarly, as a result of reciprocal competition, adjustments will be required in Latin America, together with the safeguards later mentioned in this document. If we are not prepared to make these adjustments to expedite growth, how can we expect the major industrial centres to agree to do so? Will we have the authority to impress upon them the need to transform the traditional structure if we do not show our decision to do likewise in the reciprocal trade between our own countries?

II. INTEGRATION POLICY

As has been previously mentioned, this document conceives the general policy of Latin American integration to be a series of measures covering commercial policy, regional investments, monetary and payments policy, and certain basic principles required for the proper functioning of the common market. Each of these aspects will be dealt with separately in the following pages.

Trade Policy

It was already stated that the Montevideo Treaty has put a very important trade policy instrument in the hands of the signatory Governments. It would not be fair to examine the best way of using that instrument for the gradual attainment of the common market without a frank and explicit recognition of the significance of everything that has been accomplished at Montevideo during the nearly four years of the Treaty's existence.

A common list of products has been agreed upon with a firm commitment to eliminate completely, by 1973, the customs duties and other restrictions on zonal trade in these products. That common list is subsequently to be gradually enlarged every three years. In addition, the annual negotiations have resulted in the inclusion in the national lists of a much larger number of products for which lower duties of differing degrees have been established. All this has created favourable conditions for encouraging industrial investments in the next few years. And reciprocal trade has grown by 38 per cent in the three-year interval between 1959/61 and 1962/63, even though the $950 million recorded in 1963 still represents only a small proportion of the total trade of the LAFTA countries.

At the technical level, very useful work has been carried out, such as the adoption of basic criteria and the clarification of various problems regarding the definition of the origin of goods and others connected with customs technique, and progress is being made with the standard customs nomenclature, without which progress towards a common external tariff vis-à-vis the rest of the world is impossible.

Within LAFTA a group of technical advisers has been established, and private enterprise has been encouraged to establish representative bodies to collaborate in carrying out the Treaty. Moreover—and this is particularly important for the future—a capable and efficient secretariat has been formed with a strong sense of its responsibilities.

Some very commendable results have therefore been achieved. But if these are evaluated in terms of the major objectives of a common market, as previously defined, the enormous field of action still to be covered can be clearly seen.

The Montevideo Treaty constitutes an important step towards the establishment of the Latin American common market, and member Governments have declared their intention of doing their utmost to create favourable conditions for attaining that purpose. But the immediate objectives and the commitments assumed have so far been primarily those required in order to create the preferential instrument to which reference was previously made, within the juridical context of a free-trade area, by means of selective negotiations on a commodity-by-commodity basis.

This cumbersome procedure of miniature negotiations is showing itself to be incapable of bringing about a substantial liberalization or an important expansion of trade. As the stage of easy concessions comes to an end, it has become increasingly more difficult to include new products in the lists. Moreover, in each negotiation vested interests exert pressure on Governments to exclude products that could be exposed to competition from the rest of the area. As a general rule, the selective procedure limits tariff reductions to a specific number of items and makes it almost impossible to achieve the general liberalization of reciprocal trade. This is even more important if account is taken of the high barrier of tariffs and restrictions on the area's trade. The tariff barrier is largely a result of the improvisation to which our countries have frequently been forced to resort in trade policy under critical pressure from outside. It is estimated that the average tariff level of the LAFTA countries exceeds 100 per cent, and duties of 200 and 300 per cent are frequent.

Perhaps it would not have been possible to choose any procedure other than these commodity-by-commodity negotiations during the initial stages of the Treaty. Still, it was foreseeable, from the experience of the European Common Market, that the procedure would be inhibited by fear of the dislocations which might transpire when the market was gradually opened up to competition from other countries of the system. It might have been seen, in the light of the European experience, that this fear was without foundation, but none the less it has been impeding the advance towards the reduction and elimination of tariffs.

Today it is generally recognized that such a system of negotiations will have to be replaced by another, in which reductions take place automatically. Within LAFTA itself, the secretariat has been studying ways and means of achieving that purpose.

In order to strengthen the integration process, it is essential to determine clearly and distinctly the point to be reached within a given period of time. Accordingly, it is considered necessary for the Latin American countries to assume four closely interrelated commitments to be fulfilled within a period of ten years: firstly, to establish quantitative targets for the desired maximum level of customs duties—including restrictions of equivalent effect—to be attained and to adopt a gradual and automatic mechanism for the application of such a system; secondly, to eliminate gradually the application of quantitative and other non-tariff restrictions on intra-regional trade; thirdly, to establish a common tariff vis-à-vis the rest of the world; and, fourthly, to establish a system of reciprocal preferences for member countries to enjoy in their intra-regional trade pending the establishment of the definitive preferences in the common tariff.

As to the first commitment, it is proposed that, at the end of the specified period, participating countries should not be able to levy customs duties in their intra-regional trade exceeding 20 per cent of the c.i.f. value of each product, with the exceptions that are explained later, particularly with respect to the relatively less developed countries. For obvious reasons, those reductions should not be left until the end of the period, but should be introduced annually. Once this idea is accepted, the technicians should present appropriate formulae for bringing this quantitative target into effect within the established time-limit.

Application of this gradual and automatic process would mean that, at the end of the first half of the period concerned, i.e., at the end of five years, all customs duties not now exceeding 100 per cent would be reduced to levels equal to or lower than 50 per cent, which is considered a reasonable minimum target for the first part of the period mentioned. The case of customs duties now higher than 100 per cent is different, and it would therefore be advisable to intensify their reduction in such a way that, at the end of the first half of the period, none of them exceeds 50 per cent.

In this way the differences in customs duties that now exist between countries and even within the same country for various products would be gradually eliminated until the target is reached; this is an indispensable requirement if a common market is to be attained. It should be borne in mind that the proposed system does not exclude the desirability of continuing those commodity-by-commodity negotiations that help to accelerate the tariff reduction process.

Furthermore, establishment of the common market implies the total elimination of customs duties, and not merely a quantitative target for reduction. It would not, however, be advisable to try to do this immediately. This should rather be left for the final stage, when decisions should be taken in the light of the experience gained during the initial stage when a substantial reduction of tariffs would be obtained.

Clearly it will be necessary to anticipate the difficulties that may arise in fulfilling these commitments. For this purpose, as is explained later, the system would also include adequate safeguard clauses that would make it possible effectively to deal with such situations or possibly to correct any trade disequilibria that might arise. Moreover, countries could introduce internal taxes affecting national production and imports alike for the purpose of restricting consumption of certain items, especially luxuries.

As for the second commitment, quantitative and other non-tariff restrictions on intra-regional trade—other than safeguard clauses—should also be gradually and automatically eliminated within the same period in accordance with formulae proposed by the technicians. These formulae should enable the above-mentioned restrictions to be converted into customs duties that would be subject to the other commitments proposed in this section.

As regards the third commitment, a common external tariff, which is an essential element for the creation of a common market, should be gradually worked out. Nevertheless, the greatest efforts should be made both to attain uniform tariffs as soon as possible for raw materials and intermediate products, in order not to dislocate competition among countries of the system, and to establish common external tariffs in the sectoral complementarity or industrial integration agreements, in order to obtain a reasonable degree of protection against external competition.

With regard to the fourth commitment, until the common external tariff is achieved, a system of preferences should be introduced for products of member countries when the preferences resulting from the process of tariff reduction are insufficient to satisfy the principle of reciprocity.

Regional Investment Policy

It would be a mistake to assume that the efficient manipulation of the trade policy instruments described above is enough to put the integration policy suggested here into effect. The play of economic forces alone, stimulated by tariff reductions, would not by itself lead to this result. It would be imperative to exercise some control over those forces, in order to attain the objectives of that policy.

It is not merely a question of reducing or eliminating duties and restrictions, of creating preferences, of foresightedly introducing safeguard measures to ward off or remedy dislocations, or of having corrective expedients available. It is much more than that. Integration also requires constructive action. Trade policy measures could not be a substitute for it; their function is solely to establish an adequate framework in which integration can be attained.

This constructive action should be translated primarily into a stimulating common market investment policy. Within the broad context of development, this policy must include, in particular, a series of activities relating to integration—first and foremost, the large import-substitution industries which, in addition to their importance in the development process, must help to overcome the external imbalance which is a feature of the more advanced countries of Latin America and which will soon appear in the others if current external trade trends continue.

As is well-known, the import-substitution process is entering a new stage. Easy substitutions are wholly or nearly exhausted in the more advanced Latin American countries and technically complex industries are beginning to be set up requiring large investments and a sizable market. None of our countries, no matter how large or vigorous, could begin or continue this stage of industrialization on its own in economically viable conditions.

It is therefore necessary to plan the development of these industries on a regional scale. This planning refers principally to iron and steel, some non-ferrous metals, some groups of heavy chemical and petro-chemical industries, including the production of fertilizers, and the manufacture of motor vehicles, ships and heavy industrial equipment. This involves a limited number of industries which, in addition to being import-substitution industries, cover fields of vital importance for strengthening the economic structure and accelerating the pace of our countries' development. It is precisely in such fields that economies of scale, the advantages of suitable siting, the utilization of productive capacity and better operational efficiency will be most strikingly achieved. One of the paradoxical situations existing side by side with the Treaty of Monte-video has been that some of these industries have been established or expanded in various countries without regard to the objectives of an integration policy.

It would be appropriate for the Governments to decide now to con-clude these sectoral agreements in such industries so that a start can be made without delay on the studies needed for carrying out the relevant negotiations.

One result of the investment policy in all these industries might be the conclusion of a series of sectoral agreements within the next few years. Although these agreements are provided for in the Treaty of Montevideo, very few of them have so far been concluded, and those that exist do not relate to the industries that are of basic importance. One circumstance which may have contributed to this situation is the view originally taken that these agreements should conform to the most-favoured-nation clause. This has just been corrected by a decision of LAFTA which provides that tariff reductions negotiated under an agreement will not automatically extend to the countries not parties to the agreement in the absence of the compensatory measures stipulated.

As a general rule, complementarity agreements would have to start from a more rapid and radical reduction in customs duties than would result from the gradual and automatic lowering of tariffs. In most cases, it might be possible for tariffs to be completely eliminated even before the end of the initial period of ten years. This, of course, does not exclude the possibility of import quotas being established for limited periods so that the industries of some countries might be able to maintain a certain volume of production until such time as they became competitive within the common market.

In order to prevent combinations which, in the execution of the agree-ments, would restrict competition, it would be desirable to provide for a gradual and reasonable reduction of tariffs vis-à-vis the rest of the world as soon as the Latin American industries had been strengthened.

These sectoral agreements should be based on development plans for the various industries. Each plan should set out the production targets which would enable demand to be met and some or all of the relevant imports to be replaced. In addition, the necessary financing would have to be provided, and the broad lines of the policy to be adopted would have to be determined, especially to forestall any substantial difficulties which might arise from competition.

From another point of view, such agreements should not be exclusive or impede any other action that might be effective in the areas covered by the agreements. The scope of the agreements should, in this regard, be limited to providing incentives—particularly fiscal, technical and financial incentives—that would direct the flow of investment in accordance with the aims of each plan but would not discourage new forms of action not benefiting from such incentives.

Apart from the sectoral agreements, the regional investment policy should concentrate on the countries that are relatively less developed and on any country in which the process of integration might give rise to substantial difficulties.

On the other hand, it must be recognized that in other branches of the consumer- or capital-goods industries, too, the progressive integration of markets may require special measures as regards promotional activities, reorganization and both technical and financial assistance, which would differ in degree and kind according to the particular circumstances and be complementary to the action taken to reduce tariffs.

Agriculture presents its own very special problems. Generally speaking, agricultural production has not expanded fast enough to keep pace with a growing population and its needs. Latin America as a whole continues to import a large volume of agricultural products from the rest of the world, whereas its exports are expanding at a slow rate. Imports currently amount to $600 million, about $200 million of which is represented by United States agricultural surpluses.

There are thus three objectives to be achieved: an increase in production to improve the diet of the people and supply raw materials for industry; a reduction in the proportion of imported food and raw materials for internal consumption; and the encouragement of agricultural exports as a means of helping to eliminate the external bottleneck.

It is obvious that the solution of this problem cannot be left entirely to the corrective action of a trade policy. The problem is a complex one that has not yet been attacked in its full breadth and depth. What possibilities does Latin America have of achieving these objectives if it takes energetic action to increase productivity? In what form and to what extent will the various countries be able to take part in this action? In what way could the agricultural trade balance of each country be modified in relation to the rest of the common market? How far would it be possible to adjust whatever imbalance might arise from purely agricultural trade?

It must be confessed that the lack of systematic research in this matter makes it impossible to give any satisfactory reply to these questions. Nothing more can be done than to make certain very general statements of principle which may serve as a guide to the technicians. One paramount consideration in this regard is that the land of each country and the factors of production related to the land must be employed in the most economically efficient manner possible and that there can be no such thing as chronic unemployment, in so far as these factors are concerned, which cannot be corrected through their absorption in other sufficiently productive types of activity.

What is needed for the achievement of all these things is a programme for developing Latin America's production and agricultural trade, a programme in which special attention must be given to price policy. Such a programme would also have to make provision for the investment necessary to put it into effect.

As to the infra-structural investment of the common market, special attention must be given to investment in transport and communications and, in some cases, to investment in power production and distribution. It is not intended that a single programme should embrace the entire range of investments to be made in these fields by the countries belonging to the system; the aim is rather to co-ordinate this investment and to concentrate on carrying out those measures that require joint action.

With regard to air transport, the fragmentation and lack of co-ordination among the large number of Latin American airlines obviously impairs their efficiency and ability to compete with the airlines of the more advanced countries. This situation will become much more serious than it is now when supersonic aircraft come into use in the near future.

Joint action is also needed in the matter of shipping, which is affected by numerous complex problems ranging from the participation of Latin American fleets in traffic both inside and outside the area to the possible organizing of multinational shipping companies and the establishment of an adequate port régime.

Existing communications are generally poor and inefficient, and the need for improving, expanding and linking the various systems is obvious. The technological revolution in communications resulting from the use of satellites makes it even more imperative to unite efforts that would otherwise continue to be weak and ineffectual.

Investment policy should likewise encourage efforts for the integration of frontiers so as gradually to eliminate the consequences of an artificial division in regions where development calls for a common approach.

The Inter-American Development Bank should channel a considerable part of its resources into these investment programmes without thereby giving any less attention to the financing of national development. As the integration policy gathers momentum, however, more extensive resources will have to be forthcoming, either from additional contributions made to the Bank for this purpose, or from funds from other sources. The ICAP is destined to play a leading role in co-ordinating these various kinds of financing.

Monetary and Financial Policy

It must be recognized that the inflation prevailing in some Latin American countries is a serious obstacle to integration, besides disrupting their economic and social development.

The struggle against inflation is a long and difficult one and the policy that is being carried out in this connexion should be pursued resolutely and persistently. It would not be possible to wait for it to bring about monetary stability before putting the integration policy that is advocated in this document into effect.

In addition to the measures which are mentioned later in this document for dealing in particular with the exchange discrepancies that inflation usually causes, it would be very useful if the Latin American central banks could co-ordinate their efforts in considering the problems of monetary policy in the context of integration and, more particularly, in examining the phenomena of temporary or permanent disequilibrium in intra-regional payments and in trade relations with the rest of the world.

Such joint efforts on the part of the central banks would be important as an expression of the sense of collective responsibility inherent in the policy of integration. This same attitude should prevail in discussions of the domestic measures of one country which might affect other countries and it should also strengthen the joint support of the efforts made by the Latin American countries in the relevant international organizations with a view to solving their balance-of-payment problems.

These movements towards regional unity will be of undoubted importance in the approach that Latin America should take as regards the revision of the world monetary system that has been recently begun. The fact that we and other developing countries are not taking part in the study of problems of international liquidity that is being made by the group of ten highly industrialized countries is further evidence of the urgent need to strengthen our capacity for international negotiation.

On the other hand, there is no doubt that the lack of an adequate system of reciprocal and multilateral payments and credits is a considerable drawback in the policy of reducing tariffs and eliminating trade restrictions among the Latin American countries. This effort, and, generally speaking, the whole policy of integration, would be largely frustrated if there was no payments union, i.e., no system under which the operations of each country can be compensated by those of the other member countries and reciprocal credits can be granted to cover the balances resulting from regional trade. It is therefore necessary to provide for the periodical liquidation in convertible currencies of the balances which exceed the limits of the established credits and for the adoption of substantive measures to eliminate the causes of the continuing disequilibria.

In this connexion, the idea that has been discussed again recently of forming a joint reserve fund of the central banks should be encouraged, for various reasons, one being that it would help in mobilizing the external resources needed for the proper operation of the payments union.

A general compensatory machinery, designed to simplify payments and to enable sizable economies to be made in currencies and operational costs, would not preclude the establishment of smaller compensatory boards of groups of countries that have close trade relations.

In this regional plan it would be necessary to use the services of the existing commercial banks and, with their close co-operation, to promote the development of a system of short-term commercial loans to encourage Latin American trade.

With regard to the need to establish machinery for the medium-term financing of exports of certain types of goods, the Inter-American Development Bank has already taken a very important step in organizing a regional system for the financing of intra-regional exports of capital goods. This system should be made more flexible and should be supplemented by regional machinery for insurance and reinsurance.

III. OTHER RECOMMENDATIONS FOR THE SYSTEM OF INTEGRATION

In the foregoing pages we have considered the measures of trade policy, investment policy and monetary policy that would have to be adopted in order to promote the establishment and smooth functioning of the common market. It would, however, be advisable also to establish clear criteria for other aspects which, if disregarded, might hamper progress towards this great objective. To this end, the following recommendations are put forward concerning the principle of reciprocity, the treatment to be accorded to the relatively less developed countries, the measures needed to deal with the internal dislocations that might arise in the process of liberalizing trade, and measures designed to stimulate Latin American private enterprise within the common market.

The Principle of Reciprocity

Reciprocity of advantage within the common market is an essential principle for its smooth functioning. No country will be able to go on deriving greater advantages than it grants to others.

It is impossible to lay down specific rules for maintaining this type of balance. Information on the additional trade which each country gains as a result of the reductions and elimination of tariffs and restrictions and of the specific integration agreements will, of course, be an important factor in assessing those advantages. Each specific case, however, will have to be examined carefully, for the disequilibrium working against one country will not always be due to the other countries not having granted it sufficient advantages. It might also have its source in the actual conduct of the country in question—its exchange system, for example, or the lack of adequate action to encourage exports, or other reasons. If that were not the case, however, it would be the responsibility of all to ensure that it obtained due reciprocity. Investment policy is of the utmost importance in the fulfilment of this collective responsibility, which is vital for the proper functioning of the common market, but in order to ensure reciprocity it will be necessary also to adjust tariffs.

In this sense, the countries which persistently gain greater advantages from the common market than do the others should speed up the reduction of customs duties and elimination of restrictions, in so far as the imbalance is not due to the attitude or policy of the less favoured countries. Those countries will also have to offer a greater margin of preferences in order to promote their imports from the region in all cases where the reduction of customs duties and the preferences already granted are not sufficient.

This corrective action might prove necessary irrespective of the countries' level of development. The case of the less developed countries of Latin America, however, would have to be given preferential attention, in accordance with the following general criteria.

The Relatively Less Developed Countries

If integration is to succeed, all the countries must have in actual practice equal opportunities to profit from the establishment of the common market. For that reason, the relatively less developed countries require preferential attention and special treatment, particularly in three fundamental aspects: trade policy, technical and financial assistance, and regional investment policy.

With regard to the execution of trade policy, the less developed countries should have longer periods in which to reach the quantitative goals set for the reduction and elimination of customs duties and other trade restrictions and to establish the corresponding preferential margins for intra-regional imports. This system would have to be applied in relation to the actual expansion in the volume that these countries manage to export to the common market, on the understanding that the less developed countries will continue to fulfil the obligations they have contracted only in so far as they go on gaining specific advantages from the common market.

There is no doubt that the incorporation of the less developed countries in the regional integration process will require a special effort of technical and financial assistance. As far as technical assistance is concerned, the international organizations, the industrialized countries and the more developed countries of the region must co-ordinate their efforts in programmes with well-defined objectives that will enable the respective projects to be prepared in good time. Moreover, for the financing of the necessary investments, consideration must be given to external financial assistance on flexible conditions and favourable terms.

The regional investment programmes must also give preferential attention to the less developed countries, especially in connexion with power supply and the linking of those countries with the rest of the region, with regard both to means of transport and to communications systems. Similarly, the economic integration programmes of the less developed countries—as in the case of the Central American countries—and the border programmes between those countries and between them and the relatively more developed countries must be given special impetus. Lastly, particular attention must be given to the problems that arise in the less developed countries as regional competition becomes stronger. In this respect, the action to be taken in order to improve or adapt established industries that are not sufficiently efficient is of special importance.

Measures of Protection and Readjustment

It is understandable that countries should be reluctant to enter into agreements providing for substantial reductions in tariffs and other trade restrictions until they have a clear picture of what protective measures they will be entitled to take if their imports should involve them in serious and persistent economic difficulties. Reference has already been made to the fact that technical and financial co-operation is needed for the re-adjustment of any activities which may be affected. While this process of readjustment is going on, it is essential that member countries should have at their disposal defensive measures which they can take in cases where their compliance with the agreements entered into jeopardizes activities of obvious importance to their national economy, or seriously affects their balance of payments or level of employment. Such measures could consist, for example, in the provisional imposition of import quotas or tariff rates higher than those agreed upon.

These measures could not be left to the sole discretion of the importing countries; they would have to be authorized by the competent organs of the common market, indicated above, so that the exporting countries would have some guarantee that measures of this kind would not be arbitrary, or be continued beyond the reasonable period necessary to bring about the required readjustment.

In this connexion, the disturbing effects on trade resulting from inflation give rise to justified concern.

Until monetary stability is achieved throughout the region, any marked disparities between internal price levels and the external value of currencies will have to be avoided. Such disparities, whether they take the form of monetary over-valuation or of under-valuation, affect the entire process of trade and the entire payments system, not only our intra-regional trade.

Where a country's currency is over-valued, the harmful effects are felt by the country itself, which can rectify them by altering its rate of exchange. However, it is conceivable that the country in question could be authorized to take certain transitional measures to correct the effects of the over-valuation of its currency on its trade with the other Latin American countries.

Where a country's currency is under-valued, the harmful effects are felt by the other countries members of the system. Accordingly, these countries should have at their disposal measures to protect their internal production and their exports until the exchange discrepancy is rectified. These measures, of course, would have to be expressly authorized whenever the country whose currency was under-valued failed itself to take measures of readjustment or compensation, as would be highly desirable.

In any event, the Governments concerned will have to avoid or correct these disparities until such time as success has been achieved in removing their causes, whether these are to be found in inflation or in any other phenomenon.

Difficulties may also be caused by the varying tariff treatment given by different countries to imports of raw materials and intermediate products, since this gives rise to cost and price differences which interfere with normal conditions of competition. Until a common tariff—the fundamental solution to this problem—has been achieved, authorization could be given for transitional measures of a compensatory character.

The Problem of Stimulating Latin American Initiative

The signatories to this document share a concern which is extremely widespread in Latin America: that in the most complex and investment-attracting sectors of the common market—i.e. in basic industry—private initiative in the great industrial centres enjoys so great a technical and financial superiority that it may well acquire a predominant position, to the decided detriment of Latin American entrepreneurs. This serious problem, while not the sole problem of the common market, may prove an obstacle to its progress.

Accordingly, solutions must be sought which will effectively dispel this concern. Two types of solutions may be conceived: the formulation of a statute providing a clear and uniform definition of the terms offered by Latin American countries and the common market to extra-regional investors; and the adoption of a policy providing regional entrepreneurs with solid technical and financial support.

Proposals were recently made for the establishment of an international system to do away with the conflicts of interest which face foreign investors. In refusing to support these proposals, the Latin American countries have implicitly assumed responsibility for creating a system of their own offering practical and stable safeguards, within a code of principles rooted in an entire tradition of independent life.

Foreign capital undoubtedly has an important part to play in the development of our economies, particularly when it operates in association

with local entrepreneurs in industries which are so technically complex or
so capital-intensive that access to them is difficult for Latin American
entrepreneurs alone at their present stage of development. Foreign firms
generally have considerable exporting experience, and this experience,
in conjunction with the efforts of our own entrepreneurs, could be of great
use in ensuring better exploitation of the opportunities offered by the
common market, and, particularly, in promoting the export of industrial
goods to the rest of the world. There are already a number of highly
positive examples of these forms of association in various Latin American
countries.

If the Latin American entrepreneur is to be enabled to take an efficient
and equitable part in this type of association, the rules for foreign investment will have to be founded on the principle that the regional market
must be an instrument to strengthen the position of our entrepreneurs and confirm their paramount role in the development of Latin
America.

Thus foreign investment must be brought into line with the fundamental objectives; that is, it must bring with it modern techniques of
production and it must serve increasingly as an efficient vehicle for the
transfer of such techniques to our technicians and entrepreneurs and their
genuine incorporation in the processes of business management.

But if the Latin American entrepreneur is to be able fully to fulfil his
function, this is not enough; he must also be given solid technical and
financial assistance. This is a responsibility which will have to be shared
by the actual countries concerned and by the international organs and
industrialized countries which are participating in the development of
Latin America. The former will have to organize themselves with a view
to mobilizing their own technical personnel—frequently dispersed
among a variety of secondary activities—and setting up credit instruments and capital markets which will be of help in the preparation of
projects and will contribute to financing the local costs of the resulting
investments.

External financial assistance is a fundamental element in our development process. While the tremendous progress made in the last decade in
the volume and quality of international financial co-operation—particularly in the financing of public investment—must be recognized,
much remains to be done to create credit instruments by means of which
similar finance can be rapidly channelled into the private sector. This is a
problem demanding urgent attention, for until it is solved the very high
proportion of total investment in Latin America represented by private
investment will for the most part go to financing suppliers, frequently in
respect of purchases of capital equipment at prices higher than the market
prices and on amortization and interest terms incompatible with the
capacity to pay of the lending countries. To solve this fundamental prob-

lem, concerted and tenacious efforts on the part of all international financial organs and the active co-operation of the competent authorities of the capital-exporting countries will be essential.

IV. THE INSTITUTIONAL MACHINERY OF THE COMMON MARKET

In order to pursue systematic integration policy culminating in the establishment of a Latin American common market, it is necessary to set up institutional machinery which will make use of the various agencies and facilities already in operation and will thus make it possible to co-ordinate all action taken in connexion with the objectives and general criteria stated above.

Council of Ministers

The supreme power of decision should vest in a Council composed of a Minister of State and an alternate representing each member country. The Council would hold regular meetings at least twice a year and special meetings when circumstances so required. When specialized subjects were under examination, the competent Secretaries of States should be present. Without prejudice to the foregoing, the alternates would meet more frequently in order to keep one another informed and to facilitate the work of the Executive Board and specialized bodies referred to below.

It would be desirable that the right to veto the Council's decisions should be restricted from the outset.

It would also be desirable for the Council to have the help of advisory committees composed of high-level technical officials from the member countries, and that of a committee composed of representatives of the workers, entrepreneurs, universities and technical and professional organizations.

Executive Board

The executive authority of the common market would vest in a Board composed of a Chairman and a limited number of members—preferably four and in any case no more than six—appointed by the Council. The Chairman and members of the Board should be nationals of member countries, would be eligible for reappointment and should be selected mainly on their technical qualifications.

The members of the Board would represent, not the Governments appointing them in the Council, but the community itself. They would accordingly be forbidden to receive orders or instructions from countries individually and would be required to exercise complete independence of judgement in the performance of their duties.

The principal functions of the Board would be: to ensure that the objectives of the integration policy were attained and that the general criteria of that policy, including the principle of reciprocity and the necessary tariff-adjustment and preferential measures, were applied; to propose to the Council measures designed to accelerate that process; to promote the negotiation of sectoral complementarity agreements; to promote, or to have carried out under its direction, the studies required for the application of the general policy of integration; to decide on the application of safeguards and readjustments when required; to act as a court of first instance in disputes on interpretation; and lastly, to coordinate activities relating to commercial and investment policy, monetary and payments policy and foreign trade financing policy.

In addition, the Board should promote or carry out studies designed to co-ordinate the action of the Latin American countries in negotiations for the expansion or diversification of exports, should protect the prices of products exported to the rest of the world, and should play an effective part in devising other measures of international co-operation.

Latin American Parliament

The establishment of a Latin American Parliament, composed of representatives of the region's Parliaments, would give great impetus to the integration process. At the recent meeting at Lima, Latin American parliamentarians gave this fundamental decision their unanimous support. The Latin American Parliament would be a regional forum in which the major currents of public opinion would converge to elucidate the most important problems of integration. A climate of opinion would thus be created which would be favourable to the political decisions needed to set the process in train and to maintain steady progress towards regional integration.

Instrument for the Promotion of Regional Investment

In the matter of regional investment policy, the Board should reach agreement with the Inter-American Development Bank on the establishment of an instrument which would actively promote the preparation of studies and projects in connexion with the regional market, taking advantage of the work already being done in this direction by various organizations and drawing upon the experience they have gained. This instrument should form part of the IDB system and be under the joint direction of representatives of IDB and of the Board.

Its main function would be to carry out pre-investment studies and to prepare programmes and projects in the following fields: basic industry; border programmes; regional infra-structural investment; and investment in relatively less developed countries, or investment designed to correct maladjustments.

With these studies and projects in its possession, the Board would be

V

able to promote the sectoral complementarity agreements required to negotiate the financing for the required investment. It should be made clear that the choice of functions for this body implies no disregard of the important contribution currently being made in this field by organizations of the inter-American system and by international agencies. On the contrary, the aim should be to encourage closer collaboration among all concerned, so that their efforts may be put to better use.

Conciliation Procedure

Disputes on interpretation may arise in the course of the integration process. Problems not solved by direct negotiation between the parties should be referred, in the first stage of the conciliation procedure, to the Board. If no agreement were to be reached, the problem would be solved by an *ad hoc* conciliation committee acting as a supreme court; its members would be drawn by lot from a list of persons designated for the purpose by the member countries beforehand. This experiment might lead to the establishment of a regional court of justice.

V. FINAL OBSERVATIONS

These are the proposals which are being submitted to the Latin American Governments for their consideration. What is needed, more than technical studies, is a definition of major objectives and the adoption of political decisions at the highest level. However, once these decisions are taken by Governments, there will have to be technical discussions on the best means of translating them into specific agreements and commitments which will ensure their implementation. Without these prior political decisions, there is a danger that the technicians will unduly prolong their deliberations for want of a complete picture of the aims and objectives to be achieved.

These proposals call for a vast programme of work. Our countries must set about this programme without delay, however much effort this may require of them, and resolutely mark out the path of Latin American integration. It would be useless to seek another solution. None exists, nor will one appear with the passage of time; indeed, time will make the task more difficult.

Integration is not something that can equally well be done or left undone. It is of fundamental importance for expediting Latin America's economic and social development, which is so gravely threatened by internal and external factors which must be dealt with most decisively.

We must realize, however, that the solutions which will lead us to that goal are not simple or easy ones. Ever since the great world depression, we have been seeking such simple and easy solutions, but we have not found them. Nor shall we find them, for our ills do not respond to contingent or transitory factors. They are basic ills, and they require basic remedies. In those earlier times, we lacked the experience to undertake this task on a regional scale. To fail to try now, after a long succession of frustrations, would be unpardonable.

Nevertheless, we must not underestimate the serious obstacles barring the way to these solutions. A multitude of immediate problems urgently demand the attention of our Governments, leaving little time or energy to attack their fundamental causes. Thus, we are caught in a vicious circle. The immediate problems are becoming more serious and more acute because no basic decisions have been taken, while such decisions are not being taken because of the constant pressure of the immediate problems. An extraordinary effort is required in order to break this vicious circle, and it is an effort which can no longer be postponed.

There is no doubt that the course of action advocated here—action leading to a common market—is fraught with dangers. However, there are also risks in inaction, and they are far greater. It would be the height of folly to run the risks of inaction in a Latin America which is in the throes of such profound social upheaval.

Moreover, the risks of action should not be exaggerated. There is no risk in the advance towards economic integration which cannot be averted or overcome, nor is there any dislocation which cannot be corrected. Why should the emphasis be placed on all these things rather than on the positive aspects of this great policy? Will it not offer our countries the most promising opportunities for action? Indeed, confined within the narrow limits of a national market, that action lacks broad horizons. Its frontier must be extended so that it can develop as effectively as possible until it reaches the 230 million inhabitants of Latin America.

We must also extend the frontier at the higher levels of Latin American educational and technical and scientific development as an essential part of the vast integration process.

This represents a tremendous challenge. It is a challenge to Latin American statesmen. It is a challenge to entrepreneurs with a spirit of determination and pioneering. And it is also a challenge to the Latin American workers, to technicians, and to the new generations which will find a great vital stimulus in the eager effort to create a Latin American community.

All this must be done now, without delay and with broad vision and constructive boldness. For a great deal is at stake. It is not simply a question of markets and competition. What is threatened in Latin America, given the imperious social demands of development, is the dynamic effectiveness of the system under which we live and the survival of our own values. What is at stake is our ability to step up the pace of development in order to achieve, on an impressive scale, a better life for the entire community through the vast potentialities of technology, within the broad and promising framework of an integrated Latin America which is conscious of its destiny and of the weight it carries in the modern world.

The recommendations appearing in this document represent the unanimous opinions of the authors and are their own and exclusive responsibility. They wish to point out that they had the co-operation of various persons, including the very valuable collaboration of Mr. Ángel Alberto Solá, Executive Secretary of LAFTA.

APPENDIX III: SELECTED RESOLUTIONS OF CONTRACTING PARTIES

1. *Resolution 17 (I): Application of the Provisions of Chapter VIII of the Treaty of Montevideo*

The Conference of Contracting Parties, at its first session,

In view of the provisions of Chapter VIII and Article 34 of the Treaty of Montevideo; and

Considering the need to establish uniform standards for a more effective application of the provisions of Chapter VIII of the Treaty

Resolves that

1. Entitlement to benefit from the provisions of Chapter VIII of the Treaty shall be limited to those countries members of the Latin American Free Trade Association whose situation as relatively less developed countries within the Area is recognized by the Contracting Parties.

2. A request for the application of one or other of the advantages envisaged in Article 32 shall contain:

(a) a specification of the advantage or advantages requested;

(b) an account of the factors that would permit a judgement to be made whether the benefits requested are necessary for the Party concerned, and adequate for the achievement of the desired objectives;

(c) an indication of the period for which authorization is requested—in the case of benefits under paragraph (a) of Article 32—as well as of the products in respect of which advantages not extended to other Contracting Parties are sought, the extent of such advantages, and the nature of the productive activities the installation or expansion of which it is desired to stimulate;

(d) the manner and rate at which the relatively less developed Contracting Party concerned proposes to comply with the programme for reduction of duties, if the benefits requested are those of paragraph (b) of Article 32.

(e) a demonstration of the existence or prospect of balance of payments disequilibrium and a specific indication of the measure or measures for which authorization is requested, if the benefits are those of paragraph (c) of Article 32.

(f) in the case of the benefits envisaged in paragraph (d) of Article 32, an indication of the productive activities of basic importance which it is considered necessary to protect, immediately or in future, an enumeration of the measures for which authorization is sought and the period for which they would be applied. In addition, data should be supplied concerning the consumption, production, and imports of the products concerned.

3. The Contracting Parties may authorize a relatively less developed Contracting Party to be granted simultaneously all or some of the benefits envisaged under Article 32 of the Treaty. The fact that a Contracting Party may have previously been granted one or more of these benefits shall not prevent the authorization of a new benefit.

4. The Contracting Parties, in authorizing the granting to a relatively less developed Contracting Party of advantages not extended to other Contracting Parties, shall fix the period during which such authorization shall be effective.

5. During the period in which the authorization is effective, any Contracting Party which has granted the benefits indicated in paragraph (*a*) of Article 32 may include in its programme of liberalization the products to which such benefits relate, and may negotiate the whole or part of the benefits affecting each product with the remaining Contracting Parties, except in so far as it may have been agreed with the relatively less developed country concerned that such negotiations should not take place for a certain time.

In the latter event, the Contracting Party concerned, in requesting the authorization provided for in the paragraph under reference, shall indicate the benefits that are not subject to negotiation and the period during which this situation will be maintained.

6. The Contracting Parties may extend the period of authorization laid down under paragraph (*a*) of Article 32 with respect to all or some of the benefits provided if, at the end of the period, the Contracting Party receiving the benefits is still in the position of a relatively less developed country within the Area and if the objectives for which the benefits had been granted have still not been realized.

A request for extension shall be presented at the session of the Conference immediately preceding the expiration of the period initially provided.

7. If the authorization granted in conformity with paragraph (*a*) of Article 32 is not extended at the end of the period provided, the benefits shall be automatically extended to the remaining Contracting Parties, in accordance with the provisions of Article 18 of the Treaty, except in those cases in which a Contracting Party which had given such concessions withdraws them at the end of the period concerned—providing that such withdrawal is in accordance with what has been agreed or resolved by the

Contracting Parties—or incorporates the products concerned in its programme of liberalization, negotiating for similar concessions iself.

8. The Contracting Parties, in granting the authorization referred to in paragraph (*b*) of Article 32, shall indicate specifically the particular rate at which the relatively less developed Contracting Party may comply with the minimum requirements of the programme for reducing duties, laid down in Article 5 of the Treaty, noting the stages and percentages by which that programme shall be carried out.

The period for such reductions may not extend beyond that laid down in Article 2 of the Treaty, except as agreed under Article 61 of the Treaty.

9. The authorization indicated in paragraph (*c*) of Article 32 may be granted by the Contracting Parties if the provisions of Chapter VI of the Treaty would not be sufficient for the correction of a disequilibrium in the balance of payments of a relatively less developed Contracting Party.

10. In granting the authorization referred to in paragraph (*d*) of Article 32, the Contracting Parties shall fix the period during which the relatively less developed country shall be allowed to impose the measures indicated in that paragraph and the period for which such measures, once applied, may be maintained.

The measures referred to may include, among others, quantitative restrictions on imports, the modification of tariffs, and price fixing arrangements.

11. The collective steps and the promotion of special programmes indicated in paragraphs (*e*) and (*f*) of Article 32 shall be undertaken at the request of the relatively less developed country concerned. Without prejudice to the above, the organs of the Association may make whatever recommendations they consider appropriate.

The Contracting Parties shall facilitate the practical application of these provisions of the Treaty.

12. The Contracting Parties may, at the request of one or more of the Parties, suspend any of the authorizations granted for the application of the measures envisaged in Article 32 of the Treaty, when

(*a*) it is agreed to withdraw recognition as a relatively less developed country owing to the cessation of the circumstances in which such recognition was granted; or

(*b*) it is proved that the special circumstances justifying the provision of the benefits in question have ended.

The suspension envisaged in the present Article, where necessary, shall be applied taking into account the provisions of Article 7 of the present resolution.

13. The Committee shall propose to the Conference whatever modifications in the present provisions may appear to be necessary in practice for the more effective application of the provisions of Chapter VIII of the Treaty.

Explanatory Notes

During the elaboration of the preceding provisions, certain clarifications have been achieved which it is convenient to set forth in explicit form, so as to ensure the fullest realization of the objectives of Chapter VIII of the Treaty, and avoid as far as possible difficulties of interpretation.

For this reason, and in view of the fact that the clarifications referred to cannot be included within the text of the resolution itself, it has been considered appropriate to add the present Explanatory Notes, which should stand annexed to the resolution.

1. Article 32 of the Treaty does not constitute an exception to the general provisions of the Treaty. Nevertheless, paragraphs (*a*) and (*b*) of that Article are exceptions to the provisions of Articles 5 and 18 of the Treaty, just as paragraphs (*c*) and (*d*) constitute exceptions to the provisions of Chapter VI.

Consequently, the relatively less developed countries, without prejudice to the benefits accorded to them by Article 32, shall, in common with the other Contracting Parties, enjoy all the rights and be subject to all the obligations emanating from the Treaty.

2. Paragraph (*a*) of Article 32 enables the Contracting Parties to authorize any Contracting Party to concede certain benefits, in addition to those contained in its liberalization programme, to another Contracting Party at a relatively less developed stage of economic development within the Area, which benefits shall not be affected by the provisions of Article 18 of the Treaty. Consequently, the Contracting Party granting any benefit may, within the limits of the authorization concerned, provide and maintain such benefit in a manner and for a period which it considers appropriate, and may even reach agreement with the relatively less developed country concerned not to withdraw nor negotiate nor modify in any other way the exclusive character of such benefit.

3. In order to avoid the application of measures restricting trade in products included in the liberalization programme, it is considered necessary to reserve the provisions of paragraph (*c*) of Article 32 for those cases in which the correction of a disequilibrium cannot be achieved through the application of Chapter VI of the Treaty.

4. The provisions of paragraph (*b*) of Article 32 are independent of those of Chapter VI, and the Contracting Parties may therefore authorize the joint application of the measures indicated in both places.

11 October 1961

2. *Resolution 68 (III): System of Voting of the Conference*

The Conference of the Contracting Parties, at its third session,

In view of Article 38 of the Treaty of Montevideo,

Considering that since the first two years of the operation of the Treaty have elapsed, it is necessary to establish the system of voting in the Conference of the Contracting Parties that will apply henceforth; and

That experience in the application of the Treaty suggests the need for gradual elimination of the provision whereby the adoption of decisions by the Conference is subject to there being no negative vote.

Resolves that

1. Except in the case of explicit provision to the contrary, decisions of the Conference shall continue to be adopted when affirmative votes are cast by at least two-thirds ($\frac{2}{3}$) of the Contracting Parties provided that no negative vote is cast.

2. The Contracting Parties shall determine, as they consider necessary, the cases to be added to those envisaged in paragraphs (*a*), (*b*), and (*c*) of Article 38 of the Treaty, which provide for decisions to be adopted by the affirmative votes of at least two-thirds ($\frac{2}{3}$) of the Contracting Parties.

4 October 1963

3. *Resolution 70 (III): Criteria for Drawing Up the Common Schedule*

The Conference of Contracting Parties, at its third session,

In view of Articles 4, 7 and 8 of the Treaty of Montevideo and the Protocol on Norms and Procedures for Negotiations,

Considering the need to define certain concepts so as to facilitate the negotiation of the Common Schedule,

Resolves that

1. The inclusion of a product in the Common Schedule binds each of the Contracting Parties to eliminate completely, before 2 June 1973, duties and restrictions of any kind affecting the import of that product if it originates in the territory of any other Contracting Party. Consequently,

the inclusion of a product in the Common Schedule does not in itself imply an obligation to reduce or eliminate restrictions on the import of that product before the above-mentioned date.

2. The products which may be included in the Common Schedule at each stage of its drawing up do not necessarily have to appear in the National Schedules and their inclusion shall be effected without indication of the import regime to be applied.

3. The irrevocability referred to in Article 8 of the Treaty shall begin to apply from the date of signature of the Act of Negotiations in which the first Common Schedule is drawn up, in relation to the products included in that Common Schedule and the import régime agreed for these products in so far as they appear in the National Schedules.

21 November 1963

4. *Resolution 71 (III): Situation of Countries with Inadequate Markets*

The Conference of Contracting Parties, at its third session,

Considering that the Contracting Parties, in the Preamble to the Treaty, have recognized that the economic development of the Area should be attained through the maximum utilization of available factors of production and the more effective co-ordination of the development programmes of the different production sectors in accordance with norms which take due account of equitable conditions of competition and of the interests of each and every one of the Contracting Parties;

That the principle established in that Preamble whereby the expansion of present national markets is a fundamental prerequisite for the acceleration of the economic development of the Contracting Parties has particular relevance for certain sectors of production in those countries whose internal demand is insufficient for the expansion of these activities;

That in consequence, in order to facilitate the achievement of the objectives of the Treaty it is necessary to make special provision for the situation of those countries having sectors of production that are insufficiently developed or that are confronted with national markets insufficiently large for the expansion or establishment of the productive activities concerned;

That at the same time in the above-mentioned Preamble it is stated that, by the adoption of suitable formulae, conditions can be created that will be conducive to stimulating the expansion of existing productive activities, formulae that may be extended to apply also to new industries of region-wide importance;

That in addition to the case of countries already designated as relatively less advanced, the narrowness of the national market for the development of certain industrial activities is common to Chile, Colombia, Peru and Uruguay, and

That it is indispensable to adopt joint measures enabling the countries mentioned in the previous paragraph to develop their economies in harmony and in parallel with the remaining Contracting Parties,

Resolves:

1. To recognize that in order to achieve a balanced and harmonious economic development of the Area it is necessary to adopt joint measures in favour of Chile, Colombia, Peru and Uruguay which would stimulate the establishment or expansion of certain productive activities for which the size of the respective national markets is inadequate or the development of which is of region-wide interest.

The countries already designated as relatively less advanced shall benefit from the provisions of the preceding paragraph.

2. To declare the firm intention of the Contracting Parties to assure the effective participation, through a fair distribution of benefits, of the countries mentioned in the preceding Article, as well as those already designated as relatively less advanced, in the Complementarity Agreements and any other type of multi-national arrangements providing for the initiation or expansion of regional productive activities. To this end, the Contracting Parties shall take into account the possibility of applying, where relevant, the principles established in Article 3, paragraph (*b*) of Resolution 48 (II) and in Article 8, paragraph (*c*) of Resolution 49 (II).

3. The Contracting Parties consider that within the framework of the Treaty it is possible to adopt joint measures adequate for the execution of a specific programme for the establishment or expansion of productive activities for the countries referred to in Article 1, the soundness of that programme being recognized by the Committee[1] in accordance with the information and advance plans presented. At the same time, the Contracting Parties undertake to do everything necessary to facilitate the execution of such a programme.

4. The Committee, in its programme of sectoral meetings and of activities of the Advisory Committee on Industrial Development, shall give priority to the examination of any initiatives presented by the Contracting Parties mentioned in Article 1 and those already designated as relatively less advanced, in accordance with the objectives of this Resolution, and shall determine the respective solutions or, where the situa-

---

[1] References to 'the Committee' in this and other resolutions are to the Standing Executive Committee established under ch. ix of the Treaty of Montevideo.

tion so requires, shall propose to the Conference the adoption of any measures that it may consider appropriate for implementing these solutions.

21 November 1963

5. Resolution 74 (III): Application of Chapter VIII of the Treaty. Plan of Operations and Special Measures in Favour of Countries at a Relatively Less Advanced Stage of Economic Development

The Conference of Contracting Parties, at its third session,

In view of Chapter VIII of the Treaty of Montevideo and Resolution 62 (II) of the Conference

Considering that the Committee,[1] in fulfilment of the recommendations of Resolution 62 (II), has proposed certain practical and effective rules for fostering, through special operations and concrete measures, the growth of the economies of countries at a relatively less advanced stage of economic development within the Area, and

That the Contracting Parties have repeatedly affirmed their readiness to consider the application of measures favouring the relatively less developed countries to the fullest extent possible, so as to permit these countries to overcome the inequalities in which they find themselves in relation to other Contracting Parties,

Resolves:

I. To approve the following Plan of Operations and Special Measures which the Contracting Parties may apply in favour of relatively less developed countries within the Area:

(a) Special Operations

When a relatively less developed country wishes to take advantage of the Plan, it shall submit for the study and approval of the Committee, a Programme of Special Operations which would permit it to accelerate its rate of economic development by means of:

1. Financial Assistance

Through loans or special operations, the Contracting Parties, may give aid, in accordance with their capacity to do so, to each one of the relatively less developed countries within the Area, principally by:

(i) Supplying machinery, equipment, installations, tools and instruments required for infrastructural projects (roads, bridges, airfield runways, transport and communications media, power facilities and others);

[1] See footnote to Resolution 71 (III).

(ii) Supplying equipment and installations for industrial and agricultural schools for the training of skilled labour;

(iii) Supplying basic texts, installations and equipment for technical courses in the universities and other specialized centres;

(iv) Establishing lines of development credit for financing imports from within the Area, of seed, insecticides, fertilizer, raw materials or other goods required in the basic productive activities of the relatively less developed countries; and

(v) Facilitating financial agreements aimed at the creation of a fund, composed of cash contributions, with the objective of supplementing the resources of the development banks of the relatively less developed countries so as to supply working capital for productive activities of region-wide interest.

2. *Technical Assistance*

The Contracting Parties shall provide technical assistance, in accordance with their capacities, corresponding to the needs of each one of the relatively less developed countries in the Area, principally by:

(i) Supplying experts, technicians and instructors to work within the countries concerned;

(ii) Providing fellowships for the training of technicians, skilled workers and business administrators from the relatively less developed countries, at the centres for professional and technical training of the other Contracting Parties.

(iii) Preparing and executing specific projects, such as: highly specialized engineering works; programmes of plant and animal health; works of irrigation, drainage, canal building and dam building; rural urbanization; agricultural colonization; reafforestation; the care and conservation of the navigable courses of rivers, and

(iv) Studying market possibilities and identifying industries, of region-wide interest, with a view to locating them on the territory of the relatively less developed countries within the Area.

(b) *Special Measures*

1. The Standing Executive Committee is authorized to study and approve collective negotiations with international financial institutions such as the Inter-American Development Bank, the International Bank for Reconstruction and Development and the Alliance for Progress, in support of requests for financial and technical assistance that have been or may be presented to these bodies by relatively less developed countries, with a view to obtaining finance for the expansion of existing productive activities or the development of new ones, including initiatives for the development of infrastructural projects.

2. The Standing Executive Committee is authorized to study and pre-

sent for the consideration of the Contracting Parties any requests which relatively less developed countries may present for maintaining margins of preference for a certain time in respect of one or more products mentioned in such requests and which had been the subject of negotiations in accordance with Resolutions 12 (I) and 38 (II).

3. The Committee is authorized to carry out studies and, on the basis of such studies, to adopt measures or prepare draft resolutions, as the case may be, which relatively less developed countries may request in the application of other provisions envisaged in Article 32 of the Treaty dealing, in particular, with the following:

(i) The identification of industries which would produce exportable products, principally intended to supply the regional market, which could be located in countries declared as being at a relatively less advanced stage of economic development under Resolutions 12 (I) and 38 (II), and

(ii) The programme of expected liberalization which would permit the installation and ensure the effective operation of the industries referred to in the preceding paragraph.

II. The operations contemplated in paragraph (*a*) of Article I are intended to supplement and not to replace the normal sources of financial or technical assistance which each relatively less developed country may obtain directly from the appropriate international agencies.

III. The Committee shall include a chapter dealing with the implementation of the present Resolution in its annual report to the Conference of the Contracting Parties.

21 November 1963

6. *Resolution 75 (III): Programme for Coordinating Economic and Commercial Policies and for Harmonizing Systems of Foreign Trade Control*

The Conference of Contracting Parties, at its third session,

In view of the provisions of Articles 15, 16, 27 and 54 of the Treaty of Montevideo, Agreement No. 2 of the first meeting of Central Banks on commercial policy and Agreements Nos. 1 and 2 of the first meeting on the planning, development and orientation of industrial development.

Considering that the diversity in the economic policies of LAFTA countries imposes grave limitations on economic integration and on the process of liberalizing the intra-regional trade of the Contracting Parties;

That, in particular, diversity in the treatment of imports from third countries gives rise to the following problems among others:

(a) Growing complexity of the process of negotiation because of the multiplicity and heterogeneity of duties and restrictions applied to the same product in different countries;

(b) Differences in the margin of preference and, consequently, in the commercial stimulus provided in the various countries by the liberalization of the same category of products;

(c) Difficulty in the application of the principle of reciprocity, laid down in the Treaty of Montevideo, to give fundamental orientation to the negotiations;

(d) Distortion of normal conditions of competition between producers in the region;

(e) Difficulties arising from differences in the cost of inputs imported from outside the region, affecting the location of new investments, and

(f) Extreme complexity of the problem of defining and controlling the regional origin of products subject to liberalization;

That in order to achieve the balanced economic and social development of the Area and to comply with the objectives laid down in the Treaty Articles and Agreements mentioned above it is necessary to correct the anomalies in question, by harmonizing the economic and commercial policies of the Contracting Parties;

That these objectives should be achieved gradually by means of adequate norms taking into account the interests of each and every Contracting Party.

Resolves:

1. The Contracting Parties, in accordance with the provisions of Articles 15 and 54 of the Treaty, agree to undertake the studies required for the elaboration of a programme of co-ordination of their economic and commercial policies and for harmonizing their systems of foreign trade control.

2. This programme, which shall be carried out in stages, shall take into account all aspects of economic policy relevant for the process of integration. To assist in formulating the programme, the Committee[1] shall request the Advisory Committees on Industrial Development, on Agricultural Questions and on Monetary Questions to carry out during the first five months of 1964 an examination of the policies of the Contracting Parties in the areas of their respective competence and the identification of the problems which, in each case, have a bearing on the process of integration.

[1] See footnote to Resolution 71 (III).

The results of the work of the Advisory Committees mentioned above shall be analysed by the Special Committee envisaged in the present Resolution, which shall produce a report for consideration by the Conference at its fourth regular session.

3. The first phase of the programme shall aim at harmonizing commercial policies, beginning by an analysis of the customs arrangements of the Contracting Parties. To this end the Committee shall entrust the Advisory Committee on Customs Questions, which shall be convened in the month of February 1964, with the following studies:

(a) Revision of NABALALC[2] so as to make it suitable for adoption as the Common Customs Nomenclature;

(b) Identification of the customs duties and charges of equivalent effect and of restrictions applied to the importation of each product in the various countries;

(c) Conversion of these customs duties and charges with equivalent effect into ad valorem terms, based on the c.i.f. value of the products;

(d) Classification under NABALALC of the charges and restrictions emerging from the work envisaged under paragraphs (b) and (c) above;

(e) Comparison of the charges and restrictions in force in each of the Contracting Parties in respect of each product, and

(f) Other studies considered necessary for examining the possibility of establishing a Common External Tariff.

4. The Committee is requested to create a Special Committee, composed of high level experts from each of the Contracting Parties to undertake the examination of the results of the work of the Advisory Committees referred to in Articles 2 and 3 of the present Resolution and to prepare a report proposing the basic measures considered necessary for achieving the objectives of the present Resolution, for consideration at the fourth regular session of the Conference.

5. The Contracting Parties shall designate the representatives of the Advisory Committee on Customs Questions and shall complete the establishment of the Advisory Committees mentioned in Article 2 before 31 December 1963.

6. The Contracting Parties shall furnish the Committee with the information necessary for the carrying out of the present Resolution and shall ensure the participation of the national technicians required for undertaking the work in question.

21 November 1963

---

[2] NABALALC is the common customs nomenclature adopted by LAFTA.

7. *Resolution 77 (III): Coordination of Agricultural Policies*

The Conference of Contracting Parties, at its third session,

In view of Articles 27 and 29 of the Treaty and Resolution 41 (II) of the Conference

Considering that under Resolution 11 (I) the Conference recommended the Committee[1] to convene meetings of experts to study regional problems in the field of agriculture;

That the Committee, under Resolution 36, created the Advisory Committee on Agricultural Questions, to carry out technical studies for the agricultural sector and to accelerate effective compliance with the provisions of the Treaty regarding agricultural complementarity;

That a harmonization of the agricultural development policies of the Contracting Parties would tend particularly to bring about overall utilization of the possibilities for trade in agricultural products within the Area;

That the co-ordination of these development policies can only be achieved in the light of a full understanding of the present situation of agriculture in each country in the Area, and

That although the work of the Advisory Committee will have to include the examination of all questions relevant to the above-mentioned objectives, it is convenient to establish an agreed tentative programme of prior studies, as a basis for an immediate plan of action,

Resolves:

1. To request the Standing Executive Committee to carry out the following tasks, with the assistance of the Advisory Committee on Agricultural Questions:

(*a*) The study and evaluation of programmes of agricultural expansion and investigation in member countries, related to the existing agricultural situation, as a basis for regional co-ordination;

(*b*) The study and analysis of requirements and availabilities of basic production equipment, with a view to increasing regional trade in these products;

(*c*) The examination of seasonal characteristics of regional production, with a view to an orderly increase in commercial transactions to supplement local supplies;

(*d*) The establishment of priorities for sectoral meetings on agricultural products, and

(*e*) The study of measures for expanding regional trade in agricultural products and stimulating the exports of these products to extra-regional markets.

[1] See footnote to Resolution 71 (III).

W

2. Without prejudice to the carrying out of the work indicated in the preceding Article, which has high priority, the Advisory Committee on Agricultural Questions is requested to analyse the present structure of agriculture and cattle-raising in each of the member countries of the Area, with special reference to the conditions of production, distribution and marketing.

3. The Committee[1] shall prepare a minimum plan of action embodying measures designed to achieve the co-ordination of the agricultural development policies of the member countries of LAFTA.

21 November 1963

8. *Resolution 99 (IV): Norms and Procedures for Complementarity Agreements*

The Conference of Contracting Parties, at its fourth regular session,

In view of Articles 15, 16, and 17 of the Treaty

Decides to approve the following norms and procedures for Complementarity Agreements.

I. *Nature and Objectives*

1. Complementarity Agreements, which constitute a means of promoting economic integration, should lead to the harmonious economic development of the Area and have the following objectives, among others:

(*a*) To accelerate the fulfilment of the programme of liberalization of duties and restrictions on industrial products;
(*b*) To facilitate the inclusion in the liberalization programme of products which do not yet form part of intra-regional trade;
(*c*) To create conditions favourable for the promotion of investments which would tend to accelerate economic and social development, raise the level of employment and improve the utilization of the resources of the Area;
(*d*) To make possible the maximum utilization of the available factors of production in the sector concerned and an adequate co-ordination of the relevant development plans;
(*e*) To facilitate programmes of sectoral integration that may be established by the Contracting Parties;
(*f*) To contribute, through the adoption of specific norms, to the narrowing of differences between the levels of economic development of the countries of the Area;

[1] See footnote to Resolution 71 (III).

(*g*) To give special attention, in planning and drawing up Complementarity Agreements, to the situation of the relatively less developed countries and to the need, in compliance with the provisions of Article 32 of the Treaty, to create opportunities for them to participate adequately in such Agreements;

(*h*) To stimulate complementarity between industrial activities designed to supply the needs of the Area; and

(*i*) To ensure equitable conditions of competition so as to increase industrial productivity, promote an improvement in quality and a reduction in prices and to enhance the competitiveness of the products of the Area in world markets.

II. *Content of the Agreements*

2. Complementarity Agreements drawn up under the provisions of Articles 15, 16 and 17 of the Treaty, shall without fail contain norms to govern the programme of liberalization to be established for the products included in such Agreements.

3. The programme of liberalization of each Complementarity Agreement shall:

(*a*) Specify the products included in the Agreement, in conformity with the specifications and corresponding code-numbers of NABALALC;

(*b*) Indicate the manner in which duties and restrictions applying to the products specified shall be eliminated, it being understood that the rate of liberalization may differ as between countries and products included in the Agreement;

(*c*) Provide for the maintenance of the margins of preference agreed upon for the products included in the liberalization programme; and

(*d*) Define the requirements as to origin to which the products concerned shall be subject, in accordance with the general norms approved by the Conference.

4. Complementarity Agreements shall contain clauses providing for accession to the Agreements which shall be such as to facilitate the participation of other Contracting Parties.

5. Contracting Parties participating in a Complementarity Agreement shall endeavour to include in such Agreement provisions relating to:

(*a*) Harmonization of treatment accorded to imports from third countries related to products included in the sector concerned, as also of raw materials and components employed in the manufacturing process in question;

(*b*) Co-ordination of governmental programmes and incentives, with a view to facilitating sectoral complementarity and harmonizing the treatment accorded to capital and services originating either within or outside the Area and involving the sector in question; and

(*c*) Regulations to prevent unfair trade practices, in line with the general norms adopted by the Conference.

6. Complementarity Agreements may include, among others, clauses relating to:

(*a*) Irrevocability of concessions or conditions regulating the withdrawal of concessions relating to one or more products of the sector;

(*b*) Special treatment in application of Chapter VIII of the Treaty;

(*c*) Treatment to be applied in implementation of Article 2 of Resolution 71 (III);

(*d*) Denunciation of the Agreement;

(*e*) Special procedures for settling disputes; and

(*f*) Administration of the Agreement.

7. A Contracting Party at a relatively less advanced stage of economic development participating in an Agreement may, in accordance with Article 32, paragraph (*a*) of the Treaty, be granted benefits through concessions not extended to other Contracting Parties, under conditions laid down in the relevant Resolution of the Conference.

8. Clauses providing for denunciation shall deal with the following points *inter alia:*

(*a*) Formalities of denunciation;

(*b*) The period at the end of which the denunciation shall begin to take effect; and

(*c*) Effects of the denunciation in respect of the liberalization programme contained in the Agreement and of the rights and obligations of participating Contracting Parties deriving therefrom.

III. *Conclusion of Agreements*

9. Negotiations for the conclusion of Complementarity Agreements shall be open to the participation of all Contracting Parties.

10. The Contracting Parties proposing to conclude a Complementarity Agreement shall communicate its text to the Standing Executive Committee through their representatives, and shall provide the most complete information possible on the nature of the Draft Agreement. The Committee shall in turn inform the other Contracting Parties of the intention to conclude the Agreement.

11. The negotiations shall not begin before forty-five days have

elapsed from the date that the Committee receives the communication referred to in the preceding Article.

12. At the request of any Contracting Party, the beginning of the negotiations shall be deferred for a supplementary period of up to sixty days.

13. The periods referred to in Articles 11 and 12 above may be reduced or eliminated by decision of the Committee, in accordance with the system of voting laid down in Article 38 of the Treaty.

14. Between the date of the communication and the commencement of negotiations, the Committee shall analyse the material presented, and supplement it with the necessary technical studies for the information of the Contracting Parties; it shall examine the possibilities for other Contracting Parties to participate in the Agreement; it shall formulate, where appropriate, any recommendations which it may consider advisable; and to this end it may request of the sponsoring Parties any additional information that it may consider necessary.

15. In the negotiations for drawing up Complementarity Agreements and for accession to such Agreements, the Contracting Parties shall take full account of the situation of the relatively less developed countries, as well as of conditions of production in the countries of the Area, especially in the cases envisaged in Resolution 71 (III).

16. Agreements shall consist of Protocols signed by plenipotentiaries duly accredited by the Contracting Parties.

17. The Secretariat of the Committee shall be the depositary of the Protocols, of which it shall supply authentic copies to all Contracting Parties.

18. Immediately after the respective Protocol has been signed, the Complementarity Agreements shall be submitted for the examination of the Committee, which shall pronounce on their compatibility with the general principles and objectives of the Treaty within a period of thirty days from the date on which the Standing Executive Committee received the Protocol in question.

19. Complementarity Agreements may enter into force only after they have been declared compatible with the general principles and objectives of the Treaty, in the manner provided in Article 17 of the Treaty, and in accordance with the terms of Article 18 of the present Resolution.

20. Complementarity Agreements shall remain open to the accession of the remaining Contracting Parties. Such accession shall take effect definitively as soon as the requisite negotiations have been completed

and the necessary Protocols have been signed by the countries participating in the Agreement and by the acceding Party, which Protocols shall
be deposited with the Secretariat of the Association.

21. The Contracting Parties expressly agree that those Contracting
Parties not participating in a Complementarity Agreement shall enjoy
the benefits granted reciprocally between the Parties participating in the
Agreement only if they provide adequate compensation.

22. Contracting Parties proposing to accede to a Complementarity
Agreement shall initiate the negotiations referred to in Article 20 not
earlier than thirty days nor later than 120 days from the date on which
they communicate their intention to the Standing Executive Committee.

23. The obligations required of an acceding Contracting Party shall, as
a maximum, not exceed the cumulative obligations undertaken since the
entry into force of the Agreement by the Contracting Party that has
assumed the greatest such obligations, taking into account the provisions of Article 15 of the present Resolution.

24. In case of any dispute regarding the interpretation of the conditions required for the entry into force of the Agreement in respect of an
acceding Contracting Party, the latter may submit the case to the Committee, which shall undertake the necessary negotiations for conciliation.

25. In all cases, benefits negotiated under Complementarity Agreements shall be automatically extended, without the provision of compensation, to the relatively less developed countries, independently of
any negotiation or accession to the Agreements.

IV. *Relation to the Liberalization Programme of the Treaty*
26. Liberalization programmes established by Complementarity
Agreements shall be formulated taking into account their auxiliary
character in relation to the liberalization programme instituted under
Chapter 2 of the Treaty of Montevideo. They shall therefore be limited to
the period indicated in Article 2 of the Treaty.

V. *Execution of the Agreements*
27. Contracting Parties participating in a Complementarity Agreement shall supply information periodically on the progress of the Agreement to the Committee, which shall render an annual report on this
matter to the Conference at its regular sessions, including in such report
an account of experience gained in the application of this Resolution.

28. A Contracting Party not participating in an Agreement may at any
time request additional information on the progress of such Agreement,
through the Committee.

29. At the request of any Contracting Party participating in a Complementarity Agreement, the organs of the Association shall endeavour to take such measures as would be necessary to correct any anomalies arising in the course of its execution, particularly in the event that one or more Contracting Parties, whether or not they are participants in the Agreement, adopt measures which cause or threaten to cause disturbances in the normal functioning of the Agreement.

30. If as a consequence of the application of the norms laid down in the present Resolution serious and persistent imbalance occurs in the industrial development of the Contracting Parties affecting the harmonious economic development of the Area, the means of correcting such imbalance shall be examined by the Standing Executive Committee, at the request of any Party that considers it has suffered damage, with a view to adopting measures that it regards as adequate for this purpose.

VI. *Special Clause*

31. The present Resolution supersedes Resolution 48 (II) of the Conference.

8 December 1964

SELECT BIBLIOGRAPHY

Allen, Robert Loring. 'Integration in Less Developed Countries', *Kyklos* (Basle), no. 3 (1961).

Association of the Bar of the City of New York, Committee on Foreign Law. *Economic Integration in Latin America.* New York, 1962.

Balassa, Bela. *El desarrollo económico y la integración.* CEMLA, 1965.

Banco Nacional de Comercio Exterior. *La integración económica latinoamericana.* Mexico City, 1963. (Articles published in *Comercio Exterior*, 1957–63.)

Brown, A. J. 'Economic Separatism versus a Common Market in Developing Countries', *Yorkshire Bulletin of Economic and Social Research*, May and Nov. 1961.

Business International. *Latin America's Merging Market.* New York, 1964.

Centro de Estudios Monetarios Latinoamericanos. *Cooperación financiera en América Latina.* Mexico City, 1963.

—— *Problemas de pagos en América Latina.* Mexico City, 1964.

Dell, Sidney. *Problemas de un mercado común en América Latina.* Mexico City, CEMLA, 1959.

—— *Trade Blocs and Common Markets.* London, Constable, 1963.

Ferrero, Rómulo A. 'Purposes and Realities of the Latin American Common Market: a Peruvian Viewpoint', *Statist* (London), Mar. 1960.

García Reynoso, Plácido. 'La Asociación Latinoamericana de Libre Comercio', *Cuadernos Americanos* (Mexico City), xix/3, May–June 1960.

—— 'Dos conferencias sobre el mercado común latinoamericano', *El Trimestre Económico* (Mexico City), Oct.–Dec. 1959.

Hoselitz, Bert F. 'Economic Development in Central America', *Weltwirtschaftliches Archiv* (Jena), 1956.

Laris Casillas, Jorge Eduardo. *La integración económica latinoamericana.* Mexico City, Consejo Nacional de Comercio Exterior, 1960.

Latin American Free Trade Association (LAFTA). *Tratado de Montevideo, resoluciones de la Conferencia.* Montevideo, 1963.

—— *Resoluciones del Comité Provisional de Montevideo, resoluciones del Comité Ejecutivo Permanente.* Montevideo, 1963.

Lindeman, John. *Preferential Trading Systems in Latin America.* Washington, D.C., International Economic Consultants, 1960.

Mikesell, Raymond F. *Liberalization of Inter-Latin American Trade.* Washington, D.C., PAU, 1957.

—— 'The Movement Towards Regional Trading Groups in Latin America', in A. O. Hirschman, ed., *Latin American Issues: Essays and Comments.* New York, Twentieth Century Fund, 1961.

Perloff, Harvey S., and Romulo Almeida. 'Regional Economic Integration in the Development of Latin America', *Economía Latinoamericana* (PAU), Nov. 1963.

Pincus, Joseph. *The Central American Common Market*. Mexico City, AID, Sept. 1962.

Plaza, Galo. 'For a Regional Market in Latin America', *Foreign Affairs* (New York), July 1959.

Prebisch, Raúl. 'El mercado común constituye una de las grandes reformas estructurales de América Latina', *Revista de Ciências Econômicas* (São Paulo), June 1962.

—— 'Ten-year Plan for South American Free Trade Zone', *Review of the River Plate* (Buenos Aires), 19 May 1959.

—— *See also under:* United Nations, ECLA.

Proposals for the Creation of the Latin American Common Market. By Felipe Herrera, Carlos Sanz de Santamaría, José Antonio Mayobre, and Raúl Prebisch (UNCTAD TD/B/11; see above, pp. 284–310).

Sammons, Robert L. 'Proposals for a Common Market in Latin America', in Harvard Univ., Graduate School of Administration. *Public Policy, 1959–60: a Yearbook.* 1960.

United Nations, Economic Commission for Africa. *The Significance of Recent Common Market Developments in Latin America* (E/CN.14/64, 6 Dec. 1960).

—— Economic Commission for Latin America (ECLA). *The Economic Development of Latin America and its Principal Problems.* By Dr R. Prebisch (UN Sales No. 1950.II.G.2).

—— *Exposición en la Comisión Económica para América Latina.* By Dr R. Prebisch (E/CN.12/IX/D.1.6, 5 May 1961).

—— *Towards a Dynamic Development Policy for Latin America.* By Dr R. Prebisch. 1963 (UN Sales No. 64.II.G.4).

—— *The Latin American Common Market* (UN Sales No. 59.II.G.4).

—— *Multilateral Economic Co-operation in Latin America* (UN Sales No. 62.G.3).

—— *Possibilities for Integrated Industrial Development in Central America* (UN Sales No. 63.II.6.10).

—— Library, Mexico City. *Mercado común latinoamericano, integración económica centroamericana: bibliografía inicial.* 1961.

Urquidi, Victor L. *Free Trade and Economic Integration in Latin America.* Berkeley, Univ. of Calif. Press, 1962.

Wionczek, Miguel S. *Latin American Free Trade Association.* New York, Carnegie Endowment for International Peace, 1965.

—— 'The Montevideo Treaty and Latin American Integration', Banco Nazionale del Lavoro, *Quarterly Review* (Rome), June 1961.

—— ed. *Integración de América Latina.* Mexico City, Fondo de Cultura Económica, 1964. (With bibliography.)

INDEX

Abs, Dr Hermann J., 182
Access to markets, 13–14, 17–18, 144, 171
Africa, 3, 30 f., 33, 37 n., 184, 190, 214
Agriculture, 2–3, 13, 95, 142, 177, 196, 211; LAFTA &, 40–41, 82 ff., 98 f., 199, 209; -resolution, 323–4; Central American integration &, 52, 63; EEC &, 96, 147–8, 208
Aid, 8, 12–13, 22, 65, 67, 137–8, 210
Alexander, Prof. Robert, 178
Alliance for Progress, 33, 61, 106, 123–5, 175, 183–6, 195, 202
Angulo, Enrique, 101 n.
Aranha, Graça, 214
Argentina, 1, 4–5, 11, 18, 20, 79, 94, 119, 158, 204, 206, 208; industry, 23 f., 189; automobile industry, 23–24, 74, 134, 136, 187; & Montevideo Treaty, 26, 28, 36, 70 ff., 110, 119; share of intra-regional trade, 27, 71–72, 102, 119, 158, 206; roads, 100; & shipping, 101; complementarity agreements, 128, 129–31, 133; & foreign capital, 187, 189, 194 f.
Armaments, 7–8
Asia, 3, 33, 184, 214
Assembly, 21, 64, 130, 133–4
Australia, 19, 181
Automaticity: of access to credit, 156–7, 161–4; of tariff reductions, 76–77, 207–9, 211
Automobile industry, 19, 23–24, 68, 134–6, 182, 186–7, 191, 198
Azuela, Mariano, 8–9

Balance of payments, ch. ix *passim*, 176 n., 182
Balassa, Prof. Bela, 165 n.
Benelux countries, 77, 106
Betancourt, President Rómulo, 175, 186
Blessing, Karl, 166 f.,
Bolívar, Simon, 213
Bolivia, 1, 4, 28, 36, 42, 47, 109, 114–16, 149
Brand, P. J., 60 n., 158 n., 172 n.
Brandenburg, Frank, 151 n., 183, 224

Brazil, 4, 11, 18, 20, 158, 169, 204, 208, 214; automobile industry, 19, 23–24, 134–5, 187; industrial development, 23 f., 79, 189; & Montevideo Treaty, 26, 28, 36, 70 ff.; share of intra-regional trade, 27, 74, 102, 115, 119, 158; complementarity agreements, 129–31, 133; & foreign capital, 176, 178, 189, 193 ff.
Brewster, Prof. Kingman, 179–80
Business International, 74 n., 189, 223

Canada, 32 n., 179–81, 187
Capital flow, 11–12, 22, 174, 180–1, 189, 213
Capital goods, 21–23, 90, 143, 198
Caribbean, 5, 18
Carroll, Thomas F., 2 n.
Cartels, 132, 180
Carter, Prof. C. F., 78–79
Central America, 5, 29, 31, ch. iv *passim*
Central American Bank for Economic Integration, 57 f., 60, 66
Central American Clearing House, 59–60, 172
Central American Committee for Economic Co-operation, 51–52
Central American Economic Council, 57, 61
Central American Monetary Union, 61–62
Central American Secretariat, 57, 64
Central American Treaties, 53 ff., 256–75
Checchi, Vincent, 3 n.
Chemicals, 24, 54 n., 63, 65, 74, 143, 155, 198
Chile, 11, 79, 100, 158, 165, 176, 208; industry, 23 f.; automobile industry, 23, 134–6; & Montevideo Treaty, 26, 28, 36, 49, 72, 74, 84, 85 n., 117–19; share of intra-regional trade, 27, 102, 119; & shipping, 102, 104; complementarity agreements, 129–31; & closer integration, 204, 275–84
China, 13, 21, 180
Coffee, 5, 10, 52 f., 85